MUSIC
IN THE
RENAISSANCE

second edition

MUSIC
IN THE
RENAISSANCE

HOWARD MAYER BROWN
LOUISE K. STEIN

PRENTICE HALL, Upper Saddle River, New Jersey 07458

Library of Congress Cataloging-in-Publication Data

BROWN, HOWARD MAYER.
  Music in the Renaissance / Howard Mayer Brown, Louise K. Stein.—
2nd ed.
    p. cm. — (Prentice Hall history of music series)

  Includes bibliographical references (p.   ) and index.
  ISBN 0-13-400045-5 (paper)
    1. Music—15th century—History and criticism. 2. Music—16th
century—History and criticism. 3. Renaissance. I. Stein, Louise
K. II. Title. III. Series.
  ML172.B86   1999
  780'.9'031—dc21
                                                        98-12248
                                                           CIP
                                                           MN

Editorial director: *Charlyce Jones Owen*
Publisher: *Norwell F. Therien*
Editor: *Marion Gottlieb*
Project manager: *Carole R. Crouse*
Prepress and manufacturing buyer: *Bob Anderson*
Marketing manager: *Sheryl Adams*

This book was set in 10/12 Caledonia by Preparé / Emilcomp
and was printed and bound by Courier Companies, Inc.
The cover was printed by Phoenix Color Corp.

Cover art: Engraving from *Los seis libros del
            Delphín de música*, by Luis de Narváez
            Courtesy of Biblioteca Nacional de España, Madrid

Printed in the United States of America

10 9 8 7 6 5 4 3

ISBN 0-13-400045-5

PRENTICE-HALL INTERNATIONAL (UK) LIMITED, *London*
PRENTICE-HALL OF AUSTRALIA PTY. LIMITED, *Sydney*
PRENTICE-HALL CANADA INC., *Toronto*
PRENTICE-HALL HISPANOAMERICANA, S.A., *Mexico*
PRENTICE-HALL OF INDIA PRIVATE LIMITED, *New Delhi*
PRENTICE-HALL OF JAPAN, INC., *Tokyo*
PRENTICE-HALL ASIA PTE. LTD., *Singapore*
EDITORA PRENTICE-HALL DO BRASIL, LTDA., *Rio de Janeiro*

TO THE MEMORY OF HMB AND RWW

CONTENTS

ix

ILLUSTRATIONS

FOREWORD

Students and informed amateurs of the history of music have long needed a series of books that are comprehensive, authoritative, and engagingly written. They have needed books written by specialists—but specialists interested in communicating vividly. The Prentice Hall History of Music Series aims at filling these needs.

Six books in the series present a panoramic view of the history of Western music, divided among the major historical periods—Medieval, Renaissance, Baroque, Classic, Romantic, and Contemporary. The musical culture of the United States, viewed historically as an independent development within the larger Western tradition, is discussed in a separate book. The rich folk and traditional music of the Western hemisphere and the rest of the world are treated in two volumes, and the nine volumes of the series are a distinctive and, we hope, distinguished contribution to the history of the music of the world's peoples. Each volume, moreover, may be read singly as a substantial account of the music of its period or area.

The authors of the series are scholars of national and international repute—musicologists, critics, and teachers of acknowledged stature in their respective fields of specialization. In their contributions to the Prentice Hall History of Music Series their goal has been to present works of solid scholarship that are eminently readable, with significant insights into music as a part of the general intellectual and cultural life of human societies.

H. WILEY HITCHCOCK, *Editor*

PREFACE

Howard Mayer Brown (1930–1993) wrote this book to introduce the music of the Renaissance period of Western civilization to college and university students, colleagues in other disciplines, and interested music-lovers. He sought to answer several fundamental questions: What were the most significant features of Renaissance music? Who were its greatest composers? How were they great? What is there about this music that still makes it meaningful for us today?

Though we may question the value judgments implicit in the words "significant" and "greatest," Howard Brown believed, even in his last years, that the history of music was shaped by the accomplishments of individuals. In the preface to the first edition (1976), he wrote:

I have placed much emphasis on the contributions of the greatest composers for two reasons. The first is that many (though by no means all) musical scholars in the past have tended to stress secondary figures of the fifteenth and sixteenth centuries almost as much as the principal composers. We have studied the Renaissance differently from almost every other period in music history, and hence we know more about Palestrina's lesser contemporaries, say, than about Beethoven's. Consequently, the contribution of the most important

composers has not always been as sharply focussed in the minds of music students as it should be. I hope that this book may help to reverse that trend.

These remarks were intended to explain why he had produced a text
very different from the leading one in English at the time, Gustave Reese's
Music in the Renaissance (rev. ed., New York, 1959). The book challenged the
general approach taken by scholars and teachers of Renaissance music in the
1950s, 1960s, and 1970s, just because it stressed "major composers and great
accomplishments rather than genres, conventions, and lesser figures," and in
doing so invited a more deeply probing analysis of music than had been typical
of the field.

By the late 1980s, Brown was among those who acknowledged that there
is much more to historical inquiry into the Renaissance than comparison of
"great" composers with their "lesser" contemporaries. This was ever present in
the discussions that he and I had beginning in 1992 about our collaboration in
revising this book. Brown was among those asking penetrating questions about
music as a cultural and political force in the Renaissance, about the place of
music in Renaissance society, and about the extent to which patronage by individuals and institutions shaped musical genres and even specific pieces of
music. He helped us to understand that even the creations of the leading composers were shaped in myriad ways by the situations in which they worked—by
the tastes of their patrons, the requirements of the liturgy, the demands of particular occasions, the talents of the performers for whom they composed, and
the intellectual trends that influenced music as well as the other arts. In the case
of music in early modern culture, we might go so far as to suggest that even the
written records of musical life that have survived—the products of the "great"
composers and their peers—are incomplete. They do not reflect the essentials
of music-making of the fifteenth and sixteenth centuries: improvisation and oral
transmission.

Though a general book about Renaissance composers and musical styles
would seem to run counter to recent trends in academe, I accepted the invitation to revise Brown's *Music in the Renaissance* knowing that I could not
attempt to rewrite the book in a way that would preserve all the best features of
the first edition and, at the same time, change the book's orientation so that it
would wholly answer the new questions asked by specialists. There is a great
deal of merit to the approach of the first edition, since even the most thoughtful consideration of the historical, social, literary, political, and economic context of Renaissance music cannot replace the kind of study that aims to shape
our hearing of the music and tighten our grasp of early modern musical genres.
Students of Renaissance music need in the first place to try to understand
pieces of music, aspects of musical style, and the conventions and technical
norms that define genres. Convictions about this were fundamental to Brown's
text, and in preparing its second edition I have been eager to preserve those
qualities of his approach and his prose that made the first edition such a congenial presentation of Renaissance music.

Chief among the virtues of the first edition were the many analyses of musical examples. These analyses describe important aspects of individual pieces and help to illustrate general points about musical styles and genres; they also speculate about compositional choices and strategies in ways highly characteristic of Brown's thinking as a scholar and his method as a teacher. He was a highly effective mentor; if *Music in the Renaissance* has succeeded as a text for more than two decades, much of that success has to be attributed to its author's musical insight. In my revision, I have preserved these analyses, editing them only as necessary in light of new information or where I believed that my own musical insights might be useful. I have added a few sections devoted to individual pieces and genres, along with some new musical examples to illustrate these. I have tried throughout the book to clarify the relationship between composers and musical conventions—to distinguish between individual choices and generic norms—keeping in mind Brown's conviction that "at least a part of the task of conceiving of our past has to do with judging those great achievements against the conventions of an age."

This second edition brings the book up to date in matters of historical record, such as the dates and places in composers' lives and the dating of musical sources. Concerning those points on which scholars differ or around which swirl important controversies, I have tried to present succinctly the conflicting views and then present my own readings of the evidence. Revision of the bibliographical notes that follow each chapter was a central task in the preparation of this new edition, and I hope that the articles and books suggested there will encourage students and instructors to delve into the literature on problems and topics that could not be treated in depth in the text proper. The bibliographical notes also point to scholarly editions of Renaissance music treated in the text, as well as facsimile editions, which have opened up new opportunities for performers and others to study the sources virtually at first hand.

I have dealt only incidentally with certain topics of interest to specialists in Renaissance music, especially issues of mode and proportion (so important to Renaissance theorists), of modality as concept and practice, and notation and scribal practice. Figures 2 and 9 of this edition provide excerpts of notation from primary sources that may serve as the basis for useful exercises in transcription. I assume on the part of readers an elementary knowledge of the modes of Western polyphonic music—Dorian, Phrygian, Lydian, and Mixolydian—and thus have felt free to discuss the music in slightly broader conceptual terms. Those who are uncertain of the character of the modes should consult such articles as "Mode" in *The New Harvard Dictionary of Music,* ed. Don Randel (Cambridge, Mass., 1986), or Harold S. Powers's "Mode" in *The New Grove Dictionary of Music and Musicians.* I refer to note values and time signatures by modern terms, relevant to the musical examples as transcribed here. Many modern editors have translated the note values of the fifteenth and sixteenth centuries—for example, breve, (◻), semibreve (◊), minim (⌊), and semiminim (⌊)—into modern values that imply a reduction by half, into whole notes (○), half notes (♩), quarter notes (♩), and eighth notes (♪). Moreover, earlier mensuration signs do not mean precisely the same thing as modern time signatures; the differences are explained in Willi Apel, *The Notation of Polyphonic Music, 900–1600*, 5th ed. (Cambridge, Mass., 1961).

This book represents a chain of mentoring that extended from Howard Brown to me and my students at the University of Michigan. I could never have completed this revision without the expert advice and hard work of two sterling scholars, Todd Borgerding and Paul Wiebe. Amanda Eubanks, Rose Pruiksma, and Jennifer Smith contributed in important ways to the preparation of the typescript and index.

I am grateful to a number of scholars who shared with me their work in progress or offered critical readings of parts of the book; they include Claudio Annibaldi, Thomas Brothers, Victor Coelho, Cathy Elias, Richard Freedman, John Griffiths, John Walter Hill, Donna Cardamone Jackson, John Kmetz, Tess Knighton, Michael Noone, Jessie Ann Owens, Keith Polk, Luis Robledo, Emilio Ros-Fábregas, and Robert Snow. Herbert Kellman gave generously of his valuable insight and very special expertise. To Bonnie Blackburn I extend my deepest gratitude for her reading of the entire text, astute criticisms, and helpful suggestions. Finally, I am grateful for the patience and wise counsel of the Series editor, H. Wiley Hitchcock.

The author and the publisher would like to thank the following institutions for graciously providing photographic material for use in this book: Florence, Kunsthistorisches Institut; Madrid, Biblioteca Nacional de España; Minneapolis, University of Minnesota Library; Munich, Bayerische Staatsbibliothek; New Haven, Beinecke Rare Book and Manuscript Library, Yale University; Paris, Bibliothèque Nationale de France; Paris, Musèe du Louvre, Rèunion des Musèes Nationaux; Rome, Biblioteca Vaticana.

LOUISE K. STEIN

COVER ART: In ancient Greece a virtuoso musician named Arion earned his living as an itinerant singer. On return from his travels, the crew of the ship in which he was traveling conspired to rob and murder him. He called upon the god Apollo (another singer) for aid. As Arion sang for what he feared might be the last time, the enchanting power of his song attracted a school of dolphins (favorites of Apollo), who surrounded the ship. Arion leaped into the waves and a dolphin carried him safely to shore. In this engraving from Luis de Narváez, *Los seis libros del Delphín de música* (Valladolid, 1538), Arion does not play an ancient lyre but a perfectly modern sixteenth-century vihuela as he rides on the dolphin's back. (Madrid, Biblioteca Nacional de España)

INTRODUCTION
MUSIC IN THE RENAISSANCE

The fifteenth and sixteenth centuries were a time of discovery for Europeans. Their ships and advances in the science of navigation carried them farther than they had ever gone before to explore new lands and cultures (especially parts of Asia and the Americas). Their appetite for discovery fueled the humanist rediscovery of antiquity, though the legacy of classical learning was also a firm anchor for both speculative intellectual forays and practical experiment. The confidence and boldness of Renaissance Europeans allowed them to reinforce, reinvent, renovate, and reinterpret their history, contemporary practices, and notions about themselves. But though they often described themselves as the blessed inhabitants of a new Golden Age, they did not recognize their music, art, and literature, for example, with the word "Renaissance."

The term "Renaissance" is used in our time to designate this period in Western history. It was first used in this way by mid-nineteenth-century European historians, who found signs of a "renaissance," or "rebirth," of secular culture in the late fourteenth through sixteenth centuries, in which human learning and endeavor, freed from the constraints of an overly religious Middle Ages, became more focused on human achievement. Music historians of the early twentieth century took up the word and the concepts associated with it largely because of the influence of Jacob Burckhardt's *The Culture of the Renaissance in Italy* (first published in German in 1860) and, later, Johan Huizinga's *The Waning of the Middle Ages* (English trans. 1924). Although the term was convenient for cultural historians, in that it invited music into the field of Renaissance studies, their picture of Renaissance culture did not easily accommodate what music historians knew about the style, technique, and geography of much fifteenth- and sixteenth-century music.

The notion of a "Renaissance" in music was and continues to be problematic. Historians of music have no need to discredit the accomplishments of the Middle Ages or to characterize that period as a "dark age" in which musical creativity was somehow suppressed or crippled by the dominance of the church and medieval authority; therefore, it makes little sense to represent the fifteenth and sixteenth centuries as bringing forth a more "human" (as opposed to "God-centered") approach. Further, because we are now more accepting of the fact that history is what historians create and is not an absolute science, we do not expect all aspects of musical culture in a given time to conform to a unified principle. Historians of music today do not feel as compelled as their earlier counterparts to draw a sharp line of demarcation between the Middle Ages and the Renaissance, or to claim that the latter was characterized by a radical and all-encompassing shift in attitude. Musical scholars and some composers in the later Middle Ages were making discoveries and developing techniques that were the basis for innovations usually credited to musicians of the Renaissance.

Another touchy question for twentieth-century historians has been the geography of music in the Renaissance. From the time of Burckhardt and Huizinga on, descriptions and definitions of "Renaissance" as a historical period have rightly centered on artistic, intellectual, and philosophical events in Italy. The centrality of Italy in the accounts of historians outside music has caused some difficulty for music historians. If the Renaissance is taken to be a largely Italian phenomenon, and "music" is taken as represented by the work of major composers, then music in Italy seems an impoverished art that lagged behind the other arts in this period: the written artifacts and records that tell us about music (archival documents and collections of music) probably do not give an accurate picture of the art of music as it flourished in Italy. Indeed, they do not adequately present the multifaceted coexistence of styles and kinds of music that were heard all over Europe, and they tell us little about musical performance. Much that was essential in musical culture was improvised, orally transmitted, and not written down. What is known about composed and written-down music in the Renaissance indicates that it was a northern art, or at least an art of northerners. All the great composers of the fifteenth and early sixteenth centuries were born in what is today northern France, Belgium, and Holland. It does not follow, however, that Italy was a provincial backwater; on the contrary, Italy was the center of a brilliant and flourishing musical culture. Curiously, though, few if any of the composers working there after about 1420 were native-born, and even if a few Italian composers did emerge about 1490, they did not threaten the artistic hegemony of the foreigners.

Flanders, Burgundy, and Italy were the principal centers of musical life in the fifteenth and sixteenth centuries. Although many of the great composers of the period were trained in Burgundy and Flanders, Italy supported more than a few of them, and many of the most elegant and elaborate musical sources of the period were copied and presented to Italian patrons or institutions. The musical culture in Italy was attractive to northern composers (whether for intellectual or economic reasons), and they flocked to the Italian courts. In short, although a history of musical style in the Renaissance must focus largely on the music of northern composers and look to northern culture to understand the relationships among composers, the models of princely patronage, and the system of musical education, Italy was central to the social and intellectual history of Renaissance music.

The term "Renaissance" is useful in describing the principal intellectual trends of the fifteenth and sixteenth centuries, if we understand "rebirth" to refer to the revival of interest in classical antiquity. By and large, however, Renaissance composers did not model their compositions on the very few fragments of ancient Greek music that had been discovered—at least, not until the later sixteenth century (when they were avidly discussed in some circles). Musicians were, however, profoundly influenced by the currents of classical humanist thought that shaped so many aspects of early modern European culture in the other arts and in philosophy, mathematics, the natural sciences, and even daily discourse. Descriptions of the effects produced by music in the ancient world played a role in forming composers' attitudes. The ways in which composers structured their compositions were influenced by procedures derived from classical rhetoric. Debates on the basic materials of music—scales, intervals, rhythmic patterns, temperaments and tuning systems for instruments—were conditioned by classical learning, habits of thought, and ways of viewing those subjects. The entire body of Renaissance treatises on music, in fact, is incomprehensible without understanding the fascination that writers on music had for classical authors. Perhaps most important, we can better understand how composers throughout the Renaissance, from Dufay to Monteverdi, approached the texts they set by continuing to investigate what Claude Palisca has described as "the transformation of musical thought brought about by the renewed pursuit of ancient learning" and its effect on poets, composers, patrons, and listeners.

Though it attempts to understand music as an expression of the culture of the Renaissance, this book is chiefly a history of musical style, and its first task is to describe how composers' attitudes toward the written, composed music changed over two hundred years. Sacred Mass settings and motets and settings of secular lyric poetry were the chief kinds of music written in the fifteenth and sixteenth centuries. The brevity of this list does not, however, suggest that composers were limited in creativity or that the musical compositions of the Renaissance are boringly homogeneous. Composers devised diverse ways of approaching the invariable words of the Mass, and during the fifteenth century they began to conceive all five sections of the Mass Ordinary—Kyrie, Gloria, Credo, Sanctus, and Agnus Dei—as a cycle by basing each movement on the same musical material. They devised ingenious musical solutions for setting many kinds of motet texts: although motets had existed since the thirteenth century, their character and function had changed over the years, and many of the most influential changes in musical style between 1430 and 1600 can best be examined by studying this genre. Composers' responses to literary trends sparked a process by which national dialects gradually fragmented the central pan-European language of music in settings of secular poetry. Chansons—settings of stereotyped French courtly lyrics—constituted the principal sort of secular music in the fifteenth century, regardless of the composers' nationalities. The sixteenth century also saw a flowering of secular song (and vernacular religious song) in other languages—the Italian madrigal above all, but also settings of Spanish, German, Dutch, and English poems.

The extent to which composers, who are the chief protagonists in the history of musical style, were conditioned by their environment and responsive to the forces of society (political, economic, personal, religious, geographical) cannot be accounted for in a single generalization. Nor can we come up with a single generalization to include all the ways in which musicians and their performances and compositions affected society and historical events. It is clear, though, that music was a potent cultural force: music and musicians were, in some cases, active agents in the definition of princely or religious identity; and the institutional and social structures that governed musical employment, and the activities of musical patrons, surely influenced composers and the development of musical genres and styles in important ways. Among social processes in the early modern period, patronage was one that had far-reaching consequences in the history of music. Musicians in the fifteenth and sixteenth centuries were employed by the church, by a court, or by a municipal or civic administration. They worked in large cathedrals, in busy parish churches, and at the papal chapel in Rome, or in monasteries and convents and collegiate churches. They also worked for confraternities and guilds. The institutions that employed musicians and vied for the best composers, singers, and players included royal chapels and royal households, princely courts and those of lesser nobility, as well as municipal and civic organizations (such as those that routinely employed wind players). Each institution had its own needs and administrative structures, so that composers and performers throughout the era were called upon to meet a variety of demands. The nature of institutional demand helps to explain, for example, why the sacred music of Binchois is distinctly less elegant than his chansons and certainly less elaborate than Dufay's: Binchois worked for the Burgundian court chapel, which did not require elaborate sacred music for daily worship. Similarly, the commissions received by Dufay provide an essential context for understanding his musical choices and accomplishments, especially in the genre of the isorhythmic motet. The point is that the musical personalities of these two composers, though certainly different for other reasons, are revealed to us as distinct partly because of their differing spheres of activity.

Historians do not describe the past merely to picture it as it really was but also to attempt to impose some order on it so that they may comprehend it better. Were we able to reconstruct the continuum of daily events during the Renaissance, we might even be tempted to argue that it never really existed: the fifteenth century was simply a continuation of the Middle Ages, and the sixteenth century, without any sharp break with the past, prepared the way for the baroque era of the seventeenth. But such an argument is not satisfactory: to understand the past, we try to find the characteristics common to many diverse phenomena and decide which events were most significant or typical.

The past may be divided into comprehensible segments by singling out those original inventions and accomplishments of individuals that influenced future generations. Dufay's brilliant realization of the possibilities for organizing gigantic musical structures around borrowed melodies and his consummate skill in using the mellifluous English sonorities, for example, bespeak a genuinely new attitude toward the art of music. So also do Josquin's synthesis of musical idioms into a highly supple and expressive texture, and Monteverdi's stunning demonstration of the musical and dramatic potentials of the new techniques of basso continuo and recitative, which had been invented by musicians with less command than his of the technical resources of polyphony. These are among the musical achievements that have determined the major divisions of this book.

The invention of a new technique has little importance unless a composer respected and influential in the mainstream demonstrates its artistic significance, or unless it raises aesthetic problems and implies a challenge to existing technical limitations. The historian, then, seeks the most influential as well as the most artful music to determine the specific shape of a period. In singling out the most novel and characteristic features of the music of the fifteenth and sixteenth centuries, the authors of this book have, in effect, outlined the history of music during the Renaissance, a necessary preliminary step toward understanding the common and contrasting elements that coexist as music and in musical culture of the two centuries.

BIBLIOGRAPHICAL NOTES

The standard work on music in this period, though now considerably dated, is Gustave Reese, *Music in the Renaissance* (New York, 1954; rev. ed. 1959). A more concise survey may be found in Donald Jay Grout and Claude Palisca, *A History of Western Music,* 5th ed. (New York, 1996). Students should also consult *The New Oxford History of Music,* ed. Dom Anselm Hughes and Gerald Abraham (London, 1960–68), especially vol. 3, *Ars Nova and the Renaissance, 1300–1540,* and vol. 4, *The Age of Humanism, 1540–1630.* A new edition of the *New Oxford History of Music,* vol. 4, ed. James Haar, is forthcoming. An excellent set of essays, including an introductory essay by Iain Fenlon on music and society, is contained in

The Renaissance from the 1470s to the End of the Sixteenth Century, ed. Iain Fenlon (Englewood Cliffs, N.J., 1989), the second volume in the Music and Society series, under the general editorship of Stanley Sadie. The introductory chapters of Reinhard Strohm, *The Rise of European Music, 1380–1500* (Cambridge, 1993), are also extremely useful for their description of music in late medieval culture and the pan-European situation in the fifteenth century. The first three chapters of Tim Carter, *Music in Late Renaissance and Early Baroque Italy* (London, 1992), offer an intelligently concise consideration of the intellectual and social background of music in the sixteenth century. The concerns and contributions of Italian musical theorists in the Renaissance are explored in Claude V. Palisca, *Humanism in Italian Renaissance Musical Thought* (New Haven, 1985); its first chapter argues passionately and eloquently for the importance of humanism in Renaissance music.

Oliver Strunk, *Source Readings in Music History* (New York, 1950), Carol MacClintock, ed., *Readings in the History of Music in Performance* (Bloomington, 1979; 1982), and Piero Weiss and Richard Taruskin, eds., *Music in the Western World. A History in Documents* (New York, 1984), contain very useful English translations of well-chosen extracts from music theory treatises and other writings from the period.

The Companion to Medieval and Renaissance Music, ed. Tess Knighton and David Fallows (London, 1992), contains easily readable essays on Renaissance music. Two guides to performing practice, *A Performer's Guide to Renaissance Music*, ed. Jeffrey T. Kite-Powell (New York, 1994), and *Medieval and Renaissance Music, a Performer's Guide*, ed. Timothy J. McGee (Toronto, 1985), provide helpful insights into the sound of Renaissance music and the practical problems encountered by performers today. The standard text in English on the notation of early music is Willi Apel, *The Notation of Polyphonic Music 900–1600* (Cambridge, Mass., 1953).

For anthologies containing score examples of the music of the period, see Sarah Fuller, *The European Musical Heritage 800–1750* (New York, 1987), which includes a lengthy and insightful annotation for each excerpt; *Historical Anthology of Music*, ed. Archibald T. Davison and Willi Apel, vol. 1, rev. ed. (Cambridge, Mass., 1966); *An Anthology of Early Renaissance Music*, ed. Noah Greenberg and Paul Maynard (New York, 1975); and *The Penguin Book of Early Music: An Anthology of Vocal and Instrumental Songs and Dances from the Renaissance (1480–1620)*, ed. and annotated by Anthony Rooley (New York, 1980). See also Arnold Schering, *Geschichte der Musik in Beispielen* (Leipzig, 1931); Carl Parrish and John F. Ohl, *Masterpieces of Music before 1750* (New York, 1951); and Carl Parrish, *A Treasury of Early Music* (New York, 1958). Note as well the scholarly editions and facsimiles cited in the chapter bibliographies that follow.

ONE

THE BEGINNINGS:
DUNSTABLE AND
THE CONTENANCE ANGLOISE

"Although it seems beyond belief, there does not exist a single piece of music, not composed within the last forty years, that is regarded by the learned as worth hearing." So wrote Johannes Tinctoris, music theorist, composer, and chapelmaster to the King of Naples, in 1477 in the preface to his treatise on counterpoint. Tinctoris's remarks were intended to help him argue the perfection of music in his own time. Dismissing older music in favor of modern music, he pointed to the Englishman Dunstable (ca. 1390–1453) and the Burgundians Guillaume Dufay (or Du Fay, ca. 1400–1474) and Gilles Binchois (ca. 1400–1460) as the founders of a new musical style, and to Johannes Ockeghem (ca. 1420–97) and Antoine Busnoys (ca. 1430–92) as the most distinguished heirs to their innovations.

Tinctoris criticized the music produced before his own day largely because its high degree of dissonance "offended the ear." Because his view was biased, and because we cannot know just how much of earlier music Tinctoris knew, his rejection of fourteenth- and early-fifteenth-century music is doubly suspect as historical evidence. But Tinctoris's view—that changes in musical style occurred early in the fifteenth century and were significant enough to mark the beginning of a new age in music—retains its significance today. The relationship among the composers of the first generation of "moderns" is also

7

alluded to in a poem, *Le champion des dames,* written by the Burgundian poet and diplomat Martin le Franc about 1441. Dufay and Binchois, wrote Le Franc, have found a new way to make elegant consonances ("*frisque concordance*"). They wear the English guise ("*la contenance angloise*"), and in following Dunstable they have made their music "gay and brilliant" (*joyeux et notable*). As historians, Tinctoris and Martin le Franc were clearly biased in favor of Burgundian culture and its achievement. Nevertheless, their testimony is valuable, for it recognizes that the sound of the English composers' music, especially Dunstable's, was not only new but also important in having been taken up by their continental colleagues.

The musical idiom identified with the *contenance angloise* was not an invention of Dunstable, for it is exemplified in the panconsonant, homogeneous sound of fourteenth-century English polyphony, notable also for its clear declamation of Latin texts and melodic fluidity. Although it was a practice of long standing in English sacred polyphony, it did not become known to European musicians until the fifteenth century, as evidenced by the numerous English pieces copied into continental choirbooks. During a period of increased musical internationalism and exchange, large areas of what is now France were for a time English dominions, and a strong English presence on the Continent brought new currents of musical interchange between English and continental composers. Although we do not know precisely who met whom, we know that the performance of English church music made a strongly favorable impression at certain important meetings of Church officials on the Continent, when English and continental musicians heard each other perform. At the Council of Constance (1414–18) and the Council of Basle (1431–49), musicians from many parts of Europe performed music of their own traditions and copied the music of others.

To the modern listener, early-fifteenth-century English music sounds sweeter and fuller than continental music of the same period, and this euphony probably constitutes the greater part of what Le Franc recognized as *la contenance angloise.* Several technical features explain the sound: full triads—those that regularly include the third—used in both melody and harmony; block chords or else lightly ornamented homorhythmic passages; a blended texture in which the voices move more or less at the same speed; and bland, uniformly consonant harmonies that avoid dissonances anywhere except as inconspicuous passing notes. Leonel Power's simple setting of the votive antiphon *Beata progenies* (Example 1–1), in discant style with the undecorated chant sung by the middle voice, and even his more complicated *Gloriose Virginis* (Example 1–2), which sets an antiphon text without any reference to the chant melody, exhibit these features characteristic of English sacred music. While the simplicity of the Power pieces is surely related to their function as music for votive services, all three "English" features contribute to this sound.

English composers of the early fifteenth century cultivated a music of strong formal design, in part achieved through textural contrast. The characteristically full sound of all three, four, or even five voices singing together is fre-

EXAMPLE 1–1. Leonel Power, *Beata progenies*, mm. 1–14.

Be - a - ta pro - ge - ni - es un -

- de Cri - stus

EXAMPLE 1–2. Leonel Power, *Gloriose Virginis*, mm. 1–20.

quently interrupted by duets for two equally melodious voices. Both voices in these duos, as well as the upper voice (and sometimes the upper two voices) in the full sections, are written as graceful arches of melody in fluid rhythms that seem always to push forward toward their cadential goals. Although the rhythms are conceived within a metrical framework—that is, the bar lines supplied by editors in modern editions often coincide with the real musical subdivisions of the melodic lines—accents are displaced within each bar, syncopations across the bar line are frequent, and the melodies are often phrased in irregular groupings of two, three, or four measures. English compositions often begin with a characteristic figure (a rising third that completes or is followed by the outline of a fifth and then a descent by falling third) or its inversion (Examples 1–3a, b, and c), revealing the triadic orientation of the melodic lines. They also consistently employ a certain cadential figure for closure, as seen in Example 1–3d. Together, these produce a very supple, English melodic style that contrasts strikingly with the highly decorated yet static melodic cells in nervous, disjointed rhythms that are found in Italian and French fourteenth-century music.

EXAMPLE 1–3. English figures.

(a) Power

Et   in   ter - ra   pax

(b) Dunstable

Pa - trem   om - ni - po -

(c) Power

Pa - trem   om - ni - po - ten -

(d) Anon.

English music of the early fifteenth century was also distinguished for its formal experiments. English composers tried in various ways to relate the movements of the Mass Ordinary to one another. Pairing two movements together—Gloria with Credo, or Sanctus with Agnus Dei—led eventually to the establishment of the cyclic Mass in which each movement is organized by means of the same structural melody, a formal ground plan that became one of the great musical conventions of the fifteenth and sixteenth centuries.

Like the continental composers of the late fourteenth and early fifteenth centuries, English musicians turned away from setting the Proper of the Mass— those sections proper only to special occasions during the church year—in favor of setting the Ordinary, the five sections that are an invariable part of the Mass each time it is sung. Similarly, the English as well as the Europeans gradually ceased to write motets that were sophisticated secular pieces (like those by Guillaume de Machaut in the fourteenth century) or that formed a part of the responsorial sections of the Mass Proper. Instead, they cultivated the votive antiphon, especially the antiphons devoted to the Virgin Mary. During the first half of the fifteenth century, English composers came to depend less and less on plainchant models in setting antiphon texts. They thus freed themselves from the restraints imposed by the practice of harmonizing a given plainchant and at the same time developed a keener sense of large-scale musical form by devising techniques for unifying long compositions by means of a cantus firmus.

LEONEL POWER AND
THE OLD HALL MANUSCRIPT

To understand what European composers might have heard of the English repertory in the early fifteenth century, we must first look at the music by Dunstable's immediate predecessors and older contemporaries—the music contained in the most important English musical source of the period, the Old Hall Manuscript, and in particular that written by the leading composer in Old Hall, Leonel Power. The Old Hall Manuscript is not the only source of English music from the period. Besides various fragments and smaller insular sources, there are a number of large continental manuscripts—the great Trent Codices and manuscripts in Aosta and Modena come to mind immediately—that contain some two hundred English pieces; many of the English compositions are copied out one after another in special sections of these anthologies, as if the continental scribes wished to signal the differences between their own and English music.

The Old Hall Manuscript was named for Old Hall College, Ware, the Roman Catholic seminary in England where it was kept until it was sold to the British Library in 1973. It was compiled about 1410–15, possibly for the king's Chapel of the Royal Household, for the Chapel of St. George at Windsor, or for Thomas, Duke of Clarence. The main portion of the anthology consists of sections devoted to settings of single movements from the Mass Ordinary, without the Kyrie; it opens with a series of Glorias, followed by one of Credos, and so on. Where space permits, scribes have interpolated a few motets and movements from the Proper. Aside from a single piece by Dunstable, two pieces by "Roy Henry" (either Henry IV or Henry V), and a number of works by Power, the composers represented in Old Hall are minor figures: Aleyn, Bittering, Burell, Chirbury, Cooke, Damett, Excetre, Fonteyns, Forest, and others.

The fact that the Old Hall contains no Kyries seems to be simple historical accident: all those originally in the manuscript were lost when its first section became detached from the rest. But English cyclic Masses often lack Kyries, especially when they are preserved in continental sources. In fact, English composers may have preferred the Kyrie sung as chant rather than polyphony, or else they chose to set Kyries to which tropes—textual interpolations appropriate to a particular liturgical occasion—had been added, making them unsuitable for general use. The recent discovery of a number of Kyries by Dunstable does not substantially alter the conclusion that the four-movement polyphonic Mass, lacking a Kyrie, is a common English convention. Moreover, the English sometimes omitted portions of the Credo, especially the clause beginning "Et in Spiritum Sanctum Dominum," or they telescoped the Credo text so that more than one portion of it was heard simultaneously, apparently to get through the Mass movement as quickly as possible with the greatest number of words.

Some of the Old Hall Manuscript is notated in score, an arrangement already out of date in most continental manuscripts of the time. Some is notated in the more conventional "choirbook format," or *cantus collateralis*—that is, with each voice written out separately, two (one above the other) on the left- and two on the right-hand side of each opening (for compositions *a 4*). This difference in notation reflects a difference in musical style. The Old Hall contains, in fact, a mixture of styles, some deriving from French and Italian fourteenth-century music, but most deriving from earlier native practice. There are simple homorhythmic English discant settings; compositions in which the top voice predominates, as in the continental chanson; pieces using canon in a manner reminiscent of the *trecento* caccia; and works based on the central French technique of isorhythm. Old Hall presents all the discant settings in score and most of the contrapuntally complex pieces in choirbook format.

The discant settings (of which Example 1–1 is a classic example) are uncomplicated and generally note-against-note harmonizations of a plainchant, which is most often to be found undecorated in the middle voice, although on occasion it appears also in one of the outer voices or even migrates from voice to voice. These simple polyphonic compositions may well represent the everyday "service music" of the later Middle Ages, but their simplicity may also represent cherished aesthetic values inherited from fourteenth-century English composers who cultivated this style for all pieces with Latin texts.

Late medieval theorists describe discant as the technique of adding a second voice against a tenor in note-against-note counterpoint, for the most part in contrary motion. Learning to improvise this second voice above a chant must have constituted an important part of the elementary training of singers and composers alike. English theorists of the early fifteenth century describe another kind of improvisation as well, "faburden" in three parts, in which the plainsong cantus firmus appears in the middle voice (the "mean"), a lower voice accompanies it in thirds and fifths, and a treble moves in fourths above the mean. Its realization was made easier by a system of "sights" or "sighting," a technique of transposition that enabled the singers to imagine their added voices on a single four-line staff. (Some slightly later pieces are said to be "on the faburden," meaning that they use the counterpoint to the chant rather than the chant itself as the cantus firmus in a new composition.) English faburden is clearly distinguishable from continental fauxbourdon, a semi-improvised music in which the chant appears in the top (not the middle) voice in a more or less decorated version and in a fluid rhythm rather like that of a freely composed treble. The bottom voice in fauxbourdon moves partly in parallel and partly in contrary motion against the treble, while the middle voice, which was not written down, follows the treble, always exactly a fourth below it. Both faburden and fauxbourdon produce many parallel $^6_3$ chords. Hence, early-fifteenth-century music that includes such parallelisms—for example, at the approach to cadences—is thought to be influenced by fauxbourdon, but the term in its strictest usage should be reserved for compositions that adhere strictly to the technique of semi-improvisation, like the hymn settings of Dufay.

The second category of compositions in the Old Hall consists of works written in chanson style, such as Example 1–4a, a *Sanctus* by Leonel Power, in which the top voice moves more quickly and with more melodic ornaments and greater rhythmic fluidity than the lower two voices. This dominating treble sometimes paraphrases a chant, as Example 1–4a does with the Sarum chant shown in Example 1–4b. The two slower-moving lower voices share the same range, generally about a fifth below that of the treble. The tenor acts as a supporting voice to the treble, usually cadencing with it and supplying either the root or the third of the appropriate chord. The contratenor, presumably composed after the other two voices, complements them, filling out bare harmonies and providing rhythmic movement when they stop; because it plays a subservient role in the texture, the contratenor could not be written with careful regard for the fine contours of its melodic shape, and so it often seems ungainly or fragmentary. Although this style may well have had its origins in the earlier English cantilena style, it resembles that of the fourteenth-century French chanson as well, though it was by no means restricted to that genre in the following century. As we shall see, many composers throughout the fif-

EXAMPLE 1–4a. Leonel Power, *Sanctus*, mm. 1–6.

EXAMPLE 1–4b. The Sarum chant Power paraphrases.

teenth century—and not just English ones—wrote in this treble-dominated texture, with its closely related tenor and superius. In the Old Hall Manuscript the style is modified in any one of several ways. If four voices take part, the upper two usually move at the same fast pace. Composers sometimes combine chanson style with discant technique to produce compositions with more nearly equal voices.

Movements in discant or chanson style, or in some combination of the two, constitute the major portion of Old Hall, but there are also isorhythmic Mass movements in Old Hall as well as some with canonic upper parts. Composers constructed their isorhythmic movements in the fourteenth-century manner, except that the fluid style of their upper voices is closer to that of the rest of Old Hall than to the nervous, static, highly decorative lines of Guillaume de Machaut and his contemporaries. In the Old Hall pieces, the plainsong cantus firmus in the tenor is invariably isorhythmic, and the upper voices often repeat their rhythms each time the tenor repeats. Other Mass movements seem to modern ears oddly inappropriate for a liturgical service because of their jaunty rhythms and their two or sometimes three canonic upper parts. These movements were apparently modeled on the trecento caccie, Italian hunting songs, in which the second and third canonic voices enter after relatively long time intervals and are supported by one or two slower-moving lower voices.

Almost nothing is known about the life of the best and most important composer in Old Hall, Leonel Power, the first great name to emerge from an enormous, longtime anonymous repertory of English sacred music. The archives reveal only that he died at Canterbury in 1445 and that he was associated with Christ Church there during his last years. All of his fifty or so compositions are sacred: Mass movements and motets. He arouses our interest not only because of the quantity and high quality of his music but also because of its varied character; he does not fit neatly into any historical scheme. Some of his music includes dissonance handled as freely as any in fourteenth-century music, but some anticipates developments of the late fifteenth century in its use of imitation and its attempt to make all three voices equal in importance and function. Most of his music, however, displays the English features, especially the euphonious sweetness and grace of melody, that so attracted continental composers of the time.

Power's motets can be grouped into three overlapping categories: simple harmonizations of plainchant in discant style, such as Example 1–1, with more or less note-against-note counterpoint; treble-dominated motets for three voices (although two are *a 4*), as in Example 1–2, in which full sections alternate with duos for two equally important voices; and a handful of presumably late works in which all voices approach equality, panconsonance prevails, passages of rhythmic and melodic imitation occur, and the text is set with a care unusual for the time. A discant setting by definition employs a plainchant as the basis for a new composition, and some of Power's treble-dominated motets incorporate a paraphrased plainsong into the fluid rhythms and arched melodies of the upper voice. In his latest works he abandoned altogether the practice of basing a new composition on chant. The music is entirely original, its formal shape determined by a free alternation of tuttis and duos.

In setting the texts of the Mass Ordinary, Power made use of a greater variety of techniques, including isorhythm. But perhaps most important are the attempts he (and his contemporaries) made to relate two Mass movements to each other and, eventually, to unify all four or five movements of the Mass Ordinary by basing them on a single cantus firmus. The relationship between paired Mass movements—normally Gloria and Credo, or Sanctus and Agnus Dei—took many different forms. In some pairs the two movements use the same plainsong cantus firmus in the tenor; in other pairs the tenors are related liturgically rather than musically (for example, when the two musically unrelated cantus firmi are taken from the same plainsong Mass). Some Mass pairs are connected by a "head motive," a melodic incipit that begins both movements. The relationship between some Mass pairs is even looser, consisting merely of laying out the two movements in the same way—for example, by dividing the movements into two roughly equal parts, the first in triple and the second in duple meter, or by using the same pattern of tuttis and duos in both or the same techniques, such as canon or isorhythm. Some Mass pairs seem not to have any musical or liturgical connection with one another, but apparently the scribes who wrote them down thought they belonged together for reasons now unknown. Although continental composers of Power's generation were also experimenting with ways of relating two Mass movements to one another, it was apparently an English invention to unite them in a musically audible and structurally important way by basing them on the same plainsong tenor. English composers seem also to have been the first to see the greater possibilities of this technique by applying it to a whole Mass.

The earliest cyclic Masses built on a single cantus firmus were composed by Power, his slightly younger contemporary Dunstable, and their contemporaries. Power's *Missa Alma redemptoris mater* is, in effect, a gigantic series of isorhythmic motets, for the tenor appears in the same rhythmic shape in each movement. The *Missa Rex seculorum*, attributed to both Power and Dunstable, abandons the isorhythmic principle. The long plainsong antiphon that underlies this Mass is stated complete once in every movement but each time in changed rhythms and with notes or even whole phrases interpolated. The composer has not even attempted to preserve the original phrasing of the chant; he treats the borrowed melody with the utmost flexibility. The rhythmic pace of every movement is approximately the same: each begins with a long section in triple meter, changes to duple, and then, near the end, changes back again to triple (the scheme in the Credo is similar to the others, though slightly more complex). On the other hand, the vocal scoring varies. Although the Gloria and the Credo resemble each other in beginning with extended duos, the placement of tuttis and duos changes in each movement, giving each its own distinctive shape and sound. Form is determined largely by the predominant top voice, which is joined by an equally melodious contratenor during the duets and supported during the tuttis by the structural tenor.

Tenors in the earliest cyclic Masses can thus be either isorhythmic or without a predetermined and repeating pattern. Some Masses of the time are built either on a freely composed tenor or on one stemming from a chant or other borrowed melody as yet unidentified. Other Masses use more extensive borrowing from polyphonic models, such as Bedingham's *Missa Dueil angoisseux* and Frye's *Missa Summe Trinitati*. Bedingham's *Missa Dueil angoisseux* is accepted by some scholars as the first known parody Mass because it is a Mass cycle that makes use of more than one voice of the polyphonic model it is based on. Here melodic material from Binchois's exquisite chanson is incorporated both as direct quotation and in highly varied, ornamented form. Thus, the parody Mass, an important genre of the sixteenth century, was cultivated in the late fifteenth century. However used, structural tenors enabled composers to build longer and more imposing musical structures than any previously possible. The importance of this technique can hardly be overemphasized.

JOHN DUNSTABLE

That Martin le Franc should single out John Dunstable (ca. 1390–1453) in praising English musicians is scarcely surprising, for Dunstable was not only the best composer of his generation but also very probably the one who had the most contact with continental musicians. His epitaph describes him as a mathematician and an astronomer as well as a musician, and he may have dedicated himself to each of these pursuits at some point in his life. He was probably employed before 1427 as a church musician and was perhaps associated with the Duke of Bedford. He later served Joan of Navarre, dowager queen of Henry IV (1427–46), and then Humphrey, Duke of Gloucester, in the late 1430s. A man of considerable means in his later life, Dunstable may have spent time in France because of the important roles that his employers played in the English government of Normandy and the lands he held in France on their behalf. It is therefore possible that he knew both Dufay and Binchois.

Dunstable belongs among those great composers who accept their stylistic heritage and refine and polish it to a high degree. The confusion of attribution of the *Missa Rex seculorum* and many other pieces both to him and to others is perhaps symptomatic. The difficulty of reaching a decision on stylistic evidence alone may suggest that Dunstable's music differs not so much in kind as in degree from that by his contemporaries. He is better rather than different, and his music shows none of the stylistic changes and "developments" that are so obvious in Power's; it is all of a piece. If Dunstable is distinguished by one quality alone, it is the incredible sweetness that Le Franc emphasized. Dunstable avoided altogether the freely handled dissonances characteristic of much music in the fourteenth century and present to some extent even in the Mass movements of Old Hall. Indeed, in a few pieces, such as his famous *Quam pulchra es,* he eliminated almost entirely any dissonances except an occasional passing tone and one or two suspensions at cadences. Careful control of dissonance is an extremely important feature of Dunstable's style and was adopted by Dufay and his continental contemporaries. This panconsonance, combined with an insistence on full triads, gives to Dunstable's music its characteristically agreeable sound.

Like most major figures of the Renaissance, Dunstable composed Mass movements, motets, and secular pieces. The least important part of his oeuvre, by far, consists of three secular pieces, two of them also attributed to John Bedingham, one of his younger English contemporaries. It would be difficult to say how *Puisque m'amour,* a rondeau setting securely assigned to Dunstable, differs from a chanson by Gilles Binchois, although its triadic orientation might point to its English origin. *Puisque m'amour* survives also in an arrangement for solo keyboard, interesting in that it demonstrates just how freely performers in the fifteenth century could add elaborate melodic ornamentation and accidentals.

Dunstable's motets, which include some of his loveliest and most immediately accessible music, may be divided into three large categories: the most complex and elaborate motets, which are isorhythmic; a few that incorporate a plainsong in the top voice; and others, the largest group, which make no use at all of chant. Only one motet, *Crux fidelis,* does not fall into any of those categories; its *cantus prius factus,* a processional antiphon, appears in the middle voice (except in a duet section). The isorhythmic motets have a special texture derived from their distinctive structure. Almost all the rest, whether or not they make reference to a borrowed chant, alternate between sections *a 3,* in which the top voice predominates, and equal-voiced duets. In the full sections the tenor supports the faster-moving treble melody; the contratenor completes the triads, keeps the motion going when the outer voices pause, and acts as a counterbalance, sometimes to the treble but mostly to the tenor. Dunstable seems to make more effort than Power to equalize the pace of all three voices; the treble never dominates quite so much as in some of Power's motets. Some passages, and even some complete pieces, move in lightly decorated blocks of chords, a texture that facilitates a clear and precise declamation of the words.

Most of Dunstable's isorhythmic motets, written in praise of a particular saint or of the Virgin, follow the same general structural outline. All voices, not just the tenor, are isorhythmic, or nearly so. In most motets, one statement of the complete chant in the tenor involves two or three repetitions of the rhythmic pattern (the *talea*); the complete pitch pattern (the *color*) is stated three times in note values that get progressively faster by simple arithmetical proportion—for example, 3:2:1. A drive to the final cadence is thus built into the structure itself. That this complicated, mathematical means of constructing a piece of music can yield graceful and apparently spontaneous results is a tribute indeed to Dunstable's superb melodic gift. The motet *Veni sancte spiritus/Veni creator* is even more ingenious in that it incorporates as well a paraphrased chant into the top voice; it is the only one of Dunstable's isorhythmic motets to do so.

The overall structure of Dunstable's treble-dominated motets, whether or not they are based on a chant melody, depends on textural and metrical contrast. Long duets for varied combinations of voices interrupt the tutti passages, and most motets are divided into several sections in contrasting meters. But it is Dunstable's melodic gift that brings these structures to life—his ability to spin out long sustained melodies without breaking them into small units by means of intermediate cadences. The treble of his *Ave Regina caelorum,* for example, displays this admirable feature, even though it is derived from chant.

Dunstable's single and paired Mass movements reveal the same stylistic traits as his motets. Whether isorhythmic or treble-dominated, and whether or not they make reference to a chant, these movements pour forth a seemingly endless flow of melody harmonized by full triads. Some of the Mass pairs reveal Dunstable's clear and obvious intent to relate two movements to each other musically, either by basing each on the same chant (the Gloria–Credo pair based on *Jesu Christe Fili Dei,* in his *Works* nos. 15 and 16) or by using the same overall structure and scoring in each (the Gloria–Credo, nos. 11 and 12). One pair uses different tenors in each movement, though they are related liturgically (the Sanctus–Agnus Dei, nos. 13 and 14). But several pairs (for example, nos. 7–8 and 9–10) exhibit no musical relationships; although they were copied side by side by fifteenth-century scribes, they may actually have been intended as separate movements.

Dunstable may have written as many as three cyclic Masses. As we have seen, the *Missa Rex seculorum* is attributed to Power as well as to Dunstable. The identity of the composer of the *Missa sine nomine* is even more ambiguous; various sources ascribe it to Power, Dunstable, or Benet. Only the *Missa Da gaudiorum premia,* based on an isorhythmic tenor, is surely by Dunstable. Although it is incompletely preserved (the Agnus Dei has not come down to us), it is perhaps the earliest Mass cycle to be based on a single cantus firmus. In light of his service to the Duke of Bedford, Dunstable's Mass was probably composed in 1420 for the marriage between England's Henry V and Catherine of Valois and performed again in 1431 for the coronation of Henry VI as King of France.

Dunstable was not the only good composer of the time. A fuller view would have to take into account not only Power and Dunstable but also John Pyamour, John Forest, John Benet, John Bedingham, John Plummer, Robert Morton, and the slightly later Walter Frye (d. 1475), as well as a host of lesser musicians. Some of their music is contained in two manuscripts of the mid–fifteenth century: British Museum, MS Egerton 3307 (which contains carols as well as liturgical settings), and Cambridge, Magdalene College, Pepys Library MS 1236. Already by the third quarter of the century, interchange between insular and continental musicians had begun to wane, and by the time of the Eton Choirbook, copied probably between 1490 and 1502, English composers seem to have gone their own way, creating a distinctly English style and formal layout, largely independent of continental developments.

ENGLISH SECULAR MUSIC

If the surviving sources reflect a true picture of their output, most major English composers of the early fifteenth century concentrated almost exclusively on sacred music. A secular musical tradition did exist in England at the time, however, in carols; this tradition was given new life in the fifteenth century when, as the culmination of a long process, English achieved acceptance as a courtly language, thanks in part to the fact that Henry IV was a native speaker of English rather than French. Most of the carols are preserved anonymously in a handful of manuscript anthologies. No polyphonic settings of carols, and only a single monophonic setting (*Lullay, lullay,* probably composed in the fourteenth century), can be dated before the fifteenth century. The early history of the genre and its origin as a monophonic dancing song can only be guessed at. By the fifteenth century, carols no longer served as accompaniment to the dance but were simply secular songs of a popular character. They were popular not by origin but by destination. Sometimes they were used as optional parts of the liturgy and especially as processional songs, perhaps for civic, school, and courtly processions as well as those in church.

Carols, with texts in English, Latin, or a mixture of the two, consist of a refrain (the "burden") and a series of uniform stanzas (often rhyming a a a b). The burden begins the carol and is repeated after each stanza. Composers commonly scored the burden for three voices (sometimes in fauxbourdon) and the stanzas for two. Some carols have a slightly more complicated formal scheme in that two versions of the burden (or occasionally of the stanza) were composed. A few explanatory rubrics suggest that the burden could be sung by full choir, the stanzas by soloists. Though the texts deal with many subjects—moral, political, and religious—most of them praise the Virgin Mary or celebrate the birth of Christ. Their religious orientation notwithstanding, the stereotyped repetition patterns, similar to the French virelai and the Italian ballata, make them the English equivalents of the continental secular *formes fixes.*

The best-known carol is doubtless the rousing *Deo gratias, Anglia,* written in honor of the battle of Agincourt. But the gentle, lyrical *There is no rose* (Example 1–5) may be more typical. Directness and simplicity in harmony, in melodic outline, and in the markedly metrical rhythms (varied chiefly by the frequent hemiolas) characterize the carol and explain the genre's great popularity.

A handful of English secular songs that are not carols survive in early-fifteenth-century manuscripts, and these are written in a remarkably clumsy and old-fashioned two- or three-part counterpoint. Composers of secular songs in the later fifteenth century seem to have followed continental models. The chansons on French texts by John Bedingham, Robert Morton, and Walter Frye fall squarely within the Burgundian tradition. Some bear such a remarkable degree of stylistic affinity to chansons by Burgundian composers that fifteenth-century scribes copying their works introduced a number of conflicting attributions. The English texts, doubtless unfamiliar to continental singers, are often omitted and French ones substituted; this technique of contrafaction may hide yet other

EXAMPLE 1–5. Anonymous English carol, *There is no rose*, mm. 1–15.

songs by English composers. The difficulty of distinguishing between English and French chansons reveals the changed position of the English. They had forged a distinctive style that had an important influence on their continental colleagues during the early years of the century. After 1450 the expatriate composers were completely assimilated into foreign cultures, and those who stayed at home continued to refine and polish older techniques and to devise new ones without regard for developments on the Continent.

BIBLIOGRAPHICAL NOTES

A densely detailed consideration of fifteenth-century music and its late medieval heritage is Reinhard Strohm, *The Rise of European Music 1380–1500* (Cambridge, 1993). Strohm, "European Politics and the Distribution of Music in the Early Fifteenth Century," *EMH* 1 (1981): 305–23, looks at stylistic exchange within Europe and between England and the Continent. Strohm, "Native and Foreign Polyphony in Late Medieval Austria," *MD* 38 (1984): 205–30, and Adelyn Peck Leverett, "Song Masses in the Trent Codices: The Austrian Connection," *EMH* 14 (1995): 205 –56, are both important contributions to our understanding of regional practices and the mid-fifteenth-century Mass repertory.

A number of important essays by David Fallows about fifteenth-century song have been reprinted in his *Songs and Musicians in the Fifteenth Century* (Aldershot, 1996). The comments of Tinctoris and Martin le Franc are the point of departure for Fallows, "The Contenance Angloise: English Influence on Continental Composers of the Fifteenth Century," *RS* 1 (1987): 189–208; the issue of musical transmission between England and the Continent is also taken up in Andrew Wathey, "Dunstable in France," *ML* 67 (1986): 1–31, which focuses on Dunstable's biography and his possible connections in France. Margaret Bent, *Dunstaple* (London, 1981), is the most comprehensive study of this composer's life and works, and the article on Dunstable by Margaret Bent and Brian Trowell in *TNG* is extremely useful and lists the older research in this area. On Leonel Power, see Roger Bowers, "Some Observations on the Life and Career of Leonel Power," *PRMA* 102 (1975–76): 103–27.

Concerning English music of the period, Frank Ll. Harrison, *Music in Medieval Britain*, 2d ed. (London, 1963), surveys plainsong and polyphony from about 1100 to the Reformation. Sylvia W. Kenney, *Walter Frye and the Contenance Angloise* (New Haven, 1964), includes an extensive discussion of early-fifteenth-century English style, discant, and the music of Frye. On English style, see also Charles Hamm, "A Catalogue of Anonymous English Music in Fifteenth-Century Continental Manuscripts," *MD* 22 (1968): 47–76, and Fallows, "English Song Repertories of the Mid–Fifteenth Century," from *PRMA* 103 (1976–77): 61–79, and "Dunstable, Bedyngham and *O rosa bella*," from *JM* 12 (1994): 287–305, both reprinted in his *Songs and Musicians in the Fifteenth Century*.

On faburden and fauxbourdon, see especially Brian L. Trowell, "Faburden and Fauxbourdon," *MD* 13 (1959): 43–78; Trowell's articles on "Faburden" and "Fauxbourdon" in *TNG*; and Ann B. Scott, "The Beginnings of Fauxbourdon: A New Interpretation," *JAMS* 24 (1971): 345–63.

The Old Hall Manuscript, now in the British Library, is available in a reliable modern edition by Andrew Hughes and Margaret Bent (3 vols. in 4, AIM, 1969–73); see also Andrew Hughes and Margaret Bent, "The Old Hall Manuscript—A Re-Appraisal and an Inventory," *MD* 21 (1967): 97–147.

The complete works of John Dunstable have been published by Manfred Bukofzer (2d rev. ed. by Brian L. Trowell, Margaret Bent, and Ian D. Bent, MB, vol. 8; London, 1970). One volume of the projected edition of the complete works of Leonel Power, ed. Charles Hamm (AIM, 1969), has been issued as CMM 1. Power's *Mass: Alma Redemptoris Mater* has appeared ed. Gareth Curtis (Newton Abbot, 1982). For music by Plummer, see *Four Motets by John Plummer*, ed. Brian L. Trowell (Banbury, 1968). Robert Morton's *Collected Works* have been issued in a modern edition by Allan Atlas (New York, 1981). Two songs by John Bedingham have been published in David Fallows, ed., *Two Mid-Fifteenth-Century English Songs* (London, 1977), and other pieces are included in the edition of the Trent codices by Guido Adler and Oswald Kooler in DTÖ (Graz, 1959). The *Missa Dueil angoisseux* is included in DTÖ 31, vol. 61 (1924). The music of Walter Frye is available in Sylvia W. Kenney, ed., *Walter Frye, Collected Works* (AIM, 1960). A selection of English sacred music is published in the series Early English Church Music (vols. 8, 22, 34) as *Fifteenth-Century Liturgical Music*, 3 vols., ed. Andrew Hughes, Margaret Bent, and Gareth R. K. Curtis (London, 1964, 1979, 1989).

British Museum, MS Egerton 3307, is available ed. Gwynn S. McPeek (London, 1963), and Cambridge, Magdalene College, MS Pepys 1236, ed. Sydney Robinson Charles (AIM, 1967). The music of the Eton Choirbook can be consulted in a modern edition by Frank Ll. Harrison as vols. 10–12 of MB.

The corpus of carols is published in *Medieval Carols*, ed. John Stevens, vol. 4 of MB (London, 1958). A few English secular songs are included in *Early Bodleian Music*, ed. John, J.F.R., and C. Stainer (London, 1901) and further examples of fifteenth-century English music are included in H. E. Wooldridge, *Early English Harmony* (London, 1897).

TWO

DUFAY AND BINCHOIS

During the first half of the fifteenth century, as we have seen, English composers cultivated a musical style highly esteemed on the Continent, yet whose "English" character was noted. Theirs was an important contribution to the mixture of styles that, by the middle of the century, blended to become a stylistic mainstream within which the most famous composers worked. Increasingly pan-European, it gradually absorbed a number of strongly regional traditions. By about 1420 the great flowering of the Italian trecento had withered away, and the rich, strange, and overly subtle style of the Ars Subtilior, which had attracted some Italian as well as many French composers (especially those under the cultural domination of Avignon during the Papal Schism), seemed to have reached a dead end. In the earlier fifteenth century, Germany remained a cultural province, content to follow the fashions of its more sophisticated neighbors. France lacked a major composer around whom musical forces could rally. Perhaps the country was too debilitated from the Hundred Years War. Whatever the reason, Paris ceased to be the musical capital of Europe. Although Italy, acknowledged as the birthplace of the Renaissance in the other arts, possessed a brilliant and flourishing cultural life, its music was dominated by foreigners, northern *oltremontani*—persons from "beyond the mountains" (the Alps)—for most of the century. Between about 1420 and 1490, Italy did not

Figure 1. Dufay with a portative organ and Binchois with a harp. Mid-fifteenth-century miniature from a manuscript of Martin le Franc, *Le champion des dames*. (Cliché Bibliothèque nationale de France, Paris)

produce any significant composers within the written tradition, although the country welcomed many of the most important musicians of the time.

Italy was extraordinarily generous in fostering composers, but the leading role in training them fell to institutions in the north, within the territory of the newly wealthy and powerful duchy of Burgundy. The vital musical culture of the Burgundian lands developed thanks to political, institutional, economic, and educational support for music at several levels. Of course, the dukes of Burgundy sought the very best musicians for their court and set an example of vigorous musical patronage. In northern cities and towns, musical education and musical practice were supported in daily activity, at church and through the local patronage of religious and civic organizations. Given the importance of music in church services and civic ritual and the availability of musical training through cathedral and church schools, it is no surprise that most of the major composers of the fifteenth and early sixteenth centuries—Dufay, Binchois, Ockeghem, Busnoys, Josquin, and Isaac, to name but a few—came from Burgundy or, to be precise, that part of it which is now northern France and Belgium. Burgundy itself, in the northeastern part of France with Dijon as its capital city, constituted only a portion of the lands ruled by the dukes. By marriage, purchase, and conquest, the four dukes of Burgundy—Philip the Bold (d. 1404), John the Fearless (d. 1419), Philip the Good (d. 1467), and Charles the Bold (d. 1477)—had put together a kingdom that included Burgundy itself, northern France, Belgium, and Holland, which they hoped to forge into a major power, a buffer state between France and the Holy Roman Empire. Their hope, as it happened, was vain. When Charles died in a battle undertaken in the continuing effort to unite geographically the disparate parts of the duchy, the Burgundian threat to France ended for all time.

The dukes were not only politically ambitious but also avid in their support of the arts. Their court became one of the most brilliant in western Europe. In *The Waning of the Middle Ages,* Huizinga described the fairy-tale atmosphere of Burgundian courtly life, with its exaggerated costumes—peaked hats with veils, long pointed shoes, and so on—polished gemlike paintings and illuminations, and fanciful poetic conceits. The well-known descriptions (by two chroniclers from the court) of the Banquet of the Oath of the Pheasant given by Philip the Good at Lille in 1454 reveal the extravagant spirit of the Burgundians. The banquet was planned to celebrate the vows undertaken, but never fulfilled, to lead a new Crusade against the Turks, who had captured Constantinople the year before. The hall was elegantly decorated with tapestries; wine flowed from fountains, and music sounded from within a mock pastry large enough to hold twenty-eight performers, and from within a model church.

Music at the Burgundian court, and indeed at all the princely courts of western Europe in the fifteenth century, centered on the chapel choir and its organist, a group of ceremonial trumpeters, a small band of virtuoso instrumentalists for chamber music (that is, *basse musique,* or soft music, with players of harp, lute, fiddle, and psaltery), and the players of *hauts* (that is, loud) instruments, such as the wind band to accompany dancing and outdoor entertainments. The singers were the intellectual leaders of these musical establishments; indeed, singing in a princely chapel or a cathedral choir became the principal occupation of composers throughout the fifteenth and sixteenth centuries.

Most composers received their initial musical training as choirboys at cathedral schools, where they undoubtedly learned counterpoint, sight-singing, musical notation, and the liturgy. Virtually every cathedral had a school, but those in Cambrai and Liège were especially famous. A number of fine musicians throughout the century, including Dufay, studied in Cambrai. After their voices changed, some young musicians went on to the university, and many took clerical orders before joining a cathedral *maîtrise* or a prince's chapel as full-fledged members. Their professional careers explain why most of them reserved their best or most ambitious efforts for sacred music, even though these were the same men who provided chansons and secular motets for courtly entertainments, state occasions, and private enjoyment.

In contemporary accounts these musicians, trained in the most complex aspects of their art, are sometimes contrasted with *ménétriers* (minstrels), who were primarily instrumentalists (although there were some *ménétriers de bouche,* or "popular singers"). Because fifteenth-century institutions such as courts, cities, and churches employed instrumentalists of various sorts, especially trumpet corps and wind bands, professional musicians were a regular feature of musical life and found steady work all over Europe. Aspiring young professional instrumentalists were apprenticed to a master player. Since their training was strictly regulated by the musicians' guild and the guilds maintained a medieval tradition of secretiveness, we know very little about their methods of education. Certainly most apprentices learned to play more than one instrument; many seem to have specialized in one range, studying treble cornett, for example, as well as treble recorder, treble shawm, and so on. Only a handful of manuscript musical sources from the period gives any evidence of the work of these apprentices and their teachers, the professional players, because musical performance did not depend exclusively on the use of written pages. They may have spent much of their time learning one by one a vast repertory of melodies along with ways to improvise polyphonic parts around them. But they occasionally played written, nonimprovised polyphony, even though they themselves almost never became composers. Once admitted to the guild as journeymen or master players, they either formed small bands to supply music for civic occasions as well as private entertainments or, if they were very proficient or very fortunate, joined a prince's musical establishment as members of a small group of virtuosi. These two kinds of professional training—at a cathedral school or through apprenticeship to a master player—constituted the principal means of acquiring a thorough musical education in the fifteenth and sixteenth centuries.

GUILLAUME DUFAY

It is no exaggeration to say that Guillaume Dufay (ca. 1400–1474) was without doubt the greatest of the early fifteenth-century composers and one of the great figures in the history of western European music. Dufay absorbed and mastered a wide range of styles and techniques; even a superficial comparison of, say, his youthful isorhythmic motet *Vasilissa ergo gaude,* with his last Mass, that on *Ave Regina caelorum,* reveals the great changes in style that took place during his long lifetime. In Dufay's music we find a sonority based on full triads, a strong sense of harmonic direction, and a careful control of dissonance; a new kind of melody composed in freely flowing rhythms and gently curving arches; newly homogeneous textures; and new methods for achieving formal grandeur.

Dufay's career, though more brilliant than most, was not atypical for a Franco-Netherlandish composer of his time. It led him frequently to Italy and put him in touch with the most advanced musical thought of the age. It differed, perhaps, chiefly in that the city where he was educated, Cambrai, played such a central role. He returned there often from his travels and eventually settled there. Although the place of his birth has not been established with certainty (it may have been in the vicinity of Cambrai or in or near Brussels), he was taught the rudiments of music at the cathedral in Cambrai, was enrolled as a choirboy in 1409, and became *clericus altaris* with a small chaplaincy in the parish church of St-Géry by 1414. It is likely that Dufay traveled to attend the Council of Constance in the retinue of a highly placed cleric from Cambrai and there gained first-hand acquaintance with English music. At Constance, Dufay seems to have come to the attention of his next employer, the Malatesta family, for by 1420 he was already established in Italy as a member of their court chapel in Pesaro and Rimini. They had enough confidence in the young composer to commission from him works commemorating important family events: the isorhythmic motet *Vasilissa ergo gaude* (1420) and the chanson *Resvelliés vous* (1423) to celebrate marriages; and the isorhythmic motet *Apostolo glorioso* (1426) to dedicate the Church of St. Andrew in Greece, newly restored by the Archbishop of Patras, Pandolfo Malatesta.

Dufay may have spent time in Laon between 1423 and 1426; his chanson *Adieu ces bons vins de Lannoy,* dated 1426 in one manuscript, sings a sad farewell to Laon and its attractions. But by April 1427 he had returned to Italy with his next patron, the influential diplomat Robert Auclou, secretary to the papal legate in Bologna, Cardinal Louis Aleman. Dufay stayed in Bologna for about eighteen months, during which time he became a priest. Dufay's motet to St. James, *Rite majorem Jacobum canamus,* and his cyclic *Missa Sancti Jacobi* seem to date from these years and may have been composed for the church of San Giacomo il Maggiore in Bologna.

In 1428 political events forced the cardinal and Dufay's patron to leave Bologna; by October 1428 Dufay was installed as a singer in the papal chapel in Rome, where he remained until 1437 (with a leave of absence from 1433 to 1435). He joined this distinguished organization just after Pierre Fontaine and Nicolas Grenon had resigned, and he belonged to it at a time when Philippe de la Folie, Barthélemy Poignare, Gaultier Libert, Guillaume Malbecque, Jean Brassart, and Arnold de Lantins were all fellow members. For the election of Pope Eugene IV in 1431, Dufay contributed the isorhythmic motet *Ecclesie militantis;* another isorhythmic motet, *Balsamus et munda cera,* was composed shortly thereafter; and yet another, *Supremum est mortalibus,* celebrates King Sigismund's entry into Rome in 1433. The chanson *C'est bien raison,* which honors the Marquis of Ferrara, may mark the peace of Ferrara in the same year. Dufay seems to have composed fewer works in Rome than we might expect of a composer in his prime, but he may also have engaged in a rigorous course of study; the degree in canon law alluded to on his tombstone may have been completed during these Roman years.

Dufay left the papal chapel in 1433 to serve the dukes of Savoy in Chambéry. His prestige was such that Duke Amadeus VIII undoubtedly hired him especially to embellish Louis of Savoy's marriage celebration, planned for early 1434. This important event would be attended by the Duke of Burgundy with his full court chapel and chief composer, Gilles Binchois. It was this event in Chambéry in 1434 that brought together Dufay and Binchois and also the Burgundian chronicler Martin le Franc of *Le champion des dames* (see Chapter 1).

By the time Dufay returned to the papal chapel in 1435, Pope Eugene had had to flee Rome, taking the papal chapel first to Florence and then to Bologna. Two of Dufay's motets from this period, *Mirandas parit haec urbs* and *Salve flos Tusce gentis,* praise Florence and its citizens; and his magnificent isorhythmic motet *Nuper rosarum flores* was composed and first performed for the dedication in 1436 of the architect Brunelleschi's masterpiece, the dome of the cathedral of Florence. During his years in the papal chapel, Dufay also undoubtedly composed many of his single Mass movements (the *Sanctus papale,* for example) and probably his collection of hymn settings.

In 1437 Dufay resigned his post as first singer in the papal chapel. His ties to both Cambrai and Savoy were as strong as ever; he was sent to the Council of Basle as a delegate from the Cambrai cathedral even as he was considered an employee of the Savoy court. During the 1440s and from 1458 to his death, Dufay resided in Cambrai as a canon of the cathedral there. He must also have been a musician in some capacity to Duke Philip the Good of Burgundy, who considered him a *familiaris.* He left his native city for about seven years—from 1452 to 1458—to reside again at the court of Savoy, where he had established cordial relations with Duke Louis and his wife, Anne of Cyprus. During the last two decades of his life, he composed some of his finest music: the lament on the fall of Constantinople, *O très piteux de tout espoir fontaine* (probably the lament sung at the Banquet of the Oath of the Pheasant in 1454); a motet in praise of St. John, *Moribus et genere,* which refers to Dijon, capital city of Burgundy; the moving antiphon-motet *Ave Regina caelorum,* which the composer asked to have sung to him during his last moments; and four of his best Masses, those on *L'homme armé, Se la face ay pale, Ecce ancilla Domini,* and *Ave Regina caelorum.*

Dufay's Chansons

Dufay composed over seventy chansons and a handful of songs on Italian texts, most of them before 1440. Their lyrical qualities, refinement, and delicacy make them an appropriate realization of the Burgundian ethos of the genre. Most of the chansons celebrate love, especially the sort of frustrated love embodied in the dying ideals of chivalry. The poems are written in the stilted and artificial language characteristic of the courtly *rhétoriqueurs* of the fifteenth century, but Dufay's settings invariably overshadow them in artistic significance.

In the fourteenth century only a few fixed poetic schemes (*formes fixes*) were thought appropriate for polyphonic chansons. Most of Machaut's chansons, for example, are either *ballades, virelais,* or *rondeaux.* Dufay continued this late medieval tradition but with a decided preference for rondeaux. Rondeaux continued to be the favorite poems for composers to set throughout the fifteenth century; the hegemony of the *formes fixes* was not threatened until about 1500. Rondeaux, in fact, make up by far the largest number of Dufay's chansons; he composed almost sixty of them. Each poem contains a refrain, part of which alternates with a stanza. Only the refrain need be set—to two sections of music, which are then used also for the stanza, according to the following pattern: AB a A ab AB (the capital letter signifies the refrain, that is, the section in which the same text is set to the same music each time it recurs). Dufay set rondeaux with four-line refrains (*rondeaux quatrains* with the repetition scheme ABCD ab AB abcd ABCD), some with five-line refrains (*rondeaux cinquains,* with the repetition scheme ABCDE abc ABC abcde ABCDE), and even one or two *rondeaux sixains.*

The longest and most serious poems set by Dufay were ballades, most of them composed in his early years. In these strophic poems, the first two couplets of each strophe were set to the same music, and the remaining lines—including the refrain that ends the strophe—received different music. Thus the musical form of the ballade is a a bC or, if a letter is assigned to each phrase of music, ab ab cdE, or ab ab cdeF, and so on, depending on the number of lines in each strophe. Sometimes in a ballade there is musical rhyme between the end of the first section and the end of the refrain (that is, the last few measures before the first double bar are the same as the last few measures of the chanson); and sometimes the traditional three strophes (not all of Dufay's ballades have been preserved with complete text) are followed by a shorter envoi, addressed to a prince. Dufay set but ten ballades, and two of them are exceptional; *Se la face ay pale* is through-composed (that is, without any repetition within a strophe), and *La belle se siet* seems to be based on a pre-existent popular tune used as a tenor cantus firmus.

The virelai is often less serious in content than the ballade; in poetic tone it still preserves something of its medieval origin as a dance song. Like the rondeau, the virelai alternates repetitions of a refrain with stanzas. A refrain opens the song; Dufay's refrains invariably contain five lines (ABCDE). The refrain is followed by a stanza consisting of a pair of couplets or tercets, each set to the same music (fg fg, or fgh fgh), and then a series of lines equal in number and similar in structure to the refrain and set to its music (abcde). The repeated middle section (fg fg) is sometimes supplied with first and second, or *ouvert* and *clos,* endings; it sometimes contrasts in meter and texture with the refrain. The refrain recurs after each stanza. Thus the musical form of a virelai of three stanzas is A bba A bba A bba A or, if the refrain consists of five lines and the first part of the stanza of two couplets, ABCDE fg fg abcde ABCDE, and so on. Virelais of one stanza (A bba A) are called bergerettes. Like Machaut, Dufay set very few of such poems, and all four of his virelais appear to be late works.

Dufay also wrote several Italian songs that seem to be in rondeau form (they may be contrafacta, originally composed in French but adapted to Italian words); some Italian ballate (a form more closely related to the virelai than to the ballade, in spite of its name); a superb setting of Petrarch's canzone to the Virgin Mary, *Vergine bella*, which should perhaps be considered a song-motet; and a handful of other shorter secular pieces in French or Latin.

By their number as well as by their high quality, Dufay's chansons constitute a significant portion of his oeuvre. Spanning his entire career, they reveal the characteristic features of his style at varying times during his life. As a young man Dufay forged a personal style amalgamating elements from the French music of his immediate predecessors with Italian and English elements. The early songs are marked by their jovial tone and use of a variety of technical experiments. During his middle years, from about 1435 to about 1450, Dufay produced fewer songs, but these reveal themselves to be mature works. His latest chansons, dating from his final years in Savoy and Cambrai, from about 1450 to his death in 1474, reveal a musical economy and seriousness of tone appropriate to the great composer's final contributions to the refined courtly genre of his time.

Most of Dufay's chansons combine three voices, although a few are for four. A more-or-less elaborate top voice carefully planned in balancing arches of melody is usually accompanied by a simpler but equally finely worked tenor and a contratenor that fills in (or sometimes determines) the harmonies and keeps the motion moving forward at cadences. Dufay, in other words, inherited the treble-dominated texture, based on the framework of the superius-tenor duet, from his immediate predecessors. During the course of his lifetime Dufay revised and refined his style, partly to make the rhythm of his melodies flow more smoothly and to bring the various strands in the texture closer together. But he never abandoned completely the concept of song as accompanied melody. This is not to say that all Dufay's chansons were intended to be performed by a solo voice with two instruments. Composers in the Renaissance did not always conceive their music with specific performance forces and timbres in mind; performers were free to adapt the composed piece to various combinations of voices and instruments. Thus many of Dufay's chansons might well be performed with two voices (presumably singing superius and tenor) and one instrument, or even with three voices with or without instrumental doubling. Many songs (see Example 2–1, for instance) include introductory, intermediate, and closing phrases suggesting that instruments played some or all of the top line as well.

The melodic style of Dufay's early chansons is metrically simpler than that of his predecessors or, indeed, than that of his own later music. Most of these early works can be transcribed in 3/4 or 6/8 with very few or no syncopations over barlines. Some of them are as straightforward as *Adieu ces bons vins de Lannoy* (Example 2–1). The melody of the top voice, ascending from D to A and then gradually descending a whole octave, shows Dufay's careful concern for architectonic planning. The tenor and the contratenor, as in many of Dufay's

EXAMPLE 2–1. Guillaume Dufay, *Adieu ces bons vins de Lannoy,* mm. 1–13.

chansons, share the same range, but the contratenor often supplies the roots of triads, and its contours emphasize the principal tones of the mode (D and A). Contratenors such as this that "carry the harmony" (*Harmonieträger,* in Heinrich Besseler's term) lend a strikingly "tonal" sound to Dufay's songs because the stressed vertical sonorities resemble tonics and dominants. Dufay's songs have a clear harmonic organization and sense of goal-directed phrasing, but these are not to be considered merely personal innovations: such "tonal" sounding harmony is heard as well in many Italian songs from the trecento and motets by Ciconia.

Whereas hemiola (that is, the juxtaposition of 6/8 and 3/4) is the chief rhythmic effect Dufay produced in the metrically regular compositions such as his early chansons, in later chansons Dufay had begun to break loose from the shackles of regular metrical stress and to conceive of his melodies in irregular groupings of two or three beats independent of metrical units (that is, measures of a modern transcription), a feature that gives his melodies their floating quality. This is only barely suggested in *Mille bonjours* (Example 2–2), where the rhythmic syncopations (note especially those at the beginning and in bars 18–19 in the top voice) tend to detract from metric regularity. Composers after Dufay took up this feature; throughout the fifteenth and, indeed, the sixteenth centuries, they continued to write melodies that unfolded in irregular rhythmic groupings.

After about 1440, Dufay abandoned the ballade and worked at refining his control of dissonance and harmonic clarity. While never abandoning the layered structure of treble-dominated texture, he took ever greater care to integrate the various strands of his texture into a homogeneous whole. In *Mille bonjours,* for example, all three voices move at about the same rate of speed; the top voice is not strikingly faster, as those in his earlier chansons are apt to be. In

EXAMPLE 2–2. Guillaume Dufay, *Mille bonjours je vous presente*, mm. 1–20.

several structurally important places (for example, in bars 12–15), the voices are knit together briefly in imitation.

Adieu m'amour (Example 2–3) is a late chanson that exemplifies these traits (tonal clarity, rhythmic independence of the voices, and integration of the texture by imitation and other means) and demonstrates that the composer handled them with masterly ease. The melody in the top voice proceeds with complete freedom from metrical restrictions; it has a memorable quality that stems

EXAMPLE 2–3. Guillaume Dufay, *Adieu m'amour*, mm. 1–6.

from the careful way the phrases are shaped, which gives form to the constantly changing rhythms. (By this time, by the way, compositions in duple meter were as common as those in 6/4 or 3/4.) Also notable is the skill with which the mode is established both melodically and harmonically in the first phrase, with the simple alternation of F and C harmonies. The opening phrases are elegant and intimate; the rising melody for "Adieu" is used sequentially with a broadening of the opening gesture for the parallelism of the poetic conceit (compare superius bars 1 and 4), and the texture is closely knit through momentary homorhythm (bar 2) and imitation (bars 3–4) between tenor and superius. *Adieu m'amour* typifies Dufay's later chanson style; it is a miniature masterpiece with few equals in the entire fifteenth century.

The harmonically coherent sound of Dufay's music does not depend merely on building individual phrases largely from definitive harmonies. Dufay connected each phrase to the structure of the whole piece by controlling the scale degrees on which the cadences occur. Most fall on important mode-defining notes, but enough occur on other degrees to provide contrast and variety and to give the music a sense of forward motion. In Dufay's music, within a style that is essentially linear in concept and technique, the composer set himself the challenge of overall planning with attention to vertical sonorities and hierarchy of cadences.

The cadences by which Dufay realizes a larger musical structure are, for the most part, those he inherited from his fourteenth-century predecessors. Most phrases end with the harmonic pattern VII^6–I, with a double leading tone in the penultimate chord (that is, a raised fourth as well as seventh degree, a mannerism that gradually disappeared in the course of the fifteenth century). This cadence is usually decorated with a melodic ornament on the scale degrees 7–6–8, which explains why it is called an "under-third cadence." Example 2–4 shows such cadences in their simplest form for each mode.

EXAMPLE 2–4. Under-third cadences in each mode.

| Dorian | Phrygian | Lydian | Mixolydian |

The more modern V–I cadence (with or without a 4–3 suspension in the top voice) also sometimes occurs in Dufay's music, especially that of his later years. More often than not, this cadence is partially disguised as an "octave-leap cadence." In such a cadence, the stepwise contrary motion that leads to an octave between superius and tenor is harmonized by the contratenor leaping up an octave from the root of the first triad to the fifth of the second (Example 2–5). This trick manages to preserve the traditional part-writing of the struc-

EXAMPLE 2–5. An octave-leap V–I cadence in the Dorian mode with 4–3 suspension.

tural voices while avoiding undesirable parallelisms that would occur between the lower voices if both leapt up a fourth to the final note.

Any of these cadences can occur on scale degrees other than the ones shown, but transpositions were most commonly made by fourths or fifths. By a convention of the time, such transpositions are indicated by a flat in the key signature. Thus a composition on G with one flat in the key signature is said to be in transposed Dorian mode, a composition on C with one flat in transposed Mixolydian mode, and so on. Two flats indicate a transposition by two fourths or fifths; thus a composition on C with two flats in the signature is said to be in twice-transposed Dorian mode. Two of our examples (Examples 2–2 and 2–3) have only partial key signatures; the first two have a flat in the lower two voices, the last only in the lowest voice.

Dufay's Motets

Dufay composed several kinds of pieces that fall into the category of motet, using a range of techniques from simple to complex. He composed a number of relatively short pieces—most of them harmonizations of plainchant—to accompany the liturgical service, and he wrote some rather more elaborate motets, some based on cantus firmi and others paraphrasing a chant in the top voice. Some of his most elegant Latin compositions fall into this last category; most of them are dedicated to the Virgin Mary, and their treble-dominated texture and lyrical charm—they resemble chansons in many ways—explain why they are called song-motets. But before the late Mass cycles, by far his most impressive and most complex compositions were isorhythmic motets, many of them written, as we have seen, for a particular historical occasion.

Fourteenth-century composers found in isorhythm a compositional technique on which they could base their most complicated musical structures; Machaut's most elaborate secular compositions, for example, are isorhythmic motets. In taking over the technique, Dufay realized that, like all ancient rituals hallowed by tradition and constant use, isorhythm was especially appropriate for official state occasions and other great events (this is true of Ciconia's isorhythmic motets and is likely the case with Dunstable's as well). Thus, the genre of the isorhythmic motet, which fell out of fashion in Dufay's own time, flourished in spectacular fashion for the last time under his care, although techniques derived from isorhythm would retain their attraction for composers in the following generation. In this respect, it would be oversimple to say that Dufay ended rather than began a tradition, for, as we shall see, his Mass cycles do carry on the older principles of the isorhythmic motet—but in a completely new and unexpected manner.

Dufay worked out the complex structures of isorhythmic motets in a variety of ways. For them he generally preferred a texture of four voices, though two have three and two have five voices. In two (*Apostolo glorioso* and *Rite maiorem*) he arranged the compositions so that they can be performed with either four or five parts, or with only the two top voices accompanied by a *solus tenor* (a lower part that can substitute for the original tenor and contratenors). All the isorhythmic motets combine a slow-moving tenor—a cantus firmus almost invariably based on plainchant—with faster-moving upper voices singing one or sometimes more texts simultaneously with the cantus firmus. In some motets only the tenor is isorhythmic; that is, it is composed of a rhythmic pattern (if an extended rhythm sometimes lasting more than forty measures can be called a pattern) that is repeated literally one or more times, on occasion in diminution or augmentation. In some, all the voices are isorhythmic. In some, Dufay added to his already elaborate design a second isorhythmic tenor also based on chant. In some, the isorhythmic voices are constructed not only with a *talea* (a repeated rhythmic pattern), but also with a *color* (a pitch pattern that repeats, but not necessarily in phase with the repetitions of the rhythm). Still others have introits, interludes, or postludes independent of any isorhythm.

The earliest motet by Dufay, *Vasilissa ergo gaude* (Example 2–6), is entirely isorhythmic, like many such ceremonial pieces by his older contemporaries. All voices are controlled by simple isorhythm, with one repetition of the *talea* (the *color* consists of the entire tenor, a cantus firmus taken from chant). Dufay's motet begins with a canonic introit independent of the isorhythmic design. The texture consists of two slower-moving lower voices and two faster melody-bearing upper voices, and the two upper voices engage frequently in imitation. Note that here even as a young composer Dufay writes smooth, long-breathed, and strongly directional melodies.

The organization of *Supremum est mortalibus* (1433), one of Dufay's most beautiful and most accessible isorhythmic motets, is at once slightly more complex and freer than that of *Vasilissa ergo gaude*. In *Supremum est mortalibus* (Example 2–7) only the tenor (apparently not based on a plainchant) is isorhythmic. The *color* in the tenor is stated twice; each statement coincides with three statements of the *talea*. The mensuration changes when the *color* is repeated, a change that seems to require a new tempo, even though that is not indicated in the modern edition of Dufay's complete works. Thus, the basic organization of the tenor is

color:	A	B	C	A	B	C
talea:	x	x	x	x′	x′	x′

EXAMPLE 2–6. Guillaume Dufay, *Vasilissa ergo gaude*, mm. 1–31, 62–70.

(a) mm. 1–31

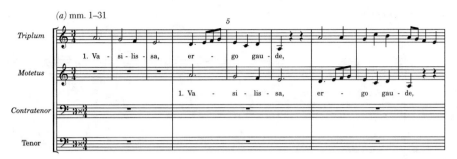

I, 1 Concupivit rex decorem tuum

EXAMPLE 2–6. (*Continued*)

(*b*) mm. 62–70

II, 1 Quoniam ipse est domine tuus

EXAMPLE 2–7. Guillaume Dufay, *Supremum est mortalibus bonum*, mm. 1–45.

I, 1

EXAMPLE 2–7. (*Continued*)

III, 1

But the motet is freer than most in a number of ways. It opens with a nonisorhythmic introit in fauxbourdon, the earliest datable composition in which that technique is specifically demanded. It closes with a similarly free postlude in which the names of Pope Eugene and Emperor Sigismund are underlined by being sung in block chords marked with fermatas. The upper voices are not isorhythmic, and the statements of the *talea* are interrupted each time by free interludes while the tenor is silent. The motet is notable for its sweetness as well, with its passages of fauxbourdon, parallel thirds in the upper parts, full triads, and many graceful under-third cadences in strong positions.

The most impressive motet of all, and one of Dufay's most complex, is *Nuper rosarum flores* (Example 2–8), commissioned for the dedication of the church of Santa Maria del Fiore, the Cathedral of Florence, in 1436. The motet's isorhythm is brought about in the repetition scheme of the two lower voices, while the two upper voices are allowed to unfold in free variation, without a predetermined rhythmic or melodic plan. The lower of the melody-bearing highest voices sometimes splits into two, enriching the sonority and increasing the sense of grandeur. The two slower-moving tenors are derived from the same chant, *Terribilis est locus iste* ("Awesome is this place"), the Introit for the Mass at the Dedication of a Church. Tenor I states the chant a fifth lower than Tenor II and in a different rhythm, so that a free canon results. The *talea* and the *color* coincide; the isorhythmic tenors are stated four times in tempos that vary in the proportions 6:4:2:3. Before each full section with all four parts, the two equally melodious upper voices sing a rhythmically free duet. Each section of duet plus tutti sets a different number of lines of the text sung by the upper voices (a four-strophe poem in Latin that Dufay himself probably wrote), such that the music reshapes the structure of the poem. The motet is thus a free set of variations based on a free canon controlled by isorhythm. The formal ground plans of this and the other isorhythmic motets are in fact their most impressive feature. The inspiration for the musical architecture of *Nuper rosarum flores* was probably the biblical Temple of Solomon, whose dimensions are reflected in the proportional relationships in the motet. Dufay's compositional challenge was to find a musical equivalent of Solomon's Temple, an important symbol in the act of consecration of the new cathedral. But the musical architecture is not the only notable aspect of this motet; its grandeur is

EXAMPLE 2–8. Guillaume Dufay, *Nuper rosarum flores*, 1–64.

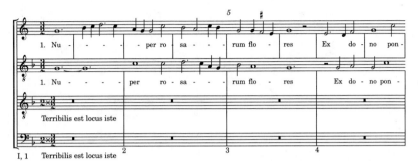

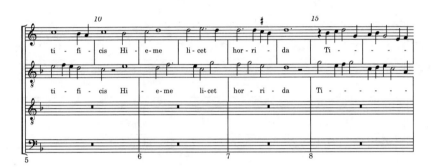

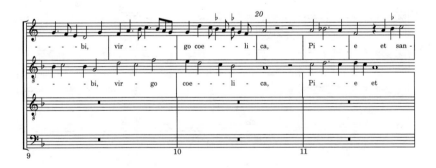

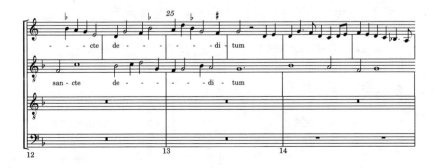

EXAMPLE 2–8. (*Continued*)

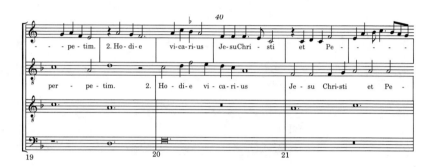

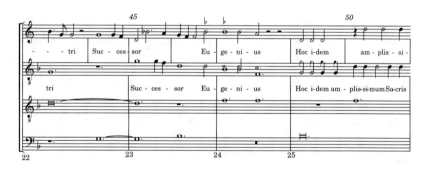

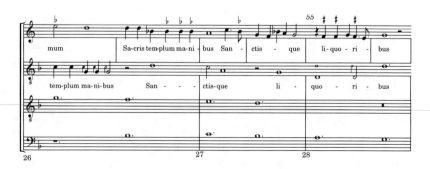

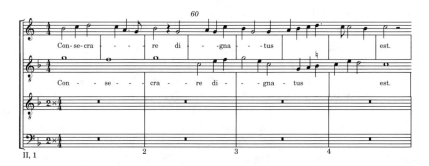

II, 1

wholly audible, especially in the series of rich triadic harmonies in root position in the extended tutti sections. Craig Wright has written that in *Nuper rosarum flores*—a "distinctly medieval creation"—"a foreground of audible sound is determined by a grand design of inaudible numerical ratios." If the structural ingenuity of *Nuper rosarum flores* belongs to the Middle Ages by virtue of its number symbolism, surely the techniques that produced the overtly full and exuberant harmony with which this motet greets the listener were ahead of their time and fundamental to the development of music in the Renaissance.

Dufay's shorter and simpler Latin pieces include those written for use in the liturgy: antiphons and sequences, for example, as well as hymns. Although cantus-firmus technique remained Dufay's principal means of constructing sacred compositions, in almost all his hymns he paraphrased the borrowed chant by presenting it in a more-or-less ornamented version in the top voice. His collection of hymns, all for three voices, consists of a cycle for the whole liturgical year, probably composed in the 1430s. They are simple, unpretentious harmonizations of the decorated chant. Four of them are written in fauxbourdon, that is, with the inner part not written out but intended to be sung a fourth below the superius. Two of these exist also in alternative versions in regular three-part counterpoint. Like various other liturgical pieces of the fifteenth and sixteenth centuries, Dufay's hymns were intended for *alternatim* performance. That is, the odd-numbered strophes of the hymn were performed in plainchant, while the even-numbered strophes were sung to a single polyphonic setting supplied by Dufay.

Cantus-firmus technique is abandoned, too, in some of Dufay's song-motets, shorter and more lyrical Latin compositions in treble-dominated texture, many of them honoring the Virgin Mary. The well-known and very beautiful *Alma redemptoris mater*—with its surprisingly effective ending in block chords—paraphrases a chant in the top voice. The very florid superius turns out, in fact, to be a surprisingly literal version of the chant, transformed rhythmically and with a few ornamental notes added. Other Marian song-motets, like *Flos florum*, were composed apparently without any borrowed material.

On the other hand, the four-part setting of the Marian antiphon *Ave Regina caelorum,* which Dufay composed in Cambrai in 1464–65, uses a cantus firmus in the tenor; but how different this paraphrase of the chant sounds from the more conventional long, slow notes of many a structural voice. Everything in the motet supports Dufay's evident desire to achieve an integrated, homogeneous texture. He gave the chant a rhythmic shape—and decorated it—so that it is indistinguishable from any of the other voices. The voices sometimes take up parts of the tenor's melody, either in imitation or in the duets and trios that vary the texture. The formal divisions of the piece are very clear: it is divided into two *partes,* the first in triple, the second in duple meter; each *pars* is subdivided according to the phrases of the original chant, but the music flows along smoothly in that free prose rhythm that characterizes Dufay's late works. Since a second contratenor moves for the most part below the tenor, the composer can control the harmonic movement more closely than he could if the chant were the lowest voice. There is one stunning expressive effect, a sudden minor chord at the textual interpolation "have mercy on thy dying Dufay," which strikes the ear as surprisingly modern.

Dufay's Masses

Dufay himself did not invent the cyclic Mass, in which all five movements of the polyphonic setting of the Ordinary are based on a single cantus firmus. This genre was created, as we have seen, by English composers in the early fifteenth century as a technique for unifying the central musical portion of the liturgy. Continental musicians developed other means to unify several sections of the Mass (for example, they used the same opening "head-motifs," or "mottoes," to link movements), and they came to know the English genre many years before they produced cyclic cantus-firmus Masses themselves. Dufay was not the first northern composer to take on the genre, but he realized brilliantly its musical possibilities and brought it into the mainstream of Franco-Netherlandish polyphony. He was apparently the first composer to use a secular melody as chief structural member in a Mass; he adapted the four-part texture of the motet to the Mass; and he was the first regularly to write a contratenor beneath the borrowed tenor, to furnish a strong bass and to free himself from the harmonic restrictions imposed by a given melody stated in the lowest voice. In a sense Dufay continued in his cantus-firmus Masses the tradition of the isorhythmic motet. Although some of his borrowed tenors—like those of his English contemporaries—are presented in new rhythmic guises each time they appear, others keep the same rhythmic identity through all five movements. The latter Masses are in effect gigantic isorhythmic structures, except for the possibility that the Mass tenor may have been intended to have an audible effect on the listener's perception of the form. One of the great formal conventions in the history of Western polyphony, the cantus-firmus Mass became the vehicle for large-scale musical thought in the fifteenth and through much of the sixteenth centuries.

Dufay's cantus-firmus Masses were all composed in his last years, after 1450. His earlier efforts at Mass compositions, between about 1420 and 1440, resulted in single movements, paired movements (Gloria–Credo and Sanctus–Agnus), two short Masses of three movements each (Kyrie–Gloria–Credo and Kyrie–Sanctus–Agnus), and three Mass cycles without a unifying cantus firmus: the *Missa sine nomine,* the *Missa Sancti Jacobi* (which includes some movements of the Proper as well as the Ordinary), and the Mass that Besseler published as *Missa Sancti Antonii Viennensis,* but which David Fallows has shown to have been dedicated instead to St. Anthony of Padua. Most of the individual movements are composed for three voices in treble-dominated style, most often without a borrowed chant, although there are some with chant (paraphrased) in the top voice. The *Missa Sancti Jacobi* includes what is probably the oldest surviving passage in fauxbourdon (although, as we have seen, the fauxbourdon in *Supremum est mortalibus* is the oldest example that can be securely dated). Some movements were intended for *alternatim* performance, with a part of the text sung as chant and the rest in polyphony supplied by Dufay. Some movements are troped, and one Gloria–Credo pair in four-part motet texture (with two upper melody-bearing voices and two slower-moving lower voices) incorporates snatches of French and Italian popular melodies into the music set to the tropes. The delightful *Gloria ad modum tubae* resembles a caccia, with a rousing canon between the top two voices and a series of fanfare-like ostinati alternating between the lower two voices, which lead the piece to a smashing climax by means of stretto and hocket.

The Mass pairs, three-movement Masses, and Mass cycles are unified in various ways. In some, each movement begins with the same phrase in one or more voices (a head-motif, or motto, opening). A distinctive final cadence ends each of the movements of one of the short Masses. The sections within many of the movements of the *Missa sine nomine* and the Ordinary of the *Missa Sancti Jacobi* follow each other with the same sequence of time signatures. Some of the multimovement works, however, are not unified by any discernible musical means; modern editions have joined them only because the original scribes did so in the manuscripts that preserve them. In short, in his earlier years Dufay experimented with a number of devices for relating one Mass movement to another. He had no fixed concept of the musically unified Mass Ordinary, nor indeed was there any need for such a concept from a strictly liturgical point of view.

Missa Caput (ca. 1440–50), the earliest of the cantus-firmus Masses once attributed to Dufay, is probably not by Dufay at all. It was composed in England by an unnamed composer about 1440–45, and within a dozen years it was known and respected on the Continent. Many subsequent Masses were modeled on its strict treatment of the cantus firmus. Its tenor was taken from a melisma in the antiphon *Venit ad Petrum,* used in the English (Sarum) service—though not in the Roman liturgy—for the ritual washing of the feet during Holy Week. Its "Englishness" seems confirmed by its appearance in several insular manuscripts. (If it had been composed by Dufay, it would be the only continental Mass of the time in an English source.) Moreover, documentary and possibly musical evidence as well suggest that the troped Kyrie—divided after the English fashion into two rather than three *partes*—was composed later than the other movements. Ockeghem and Obrecht, who both wrote Masses partly modeled on this Caput Mass, seem not to have known this Kyrie (it was attributed to Dufay in the main source, but his name was at one time erased from the manuscript).

No clear documentary evidence links Dufay with a second cantus-firmus Mass, *La mort de saint Gothard,* on a French popular tune; but Besseler was convinced enough that the style was Dufay's to include the Mass in his edition of the composer's complete works. Dufay's stature as a Mass composer rests secure on the four magnificent late works firmly attributed to him. Two of them are based on secular cantus firmi, *Se la face ay pale* and *L'homme armé,* and two on plainchant, *Ecce ancilla Domini* and *Ave Regina caelorum.*

The *Missa Se la face ay pale,* composed shortly after 1450, while Dufay was in Savoy, and the first of Dufay's Masses to be based on a secular tenor (unless *La mort de saint Gothard* is earlier and genuine), demonstrates very well Dufay's genius in planning a large-scale musical structure. For the cantus firmus, he borrowed the tenor from his own three-voice ballade *Se la face ay pale,* composed some two decades earlier (Example 2–9). As in some earlier works, the Mass has a motto opening, in this case a bit of two-part counterpoint; the first three measures of Example 2–10 show the motto exactly as it appears in all movements but the Kyrie. It is the thoroughly rational disposition of the cantus firmus that really binds all five movements together as a unit. Dufay's grand design is summarized in the following table, which shows the portion of the tenor used in each section as well as the speed at which it sounds (*integer valor* means the normal time values of notes as distinguished from values reduced or enlarged by diminution or augmentation).

EXAMPLE 2–9. Tenor of Dufay's ballade *Se la face ay pale.*

The tenor creates the form of the Mass. Its systematic repetitions impose order on the music. The way it speeds up proportionally produces a sense of climax in the Gloria and the Credo, the two movements with the most text (and the least obvious intrinsic shape). Even by dropping out for particular sections (in

THE FORMAL LAYOUT OF DUFAY'S *MISSA SE LA FACE AY PALE*

	Section of C.F. Used	Speed of C.F.
KYRIE		
Kyrie I	AB	2 × *integer valor*
Christe	c. f. omitted	
Kyrie II	C	2 × *integer valor*
GLORIA		
Et in terra pax	Complete	3 × *integer valor*
Qui tollis	Complete	2 × *integer valor*
Cum sancto spiritu	Complete	*integer valor*
CREDO		
Patrem omnipotentem	Complete	3 × *integer valor*
Et iterum venturus est	Complete	2 × *integer valor*
Confiteor	Complete	*integer valor*
SANCTUS		
Sanctus	A	2 × *integer valor*
Pleni sunt caeli	c. f. omitted	
Osanna	B	2 × *integer valor*
Benedictus	c. f. omitted	
Osanna	C	2 × *integer valor*
AGNUS DEI		
Agnus I	AB	2 × *integer valor*
Agnus II	c. f. omitted	
Agnus III	C	2 × *integer valor*

the Christe, Pleni, Benedictus, and Agnus II—sections that came traditionally to be set without cantus firmus), the tenor establishes a pattern that determines the overall form. Furthermore, in some passages within each movement the tenor is absent and the counterpoint reduced to two equally melodious voices. These changes in texture further clarify the shape of the music. Each movement except the Kyrie opens with an extended duet. In the Gloria and Credo, extended duets precede each statement of the cantus firmus, reinforcing the larger design by the alternating densities of sound, duet–tutti–duet–tutti–duet–tutti; and within each tutti the structure of the tenor melody is emphasized by the inclusion of a brief duet just before phrase C.

On a more detailed level the form of the music is determined by the length of each phrase and especially by the placement of the cadences. Example 2–10, the beginning of the Gloria, illustrates well how Dufay built up his grand structures from smaller units. The clarity of the melodic design is especially apparent in the superius during the opening duet. Its gentle arch rises several times to E before cadencing on C, and its divisions into segments are marked by strong and obvious cadences, some (at mm. 13 and 19) more important than

EXAMPLE 2–10. Guillaume Dufay, *Missa Se la face ay pale,* Gloria, mm. 1–34.

others (m. 6). After the entrance of the cantus firmus in m. 19, the next important cadence occurs at m. 31. It coincides with the end of the first phrase of the tenor (mm. 31–33 function as a codetta), and thus the force of the structural voice in determining the form is confirmed by the behavior of the other voices; the details of form reinforce the overall plan.

Even with Dufay's attention to musical detail, it is not always easy to discern a strong relationship between the words and their musical setting. In certain instances, such as the block chords to stress important phrases in several motets and the wonderfully expressive minor triads in *Ave Regina caelorum*, Dufay was clearly concerned with projection, perhaps even expression, of his text. But it is usually impossible to know precisely how he intended individual syllables to be set beneath the music, for the scribes were not careful to indicate such details, and the melodic design and frequent melismas do not usually suggest one obvious and clearly correct manner of performance. Text underlay, like instrumentation, may have been an area in which the performer was allowed a certain freedom to seek the best solution. The composer's duty was done in supplying the notes; the appropriate words could be made to fit in more than one way.

Example 2–10 is also, by the way, an excellent example of the rhythmic style of the mature Dufay. Except for the long notes in the tenor, no two consecutive bars ever present the same rhythms. Moreover, this ever-changing succession of note values can be grouped into units of two, three, four, or more beats that frequently do not coincide with the bar line. Indeed, the tension set up between the free prose rhythms and the implied metrical structure—for the cadences always come out "correctly" on the downbeat, and the dissonances always take into account strong and weak beats—gives to Dufay's later music one of its most characteristic and most exciting qualities.

In all his late Masses, Dufay wrote for four voices. To be sure, he did not keep them all active at every moment; aside from the extended duets, which function importantly in articulating form, Dufay also wrote much briefer passages for two or three voices in every conceivable combination, simply to vary the sound and to keep the texture light and transparent. In his Masses, he took over from the isorhythmic motet the idea of the repeating cantus firmus, so he adapted to them the texture of motets, with two melodious upper voices and two slower-moving lower voices, but with one important difference: in the late Masses Dufay invariably kept his second contratenor (whatever he called it—tenor bassus, contra bassus, or simply bassus) below the cantus firmus. The contratenor sounds as a real harmonic bass, in a four-part texture. This new arrangement left Dufay more freedom to determine the succession of "chords" unhampered by the notes of a *cantus prius factus* on which to build each triad. To write of triads in Dufay's music is an anachronism: he surely thought in terms of intervals between voices, in the way that all treatises of the time explain counterpoint; and yet triads are in fact the basic harmonic unit out of which his phrases grow.

The harmonic style of Dufay's Masses is partly determined by the careful way in which he handled dissonances. Intervals and chords are normally consonant on strong beats unless a suspension creates a dissonance that quickly resolves (see, for instance, Example 2–10, mm. 9, 12, 15, and 18). For the most part, dissonances occur on weak beats or subdivisions of the beat, frequently only in passing. This regularity gives to Dufay's music its characteristic sound, so much "sweeter" than that of fourteenth-century French composers and yet with a high-enough level of dissonance to keep the motion flowing smoothly forward. Controlled dissonance became a hallmark of music throughout the Renaissance. If Dufay's counterpoint is not quite as rigorously purified of unusual dissonances as, say, Palestrina's in the sixteenth century, it is nevertheless the earlier composer who established the normal practice and who made it a principle of style.

The *Missa Se la face ay pale* is, in short, a monument to rationality and order, at the beginning of the history of the cyclic Mass with unifying cantus firmus. In all Dufay's other late Masses, he used borrowed material with more rhythmic freedom, embellishing and elaborating the tenor each time it recurred.

Dufay probably wrote the *Missa Ave Regina caelorum* in the last decade or so of his life. It appears, at least, to be the work of an old and very wise musician, and it shares many stylistic features with the motet Dufay composed on the same Marian antiphon. Its most distinctive trait is the way in which all four voices begin to resemble one another. The top voice does not assert its dominance quite as much as in Dufay's earlier music, nor does the lowest voice distort its melodic line for the sake of harmonic clarity. The tenor, which states a pre-existent melody, has exactly the same contours and moves exactly as fast as the other voices, which imitate it. But the amount of imitation in the *Missa Ave Regina caelorum*—the extent to which the cantus firmus permeates the other voices—as remarkable as it is, should perhaps be emphasized less than the fact that all four voices have melodic lines virtually equal in importance. This is the texture that Dufay's successors were to adopt.

In these four late Masses, as well as in his motets and chansons, Dufay established certain norms of style for the music of the future. His method of writing melodies in free prose rhythms was taken up and refined over the next hundred or so years. His techniques for underpinning the structure of a composition by carefully planned networks of cadences were widely imitated. His chaste regulation of dissonance gave to music a characteristic sound widely adopted throughout the period. In some of his later works the hierarchical, layered texture of the Middle Ages began to be modified in favor of a homogeneous sound that later composers came to prefer. Above all, his music is distinguished for its formal clarity. In bringing the cantus-firmus Mass into the mainstream of Franco-Netherlandish polyphony and demonstrating how gigantic musical structures could be created, Dufay gave his successors one of the great formal conventions in the history of Western music.

GILLES BINCHOIS

From the time of Martin le Franc's *Le champion des dames* to the present, Dufay and his contemporary Gilles Binchois (ca. 1400–1460) have been cited together as the foremost representatives of the Burgundian epoch. Dufay, as we have seen, was a cosmopolitan composer and one of the great international figures of his time, whose penchant for compositional challenge and innovation put him in a class by himself. Binchois, on the other hand, was the *Burgundian* composer par excellence. He spent most of his mature working years, from about 1430 or even earlier, as a chaplain at the court of the dukes of Burgundy. Except for these years of service under Philip the Good, however, we know relatively little about Binchois's life. He grew up at the court of William IV, ruler of Hainaut. Ockeghem, in his lament on Binchois's death, reports that the Burgundian composer served as a soldier when a young man, before he took clerical orders. It is possible that he spent a few years during the decade of the 1420s in Paris and elsewhere working for William de la Pole, the Earl (and later Duke) of Suffolk, who was himself both poet and musician.

If we compare Binchois with Dufay, we must bear in mind that his goals as a composer had much to do with the circumscribed focus of his activity and his cultivation of a Burgundian court aesthetic. Many of Binchois's chansons are as rich and elegant as any by his contemporaries, even those by Dufay. Others merely string together favorite melodic figures that seem to us clichés. A careful evaluation of his contribution must also take into account his versatility and his breadth. Binchois was a prolific composer, and although he is known better in our time as a composer of secular songs, his sacred pieces outnumber (and are longer than) his secular ones. Some of Binchois's motets and Mass movements have the charm and sweetness that characterize much music of this epoch, though few aspire to the technical heights reached by Dufay. Binchois's sacred music is in some ways more direct than Dufay's, and certainly the Mass movements are simpler in style, with melodies that tend to be short-breathed and less intricate.

Binchois's oeuvre contains more than sixty sacred pieces: twenty-eight Mass movements (including three Gloria–Credo pairs and five Sanctus–Agnus pairs), plus settings of the Magnificat, antiphons, and motets (including a single, incomplete isorhythmic motet). Binchois's avoidance of the isorhythmic motet may stem from the demands of his position rather than from a lack of technical mastery: the Burgundian court had no use for elaborately ceremonial sacred music other than the Mass. Indeed, much of Binchois's sacred music smacks of work done in daily service to fulfill a particular set of liturgical needs. Thus many of his motets, hymns, and Magnificats are created largely from formulae or move in plain (or only slightly embellished) three-part chords. Binchois composed some music in fauxbourdon; his setting of the psalm *In exitu Israel* is virtually in fauxbourdon and moves almost entirely in $\frac{6}{3}$ chords, even though all three voices are written out. The rhythmic interest of the music depends entirely on text accents that do not correspond with the implied meter. More typical of his straightforward chordal style is a setting of the hymn *Quem terra,* which mixes parallel $\frac{6}{3}$ chords with slightly more independent part writing and adds some melodic embellishments; the chant is paraphrased in the top voice.

Aside from the incompletely preserved isorhythmic motet (*Nove cantum melodie,* written for the birth of Philip the Good's son, Antoine, in 1430, and including in its text the names of many of Binchois's colleagues among the court singers), the most elaborate of his sacred compositions are written in treble-dominated style, with or without a paraphrase of a pre-existent plainchant in the top voice. His setting of the Marian antiphon *Ave Regina caelorum, mater regis angelorum* (Example 2–11) is exceptional in that Binchois paraphrased the chant in both the superius and the tenor, thereby creating a series of points of imitation that contrast with several quite simple chordal passages. The example gives a fair impression of Binchois's treble-dominated compositions, in which the top voice is seldom as florid or as clearly distinguished from the others as in most of Dufay's comparable works. Binchois seems not to have composed cantus-firmus Masses; at least, no tenor in any of his Mass movements has yet been identified as a transformed plainchant. Nor do any cyclic Masses by him survive; at most, he created a liturgical but not a musical relationship between two movements by basing both members of the pair on chants taken from the same

EXAMPLE 2–11. Gilles Binchois, *Ave Regina caelorum, mater regis angelorum,* mm. 1–12.

Gregorian Ordinary. But his most attractive sacred compositions are those single Mass movements that most closely resemble chansons, the genre in which he excelled.

Binchois pieced together some of his chansons from musical formulae in much the same way he composed his simpler sacred music. A rondeau such as *Adieu m'amour et ma maistresse* (Example 2–12) is in this respect highly instructive, for the stereotyped nature of much of the material enables us to see

EXAMPLE 2–12. Gilles Binchois, *Adieu m'amour et ma maistresse,* mm. 1–10.

how the composer planned his chanson. The refrain of the rondeau consists of four lines of poetry, each set to a single phrase of music. A highly conventional cadential formula ends each phrase. These cadences plainly articulate the form; there can be no doubt about how each part relates to the whole. In *Adieu m'amour,* cadential formulae occupy an unusually large number of measures, and they are all harmonized in similar fashion, with parallel sixths between superius and tenor spreading to an octave. Each phrase begins with a distinctive melodic gesture; these memorable beginnings cannot be called motives, for they never return and play no part in the formal process of the composition. They are often constructed of thirds (sometimes filled in or embellished) or outline a triad. The melody in Example 2–13, taken from Binchois's famous *De plus en plus,* shows a characteristic sample from another of his chansons.

The melody of a Binchois chanson—or indeed of any Franco-Netherlandish chanson in the fifteenth century—is seldom constructed in a way that reveals or demands a single particular solution to the problem of joining the words to the notes. Nevertheless, most phrases seem to begin syllabically, the

EXAMPLE 2–13. Gilles Binchois, *De plus en plus,* superius, mm. 1–4.

distinctive opening gesture carrying most of the syllables of the poetic line. Then they broaden out into a melisma on the penultimate or antepenultimate syllable (whichever gets more stress), which leads directly to the cadential formula. In *Adieu m'amour,* instrumental interludes, separated from the main phrases by passing cadences, substitute for the nearly inevitable closing melismas. The phrases in this chanson are all short, consisting of scarcely more than an opening gesture and a closing cadential formula.

   Adieu m'amour reveals itself as an early chanson of Binchois by its rhythmic style and its texture. In the early works (composed before about 1430), the superius moves largely in eighth notes and seldom conflicts with the 6/8 time signature. The tenor is still usually the lowest voice. The contratenor's role is slightly ambiguous; it sometimes acts as a harmonic bass (for example, at the final cadence and the end of the first phrase), but it often serves as a filler voice. Both lower lines merely support the superius and take little part in the significant melodic activity of the chanson.

   The ballade *Dueil angoisseux* (Example 2–14), on the other hand, shows signs of being one of Binchois's late works. A *complainte,* or poetic and musical lament, it contains a text originally written by Christine de Pisan (ca. 1363–ca. 1431) on the death of her husband. Binchois may have set it to music to commemorate another death, perhaps that of Anne of Burgundy (1432) or of the

EXAMPLE 2–14. Gilles Binchois, *Dueil angoisseux,* mm. 1–15.

poetess herself (1431). It is written in 3/4, with movement largely in quarter notes. The melody does not run its course with the same degree of flexibility as in Dufay's late chansons, with their free prose rhythms, and yet Binchois's superius exhibits a pleasing variety of rhythms and carefully planned contours. In the first phrase the melody descends gradually from F to C (after the opening "motive") and then rises an octave before cadencing on A, staking out the musical space to be explored. The second phrase pulls the extremes together but leaves the listener suspended on the leading tone, E, which is resolved immediately after the first ending by a return to the beginning (and after the second ending by an instrumental coda cadencing on the keynote, F). This kind of careful balance and ultimate repose gives to Binchois's chansons their "classical" grace, their "Burgundian" quality, but it would be more difficult to explain their slightly melancholy charm. *Dueil angoisseux* exists in three- and four-part versions, the latter with two contratenors. In both, the tenor is principally an inner voice (though occasionally it goes below the others). The contratenor in the three-part version (or the lower of the two in the four-part version) thus serves mostly as a harmonic bass, leaping at some cadences to emphasize the roots of the principal sonorities (I and V in tonal music) but at others preserving its older function of filling out the sonority while the superius and the tenor resolve into an octave. The striking euphony of the triadic opening of the superius at the beginning of *Dueil angoisseux*, over the purposeful movement of the tenor and contratenor, leads us to hear F as an apparent "tonic." This passage would seem to demonstrate that fifteenth-century composers could at least emphasize the two most important "tonal" degrees at significant places in a form. But in strict terms, it is anachronistic to describe such a piece or the compositional thinking that produced it as "tonal." Cadences were defined not by their association with a given pitch but by their voice leading, within conventional patterns. Many chansons that open with markedly tonal gestures reveal unpredictable intermediate cadence points and finals. Binchois did not always harness the unifying force of harmonically focused and, to our ears, "tonal" procedures. In *Se je souspire,* for example, a late rondeau in G-Mixolydian, all the important cadences except the last one are on D or A, and the final resolution on G comes as something of a surprise.

Not all Binchois's chansons express the ornate and rather artificial sentiments of courtly love. *Filles à marier* wittily admonishes young girls not to marry lest jealousy destroy their love, but it is exceptional in more ways than that. Binchois wrote most of his chansons for three voices, whereas *Filles à marier* has four; the two upper voices quite unusually chase after one another in free canon (or, perhaps more accurately, highly imitative dialogue). Alone of all his songs, it is based on a pre-existent melody—most likely a popular tune—that appears in the tenor.

All the rest of Binchois's chansons set poems in one of the *formes fixes.* The vast majority are rondeaux—forty-seven of the fifty-five chansons firmly attributed to him. He composed no virelais and only seven ballades. That he wrote three chansons based on texts by the greatest poets of his time—Charles d'Orléans (*Mon cuer chante*), Christine de Pisan (*Dueil angoisseux*), and Alain Chartier (*Triste plaisir*)—may suggest that his literary tastes were more highly developed than those of his fellow musicians.

Taken as a whole, Binchois's chansons include many real masterpieces and reveal a distinct musical personality. Elegant and sophisticated musical gems, they are ornaments worthy of the most brilliant court in western Europe.

CONTEMPORARIES OF DUFAY AND BINCHOIS

Our knowledge of music by the contemporaries of Dufay and Binchois comes largely from a number of vast manuscript anthologies containing pieces by English as well as Franco-Netherlandish composers. More than 800 compositions are preserved in the three manuscripts of Italian origin that constitute the most important sources of early-fifteenth-century music—the Aosta Manuscript (Aosta is a small town in northern Italy); Bologna, Civico Museo Bibliografico Musicale, MS Q 15; and Oxford, Bodleian Library, MS Canonici misc. 213. (Since there are many concordances among the three, however, the total number of separate and distinct pieces is considerably smaller.) The 129 Mass movements (out of a total of 180 pieces) in the Aosta Manuscript constitute its most important part, but it also includes motets and smaller liturgical pieces such as antiphons and hymns. The absence of secular music suggests that the manuscript was used by chapel singers; other evidence indicates that it was compiled toward the middle of the century, perhaps in some part of the Holy Roman Empire close to the Italian border. Bologna Q 15—which, with its 323 compositions, is a much larger source than Aosta—was likewise intended for a church or chapel in northern Italy; its main part was probably copied in Padua in the 1420s, though further compositions seem to have been added during the next decade, in Vicenza. Its importance stems partly from the fact that it offers the largest collection of motets from the period, as well as the largest anthology of paired Mass movements and partial, composite, and complete Mass cycles. Single Mass movements and cycles of smaller pieces for office hours (hymns, Magnificats, and sequences) are also included; where space permitted, scribes inserted some secular music, mostly French chansons but also two Italian laude. The Oxford manuscript complements the other two. It is about the same size and date as the Bologna manuscript and appears also to have been written in northern Italy, almost certainly in Venice. It contains many more chansons than any other genre, although the scribe added almost sixty motets and Mass movements, plus a handful of Italian ballate and laude. Together, these manuscripts offer a representative cross-section of early-fifteenth-century music in every genre: Masses, motets, smaller liturgical forms, and chansons.

In addition to these three central sources, a number of smaller fragments and a few major sources compiled at a slightly earlier or later date preserve music of Dufay's generation. The seven gigantic Trent Codices (Trent, Castello del Buon Consiglio, MSS 87–93), compiled between about 1440 and 1480, must constitute the largest anthology of the century. Together the seven manuscripts contain almost 1,900 compositions of all sorts (with many concordances among them), including compositions by Dufay and his contemporaries as well as music by composers of a later generation. Some sources containing mostly earlier music also include pieces from the first years of the fifteenth century, such as the Reina Codex (in the Bibliothèque nationale in Paris), two manuscripts in Modena, and the Chantilly and Apt manuscripts. Along with mannered compositions of great rhythmic complexity and late-fourteenth-century French and Italian music, these manuscripts present some compositions by Franco-Netherlandish musicians from the very beginning of the fifteenth century.

Martin le Franc, whose poem in defense of women has already been cited for its allusion to *la contenance angloise* (see page 8), names the most important composers of the early fifteenth century when he describes how much better the Parisians of about 1440 thought the songs of Dufay and Binchois to be, in comparison with those by their recent predecessors. The composers more nearly contemporary with Dufay and Binchois moved around so much from position to position that it is difficult to group them by city, region, or even country. A surprising number of them were associated at one time in their careers with one of the two great choir schools at Cambrai and Liège. We know who were the leading composers at the Burgundian court and the papal choir in Rome during the first half of the fifteenth century, but we know only a few facts about the secondary figures. It is difficult to reconstruct the musical landscape of Europe in this period, given the paucity of historical documentation about individual composers and the conditions in which they worked. The major figures stand out even more starkly in our impression of musical Europe because so much music by secondary composers seems not to have been preserved. Most of these musicians have left us only a handful of their works—perhaps a few chansons, several motets, one or two Mass movements, or, exceptionally, a Mass cycle. Because of the paucity of material, then, if for no other reason, it would be almost impossible to draw a musical profile for each of these composers as distinct as those for Dufay and Binchois. Among the works of these lesser musicians, there are, of course, some compositions of great beauty—Brassart's *O flos fragrans,* Hugo de Lantins's *Ce j'eusse fait,* Pierre Fontaine's *Sans faire de vous departie* (with its basse-dance tenor), and his *J'ayme bien celuy qui s'en va* (with its contratenor for slide trumpet), for example—but some compositions are quite pedestrian.

Early-fifteeth-century composers set almost no virelais to music and very few ballades. Most early-fifteenth-century chansons are settings of rondeaux, and most are written in treble-dominated style, often with textless (that is, apparently instrumental) preludes, interludes, and postludes framing the sung phrases of the top voice. In general they exhibit a remarkable uniformity of style, though many of them deviate in one way or another from the norm. Most of them, for example, are written for three voices; but there are some (such as Johannes Reson's charming *Ce rondelet je vous envoye*) for two equally melodious voices moving in the same range, and some (such as Jacques Vide's *Amans doublés*) for four voices, in which the two top voices are equally important, after the manner of a tenor motet. Most early-fifteenth-century chansons consist of a more or less florid top line and two slower-moving lower lines; a tenor that forms a self-sufficient duet with the superius (and may or may not be florid enough itself and divided into sufficiently clear phrases to carry the text easily); and a contratenor that, less elegant in melodic shape than the other two voices, either fills in the gaps between the tenor and the superius and keeps the motion going forward at cadences or, in chansons written after 1430, functions as a harmonic bass and moves for the most part below the tenor. But there are also chansons in which superius and tenor sing different texts (Gaultier Libert's *Belle, plaisant / Puisque je sui de vous*), chansons in which all three voices move together more or less homorhythmically (Grenon's *La plus jolie et la plus belle*), and chansons in which the imitation between superius and tenor is so consistent and so exact that the top voice can scarcely be said to dominate (Hugo de Lantins's *A madamme playsant*).

When an early-fifteenth-century composer wished to write a large and important motet, he naturally chose to organize it according to isorhythmic principles, following the traditions established in the fourteenth century and continued, as we have seen, by Dufay. Many of these isorhythmic motets were written to honor a particular saint. Locqueville's *O flos in divo / Sacris pignoribus* was for St. Yvo of Britanny, for example, and Grenon's *Ad honorem / Caelorum / Isti semper* for St. Catherine. Some are less local in their application, such as Grossin's *Mater dulcis* for the Blessed Virgin Mary and Césaris's *A virtutis / Ergo beata nascio / Benedicta filia tua* for the Assumption. Some refer to contemporary events, such as Velut's *Benedicta viscera / Ave mater gratie / Ora pro nobis,* and Carmen's *Salve pater / Felix et beata,* both of which mention the Papal Schism. Some are isorhythmic only in the tenor, or in the two lower voices, whereas in others the rhythm of all the voices repeats according to a predetermined scheme.

Although isorhythmic motets took pride of place, composers also wrote treble-dominated motets (song-motets), such as Locqueville's *O regina clementissima,* which may in fact be a contrafactum of a rondeau, as well as simple settings of texts from the Office Hours and the Mass Proper, such as Benoit's *Virgo Maria, Puer qui natus, Lucis creator optime,* and *Tibi Christe splendor patris,* all of them composed either of a slightly embellished series of chords or in fauxbourdon. Some nonisorhythmic motets use a pre-existent plainchant as a structural tenor or paraphrase a chant in the top voice. Others are apparently free of borrowed material, such as Arnold de Lantins's two superb settings of verses from the Song of Solomon (a comparatively rare instance of motets on biblical texts so early in the century), *Tota pulchra es* (for four voices in "motet texture"), and *O pulcherrima mulierum* (for three voices in a treble-dominated style that often reverts to simple chords).

Like nonisorhythmic motets, single Mass movements were composed by early-fifteenth-century composers in all the textures in common use at the time—simple homophony, treble-dominated style, four-voice motet texture, and even canonic style in the manner of an Italian caccia. Composers gave even more formal definition to many of their single Mass movements by prefacing full sections with extended duets.

Annotations in the musical sources give us a glimpse of some of the conventions that governed how the music on the page was brought to life and given a clearer structure in performance. Some Mass movements include performing directions: annotations such as *solo, unus, duo,* or *chorus* suggest that groups of soloists alternated with a full choir. When the lower voices are marked *trompetta* (or something similar) in the musical manuscripts, instruments seem to be called for (especially slide trumpets or trombones) to play or reinforce the tenor and contratenor lines.

The most important formal innovation in early-fifteenth-century polyphonic settings of the Ordinary of the Mass involved, of course, composers' attempts to link movements together to form larger units—Mass pairs or partial or complete cycles. The solution that ultimately dominated—unification of movements by basing them all on the same chant—was only one of the methods tried, and it was by no means the most common. Composers were much more apt to begin each movement with a melodic motto, or to base each movement on the liturgically appropriate chant from a single Gregorian Mass, or even merely to lay out the movements in the same way (that is, by using the same clefs, the same sequence of mensuration signs, or the same pattern of duos alternating with full sections, or by ending each movement with the same cadential formula). There are several paired movements based on pre-existent musical material recomposed in a manner close to the fully developed parody technique of the sixteenth century.

Very few Mass cycles by Franco-Netherlandish composers survive from before the mid–fifteenth century, and none uses a recurring tenor cantus firmus. Reginald Libert's *Missa de beata virgine* (DTÖ 27/1, vol. 53), partly in fauxbourdon, is a "plenary cycle," for it includes settings of both the Proper and the Ordinary. In some movements the liturgically appropriate chant is paraphrased in the top voice (occasionally it migrates to another voice), but other movements seem to be composed without reference to borrowed material. The chant is very freely paraphrased, if it appears at all, in Arnold de Lantins's *Missa Verbum incarnatum,* in which several movements are adorned with tropes. Any real connection among the movements stems almost entirely from Lantins's use of a motto. Grossin's *Missa Trompetta* (which lacks an Agnus Dei) seems to hang together merely because of its sonority: the contratenor for slide trumpet recurs at regular intervals. In short, early-fifteenth-century composers were clearly seeking ways to create large multi-movement works unified by some readily perceptible musical principle. It took a Dufay, however, to realize the potential of the tenor cantus-firmus Mass and thus to establish it as a central genre of the musical Renaissance.

BIBLIOGRAPHICAL NOTES

Music and musical life of this period are the focus of Reinhard Strohm, *The Rise of European Music 1380–1500* (Cambridge, 1993). On Dufay and his music, David Fallows, *Dufay* (London, 1982; rev. ed. 1987) is indispensable. Several important articles are Alejandro Enrique Planchart, "The Early Career of Guillaume Du Fay," *JAMS* 46 (1993): 341–68; "Guillaume Dufay's Masses: Notes and Revisions," *MQ* 58 (1972); and "Guillaume Du Fay's Benefices and His Relationship to the Court of Burgundy," *EMH* 8 (1988): 117–71; also Craig Wright, "Dufay at Cambrai: Discoveries and Revisions," *JAMS* 28 (1975): 175–229. Pamela F. Starr, "Rome as the Centre of the Universe: Papal Grace and Music Patronage," *EMH* 11 (1992): 223–62, provides a study of petitions and benefices. Structure and significance are the focus of Craig Wright, "Dufay's *Nuper rosarum flores,* King Solomon's Temple, and the Veneration of the Virgin," *JAMS* 47 (1994): 395–439, which also corrects a great deal of misinformation associated with this motet. For a consideration of the sound of *Nuper rosarum flores* in light of musical theory, see Bonnie J. Blackburn, "On Compositional Process in the Fifteenth Century," *JAMS* 40 (1987): 210–84. Thomas Brothers, "Vestiges of the Isorhythmic Tradition in Mass and Motet, ca. 1450–1475," *JAMS* 44 (1991): 1–56, concerns an important aspect of the compositional thinking of Dufay (particularly in the *Missa Se la face ay pale*) and other composers. On Dufay's Masses, see also Christopher Reynolds, "The Counterpoint of Allusion in Fifteenth-Century Masses," *JAMS* 45 (1992): 228–57. For a controversial analysis of Dufay's approach to setting chanson texts, see Don Michael Randel, "Dufay the Reader," in *Music and Language,* Studies in the History of Music, 1 (New York, 1983), 38–78.

The complete works of Dufay are available in his *Opera Omnia,* edited by Guillaume de Van and Heinrich Besseler, 6 vols. (AIM, 1948–64; reprint, 1978); Dufay's hymn settings are also available in vol. 49 of *Das Chorwerk,* ed. F. Blume et al. (Wolfenbüttel, 1929–). An important manuscript musical source from Dufay's time, Oxford, Bodleian Library, MS Canonici Misc. 213, has been published in facsimile, ed. David Fallows (Chicago, 1995).

Binchois's complete chansons have been edited by Wolfgang Rehm (Mainz, 1957). His sacred works have been published with excellent introduction and commentary in Philip Kaye, ed., *The Sacred Music of Gilles Binchois* (Oxford, 1992). Jeanne Marix, ed., *Les Musiciens de la cour de Bourgogne au XVe siècle* (Paris, 1937), and J. F. R. Stainer and C. Stainer, eds., *Dufay and His Contemporaries* (London, 1898; reprint, 1963), are still valuable for selected works by contemporaries. Cambrai, Bibliothèque Municipale, MS 11, a choirbook used at Cambrai Cathedral and dating from the 1440s, with pieces by Dufay, Binchois, and contemporaries is available in facsimile—*Cambrai Cathedral Choirbook,* with an introduction by Liane Curtis (Peer, 1992).

An important study that clarifies the origin of the musical manuscript known as Bologna Q 15 is Margaret Bent, "A Contemporary Perception of Early Fifteenth-Century Style: Bologna Q15 as a Document of Scribal Editorial Initiative," *MD* 41 (1987): 183–201. Selections from the Trent Codices are printed in modern editions in the following volumes of the DTÖ: 14/15, 22, 38, 53, 61, and 76; and the manuscripts are also available in facsimile (7 vols.) published by Bibliopola in Rome. For other early-fifteenth-century music, see Charles van den Borren, ed., *Polyphonia Sacra* (London, 1932; reprint 1962); Charles van den Borren, ed., *Pièces polyphoniques profanes de provenance liègeoise* (Brussels, 1950); Gilbert Reaney, ed., *Early Fifteenth-Century Music,* 7 vols. (AIM, 1955–83); Laurence Feininger, ed., *Documenta polyphoniae liturgicae* (Rome, 1947–51); and Laurence Feininger, ed., *Monumenta polyphoniae liturgicae* (Rome, 1947–53).

On music at the Burgundian court under Philip the Good, see Jeanne Marix, *Histoire de la musique et des musiciens de la cour de Bourgogne sous le règne de Philippe le Bon (1420–1467)* (Strasbourg, 1939; reprint 1972), and G. van Doorslaer, "La Chapelle musicale de Philippe le Beau," *Revue belge d'archéologie et d'histoire de l'art* 4 (1934). The possible connections between Dufay (and subsequent composers) and the Order of the Golden Fleece, founded by Philip the Good in 1430, are explored in William F. Prizer, "Music and Ceremonial in the Low Countries: Philip the Fair and the Order of the Golden Fleece," *EMH* 5 (1985): 113–53. A particular Burgundian repertory, that of the anonymous chansons in the Escorial Chansonnier (known as "Escorial A," a prime source for the secular songs of Binchois and anonymous composers in the Burgundian orbit), is the subject of Walter Kemp, *Burgundian Court Song in the Time of Binchois* (Oxford, 1990). Both Kemp and Dennis Slavin, "Some Distinctive Features of Songs by Binchois: Cadential Voice Leading and the Articulation of Form," *JM* 10 (1992): 342–61, attempt to draw a stylistic profile of Binchois as a composer of chansons. The standard comprehensive article on Binchois is still David Fallows's "Binchois, Gilles" in *TNG*.

A number of studies offer local histories of music: for example, Antoine Auda, *La Musique et les musiciens de l'ancien pays de Liège* (Brussels, Paris, and Liège, 1930); Reinhard Strohm, *Music in Late Medieval Bruges* (Oxford, 1985; rev. ed. 1990); and Craig Wright, *Music at the Court of Burgundy 1364–1419: A Documentary History* (Brooklyn, 1979), although Wright's study concentrates on an earlier epoch. The standard recent work on minstrels is Walter Salmen, *Der Spielman im Mittelalter* (Innsbruck, 1983). B. Bernhard, "Recherches sur l'histoire de la corporation des ménétriers ou joueurs d'instruments de la ville de Paris," *Bibliothèque de l'école des chartes,* First Series, 3 (1841–42): 377–404; 4 (1842–43): 525–48; 5 (1843): 254–84; and 5 (1844): 339–72; and François Lesure, "La Communauté des 'joueurs d'instruments' au XVIe siècle," *Revue historique de droit français et étranger,* Fourth Series, 31 (1953), are still useful.

THREE

OCKEGHEM AND BUSNOYS

The Franco-Netherlandish composers born in the 1420s and 1430s did not introduce great technical musical innovations comparable to the invention and development of the cyclic Mass. They accepted the conventions of their time and built upon the novelties of the immediate past. Busnoys and especially Ockeghem reveal their importance and imaginativeness in the ways in which they worked out the technical questions and problems posed by an older generation. Modern scholars until recently regarded Ockeghem as a difficult, even an enigmatic, composer. Because some of Ockeghem's greatest works may, in fact, have been written before those of Dufay's last period, his music has not been easily fitted into a historical context. But it is oversimple to regard Ockeghem merely as a follower of Dufay, for he created a musical world quite distinct from that of his contemporaries.

A partial explanation for the special quality of Ockeghem's music, and to a lesser extent Busnoys's, may lie in the fact that they were heirs to the rich musical culture of the Netherlands, with its learned techniques and attitudes. Neither imitated their many contemporaries who spent large amounts of time in Italy, and there is no documentary evidence that they ever visited that country. Ockeghem was Flemish, but his native language was French and he worked at the royal court of France. Busnoys was French and spent most of his life in the service of the dukes of Burgundy. Unlike many other composers of the Renaissance, then, they cultivated their musical personalities at home, or at least close to it.

JOHANNES OCKEGHEM

Johannes Ockeghem (ca. 1420–97) was born in Saint-Ghislain in Hainaut. Perhaps he studied with Binchois at the Burgundian court; no documents reveal information about his musical education, but he did compose a lament on the older composer's death in 1460. As a young man, at least from 1443 to 1444, Ockeghem sang under Jean Pullois (or Puyllois; d. 1478) at the Church of Our Lady in Antwerp, one of the most important musical centers in the Low Countries, and here he likely came to know examples of English sacred music. Ockeghem, Pullois, and Petrus de Domarto (who sang in the choir at the same Antwerp church in 1449) all composed Mass settings based on English models, and the English "Caput" Mass was the model for both Ockeghem's *Missa Caput* and Domarto's *Missa Spiritus almus*. Ockeghem's whereabouts for the next few years are unknown, but he served from 1446 to 1448 in the twelve-man chapel choir of Duke Charles I of Bourbon in Moulins.

From the early 1450s his name is cited in French court records, and by 1456 he had become the first among the singing *chapelains* (a high position among those who were not priests). Ockeghem served, until his death more than forty years later, three French kings successively—Charles VII, Louis XI, and Charles VIII—as chaplain, composer, and chapelmaster. By the late 1450s he was highly enough esteemed to be appointed treasurer of the royal abbey of St. Martin in Tours, where the king himself was abbot. For Ockeghem this was a position of great honor, and he was given an elegant house and a number of generous benefices. It was a position he could hold, apparently, without continuous residence in Tours, for he continued as first chaplain in the royal musical establishment. Except for a trip to Spain in 1470, possibly on a mission for the king, Ockeghem spent the remainder of his life attached to the royal court, honored as a singer, choirmaster, composer, and teacher. Among his students may have been the incomparable Josquin des Prez. When Ockeghem died in 1497 an unusually large number of laments appeared, one by Guillaume Crétin and two by the poet and musician Jean Molinet—one in French, set to music by Josquin, and another in Latin; even the great humanist Erasmus composed a *Naenia*, which was later set to music by Johannes Lupi.

For such a distinguished musician, Ockeghem composed but little music. Ten complete Masses survive, along with the earliest extant polyphonic Requiem, a handful of partial Masses and Mass fragments, fewer than ten motets, and some twenty chansons. Among scholars today, his reputation as a composer of sacred music is based on his Masses, partly because his motets had not been easily accessible in modern editions until recently, but mostly because the Masses form an intriguing group of masterpieces. Ockeghem constructed about half of his Masses by means of cantus-firmus technique; his Requiem paraphrases plainchant; the remaining Masses are, quite unusually, apparently free of borrowed material.

Ockeghem's four great cantus-firmus Masses for four voices—those based on the *Caput* melisma, the plainchant *Ecce ancilla Domini,* the popular tune *L'homme armé,* and the tenor of Binchois's chanson *De plus en plus*—reveal their relationship with Dufay's procedures in their overall formal design. That is, the *cantus prius factus* is the prime agent in creating the formal structure, for it is stated completely one or more times in each movement. In the *Missa Ecce ancilla Domini,* the rational disposition of the cantus firmus is even made explicit by a pattern of alternating duets and tuttis that reinforces the formal plan, as in a Dufay Mass. Unlike Dufay, Ockeghem sometimes placed the borrowed melody in the lowest voice—for example, in his *Missa Caput*—an indication, perhaps, that he was less concerned than the older musician with consistency of harmonic planning and more concerned with independence of voices, contrapuntal complexity, and richness of sonority.

Ockeghem usually preferred to vary the rhythmic shape of the structural voice with each of its appearances (here the *Missa Caput* is an exception to his normal practice, since it presents the chant in the same form in each movement). He did not construct the highly rational systems of proportional relationships among statements of the cantus firmus that distinguish some Dufay Masses and inevitably make audible the underlying structure through their clear differentiation of the structural voice. On the contrary, Ockeghem usually transformed the borrowed melody rhythmically so that it resembles the other voices in its melodic contours and pace. Thus the texture of his music is apt to consist of four seemingly independent voices, equally fast-moving and equally florid; but, however hidden, it is the borrowed material and its repetitions that give to these works their basic structure. "Hidden structure," in fact, may fairly be said to characterize Ockeghem's form. Even on those few occasions when he used mottoes to link one movement to another (for example, in the *Missa Caput*) he disguised the relationship by varying each statement of the recurring melody.

At the beginning of the second Kyrie in Ockeghem's *Missa L'homme armé* (Example 3–1), the texture resembles relatively closely that in Dufay's music: the upper two predominantly melodic voices are supported by two slightly slower-moving lower voices, one of which states the cantus firmus. By the end of the short movement all four voices approach equality; the bass speeds up in m. 34, and from m. 38 onward the tenor states free material unrelated to the *L'homme armé* tune in rhythms like those of the other voices.

The impression that Ockeghem's voices are all equal in importance stems partly from the nature of his melodies. Individual lines are often so nonimitative and nonrepetitive that they seem more continuous, more independent of one another, and more nonstructured than they sometimes really are. In the first section of the Gloria of the *Missa L'homme armé* (Example 3–2), for

EXAMPLE 3–1. Johannes Ockeghem, *Missa L'homme armé,* Kyrie II.

instance, the cantus firmus is clearly differentiated from the other voices. Quite exceptionally, the section ends (in m. 15) with a cadence in all voices (typically one based on a VII⁶–I progression). There is even a relatively clear-cut point of articulation in mm. 6–7 after the opening statement of the text and before the series of exhortations "Laudamus te. Benedicimus te. Adoramus te. Glorifica-mus te." This caesura is disguised by the overlapped contratenor, the lack of rests in the outer voices, and the absence of unambiguous cadence formulas. Within the section (mm. 1–15) the music appears to move forward without breaks and without apparent subdivisions into phrases. Except for the tenor, the individual voices proceed without obvious cadences and, indeed, without

EXAMPLE 3–2. Johannes Ockeghem, *Missa L'homme armé,* Gloria, mm. 1–15.

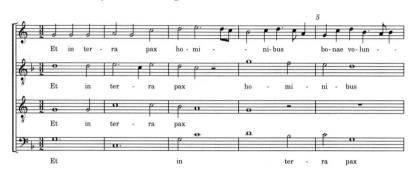

motives that relate one line to another (except for the contratenor in mm. 4–5, which echoes the cantus firmus). Instead, the endless melody flows along without pause, at a relatively steady pace, and for the most part without rational controls like imitation, sequence, or motivic work to clarify the structure and the relationships between one part and another. In this Mass, to a much greater extent than in Ockeghem's free Masses, the top voice still seems to predominate, growing in long and gently arching strands of melody. The superius in Example 3–2 reaches its high point in m. 3, for instance, and gradually descends to the cadence in m. 15 in a series of curves that does not disturb the even flow. But if the endless melody hides the points of articulation, the structure of this Mass is still fairly easily visible beneath the skin.

A few of Ockeghem's cantus-firmus Masses depart more radically than the *Missa L'homme armé* from conventional style and procedure. His *Missa Caput* retains the cantus firmus of its English model and assimilates it completely into the rest of the texture, so the top voice has scarcely more importance than the others. One voice and then another take turns in drawing our momentary attention, and this constantly shifting contrapuntal fabric appears to be built without any seams or joins. Ockeghem placed the tenor of the chanson *Au travail suis* (probably by Barbingant but also attributed to Ockeghem) in the tenor of the Kyrie of his *Missa Au travail suis,* but in the following four movements the borrowed material appears only at the beginning, in an unusually imitative texture in which some or all of the voices share the opening motive of the borrowed melody. Thereafter the music unfolds freely, without any reference to the chanson tenor. In his five-voice *Missa Fors seulement,* which includes but three movements (Kyrie, Gloria, and Credo), Ockeghem derived the well-hidden scaffolding voice from his own chanson; but he incorporated elements from both the superius and the tenor of the model into the structural line and changed it for each movement, not only its melodic and rhythmic shape but also the voice in which it appears. Moreover, he introduced from time to time more than one voice from the model.

In his free Masses—*Missa Mi-mi, Missa Quinti toni,* and *Missa sine nomine* (No. 2 in the *Complete Works*)—Ockeghem's style unfolds at its most enigmatic, revealing his full command of nonimitative counterpoint made up of strands of endless melody. In these Masses no cantus firmus, paraphrased chant, or borrowed material of any kind gives rise to a predetermined schema. At least no one has yet succeeded in identifying in them thematic material modeled on any other music; apparently they are from beginning to end entirely the product of Ockeghem's musical invention. Their style is difficult to describe precisely, because no one contrapuntal technique underlies the music. The texture constantly shifts its emphasis and changes its orientation, and the absence of systematic imitation, sequence, and motivic work prevents the listener from anticipating what musical events will happen next. The music is always new and always changing—Ockeghem's inventiveness is astonishing—and yet he gave to every movement a unity of mood that belies the apparent inconsistencies and imposes a shape unique to each work.

The final section of the Gloria from the *Missa Mi-mi* (Example 3–3) exemplifies Ockeghem's most mature contrapuntal technique, in which individual lines are subordinate to the total effect of the interplay among all voices. Because the voices are nearly equivalent to each other in speed, floridity, and function, the bass does not stand out as the voice that determines and controls the harmonic movement. Ockeghem's music sounds much less tonally oriented than Dufay's for this reason and also because it so effectively avoids prominent cadences with their propensity for establishing harmonic structure. Example 3–3 illustrates Ockeghem's modal harmonic style especially well, since the Phrygian mode, in which it is written, does not use the fifth degree as dominant.

At the smallest level of detail, Ockeghem relied on various traditional techniques to hold the texture together and to help the listener hear what is going on. In Example 3–3, for instance, there is imitative dialogue among the tenor in mm. 105–6, the bass and contratenor in mm. 107–8, and the superius in m. 109 (on the words "miserere nobis"); there are brief imitations between tenor and superius at both "Tu solus Dominus" and "Tu solus Altissimus"; and there is parallel motion in tenths between tenor and superius in mm. 141–42, and imitation between bass and superius in mm. 144–47. But these techniques are not used systematically to illuminate the structure. They vary within any one section of music so much and so quickly that they can scarcely be said to constitute the formal principle of the work, even though they do help the listener to penetrate the difficult and concentrated combination of strands of melody.

Like other fifteenth-century composers, Ockeghem subdivided larger sections of music into smaller units. Example 3–3, for instance, might be divided into the following segments, each of them setting a single phrase of the text.

1. Qui sedes ad dexteram Patris, miserere nobis.
2. Quoniam tu solus sanctus. Tu solus Dominus. Tu solus Altissimus, Jesu Christe.
3. Cum Sancto Spiritu, in gloria Dei Patris.
4. Amen.

The second of these sections might further be subdivided into three phrases, each identified with a clause of the text. But the sections are not clearly marked off from one another by cadences, as they would be in a Dufay Mass. On the contrary, some of them flow into the next ones almost imperceptibly; in some, the cadence is overlapped and disguised (as in m. 111), and in others, a new section begins precisely at the moment the preceding one cadences (as in m. 144, which is also overlapped).

Ockeghem built complete movements by writing a series of sections that meld into one another but that can be separated analytically, making it easier to hear and understand the way the music is constructed. The Gloria of the *Missa Mi-mi*, for example, divides into two large parts, marked off by a complete stop in all voices and a double bar. Ockeghem uses one of the two or three traditional ground plans in making this bipartite division and in beginning the second part at "Qui tollis peccata mundi." The first part can then be subdivided into the following sections, which quite rationally correspond with the clauses of the

EXAMPLE 3–3. Johannes Ockeghem, *Missa Mi-mi*, Gloria, mm. 97–162.

EXAMPLE 3–3. (*Continued*)

text and are either articulated by a disguised cadence or else overlapped with their neighbors.

1. Et in terra pax hominibus bonae voluntatis.
2. Laudamus te. Benedicimus te. Adoramus te. Glorificamus te.
3. Gratias agimus tibi propter magnam gloriam tuam.
4. Domine Deus, Rex coelestis, Deus Pater omnipotens,
   [which overlaps with]
5. Domine Fili unigenite Jesu Christe,
   [which overlaps with]
6. Domine Deus, Agnus Dei, Filius Patris.

That Ockeghem's schemas for every movement unfold freely and in an ad hoc manner so that each is different from the others explains why generalizations about his formal principles are so difficult to formulate. On the other hand, we can easily grasp the way in which he so often achieved a sense of climax and gave shape to a number of movements: by devising a drive to the final cadence. The end of the Gloria from the *Missa Mi-mi* (Example 3–3) illustrates this technique well. Starting with the Amen in m. 144 (or, indeed, even two measures before the entrance of the bass) the motion speeds up in all voices—the number of eighth as well as quarter notes increases markedly—and the music drives forward suddenly to the final cadence.

Ockeghem also had recourse to the traditional means of identifying each movement as belonging to a larger unit by writing motto beginnings. The melodic tag that connects the various sections of the *Missa Mi-mi* consists of a descending fifth, E to A, heard at the beginning of each movement in the bass. The interval would have been sung to the solmization syllables "mi, mi" (the third degree of the natural hexachord on C, followed by the third degree of the soft hexachord on F), which has given the Mass its sobriquet. Similarly, the

Missa sine nomine (No. 2) and the *Missa Quinti toni* both include mottoes that recur, although each time in the typically disguised manner of Ockeghem. If the *Missa sine nomine* (No. 2) was indeed composed as early as the 1440s, with its motto beginnings and no cantus firmus or other borrowed material, it may relate directly to the early stage of cyclic Mass settings, before the English composers and Dufay had established cantus-firmus technique as the central means of building gigantic musical structures.

In two of his free Masses, the *Missa Cuiusvis toni* and the *Missa Prolationum,* Ockeghem set himself technical hurdles of the utmost complexity. As its name suggests, the *Missa Cuiusvis toni* ("Mass in any mode") is written in such a way that by changing the combination of clefs it can be sung in any one of four modes, Dorian, Phrygian, Lydian, or Mixolydian. The *Missa Prolationum,* on the other hand, consists of a series of complicated double canons. They are mostly mensuration canons. Mensuration (or *prolatio*) is a general term for the relationships of smaller to larger time values. Mensuration signs, the predecessors of modern time signatures, govern the number of breves in a long, the number of semibreves in a breve, and the number of minims in a semibreve. In the *Missa Prolationum* all the voices begin simultaneously in many of the movements, each with a different mensuration and thus moving at

Figure 2. An opening from the Chigi Codex showing the initial Kyrie of Ockeghem's *Missa Mi-mi,* copied in choirbook format. The miniatures at the bottom of each folio show courtiers playing soft instruments—lute, recorder, fiddle, and harp—and singing from parts. (Foto Biblioteca Vaticana, Rome)

a rate of speed unlike that of its canonic partner. In overcoming the immense conceptual problems posed by the technical demands he placed on himself in these Masses, Ockeghem displayed compositional virtuosity of the highest order and managed at the same time to write superb music.

Ockeghem's motets for four and five voices (fewer than a dozen survive) display a variety of approaches. Some of the motets are based on plainsong, either elaborating the chant in an upper voice or using it as a tenor cantus firmus, whereas others, such as *Ave Maria* and *Intemerata Dei mater,* seem to be freely composed, without reference to a borrowed melody. *Intemerata Dei mater* is preserved in an elegantly decorated manuscript in the Vatican Library (Chigiana, C. VIII.234, the so-called Chigi Codex), which contains more of Ockeghem's Masses than any other source. The music is written out in choirbook format, not in score but with the individual voices following one after another on facing pages, the superius and the tenor on the left-hand side of the opening and the contratenor and the bass on the right. *Intemerata Dei mater* is one of Ockeghem's longest and most striking motets. Its five voices create a most solemn and majestic flow of sound, especially since they lie rather low; the bass at one point reaches the C below the staff in the bass clef. Ockeghem seems not to have used borrowed material. Instead he adopted the same technique as in his free Masses: he set each clause of the text to long, irregularly shaped melodies combined into a rich nonimitative texture, and each phrase was then overlapped with the others to make a continuous stream of music. In the second of the three *partes,* he exploited choral sonority to shape his music, writing a series of trios leading to a final section for all five voices. In the third part, after an opening duet and an unusually declamatory sequence of chords, he built up to the end by increasing the speed of each voice in his characteristic drive to the cadence. As in the free Masses, each section is assigned its own mensuration; this, together with changes in texture or density, highlights the important divisions in the piece.

Intemerata Dei mater is thought to be free of borrowed material because no chant has been discovered that sets the text, and because no one voice in Ockeghem's setting differs from the others so strikingly that it could be singled out as cantus firmus or paraphrased *cantus prius factus.* In some of Ockeghem's other Marian motets, the chant is well known and his paraphrase of it in a single voice is therefore obvious; yet the voice carrying it is completely absorbed into the contrapuntal texture. In *Alma redemptoris mater,* for example, the next-to-highest voice paraphrases the well-known Marian antiphon, but the texture sounds as though it were composed of four equally important strands of melody. *Alma redemptoris mater* has an unusually bright and clear sound, partly because it is pitched so high (for Ockeghem) and partly because the tutti sections are interrupted from time to time by duets for varying combinations of voices. In this motet the other voices, too, occasionally paraphrase the chant, but they usually do so without producing imitation. Ockeghem wrote several other Marian motets as well, some with paraphrased chant and some apparently without. One of his motets, *Ut heremita solus,* is preserved without text in the only two printed sixteenth-century sources that contain it, but with a complicated set of instructions (a "canon") explaining how to sing its tenor, by no means obvious from the arcane way in which it is notated.

Ockeghem's beautiful lament on the death of Binchois is really a chanson rather than a motet (in spite of the Latin cantus firmus in the tenor), since the French ballade text, beginning "Mort, tu as navré de ton dart," which the top voice sings, governs the work's repetition scheme and has the most active and the most carefully wrought melody. With its treble-dominated texture and its succession of $^6_3$ chords in the lower voices, this is a rather old-fashioned work, doubtless because Ockeghem paid homage to the dead master by imitating his style. Ockeghem wrote one other cantus-firmus chanson, also for four voices, but of a very different sort. While the tenor sings the popular tune *Petite camusette*, imitated by the contratenor and the bass, the superius, which shares melodic material with the other voices, is set to a conventional love lyric in rondeau form, *S'elle m'amera je ne scay*. (The piece has been published several times without the rondeau text in the superius.)

Most of Ockeghem's chansons are three-voice settings of rondeaux, though a few are virelais (or, to be more precise, one-stanza bergerettes), and several have four voices. In addition to the twenty-odd chansons entirely of his own composition, Ockeghem also rearranged the Spaniard Juan Cornago's three-voice *Qu'es mi vida preguntays*, turning it into a four-voice song but retaining only its tenor and superius; and he added a new top line to an older arrangement of the Italian song *O rosa bella*, incorporating the pre-existent superius. He also wrote, to a French text, one *catholicon* (that is, a piece that, like the *Missa Cuiusvis toni*, may be performed in more than one mode), the famous three-voice canon *Prenez sur moy vostre exemple*, cited by various theorists into the sixteenth century and even worked in intarsia (wooden inlay) for Isabella d'Este's study in the ducal palace at Mantua.

His chansons reveal a slightly simpler and lighter side to Ockeghem's musical personality, a side well known to his contemporaries, for his early fame as a composer was built on the popularity of pieces like *Ma maistresse, Fors seulement,* and *Ma bouche rit;* the last was surely one of the biggest hits of the day, since it survives in an astonishing number of musical sources. In most of Ockeghem's chansons, as in the chansons of Dufay's generation, the top voice predominates and the tenor sings an equally good countermelody against it, so that together they make self-sufficient two-part counterpoint. The contratenor may be better integrated into the texture than in many chansons from the first half of the century, and imitation may play a greater role in enriching the texture, but the earlier principle still holds good that form in chansons is determined largely by the repetition scheme of the poem and by a carefully controlled network of cadences on important scale degrees. The melodies themselves generally avoid constructive devices such as sequences, sharply profiled motives, and other repetitive elements; they unfold as complete pieces rather than as series of isolated phrases because Ockeghem took such care to balance high points against low points, and because he built into his complex arches of melody a long-range sense of directional thrust toward a final goal. The first two phrases of *Ma bouche rit* (Example 3–4), for instance, while tracing a satisfying curve in rising to high D and then gradually descending through a series of looped curves down to the final C, nevertheless leave several gaps in the middle range to be filled in by later phrases. (The chanson begins with an uncharacteristic sequence in the superius that propels the motion forward.) Ockeghem's chansons are subtle and delicate miniatures; taken as a group, they help to explain why Ockeghem was renowned for the sweetness and beauty of his music, and they remind us that he was not as austere as he has sometimes been described.

EXAMPLE 3–4. Johannes Ockeghem, *Ma bouche rit,* mm. 1–10.

ANTOINE BUSNOYS

Both in his own time and after his death, the composer and poet Antoine Busnoys (ca. 1430–92) was almost as famous as Ockeghem. Ockeghem and Busnoys surely knew each other and probably coincided for a time in the early 1460s, through their association with the Church of Saint Martin in Tours. Yet their musical personalities were very different, perhaps because Busnoys was trained in France, was employed for most of his life by the Burgundian court, and traveled extensively in the Burgundian realms with the ducal chapel. He worked for Charles the Bold (r. 1467–77), both before and after Charles became duke, and accompanied him on military campaigns. He served Charles's duchess, Margaret of York, and he sang in the chapel of their daughter, Mary of Burgundy, during the last five years of her life, after her father had died in battle in 1477 and she had married Archduke (later Emperor) Maximilian. He was a courtly artist through and through, and several of his chansons allude by acrostic or pun to Jacqueline d'Hacqueville (either a lady in waiting to the Scottish princess Margaret Stuart [d. 1445] or the wife of a Parisian parliamentarian), suggesting that Busnoys may have had some contact with Parisian circles. Like Ockeghem, Busnoys never worked in Italy, and we know of no document recording a trip south of the Alps. He spent his last years at the Church of Saint Sauveur in Bruges and died there in 1492.

Busnoys wrote poetry as well as music and exchanged poems with the Burgundian court chronicler, Jean Molinet, a poet who also wrote some music. Perhaps this versatility is not as unusual as it seems. Very few of the poems set to music in the fifteenth century can be identified as the work of recognized poets; most are anonymous, and many may have been written by the very composers who set them to music.

Busnoys was preeminently a composer of chansons. He wrote at least two Masses and a handful of motets, but his more than sixty-five chansons constitute the corpus of works by which he is best remembered. Most of them set rondeau or bergerette texts, the two most common *formes fixes* by the second half of the fifteenth century, but a few are polyphonic arrangements of popular tunes, and in some, one or two popular tunes serve as cantus firmi. Normally, three voices sufficed, but in about a third of his chansons, Busnoys wrote for four voices, a texture that was to become standard for secular as well as sacred music by 1500. Some chansons, such as *Je ne fay plus* (Example 3–5), were originally conceived for three voices, but at a later time Busnoys or another musician added a fourth, optional (*si placet*) voice to bring the texture up to date.

Je ne fay plus (Example 3–5) was almost certainly composed by Busnoys, even though it is attributed in some sources to a minor composer, Gilles Mureau. Indeed, it resembles Busnoys's other chansons so closely that it can serve as a representative example of his style. It reveals him to be a great melodist, a composer not of catchy tunes but of long and elaborately shaped vocal lines. Often, it is true, they are composed of melodic clichés, cadence formulae, and turns of phrase common to all Franco-Netherlandish composers of his time, but Busnoys filled his melodies with finely wrought details and organized them in carefully balanced segments. Many of his chansons, like *Je ne fay plus*, open with the first phrase of the superius divided into two parts by a rest that coincides with the poetic caesura in the middle of the first line of text. The distinctive opening motive, thus isolated from its continuation, sets the first four syllables of the poem syllabically and moves more slowly and with greater metric emphasis than the remainder of the phrase. The second half acts as a melodic extension; it moves in smaller note values than the opening, includes syncopations and rhythmic figures that conflict with a regular metric pulse, and ends with a long melisma on the penultimate syllable. Busnoys's technique of beginning each phrase syllabically and with a clear-cut motive and continuing with faster motion and a long melisma on the penultimate or antepenultimate syllable derives from earlier masters. He normally took greater pains than they to contrast the differing formal and melodic functions of phrase beginnings and

EXAMPLE 3–5. Antoine Busnoys, *Je ne fay plus,* mm. 1–18.

endings, demonstrating his awareness of the possibility of writing melodies that reflect in detail the metrical structure and the accent pattern of the text. That he was not greatly concerned with reflecting the emotional content of the words is suggested by the superius's melisma on "ne" ("not") beginning in m. 7f, and the tenor's in m. 9f, for a neutral word that is given such emphasis for purely musical reasons.

The way Busnoys linked the first two phrases of *Je ne fay plus* exemplifies his method of achieving formal clarity without sacrificing continuity. The superius and the tenor cadence together, so that the overall form of the composition is crystal clear; the contratenor keeps the motion going by imitating rhythmically the opening motive of the second line. *Je ne fay plus* is a *rondeau layé,* that is, one with short lines of text alternating with longer ones. As an exception to the rule that each poetic verse gets a separate phrase of music, the short second line, "En mes escrips," serves as the opening motive for the longer third line, beginning "L'on trouvera." On the other hand, the short fourth line (which begins the second half of the composition) is set as a full-fledged phrase, doubtless for purely formal reasons; the composition as a whole has the proportions and balance among phrases typical of a normal *rondeau quatrain.*

Busnoys made an effort to weld the three voices together into a homogeneous texture, understating the conventional hierarchy of principal melody (superius), supporting melody (tenor), and filler voice (contratenor). Not infrequently two of the three voices move in parallel thirds or tenths, a mannerism associated with Busnoys as well as his younger contemporaries, Obrecht and Agricola. Both the tenor and the contratenor of *Je ne fay plus* imitate the superius from time to time (for example, the tenor in mm. 5–6 and the contratenor in mm. 13–14) but seldom at the beginnings of phrases, where the technique would draw most attention to itself. The amount of imitation Busnoys wrote in any one chanson varies greatly. Some have as little as *Je ne fay plus;* others, such as *Cent mille escus,* include fully developed points of imitation between two or even all three voices at the beginnings of each or nearly every phrase. In *Ha que ville et habominable* (one of the chansons that alludes to Jacqueline d'Hacqueville), the superius may either be accompanied by two freely invented lower voices or be set to itself as a three-part canon, the ultimate stage of imitation. The consonant, almost bland, harmonies of *Je ne fay plus,* with 4–3 or 7–6 suspensions furnishing the only dissonances, typify Busnoys's style, as does its clear scheme of tonal cadences exclusively on I and V.

The voices in *Je ne fay plus* seldom cross; each voice operates in its own territory. Busnoys and his contemporaries extended the range downward even to notes below gamma ut (the G at the bottom of the staff in the bass clef), and they also extended it upward to the top of the staff in the treble clef, in effect distributing the melodic lines more evenly over the whole available compass.

Along with delicate and refined courtly lyrics, Busnoys also set rather more earthy and direct poems, the popular songs of their day, associated with relatively simple monophonic melodies. Sometimes he used one of these melodies as a cantus firmus for a rondeau setting. In *Mon mignault musequin / Gracieuse plaisant munière,* the rondeau in the superius is perhaps more explicitly amorous than usual, but with a completely different tone from the wryly equivocal cantus firmus extolling the virtues of the milleress's mill. The imitation between the tenor (stating the cantus firmus) and the contratenor might more accurately be called free canon, so closely do the two voices resemble each other. In *Amour fait moult tant que argent dure / Il est de bonne heure né / Tant que nostre argent dura,* two popular cantus firmi are combined beneath a rondeau setting without destroying the elegance of the counterpoint. In other chansons, such as *On a grant mal par trop aimer* and *Vous marchez au bout du pied,* Busnoys set popular tunes more simply and without any interference from a second text. In these four-part popular arrangements, the tune appears in its simplest form in the tenor; the other voices imitate it and also sing rhythmically complex counterpoints around it.

  Busnoys made use of cantus-firmus technique, too, in most of his sacred music. His *Missa L'homme armé* presents the popular melody once or twice in each movement; each is also related to the others by means of a motto beginning. The motet *Anima mea liquefacta est* is built on the plainsong tenor *Stirps Jesse*, and one of Busnoys's two settings of *Regina coeli laetare* presents the Gregorian chant in a free canon at the fourth in the lower two of the four voices. In his *Magnificat* and his relatively short but rhythmically complicated setting of *Conditor alme siderum,* Busnoys paraphrased the chant in his superius. At least some of his motets, such as *Noel noel,* are thought to have been freely invented without any reference at all to pre-existing melodies. Two of the presumably free motets are, however, based on cantus firmi apparently of Busnoys's own invention. *In hydraulis,* with a curious Pythagorean text in praise of Ockeghem, is organized around a simple ostinato figure, D–C–D, presented repeatedly at that pitch and transposed a fifth or an octave higher. The text of *Anthoni usque limina* alludes to the composer, who must have chosen it to link his name with that of his patron saint, St. Anthony Abbot. In the manuscript that preserves the motet, a scroll with an image of a bell, one of St. Anthony's attributes, hints obscurely that the tenor consists of the single note D, possibly intended to be sounded on an actual bell.

  Perhaps Busnoys's brilliance in creating chansons that are exquisite gems reflects the predilections of the court of Burgundy and his mastery of the courtly aesthetic. Busnoys is one of the great masters of the fifteenth-century chanson, whom even Ockeghem can scarcely rival. His sacred music exhibits the same delicacy, refinement, and melodic gift that mark his chansons, and although his few motets and Masses cannot compare in breadth of conception or depth of realization to Ockeghem's greater achievement in this field, it is possible that Busnoys's historical significance as a central figure in the advancement of imitative polyphony and counterpoint has not yet been fully appreciated. After all, his *Missa L'homme armé* may be the foundation for the entire tradition of Masses on this tune, and the famous chanson on which the *L'homme armé* Masses are based may be his as well (as the Italian sixteenth-century writer Pietro Aaron suggested).

CONTEMPORARIES OF BUSNOYS AND OCKEGHEM

  Large choirbooks that stood on lecterns supplied church choirs in the fifteenth century with the music they sang. A number of small and precious songbooks, most of them scarcely large enough for two people to sing from, survive from the second half of the century and contain the secular music of Busnoys and his contemporaries. Some of these "chansonniers" are elegantly illuminated; most of them once belonged to princes or rich collectors and have been saved because they are handsome examples of bookmaking, not because they preserve an important part of our musical heritage. Nor were they manuscripts from which courtly musicians sang and played daily.

Chansonniers adorned rich libraries everywhere in western Europe and especially in France, Burgundy, and Italy. A few that survive can be associated with the central Burgundian tradition and were compiled for the court of Burgundy or the French royal court: the Copenhagen Chansonnier (edited in a modern edition by Knud Jeppesen); the Dijon Manuscript (Dijon, Bibliothèque Municipale, MS 517, published in facsimile by Dragan Plamenac); the Laborde Chansonnier in the Library of Congress in Washington; the Wolfenbüttel Chansonnier (Wolfenbüttel, Herzog-August-Bibliothek, MS 287 extrav., published in a modern edition by Martella Gutierrez-Denhoff); and the Chansonnier Nivelle de La Chaussée (Paris, Bibliothèque Nationale, Département de la Musique, Rés. Vmc. MS 57, formerly belonging to Mme. H. de Chambure in Paris, and published in facsimile with an introduction by Paula Higgins). One of the most beautiful of all is the Chansonnier Cordiforme, prepared in Savoy about 1470 and so called because the manuscript itself takes the shape of a heart (Paris, Bibliothèque nationale, Collection Rothschild, MS I.5.13; available in a partial edition by Edward L. Kottick). Some of the chansonniers from Italy are equally elegant. A Florentine chansonnier from the time of Lorenzo de' Medici, "the Magnificent" (Florence, Biblioteca Nazionale Centrale, MS Banco rari 229, published in a modern edition by Howard Mayer Brown), is sumptuously decorated with miniatures; it is only slightly more beautiful, though, than two other Florentine chansonniers from the last quarter of the fifteenth century, the Pixérécourt Manuscript (Paris, Bibliothèque nationale, MS fonds fr. 15123) and the Cappella Giulia Chansonnier (Vatican City, Cappella Giulia, MS XIII.27; study and partial edition by Allan Atlas). Several chansonniers were probably prepared in Naples, among them the Escorial Manuscript (El Escorial, Biblioteca de S. Lorenzo, MS IV.a.24; published in an edition by Martha K. Hanen) and the Mellon Chansonnier (Yale University Library, available in facsimile and modern edition by Leeman L. Perkins and Howard Garey). One chansonnier from the Este court at Ferrara (Rome, Biblioteca Casanatense, MS 2856) was probably intended for Isabella d'Este's establishment in Mantua. Also of Italian origin is the Seville Chansonnier (Seville, Biblioteca Colombina, MS 5-I-43, to which was originally joined Paris, Bibliothèque nationale, MS nouv. acq. fr. 4379, both parts of which are available in a facsimile edited by Dragan Plamenac). There are even some German chansonniers, notably the Glogauer Liederbuch (available in facsimile with an introduction by Jessie Ann Owens, and in a partial modern edition in *Das Erbe deutscher Musik,* vols. 4 and 8) and the Schedelsches Liederbuch written down in the 1460s by a doctor and historian, Hartmann Schedel (Munich, Bayerische Staatsbibliothek, MS 3232; published in a facsimile edition by Bettina Wackernagel).

No matter where they were written, these anthologies contain mostly French chansons. French culture was foremost in courtly circles everywhere in western Europe at the time, at least so far as secular music was concerned, and the interest in French chansons at Italian courts is attested to by the considerable number of chanson manuscripts prepared in Italy. The first book of polyphonic music printed with movable type, Petrucci's *Harmonice musices odhecaton A,* printed in Venice in 1501 and known simply as the *Odhecaton* (modern edition by Helen Hewitt), is an anthology dominated by chansons for three and four voices by Busnoys and younger composers such as Agricola and Josquin. But the manuscript chansonniers are true miscellanies and reflect local tastes and customs. Along with chansons they include song-motets in Latin; compositions with Italian, German, Spanish, English, or Dutch texts; and even a few compositions apparently originally conceived for instruments.

Chansonniers and other sorts of manuscripts prepared for use in churches, cathedrals, and princely chapels include music by the great composers of the century—Dufay and Binchois, Ockeghem and Busnoys, and their younger contemporaries, such as Agricola, Obrecht, Isaac, and Josquin—as well as compositions by a host of minor composers about whom little is known. Manuscript sources preserve music by some of the composers who worked with Busnoys at the Burgundian court—his slightly older colleagues, Gilles Joye and the Englishman Robert Morton, and his friend, Jean Molinet, the court chronicler. Chansonniers include a number of chansons by Hayne van Ghizeghem, a Burgundian composer of considerable charm, whose *De tous biens plaine est ma maistresse* (preserved in the *Odhecaton* and the Copenhagen and Wolfenbüttel chansonniers) is among the best loved and most widely distributed chansons of the entire fifteenth century, surpassed perhaps only by the highly successful but anonymous *J'ay pris amours en ma devise.*

A certain amount of mystery surrounds the composer Petrus de Domarto (d. 1477?), an older contemporary of Ockeghem whose music is cited and criticized in the treatises of Johannes Tinctoris. Of Domarto's works, only two Masses and two songs survive. His *Missa Spiritus almus* was in demand, to judge by the number of sources that preserve it today, and from it Ockeghem, Busnoys, and even some later composers in the Netherlands may have learned something of their cantus-firmus technique; certain features of the *Missa Spiritus almus* help us to understand the anomalies in Ockeghem's *Missa Caput.*

Johannes Tinctoris (ca. 1435–1511), associated in his younger days with the cathedrals of both Cambrai and Chartres, settled in the 1470s in Naples, where he worked for King Ferrante, taught the king's daughter, Beatrice of Aragon, before she became Queen of Hungary, and wrote a series of treatises that forms the most substantial corpus of theoretical work we possess from the fifteenth century. Less important as a composer than as a writer on music, Tinctoris nevertheless composed at least four Masses, two motets, and a handful of chansons.

Like Tinctoris, Philippe (or Firmin?) Caron, Jean Cornuel (called Verjust), and Johannes Regis were all associated with Cambrai at some time in their lives. Caron seems to have spent much of his life in Italy, where he composed some charming chansons—among them *Helas que pourra devenir* and *Accueil-*

lie m'a la belle, which were widely distributed throughout western Europe—as well as longer and more ambitious works. Regis (d. 1496) stayed north, working in Soignies and acting for a time as Dufay's secretary, probably in the 1440s. Five of his tenor motets for five voices are preserved in the Chigi Codex. His *Missa L'homme armé* uses the cantus firmus to illustrate the liturgical occasion for which the work was intended, the Feast of St. Michael the Archangel, the "armed man" in this context.

Tinctoris certainly knew Johannes Stokhem, Beatrice of Aragon's chapelmaster in Budapest, for the theorist sent the composer a copy of the printed section of his treatise *De inventione et usu musicae*. In another treatise, Tinctoris cited with admiration the work of Guillaume Faugues, who composed several Masses of considerable interest. One is based on a *basse danse* tenor; another uses as its cantus firmus the tenor of Dufay's chanson *Le serviteur* and also quotes other voices of the model—at times all three voices simultaneously. And Tinctoris surely knew Gilles Mureau, since the two worked at the cathedral in Chartres at the same time.

Of the papal singers during the second half of the fifteenth century, Bertrand de Vaqueras, who had spent some time in Liège, and Jean Sohier (called Fedé), a native of Douai who also sang for a while at the Sainte Chapelle in Paris, won considerable fame as composers. Among the many other contemporaries of Busnoys and Ockeghem, the "three B's"—Barbingant, Jacob Barbireau, and Philippe Basiron ("Philippon")—are easily confused because of their names. Collinet de Lannoy, a northerner who worked in Italy, achieved notoriety because he left Isabella d'Este's service without her permission, as is made clear in correspondence between the marchesa and her music teacher, Johannes Martini. Collinet's chanson *Cela sans plus*, though to modern ears thin and lacking in invention, appealed to contemporary musicians enough to find its way into numerous sources and inspired Pope Leo X to write a five-voice version around the original tenor. Cornelius Heyn's *Missa Pour quelque paine* is of high enough quality to have been mistaken in one source for a work by Ockeghem.

BIBLIOGRAPHICAL NOTES

A detailed study of music and musical life in this period, with particular attention to the role of the many lesser-known composers as well as the major figures, is Reinhard Strohm, *The Rise of European Music, 1380–1500* (Cambridge, 1993).

The complete works of Ockeghem are published by the AIM as the *Collected Works*, ed. Dragan Plamenac and Richard Wexler (vol. 1: 2d corrected ed., 1966; vol. 2: 2d rev. ed., 1966; vol. 3: 1992). Ockeghem's *Missa Cuiusvis toni* is now available in a performing edition and realization in each of the modes, with an introduction by George Houle (Bloomington, Ind., 1992). The Chigi Codex is available in facsimile, with an introduction by Herbert Kellman (New York, 1987). Ockeghem's *Fors seulement* and the compositions by other composers based on it have been published as *Fors seulement: Thirty Compositions for Three to Five Voices or Instruments from the Fifteenth and Sixteenth Centuries,* ed. Martin Picker (Madison, Wis., 1981). Lists of Ockeghem's works and an excellent annotated bibliography of the scholarly literature on the composer and his music are included in Picker, *Johannes Ockeghem and Jacob Obrecht. A Guide to Research* (New York, 1988), which, together with Daniel Van Overstraeten, "La Lieu de naissance de Jean Ockeghem (ca. 1420–1497): Une e'nigme e'lucide'e," *RBM* 46 (1992): 23–32; Leeman L. Perkins, "Ockeghem, Johannes" in *TNG;* and Perkins, "Musical Patronage at the Royal Court of France under Charles VIII and Louis XI (1472–83)," *JAMS* 37 (1984): 507–66, brings together all the available documentary evidence. A classic essay on Ockeghem's style is that on the *Caput* Mass in Manfred Bukofzer, *Studies in Medieval and Renaissance Music* (New York, 1950). David Fallows's article, "Johannes Ockeghem. The Changing Image, the Songs and a New Source," *EM* 12 (1984): 218–30, sheds new light on the secular works, and Andrea Lindmayr, *Quellenstudien zu den Motetten von Johannes Ockeghem* (Heidelberg, 1990), brings long-needed attention to the motets. Concerning Pullois and Ockeghem, see Pamela F. Starr, "Rome as the Centre of the Universe: Papal Grace and Music Patronage," *EMH* 11 (1992): 223–62. On Ockeghem and Petrus de Domarto, see Rob C. Wegman, "Petrus de Domarto's *Missa Spiritus almus,*" *EMH* 10 (1991): 235–303. Concerning the career of Johannes Regis, see David Fallows, "The Life of Johannes Regis, ca. 1425–1496," *RBM* 43 (1989): 143–72.

For the standard life and works of Busnoys, see the extensive article by Martin Picker, "Busnois, Antoine," in *TNG.* Two articles by Paula Higgins, "*In Hydraulis* Revisited: New Light on the Career of Antoine Busnoys," *JAMS* 39 (1986): 36–86, and "Parisian Nobles, a Scottish Princess, and the Woman's Voice in Late Medieval Song," *EMH* 10 (1991): 145–200, and the collection *Antoine Busnoys: Method, Meaning, and Context in Late Medieval Music,* ed. Paula Higgins (Oxford, 1997), significantly revise our picture of the context for Busnoys's music and enhance our understanding of it. Richard Taruskin, "Antoine Busnoys and the *L'Homme Armé* Tradition," *JAMS* 39 (1986): 255–93, argues for the centrality of Busnoys's Mass and explores its Pythagorean proportions. On motets of this period see Wolfgang Stephan, *Die burgundisch-niederländische Motette zur Zeit Ockeghems* (Kassel, 1937; reprint, 1973); and the always valuable *Cantus Firmus in Mass and Motet 1420–1520* by Edgar Sparks (Berkeley, 1963). Bonnie J. Blackburn, "On Compositional Process in the Fifteenth Century," *JAMS* 40 (1987): 210–84, provides an extremely detailed analysis of information from Tinctoris and other writers concerning the "harmonic conception" of Renaissance music from the early fifteenth century on. Also on Tinctoris, see Ronald Woodley, "The Printing and Scope of Tinctoris's Fragmentary Treatise *De inventione et usu musicae,*" *EMH* 5 (1985): 239–68.

The first part of the *Collected Works* of Busnoys, dedicated to *Latin Texted Works,* 2 vols., has appeared in an edition with valuable commentary by Richard Taruskin (New York, 1990). An important source for Busnoys's sacred music, Brussels, Royal Library MS 5557, has been issued in facsimile as *Choirbook of the Burgundian Court Chapel* (Peer, 1989) with an introduction by Rob C. Wegman. The choirbook Verona, Biblioteca Capitolare, MS DCCLVII, is also available in facsimile in vol. 24 of RMF, ed. with an introduction by Howard Mayer Brown (New York, 1987). Some of Busnoys's chansons are published in the editions of chansonniers cited in the text above.

Particularly useful information on the chansonniers is included in Allan Atlas, *The Cappella Giulia Chansonnier* (Institute of Medieval Music, 1975); Leeman L. Perkins, ed., *The Mellon Chansonnier* (New Haven, 1979); and Howard Mayer Brown, *A Florentine Chanson-*

nier from the Time of Lorenzo the Magnificent (Chicago, 1983). See also Leeman Perkins, "Modern Methods, Received Opinion and the Chansonnier," *ML* 69 (1988): 356–64. Pieces from the Escorial, Pixérécourt, and Dijon chansonniers are included in *The Combinative Chanson: An Anthology*, ed. Maria Rika Maniates, RRMR, vol. 77.

Petrucci's earliest anthologies of secular music have been published in modern editions by Helen Hewitt, as *Harmonice Musices Odhecaton A* (Cambridge, Mass., 1942; reprint, New York, 1978) and Ottaviano Petrucci, *Canti B, numero cinquanta, Venice, 1502*, MRM vol. 2 (Chicago, 1967). Facsimile editions of *Harmonice Musices Odhecaton A (1504)*, *Canti B, numero cinquanta (1502)*, and *Canti C numero cento cinquanta (1503/4)* have been issued by Broude Bros. (New York, 1973, 1975, and 1978), in the series Monuments of Music and Music Literature in Facsimile.

The *Opera Omnia* of Hayne van Ghizeghem can be consulted in a modern edition by Barton Hudson (AIM, 1977); the *Oeuvres complètes* of Philippe Caron have been edited by James Thomson (New York, 1971–76); secular pieces by Johannes Martini are in a modern edition by Edward G. Evans (Madison, Wis., 1975); the musical output of Johannes Tinctoris has been published as his *Opera Omnia*, edited by William Melin (AIM, 1976); see also Johannes Regis, *Opera Omnia*, ed. C. W. H. Lindenburg (AIM, 1956); and Bertrandus Vaqueras, *Opera Omnia*, ed. Richard Sherr (AIM, 1978).

Detailed descriptions of all the manuscripts mentioned in the text can be found in the *Census Catalogue of Manuscript Sources of Polyphonic Music, 1400–1550*, ed. Herbert Kellman and Jerry Call of the University of Illinois Archives for Renaissance Manuscript Studies, 5 vols. (AIM, 1979–88). In addition to the editions noted in the text, see Eugénie Droz, Yvonne Rokseth, and G. Thibault, eds., *Trois chansonniers français du XVe siècle* (Paris, 1927); E. Droz and G. Thibault, eds., *Poètes et musiciens du XVe siècle* (Paris, 1924).

FOUR

MUSIC OF THE COURTS
AND CHAPELS IN ITALY,
1490–1520

During the fifteenth and sixteenth centuries the area we now refer to as Italy did not constitute a single country but contained a number of separate political entities (the courts of northern Italy, the Papal States, the Kingdom of Naples, etc.), each with its own ruler or ruling family, government, and cultural institutions. The musical life of the prosperous courts and cities in Italy was dominated by foreign musicians, called *oltremontani,* whose contributions as composers and singers were a distinguishing feature of Renaissance musical culture. By 1474, for example, Galeazzo Maria Sforza, Duke of Milan, had assembled a brilliant group of musicians that included Gaspar van Weerbecke, Johannes Martini, Loyset Compère, Alexander Agricola, and the young Josquin des Prez. Martini also worked in Ferrara for many years, but he was only one of the many northerners—among them Jacob Obrecht, Josquin, Collinet de Lannoy, Antoine Brumel, and Johannes Ghiselin (called Verbonnet)—who came to the city while Ercole d'Este (r. 1471–1505) was duke. Agricola, Collinet, Ghiselin, Johannes Stokhem, and others spent some time in Florence, where Heinrich Isaac, the most distinguished composer in the city, had settled about 1484. The papal chapel in Rome, not surprisingly one of the leading musical centers in all of Italy, boasted among its singers a number of accomplished foreigners—

Josquin, Weerbecke, Marbriano de Orto, and, under Leo X, Antoine Bruhier and Elzéar Genet (called Carpentras).

It is one of the greatest oddities of musical history that we know of so few Italian composers active during the century that saw in that country the birth of the Renaissance in painting, sculpture, and architecture. Yet after about 1420, when the great musical efflorescence of the trecento had died down, no native-born composers could compare in stature and achievement with visual artists such as Alberti, Fra Angelico, Brunelleschi, Donatello, Filippo Lippi, and Masaccio. Even after 1490, when some Italian composers finally began to make a name for themselves—Tromboncino, Cara, and the other frottolists in northern Italy, and Coppini, Bartolomeo degli Organi, and others in Florence—Franco-Netherlandish musicians still held the most important positions in courts and cathedrals. Italian princes vied with one another to secure for themselves the best foreign talent they could afford. Perhaps this situation developed simply because Italian princes emulated the Burgundian court and it was fashionable to import musicians from the north. Although a number of Italian cathedrals employed professional singers for the performance of polyphony in the later fifteenth century, the Italian cathedral schools also depended on the services of foreigners when it came to the training of young musicians. Perhaps the music heard at Italian courts before the late fifteenth century was largely improvised and orally transmitted, so that almost no written record of it has survived. Or perhaps Italian humanists rejected elaborate "Gothic" polyphony when setting vernacular poems, since its sound was so clearly "sacred" and its practitioners clerics; could it be that this discouraged native-born composers from composing in that style?

The musical patrons of fifteenth-century Italy surely cultivated foreign music and hired northern musicians for the same reasons that they read French romances and imported Flemish pictures to adorn their palaces. French courtly culture was in style; it dominated Italian courts, and northern polyphony was thoroughly integrated into the elite culture of fifteenth-century Italy. Thus, French chansons predominate even in the secular musical collections prepared in Italy. But late-fifteenth-century chansonniers also contain some compositions with Italian texts or titles, many of them written by northern composers. Some Italian incipits, though, turn out to be garbled versions of French titles; thus Busnoys's rondeau *Cent mille escus* is called in one source *Cento milia scuti*. In some manuscripts, Italian incipits begin compositions that can be identified as French chansons; the incipits apparently refer to contrafacta, Italian texts that replaced the original French in performance. Thus Caron's *Le despourveu infortuné* is labeled in one manuscript *Tanto è l'affanno* (no further text is given), and Busnoys's *M'a vostre cueur* is called *Terribile fortuna*. On closer examination, even more of the Italian compositions in chansonniers will doubtless turn out to be French chansons in disguise. Some compositions in late-fifteenth-century manuscript anthologies have Italian titles rather than text incipits, but some of these, though seeming to be compositions originally conceived for instruments, are written in more or less the same style as chansons. Many of the titles refer to people's names—for example, Ghiselin's *La Alfonsina,* Josquin's *La Bernardina,* Martini's *La Martinella* (a title used by several other composers as well), and perhaps even Isaac's *La Morra.* These compositions pay homage to the composers' friends or patrons.

The fifteenth-century chansonniers also include some original settings of Italian poems. A few are based on popular monophonic tunes, which the northern composers worked into elaborate polyphonic arrangements; both Josquin and Compère, for example, perhaps in competition, devised witty contrapuntal versions of *Scaramella va alla guerra.* A few fifteenth-century Italian songs are altogether exceptional, compositions that do not follow any established tradition—such as Dufay's extraordinary setting of the first stanza of Petrarch's canzone *Vergine bella*—but many of the Italian songs in secular anthologies do relate to an older convention in that they are *ballate,* one of the chief forms of secular music carried over from the trecento into the fifteenth century. The repetition scheme of the ballata, A b b a A, resembles that of the virelai. Composers as early as Dufay composed Italian songs in this form, and settings of ballate or closely related poems make up most of the Italian compositions in a number of later-fifteenth-century chansonniers, like the Neapolitan anthology now in the library at El Escorial in Spain (Escorial MS IV. a. 24; modern edition by Martha K. Hanen).

Some of the songs with Italian texts in the Escorial chansonnier and other fifteenth-century anthologies are *strambotti,* poems in *ottava rima* (eight-line stanzas rhyming abababcc or abababab). This verse form was adopted for the epic poetry of Ariosto and Tasso and also for the improvised, semipopular narratives and lyrics performed at courts and in Italian cities from the very beginning of the fifteenth century. The improvisers were poet-musicians whose reputations were based primarily on their ability to declaim improvised poems while accompanying themselves on a stringed instrument. The Brandolini brothers, Leonardo Giustiniani in Venice, Pietro Bono in Ferrara, Serafino dall'Aquila in the service of Cardinal Ascanio Sforza in Rome, the Spaniard Il Chariteo (Benedetto Gareth) in Naples, Bacio Ugolini in Florence (who sang the title role in Poliziano's *Orfeo* in 1480), and even Marsilio Ficino, the great philosopher, who claimed his invention of Orphic singing to the lyre as one of the great achievements of the age—all these men and more were the great native Italian musicians of their day. Many of their poems survive, not only strambotti but also *capitoli* and other narratives in *terza rima,* odes, sonnets, ballate, and so on. There are many extravagant descriptions of their talent in improvising music to these texts, but because the improvisations were not written down, only a small portion of this large repertory of songs has survived, and the art of performing them remains a challenge.

A few chansonniers include examples of strambotti by northern composers that combine a very simple melody with fairly elaborate counterpoint.

The character of pieces like Japart's *Nenciozza mia* and Obrecht's *La tortorella* suggests that strambotti were associated with monophonic formulae repeated for each couplet in a stanza. (Example 4–1 shows one such setting, with the chanting formula in the tenor; in the second half of the piece, the same formula appears in the superius.) Although the counterpoint in these arrangements is Franco-Netherlandish, the stereotyped and conventional nature of the Italian formulae that inspired the composers is clear. We can get a further idea of the style of fifteenth-century improvised music by carefully examining the straight-forward settings of strambotti that do survive and also by inferring the style from literary descriptions and by extrapolating backward from that of the slightly later Italian repertory of Mantuan *frottole*, Florentine *canti carnascialeschi* and other songs, and Latin *laude*.

EXAMPLE 4–1. Japart, *Nenciozza mia*, mm. 1–9.

One important clue to the nature of the Italians' improvisations comes from the fact that we know they accompanied themselves on the lute or harp, or, more characteristically, on the *lira da braccio*, a violinlike fiddle with seven strings (five on the fingerboard and two drones off the fingerboard) that was adept at playing chords. The number of strings on the lira da braccio is the only feature it shares with the ancient lyre, and yet the name was given to the instrument because it was associated with the declamation of epic and narrative poems in a style that apparently reminded fifteenth-century listeners of the ancient world. When the instrument is shown in fifteenth-century Italian art, it is often seen in the hands of Orpheus, Apollo, or another of the more musical ancient gods or heroes.

Aside from a few musical examples in theoretical treatises, the only source of lira music dating from the late fifteenth century (Pesaro, Biblioteca Oliveriana, MS 1144) reveals that when the lira da braccio was used as a solo instrument, it played melodies accompanied by relatively simple chords, as in the Romanesca setting shown in Example 4–2. That the Pesaro manuscript should offer as its two specimens of lira music a Romanesca and a Passamezzo—two of the most common series of chord progressions that underlie many compositions throughout the sixteenth century—is itself significant, for these chordal patterns may originally have been invented for Italian improvisers earlier in the fifteenth century. What little evidence exists certainly suggests that these poet-musicians worked with standard patterns of chords—like twentieth-century blues and jazz musicians.

EXAMPLE 4–2. *Romanesca* for the lira da braccio, mm. 1–9.

Occasionally a formula for singing all Italian poems in a given form appears in the musical sources. The *modus dicendi capitula* (the formula for singing or declaiming capitoli), for example, taken from the first book of printed frottole of 1504 (Example 4–3), consists simply of a skeletal melody and a pattern of chords. To sing a complete narrative capitolo consisting of many stanzas (each stanza having three eleven-syllable lines in a set meter and rhyme) using this bare formula without variation would be aesthetically intolerable. The art of the *improvvisatori* must have consisted partly in their skill in varying and embellishing the bare outline from which they began. But however much these poet-musicians decorated the basic formula, they would have wished to project the words. The syllabic, declamatory style, as well as the chordal orientation of the texture exemplified in Example 4–3 and indeed in the entire frottola repertory, sharply distinguishes Italian fifteenth-century improvised music from the highly melismatic and contrapuntal inventions of the Franco-Netherlanders.

The music of the courtly poet-musicians must have been a revelation to the northern composers of the fifteenth century coming to Italy for the first time, for almost nothing in their own training within the Franco-Netherlandish tradition would have prepared them for these formulaic chord patterns, clearly declaimed texts, and *fioriture*. These two kinds of music—elegant, improvisatory southern song and refined, learned northern polyphony—existed side by side in Italy throughout the fifteenth century.

EXAMPLE 4–3. Michele Pesenti, *Modus dicendi Capitula.*

THE FROTTOLA AND RELATED TYPES

The Italian composers who began to appear on the musical scene in great numbers in the last decade of the fifteenth century set the sort of poetry declaimed by the improvisers—strambotti, odes, and capitoli, for example—as well as *barzellette,* lyrical strophic poems with refrains not unlike the older ballate. All these kinds of songs are called, rather loosely, *frottole,* a word that refers more particularly to the barzelletta. Most of the frottolists came from northern Italy: Francesco d'Ana, for example, from Venice; Michele Pesenti and Giovanni Brocco from Verona; and Antonio Caprioli from Brescia. But the frottola was identified especially with the small court of Mantua, partly because the enlightened patronage of Isabella d'Este (1474–1539), marchioness of Mantua, greatly stimulated the development of the genre, and partly because the two most distinguished composers of frottole, Bartolomeo Tromboncino (d. ca. 1535) and Marco Cara (d. ca. 1530), both established their reputations in that city and worked there for long periods in their lives.

In fifteenth-century Italy, music was judged essential to the education of the courtier and an appropriate leisure activity for aristocratic women. In Castiglione's *Book of the Courtier,* printed in 1528, for example, music is described as a decorous pastime for women because their "tender and delicate spirits are readily penetrated with harmony and filled with sweetness." This association between the supposed sweet and delicate nature of women also made it inappropriate, for example, for women to play loud instruments such as drums and trumpets or to sing certain kinds of loud songs; social conventions assigned them, rather, the soft instruments, such as the lute, one or another viol, and the harpsichord. As patrons of music, women in Italy supported only certain kinds of music. The music of the *pifferi,* or wind bands, for example, was considered masculine for its loud sounds and military associations; the physical exertion and facial distortion needed to play shawms and trumpets was also considered unfeminine. Women like Isabella d'Este, Lucrecia Borgia, and Elisabetta Gonzaga organized private musical parties, court balls, and musical or theatrical entertainments and supported the kinds of music called for by these social occasions.

Isabella d'Este is a perfect example of the enlightened patron of the Italian Renaissance with broad cultural interests. As a young girl in Ferrara, she studied music with the Netherlander Johannes Martini. After she moved to Mantua as the bride of Francesco Gonzaga, she began commissioning works of art and corresponding, in letters distinguished for their wit and intelligence,

Figure 3.   Leonardo da Vinci, portrait of Isabella d'Este, 1499. (© Photo RMN, Paris)

with painters, poets, and musicians. She had contact with most of the greatest artists of her time, including Leonardo da Vinci, Titian, Castiglione, and Ariosto. In pursuing her musical interests, she dealt not only with instrument makers and performers but also with poets like Galeotto del Carretto and Serafino dall'Aquila, encouraging them to supply poems to be set to music. She kept in her employ the tempestuous Tromboncino even after he had murdered his unfaithful wife and escaped punishment for the crime, as well as the calmer and more dependable Cara, who spent his entire career working for Isabella and her husband. Isabella was a virtuoso musician who sang and accompanied herself on the lute, even during semipublic court festivities, such as the wedding of her brother Alfonso in 1502. As patron, she supported those kinds of music that she herself could perform but also guided the best work of any kind being done around her. Her participation and vigorous patronage brought to the secular genres she cultivated the refined artistic standards of her court. Her personal musical interests and abilities and her taste in poetry clearly shaped the music composed and performed for her and thus the history of Italian secular music.

Frottole survive in a number of manuscripts and printed books from the first quarter of the sixteenth century. The largest corpus of them is contained in the eleven volumes of frottole published in Venice between 1504 and 1514 by the first great printer of music, Ottaviano Petrucci. Books of plainchant and isolated examples of polyphony had been printed before 1500, and Michel Toulouze of Paris had issued a collection of basse-dance tenors set in movable type; but Petrucci was the first to perfect the techniques necessary for publishing complete collections of polyphonic music set in movable type and printed by multiple impression—that is, each page went through the presses twice, with the staves printed separately from the note heads, stems, and texts, a procedure requiring very precise control over registration (the positioning of the sheets when they are put through the press a second time). Petrucci's first book, issued in 1501, *Harmonice musices odhecaton A* (the title, a mixture of words derived from Latin and Greek, means simply "one hundred songs of harmonic music," though in fact the volume includes only ninety-six), is the first of a three-volume set including also *Canti B* and *Canti C*. The collection represents both an end and a beginning. Whereas it is the first printed anthology of polyphonic music, it is one of the last great chansonniers, containing a comprehensive and diverse cross-section of all the kinds of secular music current in the late fifteenth century, though its emphasis is on French chansons. Thereafter, anthologies tended to cater to slightly more specialized tastes. Petrucci went on to produce a large number of beautifully printed volumes of motets and Masses and collections devoted to individual composers—among them Josquin, Obrecht, Brumel, Pierre de la Rue, Ghiselin, Agricola, Marbriano de Orto, Isaac, Weerbecke, Févin, and Mouton—as well as laude, frottole, and volumes of music for lute, lute and voice, and keyboard.

Petrucci's eleven books of frottole (only a few fragments of Book X survive) appeared more than a decade after the genre had begun in and around

Mantua in the 1490s. The volumes should be regarded, then, as a slightly retrospective view of the new music and perhaps, as Einstein suggests, as the musical equivalents of epistolary guides for the composition of letters—"suitable compositions for all occasions and situations of amorous and courtly life" that furnish models to follow in constructing similar pieces and, not least, formulae on which improvisations can be based. The utilitarian nature of the volumes explains why much of the poetry has but little literary value—it is mere *poesia per musica*—and also why the volumes are so miscellaneous in character. They contain not only frottole in the narrowest sense of the word but also settings of all the other sorts of poems in common use at the time—strambotti, capitoli, odes, sonnets, canzoni, and so on.

The frottola proper, or barzelletta, is a fixed lyrical form much like the French virelai or, more to the point, like the older Italian ballata. Typically it consists of a four-line refrain (called the *ripresa*) and a six-line stanza. Four phrases of music (ABCD) are supplied for the *ripresa*. The first quatrain of the six-line stanza is sung to the first two phrases of music and their repetition, and the final couplet to the second half of the music, as the following diagram makes clear.

	Ripresa	*Stanza*
Music :	A B C D	a b a b c d
Rhyme scheme:	a b b a	c d c d d a

The number of stanzas in a frottola is not fixed. Between each the refrain is repeated in whole or in part. If only a part of the refrain is to be sung between stanzas, the composer often supplies a special version of the truncated part consisting of the first two phrases of music plus a more or less extended coda (AB + x), and this shortened refrain is given in the sources immediately following the complete version.

Thus the performance of a typical frottola results in the repetition scheme ABCD ababcd AB + x ababcd AB + x, and so on, ending with a complete statement of the refrain.

These barzellette—charming, unpretentious settings of stereotyped lyrical poems dealing chiefly with love—make up the major part of the earlier Petrucci books of frottole. From the fourth volume onward, other forms of poetry take an ever greater share of space. Even the most complex settings of strambotti, odes, capitoli, and sonnets are often little more than patterns to follow, formulas to use in declaiming poetry, or bare frameworks on which to base presumably more elaborate semi-improvisations. The simplest are no more than a few chord progressions harmonizing a melodic formula.

The odes of the frottolists deal with a variety of subjects, moralistic or amorous, usually in a series of quatrains. They are modeled on similar poems by Horace and other classical Latin poets. In Petrucci's first book, there is even a setting by Michele Pesenti of Horace's *Integer vitae,* one of the barest of all the patterns in the frottola books, scarcely more interesting musically than some of the contemporary experiments by German humanists in setting Latin odes for use in schools. Marco Cara's ode *Udite voi finestre* (Example 4–4) is hardly more complicated than the capitolo by Pesenti. The composer's emphatic repetition of the last lines of each quatrain is unusual, but the interlocking rhyme scheme (abbc cdde effg and so on) in this slightly melancholy serenade is a feature common to the form.

EXAMPLE 4–4. Cara, *Udite voi finestre,* mm. 1–12.

Interlocking rhymes are also found in *capitoli,* in which the middle rhyme in one three-line strophe continues over into the next (aba bcb cdc and so on, as in Example 4–3). Called *terza rima,* this is the verse form Dante chose for his *Divine Comedy.* Capitoli are associated with lyrical or dramatic eclogues—pastoral poems, often pathetic in tone. Sonnets are set by the frottolists as schematically as the other poetic types. The composers often use the same four phrases of music for both quatrains of the poem and three contrasting phrases for both tercets, and some sonnet settings consist simply of three phrases of music, the first two repeated over and over for successive couplets and the last phrase reserved for the final line of the poem.

Of all the poetic forms used by the frottolists, the *canzone* shows the greatest degree of structural irregularity and the highest literary standards. Strophic like most of the other forms—though often only one strophe of poetry is included in the frottola books—canzoni consist of a varying number of alternating seven- and eleven-syllable lines in irregular rhyme schemes. In the first decades of the sixteenth century, the frottolists began to set these more sophisticated poems, including the magnificent canzoni by the great fourteenth-century Italian poet Francesco Petrarch. For these poems the musicians did not change their simple and often declamatory manner, as the excerpt from Tromboncino's setting of Petrarch's *Sì è debile il filo* (Example 4–5) makes clear; but the irregular nature of the poetry at least forced them to write through-composed music, lacking the patterned and stereotyped features that characterize most frottole. In addition to all these poetic types, Petrucci also included some examples of other sorts of music in his volumes of frottole: contrapuntal, even highly imitative settings of *villote,* or popular songs, like Michele Pesenti's *Dal lecto me levava* in the first book and Compère's *Che fa la ramacina* in Book IV; classical Latin texts, as we have seen; a few quodlibets; and various irregular forms like Josquin's *El grillo.*

EXAMPLE 4–5. Bartolomeo Tromboncino, *Sì è debile il filo,* mm. 1–9.

The style of the frottole differs markedly from that of Franco-Netherlandish polyphony of the late fifteenth century, above all in its chordal orientation and its use of patterned rhythms. Frottole are often strongly metrical, even though the mensuration sign sometimes implies a meter different from that required by the music (as in Examples 4–4, published by Petrucci in triple mensuration, and 4–6, published in duple mensuration). A rhythmic pattern once established is apt to be repeated over and over throughout most of a composition. When the meter is triple, the patterns almost always involve hemiola, the juxtaposition and combination of rhythms in 6/8 and 3/4 (or 6/4 and 3/2). Tromboncino's *Chi se fida de fortuna* (Example 4–6) displays the characteristic dance rhythms and hemiola (and its repeated notes at cadences echo the feminine ending so typical of Italian poetry).

A frottola melody is usually set to its text syllabically or with a few short melismas to accentuate stressed syllables; it cadences regularly on feminine endings; and it is supported by a bass line that usually supplies the roots of triads formed into surprisingly tonal progressions. Patterns of chords underlie the harmony of frottole in the same way that patterns of note values determine their

EXAMPLE 4–6. Bartolomeo Tromboncino, *Chi se fida de fortuna*, mm. 1–5.

rhythm. Chords built on tonal degrees of the scale—I, IV, and V—generally predominate over others (Example 4–4 in G-Dorian, for instance, is almost entirely based on those three chords except at the very beginning, where a progression of chords built on F, G, and D establishes the key clearly even though being "modal" rather than "tonal"). Final cadences are more apt to involve an octave leap in the bass, while an inner voice supplies the last root, than the more modern I–V–I bass movement of Example 4–4.

Between the principal melody in the top voice and the harmonically oriented bass line, the inner voices act as harmonic filler and keep the rhythmic motion moving forward. The special relationship between superius and tenor so often found in Franco-Netherlandish polyphony—the two-part counterpoint that forms the basis for the entire contrapuntal fabric—is absent from these Italian songs. Even when the inner voices furnish imitations or other contrapuntal refinements, their primary function is simply to fill out the texture and to keep the sound from being unpleasantly thin. They often share the same range; they are frequently written in the same clefs and cross each other regularly. But behind the chordal texture of the frottola lies a realization that is superficially contrapuntal rather than purely chordal in conception.

The distinctive texture and strong chordal orientation explain why frottole often seem to be so appropriate for solo singing with the accompaniment of a lute or an instrumental ensemble. That Italian musicians in the late fifteenth and early sixteenth centuries often performed them in this way is not surprising in view of the connection between this repertory and that of the earlier fifteenth-century courtly improvisers who accompanied themselves on lute or lira. Nor is it then surprising that two volumes of frottole arranged for solo voice and lute were published in 1509 and 1511 by the lutenist Franciscus Bossinensis; a third volume, featuring works by Tromboncino and Cara, was issued in the 1520s. In almost all these songs, the voice sings the superius and the lute plays the tenor and bass; the alto line of the four-part "original" is simply omitted in the arrangement. Frottole were also sometimes sung *a cappella,* a method that poses some problems: the text fits the lower voices very awkwardly because many of the bass lines are continuous and the inner voices filled with busy passagework. Almost certainly, then, the versions of frottole published by Petrucci do not represent the music in its fixed and immutable state; rather, they present material in a manner that is most convenient for musicians to arrange, in as many differing ways as they can invent.

Within a comparatively narrow range of style, frottole offer a surprising amount of contrast in mood and technique. Some are charming and delicate lyrics; others are so declamatory that they seem mere excuses for reciting the poetry, or perhaps for displaying the performer's skill at improvisation; and quite a few are dance songs set out in lively rhythmic patterns. Frottole reveal themselves fully only in performances that acknowledge that the printed versions merely indicate a bare framework to be filled in by singers and instrumentalists using their creative imagination.

By the second decade of the sixteenth century, Italian composers had begun to take the frottola more seriously as a vehicle for intensifying by music their perception of great poems. They chose to set texts of high literary merit, especially canzoni and sonnets. Petrucci's eleventh book of frottole (1514) contains as many as twenty poems by Petrarch, and he published in 1520 a whole volume of settings of Petrarch's canzoni by the Tuscan Bernardo Pisano. In short, the frottola began to lose its concentration on courtly trifles and its connections with the world of the improvisers as it came to serve more self-consciously serious artistic aims.

CANTI CARNASCIALESCHI
AND OTHER FLORENTINE MUSIC

Florence in the late fifteenth century celebrated the carnival time just before Lent with special intensity. Both then and during the Calendimaggio, the period between May 1 and the Feast of St. John the Baptist, the city's patron, on June 24, the citizens of Florence organized many festivities, especially torchlight parades with decorated wheeled floats, masked musicians singing carnival songs (*canti carnascialeschi*), and dancing in the streets. Some of the floats were sponsored by trade guilds; others satirized one or another of the groups that made up the colorful life of the city—the tailors, oil makers, used-clothing dealers, and bird sellers; the poor pensioners, beggars, widows, gypsies, Jews, and German soldiers (*Landsknechte*, songs about whom were written in heavily accented Italian). The singers almost always identify themselves at the beginning and then proceed to poke fun at their own customs, dialects, or stations in life. Political as well as social satire sometimes enters in, and the second meaning of the double entendres is often obscene.

The celebration of carnival and the songs associated with it flourished especially during the time of Lorenzo de' Medici, "the Magnificent," who ruled Florence from 1469 until his death in 1492. He himself wrote *canzoni a ballo* (dance songs) as well as some of the best-known canti carnascialeschi, including the mythological song of Bacchus that begins "Quant'è bella giovinezza, Che si fugge tuttavia" ("How beautiful is youth, though it vanishes all too quickly"). Lorenzo encouraged his courtiers and the city's poets to write such poems for carnival, and for setting to music. Cynical modern historians have suggested that Lorenzo arranged lavish entertainments to make the Florentine people forget their oppressed state. Whatever his motives, Lorenzo played the same role that Isabella d'Este had in Mantua; he furthered the cause of vernacular poetry and stimulated the formation of an Italian musical style distinct from that of the Franco-Netherlanders.

The tradition of celebrating carnival with extravagant entertainments declined after Lorenzo's death in 1492, when the city fell into the grip of the reforming friar Girolamo Savonarola. In his puritanical zeal he argued eloquently against foolish ornament and worldly frivolity, and secular songbooks joined playing cards, trivial literature, fans, and immodest articles of clothing on the bonfires of vanities that he organized. But opposition to his ideas soon grew, and in 1498, after the church convicted him of heresy, he was hanged and then burned in the Piazza della Signoria. The Medici were restored in 1512, expelled in 1527 when the republic was reestablished, and restored again in 1530, this time as hereditary rulers and, eventually, as Grand Dukes of Tuscany. These civic disturbances help to explain why so few sources of carnival songs survive. Our knowledge of them comes from a few manuscripts dating from after Lorenzo's death, and mostly from a retrospective collection of texts, *Tutti i trionfi, carri, mascherate e canti carnascialeschi dal tempo del Magnifico Lorenzo Vecchio de' Medici*, edited by Anton Francesco Grazzini, called Il Lasca, and published in Florence in 1559.

The two best-known composers of carnival songs during the time of Lorenzo the Magnificent were foreigners: Heinrich Isaac and Alexander Agricola, who spent long periods in Florence from the 1470s onward. But the largest number of surviving examples were written by a native Florentine—Alessandro Coppini (ca. 1465–1527), monk, Doctor of Sacred Theology, and composer and organist who worked at various Florentine churches, including the prestigious Santissima Annunziata and the Medici family's favorite, San Lorenzo. Only a few others among the many anonymous canti carnascialeschi are attributed to composers, among them the slightly younger Bartolomeo degli Organi (1474–1539), called Baccio by his contemporaries, and Ser Giovanni Serragli (fl. 1502–27).

A few canti carnascialeschi are simple strophic songs in which the through-composed music setting the first strophe is repeated for all subsequent ones. But most of the carnival songs resemble ballate, with a two-, three-, or four-line refrain (the *ripresa*) and a series of complex strophes, each of which consists of two alternately rhyming couplets (the *piedi*) and a closing section with a variable number of lines (the *volta*). The music composed to fit this poetic form does not follow a predetermined repetition scheme as rigid as those devised for the French *formes fixes* or the northern Italian barzellette. Often the two *piedi* are sung to the same music, which contrasts with that for the refrain, and the *volta* is set to a third section of music. Some canti carnascialeschi, however, do not include any repeated phrases—each strophe is through-composed—and others repeat phrases according to no preconceived pattern. Thus in his song of the bird-catchers, *Canzona degli uccellatori alle starne* (Example 4–7), Coppini used the same music for the two middle lines of the refrain (mm. 7–12 and 12–17), and he began the *volta* ("Vuolsi dunque aristiare") with a phrase he had previously set to the third line of the *piedi* ("Ci poteva insegnare").

Along with its ad hoc pattern of repetition—not an unusual feature of the canti carnascialeschi—Coppini's *Canzona degli uccellatori* displays certain other mannerisms characteristic of them. Most include brief sections in triple meter, either at the beginning of the *piedi*, as in Coppini's piece, or at the end of the *volta*. Most reduce the standard number of four voices to two or three for at least one passage in imitative counterpoint. And Coppini's composition is written in the typically homophonic texture of the canti carnascialeschi, even though the middle phrases of its *ripresa* are unusually contrapuntal.

Florentine carnival songs differ from Mantuan frottole in many ways. The main differences stem from the fact that they were conceived as vocal in all four parts. The style of the carnival songs does not show any clear-cut relationship with the techniques of the earlier fifteenth-century improvisers, and their texture is usually much plainer than that of frottole. Many sections of the carnival songs are almost completely homorhythmic; their inner voices are not nearly so active as those in frottole; and in many the superius and the tenor might almost form self-sufficient two-part counterpoint, an indication that in some ways Florentine music was closer than the frottole to Franco-Netherlandish polyphony.

No one could mistake Bartolomeo degli Organi's three-part setting of *Un dì lieto già mai* (Example 4–8), a ballata attributed to Lorenzo the Magnificent, for a Mantuan frottola or a French chanson. Yet it partakes of some features of both with, on the one hand, its clear chordal orientation and, on the other, its sensitively shaped melodic lines. The settings by Bartolomeo and other Florentine composers of ballate and closely related kinds of poetry, more serious in tone than carnival songs, are by no means models of complex and highly refined contrapuntal technique. Bartolomeo's ballata is fundamentally as chordal as any frottola and, indeed, more obviously so, since it is more starkly homorhythmic. In this respect it is not dissimilar to the setting of the same poem by the Netherlander Heinrich Isaac. Yet the words of Bartolomeo's song, unlike those in frottole, can be added to the three lower voices without any difficulty at all; they were obviously intended to be sung. A four-part or even five-part texture in which all the melodic lines are vocally conceived became a hallmark of early-sixteenth-century Franco-Netherlandish music, as we shall see. Albeit with very different effect, the Florentines adopted the same techniques in elaborating their simple harmonic schemes.

The kind of interpenetration between Italianate harmony and Franco-Netherlandish polyphony that was to characterize the sixteenth-century Italian madrigal can already be seen in Bernardo Pisano's settings, published in 1520, of Petrarch's *canzoni,* one of the first volumes printed by Petrucci to be devoted to a single Italian composer. The volume reflects the interest of early sixteenth-

EXAMPLE 4–7. Alessandro Coppini, *Canzona degli uccellatori alle starne*, mm. 1–47.

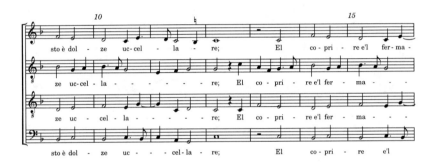

EXAMPLE 4–7. (*Continued*)

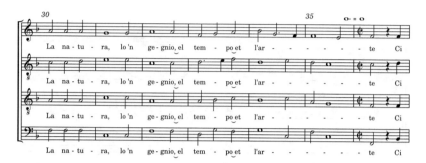

La na-tu-ra, lo 'n ge-gnio, el tem - po et l'ar - - - - - te Ci

po - te-va in-se - gna - - - re, Cer-chan - do a ton-do a ton-do in o - gni par -

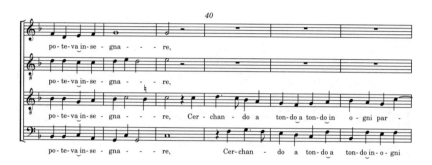

Vuol - si dun-que a-ri - stia - - - re

EXAMPLE 4–8. Bartolomeo degli Organi, *Un dì lieto già mai*, mm. 1–10.

Un dì lie - to già ma - - - i Non heb-bi A - mor, da po - i

century Italian musicians in poetry of high literary quality, and it reveals how they came to give up their schematic settings of predetermined poetic forms in favor of freer kinds of poems (canzoni and madrigals) that they could treat phrase by phrase, in through-composed settings that attempt to reflect the special shape or character of each line of verse.

LAUDE AND
OTHER ITALIAN SACRED MUSIC

Many Italian composers of the late fifteenth and early sixteenth centuries worked in princely courts where their principal responsibilities were to supply secular music for the enjoyment of the courtiers. Some, notably the Florentines Coppini and Bartolomeo degli Organi, held positions at churches as choirmasters, organists, or singers. They certainly wrote sacred music as a part of their duties, but much of it is now lost. The fragments that survive do not suggest that Italian composers of the time could rival, in the quality of their achievement, the great Franco-Netherlanders then employed in most of the leading churches and cathedrals. Petrucci published two volumes of Lamentations of Jeremiah in 1506 and included in them several predominantly chordal settings by Italians, among them one by Tromboncino and a *Passio sacra* by Francesco d'Ana that is surprisingly expressive, considering its economy of means. Manuscript sources contain several late-fifteenth-century Italian passions in which the dramatic story is told in a mixture of chant and simple polyphony. Coppini and Bartolomeo degli Organi composed motets in a polyphonic style not unlike that of the Franco-Netherlanders, and Coppini even wrote a Mass based on Alexander Agricola's three-part motet *Si dedero.*

The largest corpus of Italian sacred music written about 1500, however, consists of *laude.* These hymns of praise and devotion (most of them set to Italian words but some to Latin) were intended for performance by laymen, and especially by members of *Compagnie di Laudesi* (companies of lauda singers), which existed everywhere in Italy at that time but particularly in Florence. Saint Francis of Assisi wrote laude as early as the thirteenth century, and they were sung by the numerous penitential fraternities of the fourteenth century. But by 1500 companies of lauda singers were simply groups that met regularly for devotional purposes and for singing, especially hymns of praise to the Virgin Mary. An account from mid-sixteenth-century Florence describes how one society, made up mostly of artisans, met in a church every Saturday after the office of nones. Their procedures were probably quite typical. After singing a number of laude, their simple ceremony concluded when a picture of the Virgin was unveiled to the accompaniment of song and organ music.

In keeping with their homely social function, laude were sung to simple poems that resemble folk songs, popular songs, or fundamentalist hymns. Some are enthusiastically devotional:

> Senza te, sacra regina,
> Non si pò in ciel salire,
> L'alma sua non pò perire
> Che a te serve, a te s'inclina …

("Without you, sacred queen, we cannot go to heaven; if we serve you and bow before you, our souls cannot die.") Others have a fresh naïveté characteristic of popular poetry:

> Ognun driza al ciel el viso
> E comenza a caminare.
> Su su su, che stiam a fare,
> Su su, tutti al paradiso!

("Everyone should turn his gaze to heaven and start to walk; up, up, up, you laggards, let's all go to paradise!") Many laude borrow the formal schemes of their secular counterparts—barzellette, strambotti, odes, capitoli, and so on—and some are uncomplicated strophic poems.

Many monophonic laude survive from the later Middle Ages, and it seems likely that they continued to be sung as unaccompanied melodies throughout the fifteenth century. Lauda texts were imposed on the melodies of secular songs, both monophonic and polyphonic, throughout the sixteenth century. Several sixteenth-century collections of lauda texts exist, and they indicate the secular tunes to which the poems were meant to be sung. But polyphonic laude, too, either newly composed or based on pre-existing melodies, had begun to be written in the fifteenth century. The largest collections of them are two volumes published by Petrucci in 1507 and 1508, the first composed entirely by Innocentius Dammonis, the second consisting of works by musicians familiar to us from Petrucci's frottola books—not only Tromboncino and Cara, but also Giacomo Fogliano, Paulus Scotus, Piero da Lodi, Josquin, and others.

Musically the laude are as simple as their texts. Those based on secular forms resemble frottole. *Vengo a te, madre Maria* (Example 4–9) by Giacomo Fogliano (or Don Nicolo?) even uses the typical dance rhythms of the frottola, though the triple meter with hemiola is interrupted at some cadences by one bar in duple meter that breaks the forward motion. Like a frottola, too, the

EXAMPLE 4–9. Giacomo Fogliano (or Don Nicolo?), *Vengo a te, madre Maria,* mm. 1–4.

inner voices of *Vengo a te* are more active than the soprano or the bass. Some laude, on the other hand, are much more strictly homorhythmic and proceed at a slightly slower pace than the more frottolistic examples. The greater solemnity of their rhythm is usually matched by the greater piety of their texts.

BIBLIOGRAPHICAL NOTES

On the musical institutions of fifteenth-century Italy and the interplay between Flemish and Italian musicians, see Nanie Bridgman, *La vie musicale au Quattrocento* (Paris, 1964), and Nino Pirrotta, "Music and Cultural Tendencies in 15th-Century Italy," *JAMS* 19 (1966): 127–61, reprinted along with other essays relevant to this chapter in Pirrotta, *Music and Cultural Tendencies in Italy from the Middle Ages to the Baroque. A Collection of Essays* (Cambridge, Mass., 1984). Lewis Lockwood, *Music in Renaissance Ferrara 1400–1505* (Oxford, 1984), is an exemplary study of musical patronage at a north Italian court. William Prizer, "Music at the Court of the Sforza: the Birth and Death of a Musical Center," *MD* 43 (1989): 141–93, considers patronage of music in Milan. On Naples through the end of the fifteenth century, see Allan W. Atlas, "Aragonese Naples," Chap. 5 in *The Renaissance from the 1470s to the End of the Sixteenth Century,* ed. Iain Fenlon (Englewood Cliffs, N.J., 1989), 156–73, based on the same author's *Music at the Aragonese Court of Naples* (Cambridge, 1985). Jonathan Glixon, "Music at the Venetian Scuole Grandi, 1440–1450," in *Music in Medieval and Early Modern Europe: Patronage, Sources, and Texts,* ed. Iain Fenlon (New York, 1981), 191–208, is a study of the confraternities in Venice as supporters of music; and in the same volume see also Giulio Cattin, "Church Patronage of Music in Fifteenth-Century Italy," 21–36. For a study of music in Mantua, see Iain Fenlon, *Music and Patronage in Sixteenth-Century Mantua* (Cambridge, 1980).

On courtly improvisers, see Lewis Lockwood, "Pietrobono and the Instrumental Tradition at Ferrara," *RIM* 10 (1975): 115–29; Walter Rubsamen, *Literary Sources of Secular Music in Italy* (ca. 1500) (Berkeley and Los Angeles, 1943); Rubsamen, "The Justiniane or Viniziane of the 15th Century," *AcM* 29 (1957); and Emile Haraszti, "La technique des improvisateurs latins et de langue vulgaire au XVe siècle," *RBM* 9 (1955). Music for the lira da braccio is discussed in Howard Mayer Brown, *Sixteenth-Century Instrumentation: The Music for the Florentine Intermedii* (AIM, 1974). See also William F. Prizer, "Lutenists and the Court of Mantua in the Late Fifteenth and Early Sixteenth Centuries," *JLSA* 13 (1980): 4–34.

The first two of Petrucci's early anthologies of secular music have been published in editions by Helen Hewitt, as *Harmonice Musices Odhecaton A* (Cambridge, Mass., 1942; reprint, New York, 1978) and *Ottaviano Petrucci, Canti B, numero cinquanta, Venice, 1502,* MRM, vol. 2 (Chicago, 1967). Facsimile editions of Petrucci's *Harmonice Musices Odhecaton A (1504), Canti B, numero cinquanta (1502),* and *Canti C numero cento cinquanta (1503/4)* have been issued by Broude Bros. (New York, 1973, 1975, and 1978), in the series Monuments of Music and Music Literature in Facsimile. Petrucci's first three books of frottole are reprinted in Gaetano Cesari, Raffaello Monterosso, and Benvenuto Disertori, eds., *Le Frottole nell'edizione di Ottaviano Petrucci* (Cremona, 1954). The first and fourth books are reprinted in Rudolf Schwartz, ed., *Ottaviano Petrucci: Frottole I und IV* (Leipzig, 1935). Another volume of frottole in modern edition is Alfred Einstein, ed., *Canzoni Sonetti Strambotti e Frottole, Libro Tertio* (Andrea Antico, 1517), Smith College Music Archives 4 (Northampton, Mass., 1941). Bossinensis's arrangements of frottole for voice and lute are reprinted in Benvenuto Disertori, ed., *Le Frottole per canto e liuto intabulate da Franciscus Bossinensis* (Milan, 1964).

The classic studies of the frottola repertory are those in Einstein, *The Italian Madrigal* (Princeton, 1949); Knud Jeppesen, *La Frottola* (Copenhagen, 1968–70); and Walter Rubsamen, *Literary Sources of Secular Music in Italy (ca. 1500)* (Berkeley and Los Angeles, 1943). Important recent studies are William Prizer, *Courtly Pastimes: The Frottole of Marchetto Cara* (Ann Arbor, 1980); Prizer, "The Frottola and the Unwritten Tradition," *SM* 15 (1986): 3–37; Prizer, "Isabella d'Este and Lucrezia Borgia as Patrons of Music: the Frottola at Mantua and Ferrara," *JAMS* 38 (1985): 1–33; and Giulio Cattin, "Nomi di rimatori per la polifania profana italiana del secondo Quattrocento," *RIM* 25 (1990): 209–311.

On women's music, see Howard Mayer Brown, "Women Singers and Women's Songs in Fifteenth-Century Italy," in *Women Making Music. The Western Art Tradition, 1150–1950,* ed. Jane Bowers and Judith Tick (Urbana, Ill., 1986), 62–89. William F. Prizer, "Renaissance Women as Patrons of Music: The North-Italian Courts," in *Rediscovering the Muses: Women's Musical Traditions,* ed. Kimberly Marshall (Boston, 1993), 186–205, and Prizer, "Games of Venus: Secular Vocal Music in the Late Quattrocento and Early Cinquecento," *JM* 9 (1991): 3–56, are studies of women as patrons and amateur musicians.

Concerning the "unwritten" tradition and Italian music of this period, see James Haar, "Monophony and the Unwritten Tradition," in *Performance Practice: Music before 1600,* ed. Howard Mayer Brown and Stanley Sadie (London, 1989; New York, 1990), 240–66; Haar, "*Improvisatori* and Their Relationship to Sixteenth-Century Music," Chap. 4 in *Essays on Italian Poetry and Music in the Renaissance 1350–1600* (Berkeley and Los Angeles, 1986); and Nino Pirrotta, "The Oral and Written Traditions of Music" and other essays in Pirrotta, *Music and Culture in Italy from the Middle Ages to the Baroque.*

For strambotti, see the edition by Giuseppina La Face Bianconi, *Gli strambotti del codice estense F.9.9* (Florence, 1990). The standard work on canti carnascialeschi remains Federico Ghisi, *I canti carnascialeschi nelle fonti musicali del XV e XVI secoli* (Florence, 1937). All extant texts are published in *Canti Carnascialeschi del Rinascimento,* 2 vols., ed. Charles S. Singleton (Bari, 1936). Examples of the music appear in Paul-Marie Masson, ed., *Chants de carnaval florentin* (Paris, 1913), and K. Westphal, ed., *Karnevalslieder der Renaissance, Das Chorwerk,* vol. 43 (Wolfenbüttel, 1936). The series Music of the Florentine Renaissance, ed. Frank A. D'Accone, CMM, series 32 (AIM, 1966—), includes the collected works of Bernardo Pisano, Alessandro Coppini, Bartolomeo degli Organi, and Giovanni Serragli, plus some anonymous works. On Florentine musicians, see D'Accone, "Alessandro Coppini and Bartolomeo degli Organi—two Florentine Composers of the Renaissance," *Analecta Musicologica* 4 (1967), and D'Accone, "Bernardo Pisano, an Introduction to His Life and Works," *MD* 17 (1963). *Florentine Festival Music (1480–1520),* ed. Joseph J. Gallucci, Jr., is vol. 40 of RRMR (Madison, Wis.).

An important study of the laude to the mid–fifteenth century is Elisabeth Diederichs, *Die Anfänge der mehrstimmigen Lauda vom Ende des 14. bis zur Mitte des 15. Jahrhunderts* (Tutzing, 1986). On the laude and corporate patronage for music in Florence to 1494, see Blake Wilson, *Music and Merchants. The Laudesi Companies of Republican Florence* (Oxford, 1992). See also Jonathan Glixon, "The Polyphonic Laude of Innocentius Dammonis," *JM* 8 (1990): 19–53. Knud Jeppesen, *Die mehrstimmige italienische Laude um 1500* (Leipzig, 1935), includes a selection from Petrucci's two volumes of laude, and Jeppesen, *Italia sacra musica* (Copenhagen, 1962), supplies sacred music by Italian composers from the first half of the sixteenth century.

FIVE

JOSQUIN DES PREZ

By the last quarter of the fifteenth century, Dufay and the composers of his generation had formed the central musical language of the early Renaissance, and composers of the next generation, such as Ockeghem and Busnoys, had explored the possibilities for expansion of their musical techniques. But it is in the music of Josquin des Prez and his contemporaries—composers born in the 1440s, 1450s, and 1460s—that the word "Renaissance" is more easily applied to the musical genres we have been studying. If we accept that Renaissance culture was concerned, above all, with the search for elegance and eloquence of expression, then it is clear that these composers were Renaissance artists, working to create a music more overtly expressive of its text and more adaptable to social and religious contexts than ever before. The incredibly productive generation of northern musicians whose careers span the several decades before and after 1500—in the first place Josquin, but also Obrecht, Isaac, Agricola, Compère, Pierre de la Rue, and others—transformed music by forging new techniques that became central to the musical language of the sixteenth century, though their implications were not fully worked out until its close.

The composers of Josquin's generation took a new interest in the relationship between text and music, respecting the integrity of a text's declamation and pattern of accents, its poetic structure, and to some extent its message.

Composers began to explore the ways in which their melodies (and other aspects of a composition) could capture the shape and the meanings of the words they set. Given that so many of these composers were northerners employed in Italy, it has often been argued that the new style reflects the musical contact between north and south: the new attention to text and sensitivity of expression is something that northern composers may have learned in Italy, where a fully blown Renaissance humanist culture flourished.

A second aspect of the new sound that developed in the late fifteenth century was its greater chordal orientation and clearer harmonic structure. Perhaps the northern composers learned something about both text setting and the richness of chordal harmony from the songs of native Italian musicians (as we have seen, the northerners could have heard four-part versions of laude and frottole in the later fifteenth century). But composers of Josquin's generation might just as well have been attracted to the striking harmonies encountered quite often, for example, in Ockeghem's music; and to the marked "tonal" orientation and sensitive treatment of text in some pieces by Dufay, or the brightly consonant chordal and declamatory openings of many popular chansons. It is likely that composers north and south learned, through study and experiment with the music available to them, music of every sort and of every geographic derivation. Whether or not it was the confrontation between Franco-Netherlandish and Italian musical cultures, the rich, harmonious, and expressive sound of the music of Josquin and his contemporaries attests to a new awareness of harmony and its utility in the articulation of musical form.

Composers did not discard the principles and norms, the techniques and conventions learned, explored, and perfected over several generations. But the new style that began to coalesce in the late fifteenth century—with its freely invented, fluid, and long-breathed melodic lines assigned to more-or-less equal voices in a polyphonic web—eventually replaced the well-worn older style in which the melodic lines were worked out over a slower-moving tenor cantus firmus. The process of stylistic transformation came about by means of a series of interrelated factors. The use of cantus firmus remained an important technical resource of composers throughout the sixteenth century and even later, but musicians about 1500 made a decisive step forward by beginning to work with *motives* as the basic units of musical construction. By this means they could create long movements consisting of chains of interlocked phrases, each of them devoted to the contrapuntal exploration of a single motive. In its classical formulation in the sixteenth century, this technique produced a series of motivically based sections of counterpoint called "points of imitation," which could be interrupted for variety and contrast by occasional chordal passages. In shaping music around a text or in elucidating the meaning of a text, composers learned how to vary the texture and change the character of the music at will, shifting from full sounds to thin and from strict imitative counterpoint to dialogue among the voices to thickly scored chords, as needed. They also began to work out simultaneously the details of form and texture of a composition. This radically changed the way individual voices related to one another and hence the way music actually sounded. As we have seen, both Dufay (especially in his later years) and Ockeghem tended to deemphasize the differences among various voices. Toward the very end of the fifteenth century, in the music of Josquin and his contemporaries, the most obvious result of this compositional innovation was the change from a hierarchical texture, in which each voice has a special function, to a texture in which all the voices, though independent, are equal in importance and in melodic style. This compositional approach (sometimes called "simultaneous composition" but perhaps better termed "harmonic conception") was described and recommended early in the sixteenth century by the Italian theorist Pietro Aaron on the basis of his study of music by northern composers.

It is no exaggeration to say that the new technique of interlocked phrases, each of them unified motivically, emancipated music while at the same time opening the way for its closer relationship to words and images. The sonority it produces is sometimes described as a combination of melodic lines that are all vocal in conception. But though each line can in fact easily be sung—a feature that distinguishes the new music from many earlier compositions—pieces in the new style were not always performed exclusively by singers alone in *a cappella* choirs. Some organizations, such as the Sistine Chapel in Rome and the cathedral in Cambrai, did exclude instruments (even the organ) from the performance of sacred music, but the choirs in most chapels sometimes sang with instruments and sometimes without. The *"a cappella* ideal" (a term that used to be associated with sixteenth-century music) has little or no historical validity, even though it does draw attention to the homogeneous texture of much of this music, a texture that sounds good, it must be admitted, whether played by groups of like instruments—consorts (ensembles) of flutes, recorders, or viols, for example—or sung by consorts of unaccompanied voices.

An unusually large number of distinguished composers worked during the last several decades of the fifteenth century and the first several of the sixteenth. Of these, the greatest was Josquin des Prez. This was recognized by his contemporaries. Martin Luther, for example, wrote that Josquin alone was master of the notes, which must do as he wished: other composers did as the notes wished. The Florentine writer Cosimo Bartoli, in recounting in 1543 the recent history of music, compared Ockeghem to Donatello, both of whom rediscovered an art that was almost dead, but likened Josquin to Michelangelo: they were both wonders of nature who had brought their art to a peak of perfection. A letter of 2 September 1502 addressed to Duke Ercole d'Este I of Ferrara by his secretary acknowledged the high esteem in which Josquin was held while at the same time revealing something of the composer's personality. The duke was seeking a composer for his court, and his secretary urged him to hire Isaac rather than Josquin because Isaac "is able to get on better with his colleagues and composes new pieces quicker. It is true, Josquin composes better, but he does it only when it suits him and not when it is requested. More than this, Josquin asks 200 ducats while Isaac is pleased with 120." (In fact, when Josquin came to Ferrara in 1503, his salary was 200 ducats, the most a chapel master had ever received there.)

IOSQVINVS PRATENSIS.

Figure 4. Portrait of Josquin des Prez, preserved in a woodcut from Petrus Opmeer, *Opus chronographicum,* 1611. (Courtesy of the University of Minnesota Libraries, Special Collections, and Rare Books, Minneapolis, Minnesota)

Although his genius was recognized in his own lifetime and later, some basic questions about Josquin's life and works remain unanswered. We do not know what part he took in forging the new style during its formative years at the end of the fifteenth century. We do not know precisely where he worked during many years of his life, and we cannot yet arrange his works in chronological order with any degree of assurance. We cannot associate many works with specific events, and relatively few compositions by him are preserved in sources before 1500. We may be particularly ignorant, then, about Josquin's earliest works, perhaps because so many manuscripts have been lost or perhaps because he was extremely self-critical and destroyed or otherwise prevented his early compositions from being circulated. Petrucci printed some of them in his publications after 1501, and he devoted three volumes exclusively to Josquin's Masses. But many of his works, most unusually, were printed for the first time only years after his death. Beginning in the 1530s, Josquin's Masses, motets, and chansons appeared in publications everywhere in northern Europe. These late sources give us many compositions by Josquin that would otherwise be lost to us, though they do not always offer the most trustworthy readings, and they complicate the picture by ascribing pieces to Josquin that are clearly not his. That musicians throughout the sixteenth century were obviously still so deeply interested in Josquin's music is a remarkable tribute to the composer in an age when music went out of fashion rapidly; compositions twenty or more years old were normally considered unworthy of performance.

One of the great international figures of his time, Josquin traveled extensively and worked in various cities during his long and productive life. He cannot be associated with a single court, a single ruler, or a single locality unless it be the land associated with the river Escaut: he spent his last years as provost of the Church of Notre Dame in Condé-sur-l'Escaut, and he was probably born about 1440 near the head of the river, in the province of Picardy. It is likely that he was a choirboy at the collegiate church in St. Quentin, and later in life he became a "clerc," and eventually a priest, in the diocese of Cambrai. It is possible that he studied with Ockeghem; he certainly felt close ties with the older composer, since he based several compositions on melodies by him and wrote a lament on his death (*Nymphes des bois*, the famous "Déploration de Johannes Ockeghem").

In 1459 a young man named "Juschino" was appointed a singer at the Cathedral of Santa Maria Maggiore in Milan, a position he held until 1472. This is the first documented event in Josquin's career, although some scholars argue that this Josquin is not the composer Josquin des Prez, though this seems unlikely. He left the cathedral in 1472 to enter the service of the Duke of Milan, Galeazzo Maria Sforza, who had assembled a brilliant group of musicians at his court, including Agricola, Weerbecke, Compère, and Johannes Martini. Clearly the duke valued Josquin, because in 1473, within months of the singer-composer's appointment to the court chapel, he wrote to obtain a lucrative benefice for him. A few months later, in March 1473, the duke wrote directly to Josquin:

> We hear that you are spending your time writing something other than the work that we have given you, and you have set aside our business to serve others, which bothers us greatly. And we have been of a mind to have you locked up in prison in order to teach you to be wiser the next time, which will happen to you if you do not arrange that the work commissioned from you is expedited without delay.

From the wording of the letter we cannot know for sure whether the duke had ordered Josquin to copy music or compose music for him (or both), or whether Josquin was in the habit of working for other patrons or simply received tempting offers from time to time. Nor is it clear whether Josquin was generally tardy with his work or so only in this instance. As was usual in the relationship between patron and musician in this period, the duke asked for absolute fidelity and considered Josquin's labor (whether as composer or music copyist) and his music his property. Whether or not the duke would actually have thrown the composer into prison, it is clear that he prized his talents and jealously guarded Josquin as his possession.

After Duke Galeazzo Maria was murdered at the end of 1476, Josquin made his way to the court of King René of Anjou at Aix-en-Provence, where he is listed as a chapel singer in April 1477. But two years later he went back to Milan, in the employ of Duchess Bona Sforza, Galeazzo's widow.

During his years in Milan Josquin probably came to know Galeazzo Maria's younger brother, Cardinal Ascanio Sforza, and he was in the cardinal's entourage in Rome in the 1480s. Several frottole printed by Petrucci are attributed to "Jusquin d'Ascanio," and the poet-musician Serafino dall'Aquila addressed a poem to Josquin, his companion in service, in which he alludes to their difficulties in getting paid by the cardinal. It may have been through Ascanio that Josquin was introduced to Roman musical circles and subsequently joined the papal chapel, where he sang from 1489 through at least November 1494, perhaps keeping close contact with Ascanio, for whom he may even have worked during his frequent absences from the papal payroll. It is also possible that one or two of his absences allowed him to visit France and the Burgundian lands again. The documents containing the payrolls of the years 1495–99 are missing, so we cannot know precisely how long Josquin's papal service may have continued. It had ended before 1500, the year in which the records resume, and by that time he had surely left Rome altogether.

Where Josquin was in the next few years is not clear, but in 1499 we have the first hint that his music was especially appreciated at the court of the Duke of Ferrara, Ercole d'Este I, for a singer of the duke's sent the Marquis of Mantua one of his compositions "good [to listen to] because of its excellence." In 1501 some of his pieces were acquired by the court of Ferrara. Toward the end of that year Josquin traveled to Flanders to recruit singers for the duke's chapel. From Flanders he journeyed directly to the French royal court at Blois, where a splendid ceremonial meeting between King Louis XII and the Burgundian Duke Philip the Fair was taking place, with both chapels in attendance to celebrate the peace treaty between the two states. Josquin apparently did not belong to either chapel, but it is clear that he was known at the French court. Philip the Fair also surely knew of his skill, for he wished Josquin to join the Burgundian chapel for the rest of the ducal journey, to Spain. Josquin did not do so, but Philip's esteem for him was to be shown again a few years later. It was through the French court, however, that Josquin, who seemingly had shown some reluctance, was finally recruited for Ferrara, arriving there by way of Paris and Lyons in April 1503. His immense reputation by that time is brought out in an earlier letter to Duke Ercole from one of his musicians:

> My Lord, I believe that there is neither lord nor king who will now have a better chapel than yours if Your Lordship sends for Josquin. [Your son] wishes to write this to Your Lordship and so does the entire chapel; and by having Josquin in our chapel I want to place a crown upon this chapel of ours.

Josquin served as *maestro di cappella* of Ercole's chapel for only a year: his last payment was in April 1504. It was long assumed he had composed his *Missa Hercules Dux Ferrarie* in Ercole's honor during that period of service, but scholars now believe the work could have been written one or even two decades earlier, at the time of a previous encounter with the duke.

Josquin left Ferrara to take a position as provost of Notre Dame in Condé-sur-l'Escaut, perhaps not far from his birthplace. He seems to have kept this job at Condé during the remaining seventeen years until his death on 27 August 1521. But perhaps from this humble position he maintained his ties with the rich and powerful: his chansons were prized by Margaret of Austria at her court in Malines; and her nephew Charles V, the Holy Roman Emperor himself, seems to have had a particular affection for the composer's music. Josquin's *Mille regretz* was labeled "La canción del emperador" when it was published in Spain in 1538 in an arrangement for vihuela by Luis de Narváez.

JOSQUIN'S MOTETS

About twenty Masses, seventy-five secular pieces, and one hundred motets by Josquin survive. In many ways his greatness and individuality are displayed more clearly in his motets than in the other genres. Although he composed a very large number of motets in comparison with Ockeghem and Obrecht, his interest in the genre was not atypical of his generation; a virtual explosion of motet composition occurred in the last quarter of the fifteenth century. As yet, we know too little of what lay behind this upsurge in interest in the genre. Surely one reason was the founding of princely chapel choirs all over Europe, and the reorganization and revitalization of cathedral choirs (sometimes due to lay patronage), which produced more occasions and venues for sacred polyphony and more institutions that could support its performance. Most cathedrals, churches, and court chapels heard a variety of kinds of music on a regular basis, even within the broad category of "sacred" or "religious" polyphony. For the most part, we assume that motets were used as extraliturgical adornments of Masses and Office Hours. But we still do not know precisely how all the various kinds of motets were used or for what specific purposes they were composed, performed, and copied. In some cases, composers must have chosen to set the texts they found most stimulating or appropriate; in others, motets were composed (as they always had been) for specific patrons or occasions, whether sacred or secular—for example, for state ceremonies.

The texts Josquin chose for his motets can be divided roughly into three large categories: those found in liturgical books and thus prescribed for the Mass or Canonical Hours (most of these already had a chant setting); biblical texts such as psalms or combinations of texts not known in liturgical sources; and a miscellaneous group including prayers, poems of devotion, songs of praise, and the like, many addressed to or in honor of Christ or the Virgin Mary. The third category is necessarily the least well defined. Even its extent can scarcely be described with precision, since it is difficult to draw the line between liturgical and devotional texts. Perhaps we shall eventually discover that all Josquin's motets were intended for performance in ritual or votive services in royal chapels or collegiate churches. In the meantime, however, we must recognize that although more than half of his hundred-odd motet texts have been found in early liturgical books, few of them, if any, could have substituted for the chant settings. Nevertheless, whenever Josquin set a liturgical text that had its own plainchant, he either used the sacred melody as a cantus firmus on which to base his own polyphony or paraphrased it in all voices.

The distinction between liturgical and nonliturgical sacred texts becomes increasingly blurred by the time of Josquin's generation. Some of the devotional texts he set are personal and contemporary—for example, the two Marian compositions *Illibata Dei virgo nutrix* (incorporating Josquin's name in an acrostic) and *O Virgo prudentissima,* a rhymed prayer by the Florentine poet Angelo Poliziano. Others he could have found in books of hours, which laymen read from at Mass or at their private devotions. Some of the most intriguing texts are those gathered from various biblical sources, which may have been devised for or inspired by particular events: *Absalon, fili mi,* incorporating the words of David mourning over his slain son, may have been written either for the Emperor Maximilian I of Austria after the death in 1506 of his son, Philip the Handsome, or for Pope Alexander VI when his favorite son, Juan, Duke of Gandia, was murdered in 1497.

Josquin was among the first to set psalms polyphonically, and it was this genre (the psalm motet) more than any other that was to ensure his place in musical history, for such works appealed also to Lutherans; German printers published many of them (and a number of spurious ones as well). Josquin's interest in psalms may merely reflect the changing liturgical practices of the time, but possibly he was attracted to them for subjective reasons. The highly poetic, emotional, and colorful language of David's psalms must have appealed to him for the opportunities they afforded to invent an extraordinarily expressive music, human and personal, that was in every way worthy of the exalted words it set.

In a historical sense, Josquin's motets are important for the precedents they set and the doors they opened. They display his bold compositional inventiveness within the new style of equal-voiced polyphony built in interlocking phrases. They show the composer deploying an arsenal of techniques for the elucidation and interpretation of text, each technique developed with a musical power and coherence, a sustained level of expressive intensity, altogether new in the history of Western music. Josquin cultivated the motet throughout his long and productive life; hence it would seem natural to study the motets of his early, middle, and late years to gain some impression of his development as a composer. But scholars have discovered that simple analogies between stylistic complexity and compositional maturity break down. Josquin's most enduring trait was his diversity, and he could use certain stylistic elements—florid melismatic writing or austere declamatory homophony, for example—in a late motet or an early one. The dating of any composition by Josquin depends on a combination of factors: the dates and reliability of the sources that preserve the piece; the subject and origin of its text; and the way the form and meaning of the text are treated in its music. Josquin chose compositional devices to suit the nature of the text he set and the circumstances of a particular commission or the ceremonial or religious use associated with it.

A few motets by Josquin can be tentatively assigned a date according to what we know about them. For example, *Miserere mei, Deus,* Josquin's grand and solemn setting of Psalm 50, was almost certainly composed in 1503–4 when Josquin was in Ferrara, under a commission from Duke Ercole d'Este as a memorial tribute to Girolamo Savonarola, the Florentine Dominican priest who had preached against the corruption of the church. The night before his execution in 1498, Savonarola wrote a meditation on Psalm 50 that was later printed and widely circulated. It includes a very effective rhetorical device: the opening words of the psalm, the plea "Miserere mei, Deus," keep returning as a refrain. Perhaps because of the special nature of this commission, Josquin seems to have been inspired by Savonarola's rhetoric; in his motet, he set the words "Miserere mei, Deus" as a recurring refrain, made all the more powerful through a simple, austere musical formula.

As Lowinsky wrote in his commentary on the *Miserere mei, Deus* in the Medici Codex, Josquin "has arrived at a new concept: music as an artistic projection, elevation, and intensification of the spoken word." In *Miserere mei, Deus,* this is revealed even in the motto that underlies the composition and serves both as cantus firmus and as refrain. A syllabic recitation on two notes, it is in its simplicity a direct cry for mercy. Josquin repeated it over and over as a cantus firmus on scale degrees that descend stepwise through an octave in the first part, ascend an octave (in rhythmic diminution) in the second part, and descend a fifth in the third part. This scheme is not as rigid as it seems, since the appearances of the motto do not follow a preconceived plan: the tenor states the theme at irregular time intervals, depending on the length of the verses and the emphasis Josquin wished to put on certain parts of the text. Moreover, the other voices join the tenor each time in singing "Miserere mei, Deus" either in imitation or in near homophony, and these tutti passages, the only ones in the motet, give the composition a dramatic shape. In short, the compact and elegantly concise melodies in the motet vividly interpret the text they carry. The rhythms of these melodic lines mirror the accents in individual words, and their overall contours throw into relief important words and phrases. A master of vocal sonority, Josquin played off parts of the choir against each other. Much of *Miserere mei, Deus* is written in two- or three-part counterpoint; all five voices sing together only for the refrains. Between statements of the refrain, the texture is spare and airy, even austere. The vocal scoring helps us to hear both the words of the psalm and Josquin's interpretation of it.

The dating of Josquin's works is especially complicated because many techniques that we tend to associate with earlier epochs and composers had their place in his creative workshop. The treatment of the cantus firmus in *Miserere mei, Deus,* for example, and in other psalm settings by Josquin was hardly novel in 1503, and the duos formed of long melismatic lines that open *Illibata Dei virgo nutrix* (a motet that scholars argue Josquin may have composed in Milan during the 1470s or in Rome later on) remind us quite distinctly of

Dufay. *Illibata Dei virgo nutrix,* a rhymed prayer to the Virgin Mary, for which Josquin possibly wrote the words as well as the music (his name is revealed in an acrostic in the text), is built over a cantus firmus that translates "Maria" into musical terms by assigning a solmization syllable to each vowel, la mi la (A E A, or, as transposed in the motet, D A D and G D G). The motet contains as well a proportional treatment with successive diminutions of the tenor that can be viewed as a late manifestation of the isorhythmic procedures that underlay most of the big ceremonial motets from the fourteenth and fifteenth centuries—such as Busnoys's *In hydraulis,* which Josquin probably studied. Another of his Marian motets, *Alma redemptoris mater / Ave Regina caelorum,* paraphrases one Marian antiphon in the outer voices and another in the inner voices; here Josquin may actually quote Ockeghem, who began his paraphrase of *Alma redemptoris* in exactly the same way. Josquin's motet starts with three long melismatic duos, but in the middle of the third the other voices enter and lead to a tutti cadence that divides the first part into two halves. The high proportion of two- and three-part writing in this motet produces an open texture filled, as it were, with light and air, a texture characteristic of much of Josquin's music. Even in these pieces, with their clear debt to earlier composers, the melodic relationships among voices—in *Alma redemptoris mater,* notably the imitations between each of the pairs of voices sharing the same antiphon—create a texture unified motivically to some extent, though the voices often move at varying rates of speed and thus sound "layered." Although both pieces contain considerable passages of two- and three-part writing, the solemn and spare quality of *Miserere mei, Deus* contrasts with that of the ebulliently melismatic individual lines in *Alma redemptoris mater / Ave Regina caelorum,* just as the penitential quality of the *Miserere mei, Deus* text is worlds away from the joyful song in praise of the Virgin Mary. *Virgo salutiferi,* another Marian motet probably written several decades later than *Alma redemptoris mater / Ave Regina caelorum* but close in time to *Miserere mei, Deus,* is, however, also highly melismatic in its praise of the Virgin Mary. In all these motets, Josquin adjusted his style in response to the text, and they all display some of his characteristic mannerisms while still reflecting the compositional techniques of an earlier generation.

The "classical" formulation of the new stylistic norm that we associate with Josquin is found in those pieces in which formal coherence enhances textual clarity and smoothness of texture. A number of such pieces are tentatively assigned to the time Josquin was in Rome and other parts of Italy (ca. 1489–1504). Perhaps no motet better exemplifies Josquin's mastery of the new imitative counterpoint than his setting of a rhymed prayer to the Virgin Mary, *Ave Maria ... virgo serena* (Example 5–1), one of the best known of all his works. As the piece unfolds phrase by phrase and section by section, its form is crystal clear. Each line of the text receives new music, which is composed in points of imitation (each of the first four lines of the poem); in paired duets with or without imitation; or in homorhythmic or nearly homorhythmic style (the final three lines of the example, beginning "Solemni plena gaudio"). Indeed, the

EXAMPLE 5–1. Josquin, *Ave Maria*, mm. 1–53.

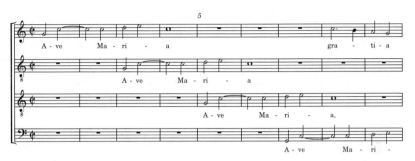

EXAMPLE 5–1. (*Continued*)

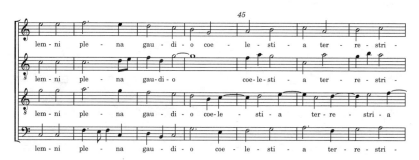

opening points of imitation are striking (and unusual) in their classic simplicity, each voice singing little more than the motive shared by all the other voices. Even in this short example the flexibility of the imitative technique is obvious. The order of entries and the time interval between them, the ways in which each voice continues the head motive, the way in which each set of entries is overlapped—all can be modified or changed in each new section; the use of interlocking sections in imitation provides a ground plan capable of almost infinite variety.

A succession of unrelated phrases, however, does not make a well-formed piece of music. In *Ave Maria* Josquin took care to fashion a shape that follows the quatrains of the text. The first quatrain ends in m. 30 with a deceptive cadence after a brief section in which all four voices sing simultaneously for the first time. That cadence, however, is merely a passing point of articulation before the first major cadence in the piece (in m. 53), the importance of which is underscored by several features: it is the first full V–I cadence (with 4–3 suspension) in the motet; a strong drive to this point of repose has been created by the sequence that builds up to a peak just before; and it occurs after the first extensive chordal section in the motet. Notable, too, is the way Josquin strove for melodic coherence by making the second couplet ("Dominus tecum," in mm. 16ff) a melodic variant of the first couplet; the two couplets paraphrase the same chant in different ways.

The second quatrain ("Ave cujus," in mm. 31ff) opens with a paired duet (in which the answer has a third voice added), one of the hallmarks of Josquin's style and one of the chief ways by which he created open and spacious textures. Similarly, the remainder of the motet contains many such antiphonal passages, in which two of the voices are answered by two others. This stylistic mannerism is one of the ways in which Josquin worked with choral sonority, pitting low sounds against high, full against half choirs, and imitative polyphony against simple chords.

Another kind of contrast is introduced in the fourth quatrain, "Ave vera virginitas" ("Hail true virginity"). For this section of the piece, the points of imitation and paired duets of the first three quatrains are replaced by a serene homophony that is combined with strict canon in a masterly, almost magical, way. Here as well a change of meter to "perfect" time (triple meter in our modern terminology) is used with great freshness to represent the idea of Mary's virginal perfection.

Beneath its beautiful surface, *Ave Maria* is wrought from a number of intricate compositional techniques; yet, perhaps the first thing to strike the ear in hearing this motet is the easy and natural way the words fit the music. There can be no doubt, for example, how the syllables of "Ave Maria" are to be sung to the notes intended for them, and the notes reinforce the natural text accents. Compared with the individual lines in *Alma redemptoris mater / Ave Regina caelorum,* those in *Ave Maria* are simple, straightforward, and eminently vocal in conception; they lack the extravagant melismas of the earlier motet and reflect Josquin's growing concern for the relationship between words and music. An interest in text declamation and a clarity of form engendered both by the technique of pervading imitation and by the use of cadential patterns and choral sonorities to shape isolated phrases into larger units characterize many of Josquin's mature works; these features help to explain why this music has lost none of its power and charm after nearly five hundred years.

Even the most contrapuntal sections of *Ave Maria* seem to be influenced by harmonic considerations, because Josquin took such great care to prepare each cadence carefully. The chordal texture and clear harmonic orientation of some passages might, in fact, remind the listener of Italian music of Josquin's time, especially the Italian laude. This is true in other motets as well—for example, *Tu solus qui facis mirabilia* and the Passion motets *O Domine Jesu Christe* and *Qui velatus facis fuisti. Tu solus* (Example 5–2) was even published

EXAMPLE 5–2. Josquin, *Tu solus qui facis mirabilia*, mm. 1–15.

as a contrafactum (that is, with a new text of a different sort) in one of Petrucci's volumes of laude as *O Mater dei*. Even though its almost unrelieved chordal texture is interrupted from time to time by contrapuntal passages including paired duets, *Tu solus* might at first seem a striking exception to the stylistic norms of Netherlandish music of the time. But *Tu solus* is a typically declamatory elevation motet, to be sung at the elevation of the host during the Mass, and its chordal texture was especially designed to facilitate the unfettered declamation of the text. Almost every sonority in the motet is a full triad; almost all its cadences are based on the progression IV–I or V–I; and its melodic interest is subjugated almost completely to the harmonies. Perhaps Josquin composed *Tu solus* while he was in Milan; during his time there, he surely would have come to know declamation motets by other composers.

Along with motets of great formal clarity and elegance, such as *Ave Maria,* and those made up for the most part of simple successions of chords, such as *Tu solus,* Josquin also composed a series of long motets in five or six voices in which contrapuntal and harmonic elements are in perfect balance. The architectural quality of some of these impressive compositions manifests itself especially in the way the structure is planned around a cantus firmus. In the six-voice *Praeter rerum seriem,* for example, the tenor and the superius sing in antiphonal dialogue the three phrases of each half stanza of the strophic sequencelike poetic text. At the same time, the cantus firmus accelerates according to a strictly proportional scheme of diminution (much as in *Illibata Dei virgo nutrix*), a plan strongly rooted in the old northern tradition of the isorhythmic motet. This, together with the fact that the poetic text (in medieval Latin) and the metrical melody that Josquin used as the basis for the structure of *Praeter rerum seriem* can be found only in sources connected to the practice of French or Flemish cathedrals and chapels, strongly suggests that the motet may have been composed in the late 1470s or 1480s, when Josquin perhaps worked in France for King René of Anjou. In *Domine Dominus noster*, for five voices, the short motto repeated five times in the tenor grows longer at each appearance (it is stated first in whole notes, then in dotted whole notes, double whole notes, and so on), perhaps to symbolize the way in which the praise of God grows in heaven and on earth. Josquin's setting of the Marian sequence *Inviolata, integra et casta es* employs a canonic cantus firmus, one of his favorite scaffolding devices, in which the time of canonic entry decreases by one measure in each of the three parts. But these constructivist devices do not produce rigid and mechanical examples of number made audible; instead, the accompanying voices seem as free to expand and develop with irregular and subtle rhythms, contrasting melodies, and ever-changing contrapuntal combinations as though they were not controlled by the progress of the structural voices, and chordal passages interrupt the tightly knit segments of counterpoint from time to time to make their effective point. At the beginning of *Inviolata*, for example, the slow, metrical head motive of the cantus firmus contrasts strikingly with the exuberant downward run in the superius that traverses a tenth and appears with a slightly different accompaniment each time it repeats (Example 5–3). The third part of the motet, on the other hand, opens in near homophony with a

EXAMPLE 5–3. Josquin, *Inviolata, integra et casta es, Maria,* mm. 1–13.

chordal progression that is stated three times to invoke the Virgin ("O benigna, O regina, O Maria") before it broadens out into a fast-moving finale. In sum, Josquin's motets demonstrate the myriad ways in which his imitative counterpoint is manipulated in the service of the texts.

The desire to express the text was surely Josquin's starting point in *Planxit autem David,* a setting of David's moving lament for Saul and Jonathan (2 Sam. 1) that is one of the great musical masterpieces of the Renaissance. It was first published in 1504 by Petrucci, although it may have been composed somewhat earlier. No scaffolding device determines its structure. At most, some of the melody in the superius is derived from the chanting tone for the Lamentations in Holy Week. At the beginning, the subject is boldly announced like a title, in a harmonically static point of imitation, "Planxit autem David" ("Thus lamented David"). From there the music flows out in a series of phrases, often punctuated by pauses, in which sections of eminently harmonic counterpoint spiced with simple yet tellingly expressive dissonances are contrasted with chordal and declamatory passages and points of imitation. The shifting patterns of texture and choral sonority play a larger role in giving shape to David's words than does any more traditional musical technique. Another freely composed and very moving lament, *Absalon, fili mi,* is set at a very low pitch and reaches new depths of expression, especially in a sequence that moves downward in a circle of fifths through progressively flatter keys (both D♭ and G♭ are actually signed in the earlier sources, though the later ones transpose the motet up a ninth), a progression that not only demonstrates the composer's success in exploring the outer limits of musical space but also symbolizes the idea of descent into the grave in a most palpable way.

A series of grand and masterly motets that Josquin seems to have composed from about 1503 through his later years is his crowning achievement. Among them are the earliest settings of complete psalms on a grand scale, works such as *Miserere mei, Deus* and *Memor esto verbi tui* (from Psalm 118), both composed in the first decade of the sixteenth century (the latter for King Louis XII of France), and *De profundis clamavi* (Psalm 129), the five-voice motet that Josquin may have written for Louis's funeral in 1515. These and such magnificent works as the sequence settings *Benedicta es, caelorum regina* and the Lord's Prayer, *Pater noster* (with *Ave Maria* as its secunda pars), display the composer's complete mastery of form and technique. *Pater noster,* the prayer Josquin wished to have sung after his own death, exemplifies his concern for clarity and simplicity; its text is declaimed with great economy of means and an apparent dramatic freedom that belies the presence of a canonic cantus firmus, which is so well integrated into the texture that it is scarcely perceived. The overall message of *Memor esto verbi tui* has shaped its form; it ends with a recapitulation of the opening material (in diminution), a structural pun that recalls the text of the first verse, "Remember thy word to thy servant." These motets do not reflect any sharp break with Josquin's past; they extend and develop tendencies found in his earlier works. Above all, they are distinguished for their expressiveness and economy of means and for the way text and music are inextricably bound together.

In his motets Josquin used all the compositional procedures available to him. As we have seen, he composed many motets over a cantus firmus, the most important structural device he inherited. Other compositions paraphrase a plainchant, and still others are completely free of borrowed material; they are organized around successive points of imitation, or they follow the dictates of the text. In some motets the cantus firmus is stated in the "classical" manner by an inner voice, usually the tenor, in note values slower than those of the other voices. Often when Josquin adopted this technique, he devised a rational plan slightly more complicated than a mere single statement of the borrowed material. In *Huc me sydereo,* for example, the plainchant *Plangent eum* occurs three times in rhythmic values that decrease with each statement in simple arithmetic proportion. Not infrequently, Josquin's cantus firmus is associated with a text different from that sung by the other voices, as in *Huc me sydereo;* and in some compositions the borrowed voice alludes to a secular melody, as in *Stabat mater dolorosa,* where the tenor sings Latin words to the tenor of the chanson *Comme femme desconfortée.* Many of Josquin's cantus firmi are ostinatos—for example, those in *Illibata Dei virgo nutrix* and *Miserere mei, Deus*—either strictly or freely handled with regard to the timing of their appearances. Josquin also had a penchant for canonic cantus firmi, such as those in *Pater noster* and in *Ut Phoebi radiis.* Some canons support the surrounding luxuriant counterpoint in an obvious way, though others are smoothly incorporated into the texture. Clearly, Josquin did not feel himself uncomfortably restricted by the use of a cantus firmus.

Far from a hindrance, cantus-firmus technique in Josquin's motets is but one element in a larger musical structure that reflects and enhances the rhetoric of the words. In the Marian motets *Virgo salutiferi* and *O virgo prudentissima,* for example, the text is interpreted not only in the layout of the cantus firmus and choice of borrowed melody but also in the relationship of the cantus firmus to the other, freely invented voices and their use of recurring themes as elements of form. The form of the music helps to clarify the meaning of the text. Most characteristic of Josquin is the way that the final section of each piece is intensified. The borrowed material in the scaffolding voices finally pervades the texture and brings all the voices together to create a highly dramatic ending—a jubilant "alleluia" in *Virgo salutiferi,* an urgent plea in *O virgo prudentissima.*

Josquin seldom paraphrased a chant melody by stating it with ornamental variation complete in one voice of a motet, in the manner of Dufay or Dunstable. Josquin's use of paraphrase technique, in fact, often does not actually influence the structure of his composition. More often than not, he used the chant as a repository, as it were, of melodic ideas, and borrowed whatever fragments he wished—to serve in points of imitation or as motives that dominate single sections of a work (as in *Domine non secundum peccata* and *Liber generationis*). In *Alma redemptoris mater / Ave Regina caelorum* he paraphrased the two chants in a variety of ways. In *Ave Maria* the chant paraphrase only shapes the opening; it is dropped after the first few phrases to suit the introduction of a text not associated with any chant, and the motet concludes without reference to borrowed material. In other settings of sequencelike texts, built in double versicles, he sometimes varied the paraphrase of each melodic phrase that is repeated, to produce a so-called variation-chain sequence, as in *Inviolata integra*. In some motets, such as *Planxit autem David,* and especially in psalm settings, he alluded to chant in only a few sections of the work.

The technique of organizing a long composition as a series of interlocked sections enabled Josquin to abandon older devices of basing new music on preexisting melodies. Many of his motets, such as *Dominus regnavit, Absalon, fili mi,* and most of the psalm settings, are wholly or mostly free of borrowed material. Form and shape are given to the music by the relationship of sections to each other or by the way in which the text is declaimed in a quasi-dramatic manner. In a number of motets, order is imposed on the music by formally significant repetitions of material, as in *Memor esto verbi tui,* with its recapitulation, or the long *Qui velatus facie fuisti* in six *partes,* with the endings of *partes* 1 and 2, and 4 and 6, being musically alike. Josquin may be the earliest composer of motets to bring back bits of melody at crucial points in a composition to give it shape and meaning.

JOSQUIN'S MASSES

If Josquin's motets reveal him to be a composer intent above all else on reflecting in his music both the outward form and the inner meaning of the words he set, his Masses show off his consummate craftsmanship, his incredible ability to build vast and magnificent structures of sound. The ritual character of the Mass Ordinary must inevitably have suggested to a Renaissance musician that he should put little stress on a subjective interpretation of the text. The very length of the Mass seldom allowed a composer to lavish on single words and idiosyncratic readings of their meanings the sort of care possible in shorter motets. Josquin's Masses thus display more obviously than do his motets the musically constructivist side of his personality.

The chronology of Josquin's Masses is a subject still being debated, and even the authenticity of some of the works ascribed to him has been successfully challenged. For example, the *Missa Da pacem* may more convincingly be attributed to Noel Bauldewyn, and Josquin probably did not compose the *Missa Allez regretz* attributed to him in the first edition of his complete works: both Masses are found only in sources prepared long after the composer's death, and neither appears among the three volumes of Masses by Josquin issued by Petrucci. These latter collections, first published in 1502, 1505, and 1514 (and reprinted several times thereafter), testify to the esteem in which the composer was held even during his own lifetime: Petrucci issued very few books devoted to the music of a single composer, and no more than one such volume for any musician except Josquin.

The Masses can conveniently be divided into three categories according to the compositional process involved. Josquin wrote some of them around cantus firmi; in others he paraphrased a pre-existing melody; and he organized two, the *Missa Ad fugam* and the *Missa Sine nomine,* around cycles of canons.

The cantus-firmus Masses make up the largest group. As scaffolding he chose secular melodies slightly more often than sacred, perhaps because the clear phrase divisions of chansons served better to support large structures. Some of these secular melodies were apparently originally monophonic popular tunes, such as *L'ami Baudichon,* which appears as a cantus firmus in what seems to be Josquin's earliest Mass. But at other times he used single voices from polyphonic compositions, such as the tenor of Robert Morton's chanson *N'aray je jamais mieulx,* which underlies the *Missa Di dadi,* so called because the earliest edition indicated the mensural proportion governing the relationship of the cantus firmus to the other voices by reproducing before each movement faces of dice (*dadi,* in Italian) with varying numbers of dots. Most of Josquin's sacred cantus firmi derive from plainchant, as in *Missa Gaudeamus, Missa Ave maris stella,* and *Missa De beata vergine,* the last based not on a single melody but on a series of chant melodies associated with the various movements of the Gregorian Ordinary (the Kyrie and Gloria of the plainchant Mass IX in the present-day *Liber Usualis,* Credo I, and the Sanctus and Agnus of Mass IV). Two of Josquin's cantus firmi involve musical puns on solmization syllables. The *Missa Hercules Dux Ferrariae* is built on the vowels of the title in the following manner:

Her-	cu-	les	Dux	Fer-	ra-	ri-	(a) e
re	ut	re	ut	re	fa	mi	re
D	C	D	C	D	F	E	D (and its transpositions)

The *Missa La sol fa re mi* unfolds over the ostinato A G F D E and its transpositions, which may ultimately refer to a line of Italian poetry, "Lassa fare a mi" ("Leave it to me").

In some of the Masses, Josquin lays out the cantus firmus following a strictly rational plan in the manner of Dufay, with rigid mensural relationships governing the time values in the recurring statements of the borrowed melody. In the *Missa Hercules Dux Ferrariae,* for example, the subject derived from the vowels (that is, the *soggetto cavato dalle vocali,* or, more simply, the *soggetto cavato*) appears three times during each movement or section of a movement—first on d, then a fifth higher on a, and last, an octave above the original statement, on d′. The only exceptions to this arrangement occur where the groups of three statements are presented in retrograde motion and in descending order, on d′, a, and d; and at the beginning of the Sanctus, where the subject is given only once. The speed of each group of subjects is regulated by a simple proportional scheme. Four groups of subjects appear, for instance, in the Credo (the third group in retrograde motion), and they move in progressively smaller (that is, faster) note values, in the relationship 3:2:2:1. Similarly, the *Missa L'homme armé super voces musicales* is organized around a strictly planned cantus firmus. The long *L'homme armé* tune is sung at least once complete in each movement but on ascending scale degrees (that is, "super voces musicales"): on C in the Kyrie, on D (in both normal and retrograde form) in the Gloria, on E (both normal and retrograde) in the Credo, and so on. The mode of the Mass remains the same throughout; Josquin composed accompanying polyphony in the Dorian mode regardless of the changing pitch level of the scaffolding voice. His other Mass based on the same melody, the *Missa L'Homme armé sexti toni* (that is, in the sixth or Hypolydian mode on F), employs a much more informal structural plan. The borrowed melody appears either in the tenor, in the bass, or in the superius, but not always in the same rhythmic shape (which changes according to the dictates of the polyphony rather than following a preconceived plan), and free melodic material is sometimes interpolated between statements of the cantus firmus. Although the borrowed melody is usually clearly distinguishable from the other voices, it does not control the structure of the music to the same extent as do the more rigidly predetermined cantus firmi. In fact, this rather informal attitude toward the disposition of borrowed material characterizes many of Josquin's Masses—for example, *Missa Ave maris stella*, *Missa Malheur me bat*, and *Missa Une musque de Buscaya*.

In planning his Masses, Josquin followed certain formal conventions that had been established by his time and continued more or less unchanged throughout the sixteenth century. For example, the Christe sections in most Masses contrast markedly with the Kyries that surround them—often the Christe is much more transparent in texture, with a greater proportion of two- and three-part counterpoint, and sometimes it proceeds under a different mensuration sign. The first phrase in both the Gloria and the Credo movements is invariably intoned in chant by the officiating priest before the polyphony begins. The Gloria is almost always divided into two parts (the second generally beginning at "Qui tollis peccata mundi"), the Credo into three (the second often beginning at "Et incarnatus est" and the third at "Et in spiritum sanctum"). Josquin, like other composers, often singled out for special treatment the solemn moments of the Credo—that describing Christ's incarnation, for example, by setting the words "Et incarnatus est" or "Et homo factus est" to block chords or in slower note values, or (less often) describing the crucifixion and resurrection by writing music for the "Crucifixus" that differs strikingly from the "Et resurrexit." In the Sanctus movement, the "Pleni" and "Benedictus" sections are almost always scored for a reduced number of voices, and the cantus firmus (if the Mass setting is based on one) is omitted. The tutti "Osanna"— often in triple meter and set only once so that the same music is sung after both the "Pleni" and the "Benedictus"—furnishes strong contrast to the two- or three-voice interludes. Similarly, if there are settings of all three Agnus Dei invocations (for sometimes a Renaissance composer included only one or two settings), the second is often scored for fewer voices than the full complement, and the third occasionally has extra voices added to it to create a final burst of sound that serves as a fitting conclusion to the whole vast musical structure.

Josquin's technique of composing these long ritual texts can best be demonstrated by considering briefly a section of one movement, the beginning of the Gloria from his *Missa L'homme armé sexti toni* (Example 5–4). Superficially it resembles one of Dufay's Masses in that, after a chanted intonation, it begins with a duet, and further duets interrupt the texture from time to time to articulate the movement's form. Moreover, Josquin writes long sweeps of melody—for example, the first three bars of the superius, which rises elegantly through an octave and then gently settles down. But the character of Josquin's melodies differs significantly from those by Dufay. The role of melodic motives is crucial in carrying the motion forward and giving to the music the exciting impetus that is one of the most characteristic traits of Josquin's style. The motives themselves are often short and simple, like those in the superius in mm. 5–8, where they are arranged to lead up to the highest point in the line and then down again to its starting pitch; and they often contradict the underlying regular metrical pulse, as here. As a consequence, the rhythm unfolds in irregular units of two or three beats each; since the units are independent of any bar lines, the music takes on a marvelous disembodied floating quality. Many of these simple motives, such as those that set the series of acclamations ("Benedicimus te. Adoramus te." and so on) and those that lead up to the climax in mm. 19–20, are treated as sequences, a technique that gives an even more compelling push to the forward motion.

Perhaps the most impressive feature of Example 5–4, though, is the careful formal control it exhibits. The cadence at m. 29 marks the midpoint of the first main section of the Gloria, which explains why it is the first prominent V–I cadence (with 4–3 suspension) for all voices. (The most important previous cadence occurs on the fifth scale degree in m. 21.) A simple description of the first three phrases of the movement (mm. 1–9, 9–21, and 21–29) as (1) an introduction for two voices, (2) a first tutti leading to a half cadence, and (3) a duet and second tutti leading to a full cadence suggests the shape of the music, the formal function of each passage, and the relationship of each to the whole. The half cadence at m. 21 is prepared by the sequences that lead up to it. The third phrase (mm. 21–29) achieves a sense of climax and of arrival at a goal by repeating the gestures of the first two phrases (that is, a duet followed by a tutti) and by reaching the highest point in the superius (m. 25) with a dramatic sweep upward from f to c″ (almost its entire range)—accomplished within the space of two measures and a half by means of a melodic line filled with repeated motives and near sequences. Moreover, the structure parallels the syntax of the words it sets; new sections of music begin with new clauses of text. In short, Josquin created an autonomous musical structure in which the relationship of each phrase to the others and to the whole is revealed by a carefully maintained cadential hierarchy, by a network of motives, and by long-range planning of the overall melodic contours; at the same time the music follows closely the form, and hence the meaning, of the words it carries.

EXAMPLE 5–4. Josquin, *Missa L'homme armé sexti toni,* Gloria, mm. 1–30.

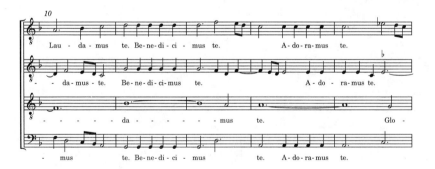

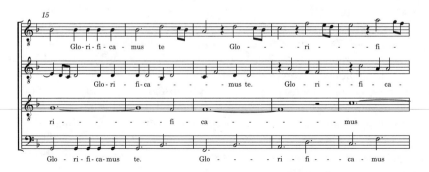

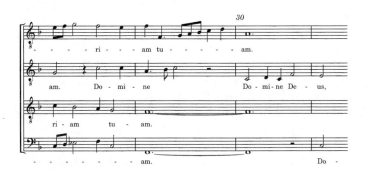

The cantus firmus, then, is not really the most important factor (as it had been in many Masses by earlier composers) in controlling the overall organization of the form in this Mass. In another way, though, the *L'homme armé* melody has far greater impact on the sound of the music than do cantus firmi in most earlier Masses, since all the parts are sometimes melodically derived from it. Josquin was not consistent throughout his life in the extent to which he used the structural voice as a source of thematic material for the strands of the polyphony. In works such as the *Missa Hercules Dux Ferrariae,* the melody derived from the vowels of the title is invariably kept separate from the melodies in the other voices. In the *Missa L'homme armé sexti toni,* the pre-existent melody influences the other voices in some sections but not in all. In some Masses, such as that based on the Gregorian hymn *Ave maris stella,* the melodic ideas of the cantus firmus thoroughly dominate the texture. In the Mass on *Ave maris stella,* though the cantus firmus is stated completely only in one voice at a time, it is often accompanied by fragments of itself in imitation.

In cantus firmus Masses in which Josquin borrowed his material from a polyphonic composition, he sometimes quoted more than a single line of the model. In other words, he occasionally approached parody technique—the practice of basing a new composition on all voices of a pre-existent polyphonic piece, which became one of the central procedures of the sixteenth century. In both his *Missa Malheur me bat* (based on a chanson by Ockeghem) and the more ingeniously organized *Missa Fortuna desperata* (based on an anonymous setting of an Italian text), Josquin borrowed various single voices of the model to use as cantus firmi for different sections of the Mass (for example, the tenor of the Kyrie in *Missa Malheur me bat* reproduces the tenor of the chanson, but the Credo is based on its superius); he sometimes accompanied the borrowed melody with material derived from the other voices of the model (as throughout the *Missa Fortuna desperata*); and he sometimes quoted all voices of the polyphonic model more or less literally in their original relationship to one another (as at the beginning of the Sanctus of the *Missa Malheur me bat* and of each movement in *Missa Fortuna desperata*).

Two of Josquin's Masses (possibly among the earliest he wrote) are based on cycles of canons: the *Missa Ad fugam* and the *Missa Sine nomine.* The canons in the *Missa Ad fugam,* between the superius and the tenor, are presented at the fifth below. Variants of the same melody, apparently of Josquin's own invention, open each movement and hence unify the Mass thematically. In the *Missa Sine nomine,* the melodic material and the interval between *dux* and *comes* change, as do the pairs of voices that state the canon; it is canonic technique as structural device that binds the Mass together.

Josquin's magnificent *Missa Pange lingua,* a late work and perhaps his only Mass that corresponds in grandeur and greatness to the splendid series of motets composed toward the end of his life, forgoes completely any rigid scaffolding device such as cantus firmus or canon. It is a paraphrase Mass that uses a Gregorian hymn merely as a source for thematic material. The chant is never stated complete in any one voice. Some quotations from it are quite literal, but in some passages Josquin merely alludes vaguely to it, deriving his music from it in a way that is not immediately apparent. Josquin's variety in paraphrasing the plainsong demonstrates how little he depended on it in planning his grand structure, but also how completely he had assimilated the chant and how skillfully he could absorb it into his overall musical conception.

Josquin wrote the *Missa Pange lingua,* like so much of his music, in a predominantly open texture, filled with two- and three-part counterpoint. Tuttis are in general reserved for important moments of structural articulation or at the most solemn moments, such as the simple and eloquent setting of "Et incarnatus est" in the Credo. Some motives in the Mass are repeated over and over, a procedure that Josquin customarily adopted to build up a powerful drive to the cadence. As in so much of Josquin's late music, the text of the *Missa Pange lingua* is set in largely syllabic fashion to project the words convincingly (though with some misaccentuations); he incorporated just enough melismas to avoid austerity and to give an impressive sweep to his melodic lines.

JOSQUIN'S SECULAR MUSIC

Like composers earlier in the fifteenth century, Josquin and his contemporaries thought of the French chanson as the principal genre of secular music. Although Josquin composed some Italian frottole and instrumental pieces, most of his works besides motets consist of chansons. As much a master in this field as in others, he was equally expert at writing chansons for three, four, five, or six voices. In applying the new techniques of imitative counterpoint to equal but independent melodic lines, all of which could be easily sung, Josquin freed himself from the invariable repetition schemes of the *formes fixes.* In doing so, he transformed the chanson from a genre limited by conventional texture and design to one capable of much greater variety in techniques and textures; it could express more moods and shades of thought than ever before and attain a much greater depth and richness of effect.

We cannot establish with confidence a chronology of Josquin's chansons any more than we can for his motets and Masses. (Petrucci published some of his chansons in Venice between 1501 and 1503, but the main corpus did not appear in print until 1545, when the Flemish publisher Tielman Susato of Antwerp issued a commemorative edition.) We can, however, point out the differing techniques he used in setting lyrical poetry, each of which may well be connected with a particular stage in his development. Thus his few rondeaux and some chansons in a style not totally unlike that of Ockeghem may have been written in his student days and during his stay in Italy. The many polyphonic arrangements of monophonic popular tunes may date from his Italian years and from the time of his connection with the French royal court, where Louis XII and his courtiers seem to have affected a great regard for popular culture. A series of somber, melancholy songs may have been written late in Josquin's life for that most unhappy of rulers, Marguerite of Austria, at a time when he may also have been composing a number of other many-voiced and rather densely scored chansons.

In addition to questions of chronology, it is sometimes difficult to determine other quite basic facts about this repertory. Some chansons, for example, are not securely attributable to Josquin, since various sources ascribe them to different composers. Others cannot unambiguously be associated with a particular poem, because the musical sources often give only the first few words; the complete text must therefore be sought in miscellaneous anthologies of poetry. These difficulties may be illustrated in considering three of Josquin's rondeaux:

La plus des plus and *Madame hélas* (both for three voices in a style virtually indistinguishable from that of Ockeghem and his contemporaries), and *Plusieurs regretz* (for five voices). Each of these songs raises unanswerable questions. *La plus des plus* is one of Josquin's few settings of a courtly poem in a *forme fixe*, and the style of this chanson does not resemble Josquin's other songs very closely. The text is problematic as well, in that a complete poem beginning "La plus des plus," surviving in a poetic anthology of the time but divorced from any musical context, may not be the poem that Josquin set. As for *Madame hélas*, the editors of the New Josquin Edition reject it on the basis of style. Although it is ascribed to Josquin in one printing of Petrucci's *Odhecaton* (1501), Petrucci changed his mind and deprived it of Josquin's name in later editions of this anthology. Moreover, *Madame hélas* survives without any text other than its first two words, so its identity as a rondeau must be inferred from its form and especially from the prominent cadence at its midpoint. *Plusieurs regretz,* for five voices, on the other hand, is certainly by Josquin, and one stanza of text, rhyming aabba (the conventional rhyme scheme for the refrain of a *rondeau cinquain*), is securely identified with the music. A poetic anthology of the time includes a complete rondeau beginning "Tous les regretz" but continuing exactly like Josquin's chanson; probably, then, that text belongs with Josquin's music. If that is so, perhaps some of the other one-stanza poems rhyming aabba and set by Josquin are also rondeau refrains for which the complete text has since been lost.

The problems posed by these three chansons should warn us to be cautious in making generalizations. The case of *Plusieurs regretz* reveals that the absence of poems in *formes fixes* from Josquin's oeuvre is not necessarily as radical a change as might at first appear. Indeed, the poets who furnished verses for the composer—among them Jean Molinet, Guillaume Crétin, Jean Lemaire de Belges, and possibly Marguerite of Austria herself—are all associated with the last generation of the *grands rhétoriqueurs,* and hence their works relate to a passing literary tradition, much as Josquin's music does to that of his immediate predecessors. Moreover, the absence of conventional repetition schemes does not mean that Josquin wrote through-composed chansons exclusively. On the contrary, he often repeated phrases in patterns that, though untraditional, are easily comprehensible, and he was especially apt to associate musical repetition with poetic lines that rhyme. Thus the music for *Plusieurs regretz* follows the pattern AABBCC, which resembles the rhyme scheme aabba, except that the composer has supplied a new musical phrase for the fifth line of verse and then repeated it.

Josquin mirrored the structure of the poem in his music especially often in chansons that, like *Plusieurs regretz,* were composed around a canon, the structural device that he used more than any other in his settings of serious courtly lyrics. Curiously, though, the device is often hidden in the middle of a highly imitative texture that is itself capable of sustaining the musical fabric; in *Plusieurs regretz* (Example 5–5), for instance, the opening double imitation

EXAMPLE 5–5. Josquin, *Plusieurs regretz*, mm. 1–12.

(involving both a subject and its contrapuntal accompaniment) and the clear motive structure separating "plusieurs regretz" from "qui sur la terre sont" not only hide the canon at the fifth between the next-to-lowest and next-to-top voice, but also make such a rigid framework superfluous. Yet Josquin wrote his other canonic chansons, such as *Incessament livre suis a martire, Douleur me bat,* and *Plaine de dueil,* in exactly the same imitative style.

In Josquin's through-composed chansons, on the other hand, the composer, without repeating any passage literally, took full advantage of the possibilities of imitative writing and vocal dialogue to vary the texture of the music and to extend each phrase by working with one or more motives, much as in a motet. The opening measures of *Je ne me puis tenir d'aimer* constitute a lengthy point of imitation in which all five voices eventually take part; in the closing phrase, in contrast, sections of the ensemble oppose one another in stating short motives in ever-changing combinations. Josquin ended the chanson with a coda over a double pedal point that eventually leads to the final plagal cadence, one of his most typical mannerisms. Of his other through-composed chansons, *Mille regretz* (one of his last compositions) is among his subtlest and most perfect, as well as simplest.

Some of Josquin's chansons are written over a cantus firmus originally associated with a separate text. His five-voice setting of *Cueurs desolez,* for example, is based on the plainchant *Plorans ploravit,* and *Fortune d'estrange plummaige* on *Pauper sum ego.* Perhaps, then, Josquin's very moving lament on the death of Ockeghem, the well-known *Déploration* in which the tenor sings the Introit of the Mass for the Dead *(Requiem aeternam)* while the other voices sing "Nymphes des bois, déesses des fontaines . . . ," should be regarded as a cantus-firmus chanson rather than a motet in French. In truth, the distinction is academic, since the composer employed the same techniques in the two genres. At least one of Josquin's cantus-firmus chansons (or "motet-chansons") uses a popular monophonic melody as its structural voice. The tune, *Adieu mes amours,* is stated as a free canon in the lower two voices while the upper two sing a rondeau also beginning with the words "Adieu mes amours" but composed in an old-fashioned melismatic style.

Popular poems similar to *Adieu mes amours* and intended to be sung circulated everywhere in France during the sixteenth century in cheaply printed books of verse. Although they are preserved today as artifacts of elite culture (courtly chansonniers), the songs may be characterized as "in the popular mode," for their texts describe people, events, and situations typical of middle- and lower-class life of the time. The melodies for some are preserved in several manuscripts (monophonic chansonniers) prepared for the court of Louis XII, where such songs, intended in the first place for the amusement and education of the urban lower and middle classes, became the rage among aristocrats. Composers before Josquin's day had occasionally set such tunes; Dufay, for example, composed an arrangement of *La belle se siet,* and Binchois used *Filles à marier.* But Josquin's generation was the first to use this material extensively, and he himself wrote a substantial number of popular arrangements.

It is not always possible to be certain that a particular chanson by Josquin borrows a popular tune. If the text or the melody cannot be traced in any literary or musical anthology and no other composer has based a polyphonic arrangement on it, then the presence of a popular song can only be inferred from the character of the melodic lines or from Josquin's treatment of them. The tenor in *Si j'avoys Marion,* for instance, is so simple and straightforward— so tuneful and easy to sing—that there can be little doubt that the composer has borrowed it from one of the melodies originally sung in the streets of Paris. The melody is treated in the manner Josquin reserved for three-part popular arrangements: the outer voices gloss or imitate the cantus firmus, but the tenor enters last of all, presenting the melody in its simplest and most complete form while the outer voices either continue their imitation or move in parallel motion. With their regular imitations of the tenor, the superius and the contratenor (or bass) move at virtually the same rate of speed as the tenor, such that the voices are heard as nearly equal and the texture is almost completely

integrated. In some of Josquin's three-part arrangements, an important technical innovation begins to emerge: the duet between tenor and superius, traditionally the self-sufficient structural scaffold of a three-part chanson, has
weakened; the countertenor, now really a bass part, is newly important for its
role in supplying the appropriate consonance.

In a number of his popular arrangements, such as the four-part setting
of *Bergerette savoyenne,* Josquin paraphrased the borrowed melody rather than
presenting it complete. He also sometimes put the popular melodies into
canons with themselves to form a solid structural framework around which the
other voices could weave complex and varied webs—as, for example, in *Faulte
d'argent,* one of his best-known chansons, and *Petite camusette,* based on a
melody that Ockeghem had also arranged. The words of these popular songs
are usually bucolic or witty, or at any rate less artificial and stilted than the
courtly lyrics. But not all Josquin's witty songs involve borrowed popular
melodies. For example, he probably invented all the musical material in the
four-voice double canon *Basiez-moy,* which a later musician less successfully
expanded into a six-voice triple canon.

If chansons constituted by far the largest part of Josquin's secular works,
he nevertheless composed several delightful frottole. Both *In te domine speravi*
(with mixed Italian and Latin words) and the formally unconventional *El grillo
è buon cantore* were published in Petrucci's frottola books as by "Jusquin
d'Ascanio." Josquin's contrapuntally witty *Scaramella va alla guerra,* based on a
popular tune similar in style to those sung in France, may date from his years in
Italy as well, since one of his colleagues at Milan, Loyset Compère, wrote a
competitive work borrowing the same melody.

Josquin arranged some of his predecessors' chansons in a way that suggests he intended to make them into compositions suitable for instrumental
performance. Beneath the superius and the tenor of Hayne van Ghizeghem's
famous *De tous biens plaine,* for instance, Josquin added a two-part canon at
the unison and at the distance of one minim, transforming this lovely lyrical
song into an impressive display of compositional ingenuity. Moreover, some of
Josquin's own works have come down to us without any literary text, and these
may have been conceived for instruments. Certainly Josquin's exploration of
imitative techniques and mastery of the art of creating structures from a series
of interlocked phrases enabled him to write interesting textless, musically
autonomous works. New concordances may, of course, reveal many of these to
have been conceived as chansons in the first place. Nevertheless, Josquin and
his contemporaries seem to have been among the first composers to create an
abstract instrumental music, and it seems unlikely that texts will ever be discovered for pieces such as *Ile Fantazies de Joskin* or *La Bernardina.* They are
surely both instrumental *carmina,* for their phrase structure, the pattern of their
cadences, and their clear networks of motives make them musically self-sufficient. *La Bernardina* seems to be a title rather than the first line of a text: it
probably refers to the person for whom it was written or to whom it was dedi-

cated, as do similar works by Josquin's contemporaries—for example, Johannes Martini's *La Martinella,* Ghiselin's *La Alfonsina,* and Isaac's *La Morra.* Josquin's works for instruments include as well the brilliant fanfare (perhaps written for the French king) based on a cantus firmus derived from the letters of "Uiue [= Vive] le roy":

U-	i-	u-	e	le	ro-	i
Ut	mi	ut	re	re	sol	mi
C	E	C	D	D	G	E

In sum, Josquin's mastery of every genre cultivated in his time—Masses, motets, chansons, frottole, and instrumental carmina—explains his preeminence in the minds of his contemporaries and his stature today as one of the greatest composers in the history of western Europe.

BIBLIOGRAPHICAL NOTES

Only three of the thirty volumes projected for the New Josquin Edition (NJE) published by the Vereniging voor Nederlandse Muziekgeschiedenis have appeared: vol. 27, "Secular Works for Three Voices," ed. Jaap van Benthem and Howard Mayer Brown (1987); vol. 8 with *Missa Faysant regretz* and *Missa Fortuna desperata,* ed. Barton Hudson (1995); and vol. 9 with *Missa Malheur me bat* and *Missa N'aray je jamais,* ed. Barton Hudson (1994). Thus the standard edition for most works is still that edited by Albert Smijers, M. Antonowycz, and W. Elders for the same publisher (Amsterdam, 1921–69). Pieces by Josquin are available in other publications, including many cited in the Bibliographical Notes for Chapter 6. See especially Howard Mayer Brown, ed., *A Florentine Chansonnier from the time of Lorenzo the Magnificent: Florence, Biblioteca Nazionale Centrale, MS Banco Rari 229,* MRM 7, 2 vols. (Chicago, 1983); Helen Hewitt, ed., *Harmonice Musices Odhecaton A* (Cambridge, Mass., 1942); Helen Hewitt, ed., *Ottaviano Petrucci, Canti B numero cinquanta, Venice 1502,* MRM 2 (Chicago, 1967); Edward E. Lowinsky, ed., *The Medici Codex of 1518,* MRM 3–5, 3 vols. (Chicago, 1968); and Martin Picker, ed., *The Chanson Albums of Marguerite of Austria* (Berkeley and Los Angeles, 1965).

The bibliography on Josquin is extensive. The article "Josquin Desprez" by Jeremy Noble and Gustave Reese in *TNG* is an excellent place to start, since it lists the pioneering research on the composer. Sydney Robinson Charles, *Josquin des Prez: A Guide to Research* (New York, 1983), is indispensable. Much fundamental work on Josquin is included in *Josquin des Prez, Proceedings of the International Josquin Festival-Conference ... New York ... 1971,* ed. Edward E. Lowinsky and Bonnie J. Blackburn (London, 1976), and in the *Proceedings of the International Josquin Symposium: Utrecht 1986,* ed. Willem Elders and Frits de Haen (Utrecht, 1991). Of the many fine scholarly articles devoted to particular aspects of Josquin's life or music, see in particular Herbert Kellman, "Josquin and the Courts of the Netherlands and France: The Evidence of the Sources," reprinted in Ellen Rosand, ed., *The Garland Library of the History of Western Music, 3, Renaissance Music Part 1* (New York, 1985), 353–88; and, among archival studies, Yves Esquieu, "La musique à la cour provençale du roi René," *Provence historique* 31 (1981): 299–312; Françoise Robin, "Josquin des Pres au service de René d'Anjou?" *RdM* 71 (1985): 180–81; Richard Sherr, "Notes on Some Papal Documents in Paris," *SM* 12 (1983): 5–16, and Lora Matthews and Paul A. Merkley, "Josquin Desprez and his Milanese Patrons," *JM* 12 (1994): 434–63.

Leeman L. Perkins, "Mode and Structure in the Masses of Josquin," *JAMS* 26 (1973): 189–239; Cristle Collins Judd, "Some Problems of pre-Baroque Analysis: Josquin's *Ave Maria ... virgo serena*," *Music Analysis* 4 (1985): 201–39; and Judd, "Modal Types and *Ut Re Mi* Tonalities: Tonal Coherence in Sacred Vocal Polyphony from about 1500," *JAMS* 45 (1992): 428–67, offer models for analysis of Josquin's sacred music; for another approach, see Howard Mayer Brown, "Notes Toward a Definition of Personal Style: Conflicting Attributions and the Six-Part Motets of Josquin and Mouton," in *Proceedings of the International Josquin Symposium: Utrecht 1986,* ed. Willem Elders and Frits de Haen (Utrecht, 1991), 185–207.

Jeremy Noble, "The Function of Josquin's Motets," *TVNM* 35 (1985): 9–22 is a thoughtful discussion, as is Howard Mayer Brown, "The Mirror of Man's Salvation: Music in Devotional Life About 1500," *RQ* 43 (1990): 747–73. Fine studies of particular pieces by Josquin include the following: Brown, "On Veronica and Josquin," in *New Perspectives on Music: Essays in Honor of Eileen Southern,* ed. Josephine Wright with Samuel A. Floyd, Jr. (Warren, Mich., 1992), 49–62; Patrick Macey, "Savonarola and the Sixteenth-Century Motet," *JAMS* 36 (1983): 422–52, which focuses on *Miserere mei deus;* Macey, "Josquin's 'Misericordias Domini' and Louis XI," *EM* 19 (1991): 163–77; William Prizer, "Music and Ceremonial in the Low Countries: Philip the Fair and the Order of the Golden Fleece," *EMH* 5 (1985): 113–53 (with particular attention to Josquin's *Ut Phoebi radiis*); Richard Sherr, "*Illibata Dei virgo nutrix* and Josquin's Roman Style," *JAMS* 41 (1988): 434–64, and Willem Elders, "Josquin's 'Gaudeamus' Mass: A Case of Number Symbolism in Worship," *SM* 14 (1985): 221–33.

On Josquin's secular music, see Christopher Reynolds, "Musical Evidence of Compositional Planning in the Renaissance: Josquin's *Plus nulz regretz*," *JAMS* 40 (1987): 53–81; Howard Mayer Brown, *Music in the French Secular Theater, 1450–1550* (Cambridge, Mass., 1963); and James Haar, ed., *Chanson and Madrigal, 1480–1530* (Cambridge, Mass., 1964).

SIX

JOSQUIN'S CONTEMPORARIES

Few periods in the history of Western music have produced so many composers of the first rank as the several decades before and after 1500. If Josquin was the great musical star of his day, his contemporaries nevertheless created an extraordinary body of music worthy to be set beside his. Some of the composers born in the late 1440s, 1450s, and 1460s—such as Alexander Agricola, Jacob Obrecht, and Loyset Compère—wrote in a style that can be related directly to the older Burgundian and Flemish traditions, whereas others—such as Heinrich Isaac, Pierre de la Rue, and Jean Mouton—composed music that more nearly resembles Josquin's and points to the new sounds and styles of the sixteenth century. Josquin's contemporaries can scarcely be studied as a group. If nothing else, their careers were too varied and too peripatetic to allow them to be grouped into a "school." The composite picture that emerges from the following brief summaries of their achievements may, however, give the reader some idea of the most important characteristics of one of the great ages of Western music.

ALEXANDER AGRICOLA (1446–1506)

By his mid-twenties, Alexander Agricola had left his native Flanders to seek his fortune in Italy, had taken a Florentine wife, and had found a position in the ducal chapel in Milan at a particularly brilliant moment in its musical history. By 1474, however, Agricola had decided to move elsewhere; in that year Duke Galeazzo Maria Sforza gave him both a letter of recommendation to Lorenzo de' Medici in Florence and permission to return to his northern homeland. During the following twenty-six years, Agricola divided his activities between Italy and the north. He served at the Aragonese court at Naples, worked for a short time for Piero de' Medici in Florence, and traveled to Rome and Mantua as well. He served at various times in the cathedrals of Cambrai and Florence and at the French royal court. In 1500 he took up his final post, as chaplain and singer in the chapel of Philip the Fair, Duke of Burgundy and King of Castile. Agricola's music must have been in demand at this time, for Petrucci issued a volume dedicated to his Masses in 1504. While in Philip's service, Agricola twice visited Spain; on the second occasion the sixty-year-old composer caught a fever and died within the same year as his ducal patron (1506).

A worthy successor to Busnoys at the Burgundian court, Agricola excelled above all as a composer of elegant courtly music. His most striking stylistic mannerism, perhaps, is his tendency to forgo long lyrical sweeps of floating melody in favor of quick, nervous lines composed of short motives fitted together with great rhythmic subtlety. The florid nature of the counterpoint, and the unexpected turns it sometimes takes, may be the traits that led one sixteenth-century musician to characterize Agricola's music as "strange in manner," a description that still strikes us as apt.

Agricola spent most of his creative energy writing secular music; some eighty chansons and other secular compositions survive by him, as opposed to eight Masses, a few isolated Mass movements, and about twenty-five motets and other smaller sacred pieces. His chansons are closer in style to late-fifteenth-century Burgundian songs by Busnoys, Ockeghem, and their contemporaries than to the new equal-voiced polyphony of Josquin and his younger colleagues. Most of Agricola's chansons are cast in one of the *formes fixes*—the majority are either rondeaux or bergerettes—and they are composed for three voices in the conventional texture of the fifteenth-century song. In a chanson such as *J'ay beau huer* (Example 6–1), the highly sophisticated imitative technique and the texture, enriched by motivic work that remains effective and individual despite its origin in the common store of late-fifteenth-century melodic material, identify the work as representing the end rather than the beginning of a tradition. The melismas, which are an inherent part of the melodic style and create an ambiguous relationship between words and music, resemble those in earlier chansons. The lack of attention to melodic cohesion and textual clarity seems somewhat old-fashioned, reminding us of Ockeghem and of Agricola's northern heritage. Yet the pervasive imitation at the beginning of both phrases of this rondeau, and the delightfully unexpected and rhythmically unsettling canon between superius and tenor at "De celle la," reveal a refinement of technique characteristic of mature, even overripe, styles and bespeak a contrapuntal ingenuity seemingly contradicted by the facility with which Agricola so often moved two of his three voices in parallel motion.

EXAMPLE 6–1. Alexander Agricola, *J'ay beau huer,* mm. 1–18.

Several of Agricola's chansons juxtapose poems in *formes fixes* with fragments of chant. The upper two voices of *Belle sur toutes / Tota pulchra es,* for
example, express in French the conventional sentiments of the lovesick suitor
while the lowest voice states as cantus firmus a related passage in Latin from
the Song of Songs, used in the liturgy as an antiphon in honor of the Virgin
Mary. Such compositions are often called motet-chansons, although they should
more accurately be considered cantus-firmus chansons, since they are really
French songs built over chants and not motets with vernacular texts. The technique Agricola used to compose them cannot have differed very much from that
involved in making polyphonic settings of popular melodies, except that Agricola's three-part popular arrangements, like those by Josquin (which they
resemble), employ one set of words in all voices. The simple tune—either with
French words, as in *Et qui la dira* and *Par ung jour de matinée,* or with Dutch,
as in *O Venus bant, Tandernaken,* and *In minen zin*—is presented in a straightforward manner, usually by the tenor, and the other two voices weave their
counterpoints around it. Fragments of imitation, motives exchanged in dialogue
and extended by variation and sequence, and ubiquitous passages in parallel
motion transform humble popular songs into elaborate and artful polyphony.

Not all Agricola's chansons, however, are so unrelievedly contrapuntal in their orientation as the examples discussed thus far. He did attempt to come to grips with the developing harmonic sense of his contemporaries. In a chanson such as *Adieu m'amour*, for instance, chordally conceived phrases are combined with old-fashioned melismatic lines, in a way suggesting that the composer had not completely assimilated the new style. His setting of the strophic poem *Amor, che sospirar,* on the other hand, is indistinguishable from any similarly chordal composition by a native Italian composer, and so, probably, was his incompletely preserved Florentine carnival song *Donne, noi siam dell'olio facitori.*

Agricola's most distinctive secular compositions, though, are his arrangements of older courtly chansons in a style that must have been intended for instrumental performance. His multiple versions of Frye's *Tout a par moy*, Binchois's *Comme femme*, Ockeghem's *D'ung aultre amer*, and Hayne's *De tous biens plaine* all pit one voice of the original (usually the tenor) against two or three newly composed lines that move primarily in smaller note values and cover a far wider range than those in Agricola's other chansons. Even his three-part popular arrangements, written similarly around a pre-existing melody in an inner voice, do not include the fast passagework that occurs, for instance, in his arrangements of Hayne's *De tous biens plaine* (the beginning of one of them is shown in Example 6–2). In the late fifteenth century, instrumentalists could and did play music in every genre; but this group of instrumental chansons instructs us in the musical styles that a virtuoso of the time (or at least a professional) found most congenial, and illustrates the kinds of figuration performers improvised over cantus firmi or added as embellishments to melodic lines. Scale fragments (some extending an octave and a fourth or more), stretto-like imitations, brief sections in triplets, and short syncopated figures repeated with little or no variation at the same or different pitches—all of which constantly recur in these pieces—do not differ radically in their nature from the figures Agricola incor-

EXAMPLE 6–2. Agricola, *De tous biens plaine,* mm. 1–8.

porated into his vocal music; they are applied more rigorously, however, without letup and in faster motion over a wider range.

The two simplest of Agricola's eight Masses, the *Missa primi toni* and the *Missa secundi toni*, were apparently written without recourse to pre-existing material. His *Missa Sine nomine* uses a chant only in the Credo, and the Easter Mass, *Missa Paschalis*, is based on a succession of Gregorian melodies. The remaining four Masses are composed on cantus firmi derived from polyphonic secular pieces: the chansons *Le serviteur* (attributed to Dufay in some sources), *Malheur me bat* (attributed to Ockeghem), Busnoys's *Je ne demande*, and Agricola's own arrangement of the Dutch song *In minen zin*. Agricola generally treated the cantus firmus quite freely. In addition to stating it in long notes in an inner voice, he sometimes speeded it up to make it indistinguishable from the other voices or interpolated newly invented material between phrases of the borrowed melody; sometimes he omitted it altogether. In one movement of the *Missa Je ne demande* he paraphrased two voices of the polyphonic model simultaneously. Agricola's Masses, save for occasional chordal passages marking off significant words or phrases, are composed in the same contrapuntally elaborate, rhythmically subtle texture that characterizes most of his chansons and, indeed, his hymns, Magnificats, and motets—both the lyrical song-motets apparently intended for private devotional use and the larger, more impressive compositions written for liturgical and paraliturgical occasions. Only his two sets of Lamentations for Holy Week proceed largely in simple chords or contrapuntally animated homophony, interrupted only occasionally by more complex polyphony.

JACOB OBRECHT (ca. 1457–1505)

Probably the only Dutchman among Josquin's most eminent contemporaries, Jacob Obrecht spent the greatest part of his life in his northern homeland. He was born in Ghent in 1457 or 1458 into a musical milieu as the son of the master city trumpeter Willem Obrecht. The earliest reliable notices of his professional activity identify him as choirmaster at the Guild of Our Lady in Bergen-op-Zoom about 1480–84, and then master of the choristers at the cathedral of Cambrai from 1484 to 1485. When the authorities at Cambrai indicated dissatisfaction with some of his financial dealings and his lack of interest in training the choirboys, he accepted appointment as *succentor* at the church of St. Donatian in Bruges. From 1485 until his death he worked mostly in Bruges (1485–91 and 1498–1500), Antwerp (at the Church of Our Lady, 1492–96 and 1501–4), and Bergen-op-Zoom (1496–98).

A number of his works can be dated or associated with a particular location. His *Missa De Sancto Martino* was most likely composed in 1486 for a fellow musician in Bruges, and the *Missa O beate pater Donatiane*, also known as the *Missa de Sancto Donatiane*, was probably composed there for another endowment in 1487; the *Missa Sicut spina rosam* may be a tribute to Ockeghem composed for the elder composer's visit to St. Donatian's; the *Missa Malheur me bat* and the *Missa Fortuna desperata* may have been composed during Obrecht's first stay in Ferrara in 1487; the motet *Mille quingentis* was composed certainly in 1488 on the death of his father.

Obrecht's career in the north was interrupted only twice, by important trips to Italy. In 1487 he was granted leave from St. Donatian to visit Ferrara, where he had been invited by Duke Ercole d'Este I. Obrecht's fame had preceded him, and he was treated like an honored guest even though he refused the duke's requests to stay longer. For more than fifteen years, the Este family tried to lure Obrecht back to Ferrara. He accepted their invitation and returned to Ferrara by the end of the summer of 1504, after stopping on his way to visit the imperial court at Innsbruck, where he composed a *Regina caeli* for the emperor's chapel. While he was in Ferrara, plague struck, and Obrecht fell victim to it in 1505.

In assessing Obrecht's music, many critics have stressed the composer's great facility—Glareanus, for example, reported that he could compose a Mass overnight—and his slightly conservative turn of mind, especially as compared with Josquin. In his music, the facile side of his character is perhaps most obviously expressed by his readiness to move contrapuntal lines in parallel motion, especially by tenths in the outer voices; by his penchant for composing sections built from short, succinct motives repeated a number of times with little or no variation; and by his willingness to extend a phrase by means of interminable sequences. Example 6–3, the beginning of the first Kyrie from his *Missa For-*

EXAMPLE 6–3. Jacob Obrecht, *Missa Fortuna desperata,* Kyrie, mm. 1–13.

tuna desperata (1491–93), shows the first of these traits (in mm. 9–11) and offers a sample of Obrecht's characteristically busy texture, with nervous and relatively fast-moving melismatic lines combined with slower-moving voices. Typically, the opening point of imitation involves four measures of two-part counterpoint (arranged like a subject and countersubject) simply transposed up an octave and rescored upon repetition. As is characteristic of Obrecht's mature style, though, the flow of this exuberant polyphony is judiciously controlled by emphatic and carefully prepared cadences: Obrecht's chord progressions and directed harmonic motion show him fully aware of the new compositional possibilities of organizing independent melodic lines by harmonic means. But the example also reveals why Obrecht is thought to be conservative: the texture of the music preserves many older features of the layered polyphony from the earlier part of the fifteenth century; Obrecht seems to have paid little attention to sensitive text declamation, that humanistic preoccupation of other composers who spent most of their careers in Italy; and he organizes the movement around a cantus firmus. Indeed, the skill and ingenuity with which Obrecht manipulated cantus-firmus technique constitutes one of the most notable features of his music.

About thirty-five Masses, twenty-five motets, and thirty secular pieces by Obrecht survive. Thus his Masses bulk far larger in his output than any other genre, and they include some of his best music. Most of them are cantus-firmus Masses in which Obrecht deployed the structural voice in several ingenious ways. In the *Missa Maria zart,* for example, he divided the monophonic tune on which the work is based (a late-fifteenth-century Meistersinger song) into several segments and presented the complete melody only as a structural climax in the Agnus Dei. The complex use of such "segmented tenors" is characteristic of Obrecht's Masses. The cantus firmi in the *Missa Sine nomine* (built on Hayne van Ghizeghem's chanson *De tous biens plaine*), the *Missa Ave regina caelorum,* and the *Missa Fortuna desperata* are at times combined with material from the other voices of the borrowed polyphonic model. Often, Obrecht incorporated borrowed musical material quite literally into his compositions. When he quoted more than one voice of his model at a time, his process of composing approached sixteenth-century parody technique, as in the Kyrie of his *Missa Rose playsante,* modeled on a chanson by Caron. Obrecht paid homage to the English "Caput" composer and to Ockeghem in his *Missa Caput* by quoting and rearranging passages from the earlier Masses on the same plainsong; and his *Missa Sicut spina rosam* honors Ockeghem by quoting from the older composer's *Missa Mi-mi.* Busnoys is acknowledged by quotation in Obrecht's *Missa L'Homme armé* and in his *Missa Je ne demande.* To organize his *Missa diversorum tenorum,* Obrecht used a number of different pre-existing melodies in the manner of a quodlibet, and in the *Missa Sub tuum praesidium,* although he employed one plainchant as cantus firmus, he added others to it after the first two movements. Moreover, in this Mass he created a sense of growing climax by adding one additional voice to each succeeding movement; three voices sing the Kyrie, four the Gloria, and so on, until the Mass ends with a seven-voice Agnus Dei.

Many of Obrecht's motets are also built over cantus firmi. But if this old-fashioned technique serves as a structural basis for the music, its style in some of the motets seems modern, since the text is set in a declamatory manner (or in any case more syllabically than in his Masses). Paradoxically, he took special care with setting the words in his five- and six-voice motets that combine more than one text, such as *Factor orbis*. Written on various chants (mostly antiphons), this work follows a variant of the standard form for responsories, aBcB; however, instead of repeating the B section literally, Obrecht varied it upon its return. In *Factor orbis,* Obrecht was much more sparing than usual in his use of melisma, and for the verses "Esto refugium pauperum" and "Alleluia, noe noe" he wrote purely chordal settings that throw the words into sharp relief. On the other hand, his Netherlandish artifices tend to obscure the text in another five-voice motet, *Haec Deum coeli,* which combines a chant-derived three-part canon in long notes with fast-moving, newly invented counterpoints. Some of Obrecht's three-part motets, such as *Si sumpsero,* are replete with imitative polyphony in which playful exchanges among the equally important voices make the compositions as apt for instruments as for voices. The structure of *Si sumpsero,* a song-motet, is determined by the layout of the points of imitation, since it does not employ a cantus firmus. In other three-voice motets, such as *O vos omnes* and *Alma redemptoris mater,* one voice usually moves in slow notes while the other two compete in rapid-fire dialogue and duets. In many of Obrecht's four-voice motets, such as the partly polytextual *Beata es, Maria,* the texture is less transparent than in Josquin's polyphony, partly because of Obrecht's generally full scoring and partly because of the relative absence of imitation between voices; but the lucid way in which the cantus firmus is laid out gives the music a strong sense of order. *Beata es, Maria* is also representative of Obrecht's skill in manipulating borrowed material; like several other motets, this one treats material borrowed from or modeled on more than one source and incorporates more than one slow-moving cantus firmus.

Ingenuity and artifice mark Obrecht's secular as well as sacred music. His instrumental carmina, which include several canonic pieces, are filled with contrapuntal science and wit. He recomposed several older chansons, such as *Cela sans plus, Fors seulement,* and *J'ay pris amours,* to make them harmonically more focused. He also delighted in placing a borrowed tune in an inner voice and pitting against it quick, nervous, playful lines filled with clever imitations, fragments of canon, motion in parallel tenths, and short motives expanded by repetitions or sequences—as in his three- and four-part arrangements of the Dutch popular songs *Meskin es hu, Rompeltier,* and *Tandernaken* and the Italian strambotto *La tortorella.* Because of the special way Obrecht applied cantus-firmus technique to them, his popular arrangements, like those by Josquin and Agricola, have a distinctive sound.

Differing markedly is a second group of Dutch songs composed in a much more chordal and harmonically focused style. These latter songs clearly reveal Obrecht's regional loyalties and the extent to which he was steeped in local Dutch culture. Unfortunately, these Dutch songs survive without their complete texts (ten of them are published by Smijers in *Van Ockeghem tot Sweelinck*), and so it is not possible to know what sorts of poems caught the composer's fancy or how he treated his texts. The music alternates between chordal sections and interludes for reduced forces, often in highly imitative polyphony. In *Laet u ghenoughen,* the interludes take the form of duets that, because of their repeated notes, seem originally to have been syllabic settings, possibly of narrative portions of the poetry. Like many of the other Dutch songs, *Laet u ghenoughen* has a refrain that is varied each time it appears. Perhaps, then, some or all of these Dutch songs are polyphonic arrangements of popular melodies; but Obrecht's technique of harmonizing what may be the pre-existing theme with simple chords, or of paraphrasing it in witty polyphony, makes the songs totally different in effect from his other, more contrapuntally ingenious but older-fashioned secular compositions.

LOYSET COMPÈRE (ca. 1450–1518)

Aside from the fact that for a year the young Compère sang beside Weerbecke, Martini, Agricola, and Josquin at the ducal court in Milan, little is known of his life. His name appears for the first time in the Milanese records for 1474, the same year that Agricola left the Sforza court. Compère is known to have served the French king, Charles VIII, as did Agricola, for he is recorded in Paris in 1486; he held benefices from Cambrai and Douai; and he spent his last years as a canon at the collegiate church of St. Quentin, where he died in 1518. He may have been educated at the famous cathedral school in Cambrai, a hypothesis suggested by the list of men included in the text of one of his earliest surviving compositions, the "singers' prayer" *Omnium bonorum plena* (which begins as a Latin translation of *De tous biens plaine,* the tenor of which serves as cantus firmus). This invocation to the Virgin Mary asks special grace for a number of musicians. Some of them, such as Dufay, Ockeghem, Busnoys, Molinet, Tinctoris, and Josquin, are among the most famous men of their time, and many among the less well known figures—Regis, Caron, Faugues, Dussart, Georget de Brelles, Hemart, and Corbet—can be associated with Cambrai.

Like Agricola, Compère was above all a composer of elegant courtly music, but to an even greater extent than his Milanese colleague he specialized in writing small lyric chansons rather than large, expansive structures. Only two complete Mass cycles by him have survived, along with several isolated or paired Mass movements, three series of motets intended to take the place of the Ordinary and the Proper in the liturgical service, some twenty-three other motets and Magnificats, and over fifty secular compositions. If he does not quite equal Isaac, Obrecht, and Josquin in stature and achievement, Compère nevertheless wrote music with considerable skill, charm, and wit. Perhaps because of his travels, and because he served a number of different institutions, he seems

to have experimented with musical styles. His several diverse manners of composition afford us an unusual opportunity to understand the process by which
the new methods of Josquin and his contemporaries were established.

Compère wrote some chansons in which the older Burgundian traditions are modified in ways that suggest he was aware of more modern attitudes
toward text setting, melodic planning, harmonic procedures, and textural homogeneity. In other chansons, especially those that reject the outworn ideals of
courtly love, he reveals that he had also completely assimilated techniques for
writing equal and independent vocal polyphony. These contrasting modes of
thought can be differentiated in comparing *Disant adieu* (Example 6–4), a
courtly rondeau quatrain, with *Mon père m'a donné mari* (Example 6–5), a
saucy popular song undoubtedly associated originally with a pre-existing
melody. Both the texture of *Disant adieu* (with self-sufficient two-part counterpoint between superius and tenor) and its conventional repetition scheme identify the work as a late Burgundian chanson, but it differs significantly from
similar songs by, say, Busnoys or Ockeghem. Its principal melody in the
superius, for example, does not trace a long and complex arch of a sort preferred by those earlier composers, nor is it filled with quick nervous motives
after the fashion of Agricola. Instead, Compère writes concise, clear-cut
phrases—half-lines of poetry are set to carefully demarcated segments of
melody, for example—and for the most part the notes have been devised to fit
the words carefully. Much of the text is set syllabically, although well-planned
melismas still have their place, especially at ends of phrases, where the music
broadens out before a cadence. In *Disant adieu* the rhythms are metrical
though contradicting the barlines. Even if the two upper lines are self-suffi-

EXAMPLE 6–4. Loyset Compère, *Disant adieu*, mm. 1–16.

EXAMPLE 6–5. Loyset Compère, *Mon père m'a donné mari*, mm. 1–13.

cient—and they alone take part in the initial imitation—the contratenor nevertheless plays an important role in stating melodic material in imitation with the
other voices and also in clarifying the harmonic progressions. The homorhythm
of the beginning emphasizes harmonic events in the music; even if the harmonies are not dominant-centered, there can be no doubt that G is established
and constantly reaffirmed as the tonic. Not all Compère's rondeaux are so formally compact and melodically succinct as *Disant adieu*. In some, such as those
built over cantus firmi from the Gregorian repertory, the melismatic lines blur
the relationship between text and melody (making it difficult for performers to
decide which syllables should be sung to which notes); in others, such as *Mes
pensées,* the texture is so transparent that much of the music proceeds in two-
part counterpoint. But *Disant adieu* differs not so much in kind as in degree
from his other courtly songs.

　　Mon père m'a donné mari, on the other hand, shows off an even more
progressive side of Compère's musical personality. All four voices of the chanson share almost equally in stating the important thematic material, mostly as a
series of imitative entries. The simple popular character of the tune doubtless
explains why it is set almost entirely syllabically and why it seems so strongly to
imply its own harmonization. The harmonic character of the counterpoint can
even be described as "tonal," if that concept can be extended to admit chords on
B♭ and F as direct support in establishing the "key" of G-Dorian. The jolly *parlando* style of this narrative chanson can be matched in a number of other com-

positions by Compère, including *Nous sommes de l'ordre de saint Babouin,* the hilarious invocation to the patron saint of bons vivants; *Je suis amie du fourrier,* which recounts the history of an unrepentant fallen woman; *Lourdault, lourdault,* a mock-stern warning against the dangers of marriage; and two settings of Italian popular songs, *Che fa la ramacina* and *Scaramella.*

The dichotomy between the Burgundian style, with its long melodic lines and counterpoint fitted to the superius-tenor framework, and the newer style, with its attention to text declamation, chordal harmony, fundamental bass motion, and equal-voiced polyphony, can be found in Compère's sacred as well as secular works. *Sola caret monstris,* for example, one of his great ceremonial motets (intended as an attack on Pope Julius II) written over a canonic cantus firmus derived from the Gregorian responsory *Videns Jacob,* is austerely contrapuntal, whereas *Quis numerare queat,* another political motet based on the antiphon *Da pacem Domine* and composed perhaps to celebrate a peace treaty between Ferrara and Venice in 1484, contains significantly more chordal, syllabically texted passages. Compère's *Ave Maria gratia plena,* which became widely known, exemplifies the young composer's concern for clear text declamation and transparent, equal-voiced polyphony, but nevertheless it is based on a cantus firmus and incorporates a plethora of borrowed material in a rhythmically consistent texture. In this case, the "Italian character" of the motet is also a matter of its underlying structure; a *lauda* melody is used as a cantus firmus. Compère's other motets—those with cantus firmus and those without borrowed material—also divide into two large, though overlapping, categories. This contrast may even be found within single large works, such as his two cantus-firmus Masses, *Missa L'homme armé* and *Missa Alles regrets;* the latter, more modern in its use of continuous imitation, is so ingenious in its treatment of various voices from the chanson by Hayne van Ghizeghem that it is an important landmark in the history of the imitation mass and parody technique. Likewise, in Compère's three substitution Masses or, as the Milanese source calls them, cycles of *motetti missales* (series of motets intended to replace the usual movements in the Mass Ordinary and Proper), older and newer styles stand side by side: passages in nonimitative counterpoint along with classical points of imitation; sections in discant-tenor technique along with four-part chordal progressions regulated by the bass; continuous layered polyphony along with textures varied by alternating duets and other sorts of choral dialogue; and traditional cantus-firmus technique along with phrases unified by repetitions and transformations of a single motive.

The curious practice of substituting motets for some movements of the Mass was followed apparently only in Milan and other places where the Ambrosian rather than Gregorian liturgy held sway. Compère's chapel master in Milan, Gaspar van Weerbecke, wrote the earliest examples, and most of the small repertory of such works are preserved together in manuscript choirbooks prepared by the theorist Franchinus Gaffurius (1451–1522) for performance in the Milan cathedral in the late 1480s. The manuscripts contain mostly pieces by Compère's northern colleagues at the Sforza court. Compère's substitution

Masses consist of up to as many as eight motets that were to be sung in place of the following Mass sections: Introit, Gloria, Credo, Offertory, Sanctus, Elevation of the Host, Agnus Dei, and Deo Gratias. Even though there are no liturgical reasons for doing so, all the motets in each cycle are written in the same mode, and thematic relationships bind some of the movements even closer together. It is probable that Compère composed these motets (whether simply as motet cycles or as *motetti missales*) in the 1470s during his time in Milan; thus they suggest that he could have been influenced by Italian music and musical practices at this early date.

HEINRICH ISAAC (ca. 1450–1517)

Isaac's career centered in Florence, where he was the leading composer during the city's golden age, and the itinerant court of the Emperor Maximilian, for whom he worked for many years. The earliest document that unambiguously refers to him dates from 1484; it records a payment made to him in Innsbruck, where he had probably stopped temporarily en route from his native Flanders to take up a position in Florence at the invitation of Lorenzo de' Medici, il Magnifico. There Isaac sang in the cathedral choir and at the church of Santissima Annunziata, and he probably tutored Lorenzo's children, including Giovanni, later Pope Leo X, in music. Isaac married a Florentine and stayed on in the city even after Lorenzo's death in 1492. The political turmoil attendant on the downfall of the Medici faction and the rise to power of the puritanical Savonarola made Isaac's livelihood as a musician precarious; already by 1492 Savonarola had had the city's music chapels disbanded. Isaac realized that he could no longer work in his adopted city, and so in 1497 he accepted a post as composer to Emperor Maximilian, an appointment that apparently did not require his residence at the imperial court. He seems to have traveled fairly extensively during the next dozen or so years but still spent much time in Florence. He may have worked for periods in Innsbruck, at the Augustinian monastery in Neustift, in Constance, and elsewhere, and he may have negotiated with Duke Ercole d'Este I for a post in Ferrara (which never materialized), but he is known to have been in Florence at regular intervals from 1499 on. When the Medici were restored to power in 1512, Isaac petitioned successfully to regain his former position, or at least his former salary, and it seems that the elderly musician no longer took an active part in regular functions but received income as a retirement benefit in recognition of many years of faithful service. He made a final trip to Vienna in 1515 to seek release from his service to the emperor, who also granted him a generous pension. Isaac returned to Florence the same year and died there two years later.

Although Isaac is one of Josquin's greatest contemporaries, and some of his compositions, especially his secular works, have been studied and performed widely, his achievement cannot yet be assessed evenhandedly because there is still no complete edition of his music. He was a prolific composer whose music exemplifies the coexistence of styles and genres that was characteristic of Europe in his lifetime. A brief evaluation is made even more difficult by the fact that no other composer before Lasso was so cosmopolitan in his approach to composition. Isaac seems to have been equally at home writing French chansons, Flemish sacred polyphony, Italian carnival songs, and German "Tenorlieder." From the nostalgic folklike hymn of praise to the emperor's favorite city, *Innsbruck ich muss dich lassen,* to the moving Italianate lament on the death of Lorenzo il Magnifico, *Quis dabit capiti meo aquam?,* to the gothic intricacies of the *Choralis Constantinus,* Isaac's works reveal understanding and mastery of the principal genres and techniques of his day.

When Isaac's music is considered as a whole, the *Choralis Constantinus* deserves pride of place, not only for the vastness of its conception, but also for the impressive technical skill the composer exhibits in it. It consists of more than three hundred polyphonic settings of Proper items for all Sundays in the year and for many major feasts and saints' days—altogether almost one hundred occasions in the liturgical calendar. Isaac was the first composer since Léonin and Pérotin in the twelfth and thirteenth centuries to attempt such an ambitious task and the only composer of the Renaissance to do so except for William Byrd, whose more modest *Gradualia* (published in two volumes in 1605–7) supplied English churches with similar material early in the seventeenth century. The *Choralis Constantinus* is a *summa* of Netherlandish polyphony about 1500, a compendium of virtually all devices, manners, and styles prevalent at the time; it is especially illuminating as a summary of the ways cantus-firmus technique could be applied to the new equal-voiced polyphony.

For most Masses, Isaac set polyphonically the Introit, the Alleluia or Tract (depending on the season or feast), the Sequence or Prosa (if one existed for the liturgical occasion in question), and the Communion; left to be performed entirely in plainchant were the Offertory and the Gradual (the remaining two sung portions of the Proper). He usually composed only one of the double versicles in Sequences, and his five settings of the Mass Ordinary appended to the collection also leave out some phrases of the text. The omitted portions of both Sequences and Mass Ordinaries (and various other sections of the Propers) were intended to be performed as plainsong, or perhaps the relevant chant would have been arranged for solo organ; thus, in each Mass, polyphony often alternated with plainsong or organ music, a performing convention called *alternatim* practice.

The history of the *Choralis Constantinus* is by no means clear. It was not published until long after Isaac's death; Hieronymus Formschneider of Nuremberg brought it out in three volumes between 1550 and 1555. In his preface the publisher stated that the diocese of Constance had commissioned the work, but doubts have been cast that the diocese had in mind any such ambitious project. Formschneider also reported that Isaac's pupil, Ludwig Senfl, completed the project, unfinished at the older master's death.

The three volumes differ somewhat from one another in style and arrangement. Book I contains fewer Sequences, doubtless because they are less

appropriate for the liturgical occasions included there. Isaac preferred to paraphrase the chant in the top voice in Book I, whereas in the later volumes he was
apt to place it in the tenor or even the bass. Moreover, the polyphony, in from
two to six but usually for four voices, grows slightly more complex and florid
from one volume to the next. This is explained partly by Isaac's use of complex
notation in Book III, which constitutes a *summa* of proportional practice and is
one of the few sources of the time in which the difficult proportional signs
explained by theorists are actually applied in practice.

In some motets from the *Choralis Constantinus* Isaac placed the chant,
in long notes or in florid style similar to that of the other voices, in only one part;
in others he divided the chant between two or more voices, or developed it in
imitation, or combined it with a second borrowed melody. Some impression of
the astounding variety of techniques to be found can be gained by comparing
briefly merely the opening few bars of each movement from a single Mass from
Book II, that for Christmas Day (Example 6–6). The Introit (a) begins with a
"classical" point of imitation in four parts; the chant is laid out in its simplest
form in the tenor voice in a rhythmic style identical with that of the other voices.
The Introit verse (b) opens with imitation by duets; the upper voice of each
duet paraphrases the chant, which appears in its simplest form in the tenor. The
first phrase of the Alleluia (c) sounds less imitative than the preceding movements because of its full sonority, but the upper two voices of the tutti imitate
each other, and the superius paraphrases the chant. The nonimitative duet that
begins the Alleluia verse (d)—in which the top voice again paraphrases the
chant—soon gives way to a chordal passage on the text "sanctificatus illuxit."
The Sequence (not shown in the example), like the Introit, opens with a classical point of imitation in four parts. The Communion (e) contrasts nonimitative
counterpoint in the upper two voices with a canon in the lower two.

At first acquaintance rather daunting because of its length and its apparent contrapuntal austerity, the *Choralis Constantinus* repays close study as well
as more frequent performance, for it is filled with some of the most magnificent polyphony of the entire period. Similarly, Isaac's settings of the Mass Ordinary deserve more attention. He composed two types: through-composed cycles
of the sort used in most Franco-Flemish and Italian chapels, and Masses in
which the *alternatim* practice prevailed. Isaac surely chose the alternation-Mass
type only when the local practice of the institutions he worked for demanded it,
as was the case in many German courts, including that of his patron, Emperor
Maximilian. Isaac's Mass cycles and movements are models of four-part imitative counterpoint that resemble Obrecht's Masses in some ways, especially the
ingenuity with which fast-moving motive-filled running passages are pitted
against slower cantus-firmus-like lines.

If Isaac impresses us, in his vast collection of Mass Propers, with a dazzling display of contrapuntal mastery, he shows himself capable of writing
motets that can also touch and move us deeply. For example, his setting of the
lament by the Florentine humanist and poet Angelo Poliziano on the death of

EXAMPLE 6–6. Heinrich Isaac, *Choralis Constantinus II,* Mass for Christmas Day.

(a) Introit, mm. 1–12

(b) Introit verse, mm. 1–5

EXAMPLE 6–6. (*Continued*)

(*c*) Alleluia, mm. 1–8

(*d*) Alleluia verse, mm. 1–9

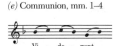

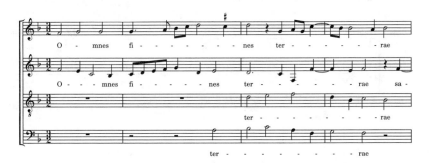

Lorenzo il Magnifico, *Quis dabit capiti meo aquam*? (Example 6–7), stands comparison even with Josquin's great lamenting motets. Many details in the composition help to produce its stunning effect: the austere and mournful beginning (a), on open fifths and octaves, that gradually broadens out into a flowing mass of sound; the poignant fragment of canon over a pedal point in an appropriately dark low register at the phrase "ut nocte fleam, ut luce fleam" ("that I may weep by night, that I may weep by day") (b); the series of nearly symmetrical declamatory statements on the words "Sic turtur viduus solet, sic cygnus moriens solet, sic luscinia conqueri" ("thus the lonely turtle-dove mourned, thus the dying swan, thus the nightingale"), with lush and unexpected harmonic progressions; and the entire *secunda pars,* built over a descending ostinato on "Et requiescamus in pace" and reduced from four to three voices to signify "the laurel [that is, Lorenzo] suddenly struck down by a thunderbolt" (c).

However impressive as a composer of sacred music, Isaac is best known today for his inventive and diverse secular music. His association with Florence and the Medici resulted in a handful of Italian songs, among the best of their kind, which show that he had completely assimilated the declamatory chordal style of his adopted country. Not only his boisterous carnival songs but also the more lyrical ballate, such as his settings of Poliziano's *Questo mostrarsi adirata* or Lorenzo the Magnificent's *Un dì lieto già mai,* could almost have been written by a native Florentine. In addition, doubtless as a consequence of his service to the Emperor Maximilian, Isaac composed a number of German songs in three and four voices, compositions that follow in the footsteps of his northern contemporaries Heinrich Finck and Paul Hofhaimer. Like theirs, most of Isaac's lieder are Tenorlieder, the principal melody being stated in the tenor, around which a web of imitative counterpoint is woven, as in the rather four-square and deceptively naive *Zwischen Perg und tieffe Tal* (based, unusually,

EXAMPLE 6–7a-c. Heinrich Isaac, *Quis dabit capiti meo aquam?*

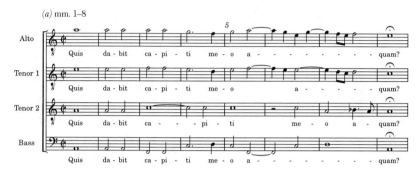

(a) mm. 1–8

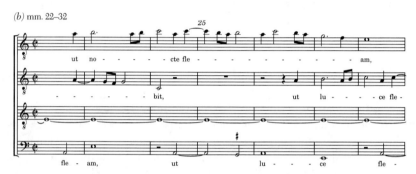

(b) mm. 22–32

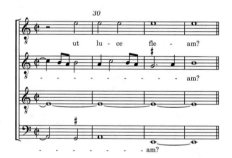

on a two-part canon in the lowest voices), the melancholy folk narrative *Ich stund an einem Morgen*, or the rollicking and lustily humorous *Es het ein Baur ein Töchterlein.*

In setting secular texts in French, Isaac took a definitely "modern" approach: he composed few new settings of traditional *formes fixes.* Like Obrecht, he neglected the graceful and delicate tradition of the Burgundian chanson in favor of lively songs distinguished for their motivic interplay and rhythmic drive, and arrangements of popular tunes such as *Et qui la dira, Par ung jour de matinée,* and *Fille vous aves mal gardé.* The few rondeaux attributed to Isaac are mostly recompositions of older songs, such as his version of the anonymous *J'ay pris amours,* in which he used the first few notes of the bor-

EXAMPLE 6–7a-c. (*Continued*)

(*c*) mm. 65–76
Secunda Pars

rowed melody as an ostinato—repeated incessantly at various pitches in the lowest voice—to accompany its complete statement in the superius, or *Le servi- teur,* where he accompanied the elegant curves of the typically Burgundian melody with fast running lines of a sort associated with instruments. A good many of his secular pieces survive without text; although some of them will surely turn out to be chansons, lieder, or Italian songs once their proper words are discovered, others were almost certainly conceived as autonomous instru- mental pieces. These include fairly short compositions in sober imitative coun- terpoint as well as extended pieces in which a singly simple motive is elaborated in witty interplay, as in *La la hö hö,* or in which the elaborate contrapuntal struc- ture is supported by a cantus firmus derived either from solmization syllables, such as *La mi la sol,* or from a simple melodic formula, such as the imposing *Palle, palle* (the *palle* being the balls in the Medici coat of arms). In his secular songs, as in his sacred pieces, Isaac was a progressive force in his time and a master of four-part counterpoint, capable of spinning out a rich and diverse tex- ture through pervasive imitation, sequences, and sections of homophony, with or without recourse to predetermined repetitive forms or structural devices such as cantus firmus and canon.

PIERRE DE LA RUE (ca. 1460–1518)

To judge by the many references to Pierre de la Rue's works in writings from the sixteenth century, he was an admired contemporary of Josquin. Petrucci's volume of Masses by La Rue (1503) was only the fifth book of Masses that he published, following books dedicated to Masses of Josquin, Obrecht,

Brumel, and Ghiselin but before books devoted to Masses of Agricola and Isaac. Born probably in Tournai, La Rue spent most of his mature life in Brussels and Malines, at the Burgundian court of the Hapsburgs; some documents place him in Siena in both 1482 and 1483–85 as a tenor in the choir of the Confraternity of Our Lady. He next appears as a singer at the cathedral in 's-Hertogenbosch, 1489–92. Before becoming emperor, Maximilian invited La Rue to join his chapel, the Burgundian *Hofkapelle,* in 1492, and La Rue stayed on to serve beside Agricola under Maximilian's son Philip the Fair and, after Philip's death in 1506, under Marguerite of Austria during the years she ruled the Nether-lands as regent for the future Charles V. In 1516 La Rue retired from the court to become a canon of the chapter of Notre Dame in Courtrai, where he died two years later. Although he worked mainly in the Burgundian orbit after his early years in Siena, he most likely came to know a number of other important composers of the time and to hear a wide range of musics on the two journeys to Spain (1501–3 and 1506) that he undertook in the entourage of Philip the Fair. La Rue was highly esteemed by his employers: after his death, Marguerite of Austria had two elegant manuscript volumes of his Masses prepared to com-memorate his achievements, and her own sumptuously decorated chanson albums contain more compositions by him than by any other composer.

No compositions by La Rue dating from his years as a singer in Siena survive, and the Netherlands sources suggest that his composing was concen-trated in the last two decades of his life. Almost all of his music comes to us in manuscripts copied by the workshop of Petrus (Pierre) Alamire (d. 1536), scribe and "keeper of books" for the Netherlands court and sometime spy for Henry VIII of England. Though it is difficult to generalize about the style of a com-poser many of whose works have yet to be published, La Rue seems to have shunned some of the "progressive" aspects of composition in his day. For exam-ple, he seldom attempted to shape his vocal lines according to the declamation of a text, and although his music often responds to its general mood or affect, it falls short of an exact projection of meaning or imagery. Nor does La Rue seem to have worked to produce the rich harmonic effects and rhythmically animated progressions of many pieces by his contemporaries. His rather somber counter-point impresses the listener instead with the individuality of its melodic lines and the complex interaction among them. In Picker's words, La Rue shunned musical rhetoric and sought "expressiveness through the tensions evoked by a linear conception."

The character of La Rue's counterpoint is well illustrated by the opening section of his motet *Lauda anima mea Dominum* (Example 6–8). After the few chords of the beginning, the texture is shot through with imitations and, espe-cially, with exchanges of short motives among the voices. But the imitations do not occur as clearly defined expositions of a central body of cogent thematic material; rather, they make the continuous flow of music sound more homoge-neous than it otherwise would. The same technique often led La Rue to repeat a single motive over and over in one or more voices as a freely recurring osti-nato. In most of his twenty-three motets and more than thirty Masses, La Rue

EXAMPLE 6–8. Pierre de la Rue, *Lauda anima mea Dominum,* mm. 1–16.

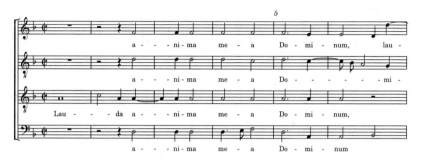

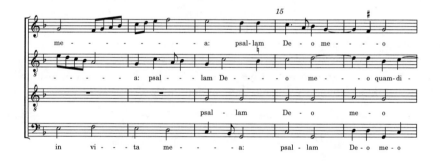

interrupted the continuous flow of music fairly frequently for extended passages of duets. Like Josquin, he tended to build movements over a canonic substructure, not least of all in his six-voice *Missa Ave sanctissima Maria,* a triple canon that parodies a motet that is also a triple canon.

No such rigid constructivist device, though, holds together his best-known Mass, the Requiem, consisting, like most polyphonic settings of the Mass for the Dead during the Renaissance, of parts of the Proper as well as the Ordinary—here Introit, Kyrie, Tract, Offertory, Sanctus, Agnus Dei, and Communion. La Rue's Requiem is remarkable in the first place for its dark sonorities. Much of the time all the voices sing in their lower registers. The first two movements, Introit and Kyrie, are especially mournful because they are scored for low men's voices, and the basses often descend to the B♭ below the staff in the bass clef. Only the Communion, with its hopeful text "Lux aeterna," makes use of appropriately bright high voices. Much of the Requiem unfolds in a characteristic full, even thick, texture in spite of frequent duets, dialogue between alternating pairs of voices, and passages in imitation.

Sobriety and contrapuntal rigor characterize Pierre de la Rue's secular as well as sacred music. He wrote chansons over sacred cantus firmi and over canonic or quasi-canonic substructures, and some of his rondeaux demonstrate how the older conventions could be adapted to the new, predominantly four-voice, vocal polyphony. But those of his thirty-odd chansons that are organized as a series of interlocked phrases without any predetermined scaffolding device or conventional repetition scheme—such as *Trop plus secret, Autant en emporte le vent,* and *Pourquoy non* (all of them in the chanson albums of Marguerite of Austria)—best demonstrate his skills at creating musical form by means of motivic imitation. In many ways they resemble those of Josquin's courtly chansons that are not bound by *formes fixes.* Like Josquin, La Rue set poems closely related to older literary traditions by their rhetoric if not their forms; he repeated musical phrases either to mirror the rhyme scheme of the poetry or merely to round off a closed form; he often overlapped phrases to ensure a continuous texture; and he wrote simpler and less melismatic music as he grew older. Perhaps La Rue's chansons differ most from Josquin's in their more concentrated use of short motives to organize and control the texture, their high level of dissonance (a characteristic of much of La Rue's music), and the generally placid character of their rhythm. They seem to move at a stately pace partly because they are filled with leisurely syncopations and partly because the composer consistently thwarted metrical stresses without counteracting the resulting loss of vigor by well-defined and sharply profiled rhythmic motives. This lack of rhythmic drive gives to these highly serious compositions their slightly melancholy calm and their smooth, unbroken flow.

JEAN MOUTON (ca. 1459–1522)

After holding positions in the churches of three provincial cities—Nesle, Amiens, and Grenoble—Mouton joined the chapel of Queen Anne of Brittany during the first decade of the sixteenth century. He remained in royal service for most of the rest of his life. When Compère died in 1518, Mouton was granted that composer's former benefice at the collegiate church of Saint Quentin, and he may have retired there to spend his final years. Mouton was apparently the official French court composer to Queen Anne and Louis XII, and then Francis I, and was commissioned to write music to celebrate important events both public and private. In his official capacity he probably took part in the conference between Francis and Pope Leo X at Bologna in 1515, and in Francis's meeting with Henry VIII of England at the Field of the Cloth of Gold in 1520. On both occasions the chapels of the rival heads of state competed with each other; at Bologna, the pope was so impressed with Mouton's genius that he rewarded the composer by appointing him an apostolic notary. Mouton may have composed his motet *Christe redemptor, O rex omnipotens* for the wedding of Anne and Louis XII in 1499, even before he was engaged at court, and a number of other motets by him can be associated with particular occasions: *Non nobis Domine,* for example, with the birth of Renée, the royal couple's second daughter, in 1510; *Quis dabit oculis* with Anne's death in 1514; *Christus vincit* with Leo X's election as pope in 1513; *Domine salvum fac Regem* with the coronation of Francis I in 1515; and *Exalta Regina Galliae* with Francis's victory at the battle of Marignano, also in 1515.

Mouton's fame in his time and through the sixteenth century was surely aided by the publication of his works; more than fifty were published in his lifetime, and Petrucci published a volume of Masses in 1515. A posthumous collection of his motets was published in 1555 by Le Roy & Ballard in Paris. Several sixteenth-century critics described Mouton as a pupil of Josquin, but in fact various other composers of the time imitated Josquin's mannerisms more closely than Mouton did. Even though the two composers employed many of the same techniques—paired imitation and canonic cantus firmi, for example—Mouton displayed a musical personality totally unlike that of Josquin. Although his one hundred–odd motets, approximately fifteen Masses, and twenty chansons include brilliant effects at times, by and large Mouton wrote serene, smoothly flowing polyphony, with great technical finish and superb contrapuntal command but without the flashes of fire of Josquin. Mouton's music seems to emphasize continuity rather than dramatic articulation, and he did not use musical motives in the same constructivist fashion that Josquin did. In short, Mouton's solid, steady craftsmanship admirably suited his position as composer for the highest official court occasions.

The smooth flow of Mouton's melody stems in large part from the stately, regular pace at which much of his music moves. He used short notes primarily to break up this slow, regular motion rather than to offer genuine rhythmic contrast. The melodic contours themselves tend to be rather short-spanned, Mouton's penchant for clear, sharply profiled motives perhaps reflecting the rational and precise spirit of his specifically French rather than Flemish heritage. Mouton was often indifferent to good text declamation: his music has many incorrect accentuations and other infelicities in the combination of words and notes. Yet at times he took care to match the text carefully to his melodic lines, particularly in his political motets, where the words are especially important. In both the motet for Francis's coronation, *Domine salvum fac Regem,* and that celebrating the battle of Marignano, *Exalta Regina Galliae,* for instance, the words can be clearly understood, and the textual and musical accents mostly coincide. Mouton was fond of full sonorities; he consistently brought in all voices soon after the initial point of imitation—although the first entrance of the cantus firmus is often long delayed—and he normally kept all voices active most of the time. In spite of this penchant for continuous full sound, though, the texture of Mouton's music is usually clear and transparent, thanks partly to his care in keeping the voice ranges separate.

Along with secular motets composed for political or other official events, Mouton set texts appropriate for particular liturgical occasions, such as Sequences (*Ave Maria ... virgo serena*), responsories (*Antequam comedam*), and antiphons (*Beata Dei genitrix*); verses honoring various saints (*Amicus Dei Nicolas* for St. Nicholas, for example); and biblical texts that had seldom been set polyphonically before Josquin's time, such as psalms and settings of the Epistle or Gospel of the Mass. There are, in addition, a number of Marian texts, several hymns, and various sacred verses not yet identified as belonging to a specific liturgical or paraliturgical occasion. Many of the texts are pieced together from various liturgical or biblical sources.

Mouton's dazzling contrapuntal skill shines in compositions in which all the voices are canonic, such as *Nesciens Mater Virgo virum,* a quadruple canon partly based on a plainchant. Frequently Mouton constructed his motets around a central canon, either derived from a Gregorian plainsong (*Salva nos, Domine*) or based on apparently free material (*Peccata mea Domine*). Motets that do not make use of some scaffolding technique sometimes paraphrase a chant (*Noli flere, Maria*), but usually quite freely; the composer assimilated the chant so well into his own melodic style that the original is sometimes difficult to disentangle. In motets apparently based entirely on free material, Mouton sometimes repeated sections in a formally significant way: by ending each of two *partes* with the same music (to produce the form aBcB); by introducing a phrase that returns in the manner of a refrain; or by reworking previously introduced thematic material in a later section, using a free variation technique. Finally, some motets (for example, the brief, lauda-like *In omni tribulatione*) are entirely free of borrowed material, scaffolding techniques, or repetition schemes; they depend for their effect on successive points of imitation, melodic coherence, or a regular and steady rhythmic flow and the interplay between harmony and counterpoint.

Mouton's Masses span the transition from cantus-firmus technique to the newer procedures of paraphrase and parody. Most of the Masses seem to date from his mature years, especially the decade between 1505 and 1515. In them, as in other genres, he mixed homophony or near-homophony judiciously with passages of imitation and adopted a more humanistic attitude toward the texts he set. He either took cantus firmi from chant (*Missa Alma redemptoris mater*) or used one voice from a polyphonic composition (for example, the tenor of Févin's motet *Benedictus Dominus Deus*). More often than not, the cantus firmus is not sharply differentiated rhythmically from the other voices but is smoothly incorporated into the texture. Some of the Masses paraphrase monophonic material, and one of them, based on Richafort's motet *Quem dicunt homines,* is a full-fledged parody Mass, one of the earliest to use that compositional process.

Like his motets, Mouton's chansons display a variety of styles. Some are canonic, such as *En venant de Lyon* and *Qui ne regrettoit,* a lament on the death of Févin. Some are three-part popular arrangements, apparently paraphrasing popular monophonic tunes. Some—for example, *Jamais, jamais* (in the *Odhecaton*) and *Resjouissez vous bourgeoises*—are wittily imitative pieces, influenced in their strongly metrical melodic style by popular tunes. Among those for five and six voices, some resemble motets in their contrapuntal complexity, and at least one chanson, *De tous regretz,* anticipates the later Parisian chanson in the manner of Claudin de Sermisy.

OTHER CONTEMPORARIES OF JOSQUIN

Some of the incredibly productive Netherlandish composers whose careers span the decades before and after 1500 have left almost no trace of themselves beyond their musical works. Little is known about the life of Johannes Japart, for example, beyond the fact that he came from Picardy and was a highly paid singer at the Sforza court in Milan in 1476–77 and in the Ferrarese court chapel in 1477–81. Probably the several Italian songs attributed to him date from his years in Italy. In his twenty or so secular works he reveals himself to be a lesser master of considerable skill, with a curious penchant for constructing musical collages by combining pre-existing melodies with one another or with music of his own invention. Various other composers in this extraordinary generation were so peripatetic that they can scarcely be associated with one place more than another. As we have seen, Josquin divided his career between northern and southern Europe, and Agricola worked in Milan, Florence, Naples, Cambrai, and Burgundy and at the French royal court. But many composers of this period, after changing posts several times in their younger years, eventually settled down to a fixed position in a cathedral, church, or princely chapel. The best musicians gravitated toward the richest and most important and active musical centers in western Europe, especially the French royal chapel or the Vatican, or toward one of the smaller but culturally rich city-states of northern Italy, or the court of the Burgundian Hapsburgs.

Wherever the French kings took up residence—at Tours, Blois, or Paris—they maintained a large and elaborate court that included, among retainers of every kind, many musicians—not only trumpeters and drummers, virtuoso chamber musicians, and expert singers but also some of the most distinguished composers of the period. After Ockeghem's death, Loyset Compère was surely the greatest musician to grace the court of Charles VIII, the king whose Italian campaigns gave such an important impetus to cultural exchange between the two countries. As we have seen, Josquin spent some time at the French royal court, and Jean Mouton served Louis XII as official court composer, a position he maintained during the first years of the reign of Francis I. But there were many other excellent composers at the French court during this period, among them Antoine de Févin (ca. 1480–1512), Johannes Prioris (fl. 1490–1512), Antoine de Longueval (died after 1523), Antonius Divitis (ca. 1475–after 1526), and Pierre Moulu (ca. 1480/90–ca. 1550).

Févin might well have been one of the greatest musicians of his age had he not died in his mid-thirties. His charming and graceful music reveals him as an attractive follower of Josquin, among the first composers to cultivate exten sively full-fledged parody technique in his Masses (including two, *Missa Ave Maria* and *Missa Mente tota,* based on motets by Josquin), and also the creator of sparkling and witty three-part arrangements of popular songs. If his transparent textures, filled with paired imitations and fragments of dialogue between parts of the chorus, sometimes seem facile, he nevertheless seldom lost sight of his ideal: a clear and elegant formal musical design. Févin's parody Masses probably predate by only a few years several others written at the French court, notably two by Févin's colleagues Mouton and Divitis, perhaps conceived in friendly competition and both based on Richafort's motet *Quem dicunt homines.* This concentration of works using parody suggests that the procedure came of age in the musical circles around the French kings. Its central importance in sixteenth-century music will be more fully considered in the following chapter.

One of Pierre Moulu's best-known works, the *Missa Alma redemptoris mater* (which paraphrases the Marian antiphon), reveals a markedly constructivist tendency in his musical personality; it can be performed either as it stands or by omitting all the rests longer than a minim. His other best-known work, the motet *Mater floreat florescat,* probably written and first performed for the triumphal entry into Paris in 1517 of the newly crowned wife of Francis I, Queen Claude, furnishes the only evidence that Moulu was connected with the royal chapel. It pays tribute to the most celebrated musicians of the time and names many of the composers from the French court. Along with Antoine de Févin and his brother Robert, Mouton, Divitis, and many others, Moulu praises Longueval, Lourdault, and Prioris. Antoine de Longueval (or, to give him his French name, Jean à la Venture) is remembered today chiefly as the composer of a Passion—actually a series of motets telling the Passion story in mostly declamatory settings of texts drawn from the four Evangelists and incorporating chant formulae—which in the sixteenth century was mistakenly thought to be a work by Obrecht, tribute indeed to Longueval's skill. Jean Braconnier may have taken his nickname "Lourdault" (meaning clown, lout, or blockhead) from a chanson with that incipit; it fits what we know of his musical personality as expressed in his raucous, witty songs. Johannes Prioris, on the other hand, is a somewhat more serious and old-fashioned composer who did not exploit the new imitative techniques to nearly the same extent as his colleagues. His best-known work, the lovely song-motet *Dulcis amica Dei,* like his delicate chansons, does not sound very different from older Burgundian music, and his Requiem Mass resembles in many ways that by his illustrious predecessor Ockeghem.

Moulu's motet also mentions Antoine Brumel (ca. 1460–ca. 1520), a sometime Parisian (he served as *maître des enfants* and canon at the cathedral of Notre Dame for a few years toward 1500) who had spent his earlier years in Geneva (1486–92) and in various French cities—Chartres, Laon, and Lyons—before moving to Ferrara late in life. Primarily a composer of sacred music, Brumel for the most part took Josquin as his model. His use of imitation, duets, and dialogue passages, however, does not always display the same fertile imagination as Josquin's—a point made by Glareanus, who compared a *Missa de Beata Virgine* by each composer, much to Brumel's detriment. Though Brumel proved his skill at the craft of composition in works like the *Missa Et ecce ter-raemotus* for twelve voices, his counterpoint, like Févin's, is often merely facile. The long passages that move in parallel tenths and the sections where the text is simply declaimed on repeated notes show that Brumel wished to write a clear and simple sort of music. Like the more contrapuntally rigorous Mathieu Gas-congne, who probably came from Cambrai to the French court during the reign of Francis I, Brumel may also have served as model for those musicians in the 1520s and 1530s who established a specifically French musical style, more lucid and direct than the rich polyphony of the Netherlanders.

We have already seen that the small city-states of northern Italy were able to attract the greatest musicians of the time. But the continuing prosperity of each court depended on uncertain political conditions, and fortunes rose and fell continually during the fifteenth and sixteenth centuries. The brilliance of Milan's musical establishment was short-lived; it scarcely survived Galeazzo Maria Sforza's murder in 1476. Music in Florence suffered at the end of the fifteenth century with the rise of the ascetic reformer Savonarola and the expulsion of the Medici family. The great musical days of Venice were yet to come. In the 1480s the cathedral at Siena began to hire Franco-Netherlandish singers in an attempt to bolster its musical establishment, but not for very long; with limited funds, republican Siena could hardly compete with the princely courts. Almost all the records of the small but unusually civilized court of Urbino have been lost, and Mantua was too poor to compete on the international scene, in spite of the lively intelligence and determination of its patroness, Isabella d'Este. During the period 1480–1520, the goddess of musical fortune smiled most warmly on the court of Ferrara, especially under the leadership of Duke Ercole d'Este I and his successor Alfonso I. To Ferrara they invited a host of great musicians, among them Obrecht, Josquin, Brumel, Collinet de Lannoy, Johannes Ghiselin (called Verbonnet), and Johannes Martini. Ghiselin (who seems also to have worked for a time at the French court) enjoyed a wider international reputation than Martini—Petrucci, for example, published many of Ghiselin's motets and chansons and devoted a whole volume to his Masses (1503)—but Martini held a place of honor at the Ferrarese court, as principal composer for many years. Both Ghiselin and Martini wrote in a style similar in many respects to that of Agricola and Obrecht. Their layered polyphony betrays a predilection for cantus-firmus technique, and their textures are often shot through with short, nervous motives or longer running passages. But both composers also made extensive use of imitation, and some of their work, such as Ghiselin's predominantly chordal motet *O gloriosa domina,* shows that they appreciated the rhetorical effect of syllabic text setting.

As brilliant as Ferrara, the papal chapel in Rome carried on its long and distinguished tradition of excellence under the pontificates of Innocent VIII (1484–92); the infamous Alexander VI (1492–1503), born Rodrigo Borgia; Pius III (1503), who reigned for less than a month; Julius II (1503–13), born Giuliano della Rovere, who established in St. Peter's the Cappella Giulia (named for him) as an organization distinct from the Sistine Chapel choir; and the great patron of the arts, Leo X (1513–21), born Giovanni de' Medici. Apart from Josquin and Prioris, the best composers in the chapel included Gaspar van Weerbecke (ca. 1440–after 1517), a Flemish composer of unusually Italianate music who came to Rome from Milan and interrupted his service at the Vatican for about ten years (1489–1500) to return to Milan and serve in the chapel of the Burgundian duke, Philip the Fair; Marbriano de Orto (d. 1529), who also left Rome for Philip's service; and Elzéar Genet (ca. 1470–1548), called Carpentras after his home town in southern France, who may more properly belong in the following chapter along with other members of the post-Josquin generation. Carpentras published most of his music at his own expense during his last years, as we know from a series of contracts between him and his printers.

Although the dream of a Burgundian empire as a buffer state between France and the Holy Roman Empire had died with Charles the Bold in 1477, the musical distinction of the duke's chapel lived on, under both Philip the Fair, Emperor Maximilian's son, and Marguerite of Austria, during the years she ruled as regent for her nephew, the future Emperor Charles V. Pierre de la Rue, Agricola, and two alumni of the papal chapel, Orto and Weerbecke, were directly involved with daily musical events at her and Philip's courts. Other notable centers of musical activity in the Netherlands included the confraternity of Our Lady (the *Illustre Lieve Vrouwe Broederschap*) in 's-Hertogenbosch, a society of clerics and musicians who numbered among their members the composers Mattheus Pipelare and Nicolaes Craen; and the church of Our Lady in the great commercial city of Antwerp, which employed Obrecht and also, as its organist from about 1515 to 1516, the lesser master Benedictus de Opitiis.

BIBLIOGRAPHICAL NOTES

Reinhard Strohm, *The Rise of European Music, 1380–1500* (Cambridge, 1993), gives an overview of this period with especially detailed information concerning musical sources. An indispensable study of sacred music is Edgar H. Sparks, *Cantus Firmus in Mass and Motet, 1420–1520* (Berkeley and Los Angeles, 1963). Strohm, *Music in Late Medieval Bruges* (Oxford, 1985), also bears on this period, especially as regards Obrecht's time in Bruges. Lewis Lockwood, *Music in Renaissance Ferrara 1400–1505* (Oxford, 1984), is an exemplary study of musical patronage at a north Italian court. The essay "North Italian Courts, 1460–1540," by William Prizer, chap. 4 in *The Renaissance from the 1470s to the End of the Sixteenth Century*, ed. Iain Fenlon (Englewood Cliffs, N.J., 1989), 133–55, is a fine brief study. Prizer's "Music at the Court of the Sforza: the Birth and Death of a Musical Center," *MD* 43 (1989): 141–93, is an extremely useful contribution on music at Milan in this period. Evelyn S. Welch, "Sight, Sound and Ceremony in the Chapel of Galeazzo Maria Sforza," *EMH* 12 (1993): 151–90, explains Sforza's patronage of an important musical chapel. Concerning Naples through the end of the fifteenth century, see Allan W. Atlas, "Aragonese Naples," chap. 5 in *The Renaissance from the 1470s to the End of the Sixteenth Century*, ed. Iain Fenlon (Englewood Cliffs, N.J., 1989), 156–73, based on the same author's *Music at the Aragonese Court of Naples* (Cambridge, 1985); for a superb essay on musical patronage at several courts, see Martin Picker, "The Habsburg Courts in the Netherlands and Austria,

1477–1530," pp. 216–42 in the same volume. William Prizer, "Music and Ceremonial in the Low Countries: Philip the Fair and the Order of the Golden Fleece," *EMH* 5 (1985): 113–53, is a valuable patronage study that bears upon not only the composers of Josquin's generation but also Dufay, Ockeghem, and Josquin himself.

The scholarly literature concerning music and musicians in Josquin's time is rich in articles dedicated to specific problems or scholarly issues, only a very few of which can be listed here. On the Milanese substitution Masses, see Lynn Halpern Ward, "The *Motetti missales* Repertory Reconsidered," *JAMS* 39 (1986): 491–523. Howard Mayer Brown, "The Mirror of Man's Salvation: Music in Devotional Life About 1500," *RQ* 43 (1990): 747–73, focuses on the large number of motets produced by Josquin and his contemporaries, especially those published in Petrucci's anthologies, and their use in votive services. The possible functions of the motet are also explored in Anthony M. Cummings, "Toward an Interpretation of the Sixteenth-Century Motet," *JAMS* 34 (1981): 43–59. Howard Mayer Brown, "Notes Towards a Definition of Personal Style: Conflicting Attributions and the Six-part Motets of Josquin and Mouton," *Proceedings of the International Josquin Symposium Utrecht, 1986,* ed. Willem Elders in collaboration with Frits de Haen (Utrecht, 1991), 185–207, sheds new light on Mouton's music and contains model analyses. Jennifer Bloxam, "*La Contenance italienne:* the Motets on *Beata Maria* by Compère, Obrecht, and Brumel," *EMH* 11 (1992): 39–90, is an extremely valuable study of the assimilation of the Italian style by northern composers. On a motet by Compère and its function, see Jeffrey J. Dean, "The Occasion of Compère's *Sola caret monstris:* A Case Study in Historical Interpretation," *MD* 40 (1986): 99–134. Two exemplary studies are Craig Wright, "Antoine Brumel and Patronage at Paris," in *Music in Medieval and Early Modern Europe: Patronage, Sources, and Texts,* ed. Iain Fenlon (New York, 1981), 37–58, and in the same volume (pp. 227–48), Lewis Lockwood's "Strategies of Musical Patronage in the Fifteenth Century: The *cappella* of Ercole I d'Este." For a selection of motets with discussion of the French royal chapel and the papal chapel, see Edward E. Lowinsky, ed., *The Medici Codex of 1518,* 3 vols., MRM 3–5 (Chicago, 1968). For chansons sung at the Burgundian court, see Martin Picker, *The Chanson Albums of Marguerite of Austria* (Berkeley and Los Angeles, 1965), together with the facsimiles ed. Martin Picker of the *Chansonnier of Marguerite of Austria* (1988) and the *Album de Marguerite d'Autriche* (1986), published in Peer, Belgium, by Musica Alamire. See also Honey Meconi, "Pierre de la Rue and Secular Music at the Court of Marguerite of Austria," in *Muziek aan het Hof van Margaretha van Oostenrijk, Jaarboek van het Vlaamse Centrum voor Oude Muziek* 3 (1987).

For chansons by contemporaries of Josquin and Ockeghem (Busnoys, Agricola, Isaac, and Martini) in an exemplary edition of the largest of the late-fifteenth-century chansonniers, with a superb study of the repertory and its courtly context, see Howard Mayer Brown, ed., *A Florentine Chansonnier from the Time of Lorenzo the Magnificent. Florence, Biblioteca Nazionale Centrale MS Banco Rari 229,* 2 vols., MRM 7 (Chicago and London, 1983). See also the essays brought together in James Haar, ed., *Chanson and Madrigal, 1480–1530* (Cambridge, Mass., 1964). Examples of Franco-Flemish music of about 1500 may be found in various volumes of the series *Das Chorwerk,* ed. Friedrich Blume (Wolfenbüttel, 1929–), and in Albert Smijers, ed., *Van Ockeghem tot Sweelinck,* 6 vols. (Amsterdam, 1939–52), in addition to more recent editions.

Editions of the complete works of many of the composers discussed in this chapter have been published or are in the course of publication in the series CMM, issued by the American Institute of Musicology—for example, Alexander Agricola, *Opera Omnia,* ed. Edward R. Lerner (CMM 22); Antoine Brumel, ed. Barton Hudson (CMM 5); Loyset Compère, *Opera*

Omnia, ed. Ludwig Finscher (CMM 15); Johannes Ghiselin-Verbonnet, ed. Clytus Gottwald (CMM 23); Pierre de La Rue, *Collected Works,* ed. Nigel Davison, J. Evan Kreider, and T. Herman Keahey (CMM 97); Jean Mouton, ed. Andrew Minor (CMM 43); Matthaes Pipelare, ed. Ronald Cross (CMM 34); Elzéar Genet (Carpentras), ed. Albert Seay (CMM 58); and others.

Jacob Obrecht, *Collected Works (New Obrecht Edition),* under the general editorship of Chris Maas (Utrecht, 1983–   ), has replaced the older editions. Barton Hudson, "Two Ferrarese Masses by Jacob Obrecht," *JM* 4 (1985–86): 275–302, and "Obrecht's Tribute to Ockeghem," *TVNM* 37 (1987): 3–13, offers important observations on Obrecht's style and the dating of some of his works. For studies of individual pieces and sources, see the commentary in each volume of the *New Obrecht Edition;* the listings in Martin Picker, *Johannes Ockeghem and Jacob Obrecht: A Guide to Research* (New York, 1988); and the bibliography included in Rob C. Wegman's definitive *Born for the Muses. The Life and Masses of Jacob Obrecht* (Oxford, 1994), a detailed documentary and musical study.

The complete works of Isaac are in the process of publication, ed. Edward R. Lerner (CMM series 65). Volume 1 of the *Choralis Constantinus,* ed. E. Bezecny and W. Rabl, was published in DTÖ Jahrgang 5, vol. 10 (Vienna, 1898); vol. 2, ed. Anton von Webern, in DTÖ Jahrgang 16, vol. 32 (Vienna, 1909); and vol. 3, ed. Louise Cuyler (Rochester, 1948). For other editions and selections, see the listings in Picker, *Heinricus Isaac, A Guide to Research* (New York, 1991).

Pieces by Agricola, Compère, Févin, Japart, Moulu, Mouton, and others are scattered through the sources produced in facsimile edition in the series Renaissance Music in Facsimile, 30 volumes, ed. Howard Mayer Brown, Frank A. D'Accone, and Jessie Ann Owens (New York, 1986–   ).

The first two of Petrucci's early anthologies of secular music have been published in modern editions by Helen Hewitt, as *Harmonice Musices Odhecaton A* (Cambridge, Mass., 1942; reprint, New York, 1978) and *Ottaviano Petrucci, Canti B, numero cinquanta, Venice, 1502,* MRM 2 (Chicago, 1967). Facsimile editions of Petrucci's *Harmonice Musices Odhecaton A (1504), Canti B, numero cinquanta (1502),* and *Canti C numero cento cinquanta (1503/4)* have been published by Broude Bros (New York, 1973, 1975, and 1978), in the series Monuments of Music and Music Literature in Facsimile. Selections from Petrucci's volumes of motets have been edited in the The Sixteenth-Century Motet, a series of volumes edited by Richard Sherr: *Selections from Motetti A numero trentatre (Venice 1502)* (New York, 1991); *Selections from Motetti C (Venice 1504)* (New York, 1991); *Selections from Motetti de la corona libro primo (Fossombrone 1514)* (New York, 1991); *Selections from Motetti de la corona [libros secundo, tertio, quarto] (Fossombrone 1519)* (New York, 1992); *Selections from Motetti libro quarto (Venice 1505)* (New York, 1991).

SEVEN

THE POST-JOSQUIN GENERATION

The geography of Western music changed in the course of the sixteenth century. Some cities and courts where music had been cultivated most intensively lost their leading positions, some preserved their reputations, and some that had never been famous for musical activities became major centers. Political events affected these changes but seem not to have determined them. Italy, for example, maintained its cultural richness and diversity in the face of overwhelming difficulties, even though the relative importance of its various cities shifted. However, divided by many rival factions and apparently unable to unite in a common cause, Italy became Europe's battleground. The terrible sack of Rome by the mercenaries of Charles V in 1527 destroyed the city but not its musical traditions; the papal chapel continued as one of the chief cultural institutions in Europe. Venice, in spite of decreasing commercial importance and political power, enjoyed a burst of creative energy that did not die down for several centuries. Ferrara, never an important pawn in the game of international politics, maintained throughout the century its rich musical and literary culture. Milan, on the other hand, never regained its musical importance after it was occupied by the French; and Florence became ever more provincial after the collapse of the republic in 1529 and the imposition of the Medici as hereditary dukes of Tuscany. In the north, the French, largely unsuccessful in the politics of war, nevertheless continued to support a court chapel of great brilliance. Despite religious persecution in the Netherlands and religious strife in the Germanic countries, the Holy Roman Emperors, Maximilian I and then Charles V, employed some of the best musicians of the time. Munich established itself for the first time as an international musical capital, especially after Albert V became Duke of Bavaria in 1550. Great patrons and enlightened policies toward the arts seem to have affected the status of music in the various cities and courts of Europe much more than political or economic trends, though the religious revolution that split Europe into warring camps—Catholic and Protestant—had far-reaching effects on music.

Wherever they worked, many of the leading composers in the years between the death of Josquin and the maturity of Lasso and Palestrina—from about 1520 until mid-century or a bit later—took up and developed the techniques of composition that Josquin and his contemporaries had first explored. But new techniques and new genres were also invented, and new factors transformed the sound of music in this generation. The process of writing new compositions by parodying old ones became for many composers a regular technical resource. Musicians intensified their quest for ways to express the meaning as well as the form of the words they set. An autonomous instrumental music grew up, not dependent in any way on literary associations or on the dance.

The second quarter of the sixteenth century also witnessed the establishment of various regional genres in music, each with individual stylistic features. The growing prominence of local styles and genres was to affect profoundly the physiognomy of sixteenth-century music, and ultimately it successfully challenged the hegemony of the Franco-Flemish pan-European musical language that had lasted for over a hundred years. For the first time, for example, it was possible to differentiate clearly between Netherlandish and Parisian chansons, and between French and Flemish sacred music; and lieder and madrigals became the predominant secular forms in the Germanic countries and Italy, respectively. Moreover, Spain and England could boast of superb composers whose music had distinctive characteristics differentiating them from the central tradition of western Europe.

Nevertheless, a mainstream of Franco-Flemish music, led by Nicolas Gombert, Adrian Willaert, and Jacob Clemens non Papa, can still be discerned through the first half of the sixteenth century. These composers were northern musicians who carried on the traditions of Josquin and his colleagues. But many features in the music of this period had little or nothing to do with these masters. Although characterizing music between 1520 and 1560 as the "age of pervading imitation" encompasses more than the individual achievements of three great musicians, doing so ignores the importance of text expression, among other things, and the growth of regional dialects. Nor can the quarter century (and more) be considered by musicians as the "age of the Reformation," crucial as the religious schism was to political and intellectual trends for the remainder of the century; that label bypasses the most important repertory of compositions and neglects the most significant changes in the history of musical style. The apparently neutral phrase "the post-Josquin generation," then, describes the salient features of the age more accurately than might first be apparent, especially if the foremost achievements of the generation are seen to have been the working-out of the implications of the new imitative techniques, the continuation of Josquin's endeavors to embody in music the essence of the texts being set, and the skill of these cosmopolitan musicians in developing local musical traditions wherever they worked in western Europe.

Along with the growth of new genres and changes in style and techniques of composition went the development of music printing, which drastically transformed the way music was distributed and the audience it reached. During the second half of the fifteenth century various attempts had been made to devise a satisfactory method for including music in books, either by printing the staves and writing in the notes by hand or by preparing entire compositions on metal blocks or woodcuts. Movable type, however, turned out to be the most practical technique, and, as we have seen, it was used for the first collection of part music, the anthology *Harmonice Musices Odhecaton A,* printed by Petrucci in Venice in 1501, and other collections published by him (see Chapter 4). Petrucci succeeded in overcoming the technical problems of music printing, and the great elegance of his many volumes set a standard unrivaled by the other Italian printers of the early sixteenth century who issued music books, even Andrea Antico, who worked in Rome and also Venice and was the only other publisher of the period to bring out a substantial number of music volumes.

In the second quarter of the sixteenth century, music began to be printed by single impression, which facilitated the beginnings of a bourgeois market for printed music because the production of multiple copies of music books became easier and less costly. In this method, pieces of type made up of small fragments of the staff already inscribed with the notes were assembled by a typesetter into a composite so that each page needed to be sent through the press only once. This was the technique used by Pierre Attaingnant in Paris beginning in the late 1520s, and it dominated music printing until the mid–eighteenth century. Attaingnant died about 1551, but his firm continued to be run by his widow for a few years. In the meantime, however, music printing in Paris had been taken over by Nicolas du Chemin and the firm of Le Roy & Ballard. In the provincial city of Lyons, Jacques Moderne began his publishing business in the 1530s. In the Netherlands, Tylman Susato of Antwerp and Pierre Phalèse of Louvain both published large quantities of music from the 1540s onward. Antwerp was the home, too, of the publishing house established by the composer Hubert Waelrant and the printer Jan Laet in 1554, and of the famous publisher Christopher Plantin, who issued several volumes of music in the second half of the century. Venetian printers dominated the Italian scene at midcentury, especially the two rival firms of Gardane, begun by an émigré Frenchman, and Scotto, run by the same family for generations. Germany, where printing had been invented, was very active in the field of music almost from the beginning of the century, and the many distinguished publishers there included Peter Schoeffer the Younger, Nicolas Faber of Leipzig, Christian Egenolph of Frankfurt, Georg Rhaw of Wittenberg, Melchior Kriesstein of Augsburg, and Hieronymus Formschneider, Johannes Petreius, and Berg and Neuber, all from Nuremberg.

NICOLAS GOMBERT

Nicolas Gombert (ca. 1500–ca. 1556), master of the choirboys in the chapel of Emperor Charles V from about 1526 to about 1540, was one of the most brilliant composers of his day. His historical position is neatly summed up by the German theorist Hermann Finck, who wrote that Gombert, the student of Josquin, showed the musicians of his time how to write in a new style that avoided pauses and was filled with harmony and imitations. In fact, Gombert's ten Masses (almost all of them parodies of motets or chansons), more than 160 motets (the majority for four or five voices), and some 60 chansons present the most classic formulation of the style of pervading imitation.

One of the great contrapuntists of the sixteenth century and, like his predecessor La Rue, heir to the Burgundian tradition, Gombert wrote melodic lines built in long arching phrases filled with ingenious syncopations that keep the motion flowing gracefully forward while avoiding obvious metrical stresses and often forgoing elaborate melismas except on the last stressed syllable of a phrase. Gombert's carelessness in planning these floating lines with little regard for the placement of text accents shows that he valued musical design and expressive sonority over clarity of text. But his music is not bland. On the contrary, his delight in unexpected, sometimes harsh dissonances is a hallmark of his style and gives to some of his part writing its delightfully gritty quality. In his setting of the Responsory for Easter Sunday, *Expurgate vetus fermentum,* for instance, even the opening point of imitation (Example 7–1), with its exposition of two motives, one for each half of the opening phrase of text, includes several pungent appoggiaturas and instances where a suspension sounds simultaneously with its note of resolution. The motet follows the conventional form for Responsories, ending both its *partes* with the same text and music (aBcB). Gombert also used this formal device in other motets, though more often in those that are based on biblical rather than strictly liturgical texts and that generally eschew Willaert's favorite scaffolding devices of cantus firmus and canon.

Gombert's formal procedures, typical for Franco-Flemish composers of the post-Josquin generation, may clearly be seen in his setting of Psalm 129, *Beati omnes* (Example 7–2). Even though the composer made no attempt to arrange the musical details of his melodic lines to accommodate the text—even the first words, "Beati omnes," are consistently misaccentuated—the form of the psalm

EXAMPLE 7–1. Nicolas Gombert, *Expurgate vetus fermentum*, mm. 1–11.

determines the form of the music. Each clause of the text is set to a separate phrase of music identified by its own distinct and individual melodic material.

> *Beati omnes qui timent Dominum,*
> Blessed is everyone who fears the Lord,
>
> *qui ambulant in viis eius.*
> who walks in his ways.
>
> *Labores manuum tuarum quia manducabis:*
> You shall eat the fruit of the labor of your hands;
>
> *beatus es, et bene tibi erit.*
> you shall be happy, and it shall be well with you.

In the first phrase the point of imitation is laid out in a leisurely "classical" manner. Successive voices enter with significant melodic material only after two or three bars, sufficient time to grasp clearly the relationship of each new voice to the whole. No clear-cut cadence separates the second from the first phrase. Instead, Gombert devises for "qui timent Dominum" a second short motive (mm. 13ff) that serves as a bridge passage. The following music, for "qui ambulant," with its characteristic rising fourth and close time interval of imita-

EXAMPLE 7–2. Nicolas Gombert, *Beati omnes,* mm. 1–47.

EXAMPLE 7–2. (*Continued*)

tion, thus overlaps the end of the first phrase. Similarly, no full cadence brings the forward motion to a halt at the end of the second phrase. Gombert makes clear that one sentence of the text has ended and another begun by cutting down the texture and by making the point of imitation on "Labores manuum tuarum" almost as leisurely in its layout as the initial exposition. All the next points—on "quia manducabis," "beatus es," and "et bene tibi erit"—are also run together. The final phrase of the excerpt, on "et bene tibi erit," broadens out, in keeping with its formal position just before an important new section and with the benign, spacious sentiments of its words; each voice states at least twice the text and the music associated with it.

In this motet—and in many compositions by other members of the post-Josquin generation—the music flows smoothly along without obvious seams or clearly demarcated points of articulation. The character of the imitation that pervades the texture changes according to its position in the larger musical design or according to the form or meaning of the words. Some points need abundant time to state their melodic material, whereas some are very compressed; in some points each voice imitates the others exactly, but in some an initial characteristic interval or even a more or less vague general shape suffices to establish the identity of the significant motives. Neither the order of entries nor the time interval between statements of a theme is fixed. The details of texture and layout can be arranged and rearranged in an infinite number of ways, although the texture or mood rarely changes abruptly from section to section. Such composers as Gombert continued to interrupt the complex polyphony from time to time with homorhythmic chordal passages that give special emphasis to individual words and phrases, but their music is seldom dramatic. In fact, many of the motives they devised for a single composition bear at least a general family resemblance to one another. None of the points of imitation in Example 7–2, for instance, is built on memorable melodic ideas that resonate obsessively in the mind's ear. But what may at first seem to be a lack of melodic invention is often, rather, the result of the composer's evident intention to maintain musical decorum. In much of the music by Gombert, Clemens, and Willaert, Josquin's ideal of clarity, elegance, balance, and symmetry was replaced by a desire to create a continuous and placid flow of sound, not well articulated formally but held together by all possible permutations of the technique of imitation.

Gombert based a Mass on his own motet *Beati omnes*, and a comparison of the two works reveals some of the procedures that composers of his generation commonly adopted in applying the advanced technique of parody to their works. The composer elaborated the borrowed composition by taking from it individual phrases and motives, or sometimes merely rhythms, chords, or chord progressions, and subjecting them to free variation. In some passages the composer took over the pre-existing polyphony with hardly any changes, but in others he recomposed the original music almost completely, extending and elaborating the musical material, combining the melodic lines in entirely new ways, giving new emphasis to motives hardly touched in the original, ignoring or underplaying motives that had been given great attention in the model, reversing or otherwise changing the order in which the themes appear, or using them in altogether new contexts.

The first petition in Kyrie I of Gombert's *Missa Beati omnes* (Example 7–3), for instance (mm. 1–12), duplicates almost exactly the opening point of imitation from his motet. Some of the melodic details are changed: in the superius, for example, a few intervals are filled in by stepwise motion, and two repeated quarter notes are combined into one half note; the end of the phrase has been adjusted to take into account the fact that the Mass reduces the motet's five voices to four, but the music remains essentially unaltered. The second petition, on the other hand (alto in m. 12), gives great attention to a motive hardly touched in the model, Gombert's alternative setting of the words "qui timent Dominum," which served as a bridge passage between the first and second phrases of the motet (Example 7–2, mm. 13–17). He recomposed and extended the original material to make an entirely new point of imitation on the same motive, a technique he also applied to the third petition of Kyrie I (mm. 19ff), which is based on the music set to the words "qui ambulant in viis eius" in the motet (Example 7–2, mm. 17–22). In the three petitions of the Christe section of the Mass, Gombert used music he originally composed for "Labores manuum tuarum," "quia manducabis," and "beatus es," and in Kyrie II he picked out three motives from the second half of the motet's *prima pars*. In other words, in the Kyrie of this parody Mass built on one of his own motets, Gombert took up some but not all of the model's most important motives, in the order in which they originally appeared, and either quoted them fairly literally or else recomposed them completely.

Certain conventions about the use of borrowed material in the overall construction of Masses become evident. More often than not, Masses take up motives in the order in which they were presented in the model. The beginning of the model usually opens each major division of a parody Mass; all five movements of Gombert's *Missa Beati omnes*, for example, begin with the motet's initial point of imitation. Often, too, the first section of the *secunda pars* of a model begins important subdivisions of a parody Mass. Gombert, for example, started the second main section of the Gloria and the second of his two Agnus Dei by parodying the opening point of imitation from the *secunda pars* of his motet, and the same material is also reworked toward the middle of the Credo (though it appears there at the words "et resurrexit," which occur midway through a section for only three voices). Moreover, the final cadence of the model often concludes each movement of the Mass cycle, a convention Gombert followed in the Gloria, Credo, and Agnus Dei of his *Missa Beati omnes*, if not in the Kyrie or Sanctus movements. In some sixteenth-century parody Masses, though not in the *Missa Beati omnes*, all the motives with which the composer chose to work appear in the Kyrie movement, which thus becomes a thematic repository for the rest of the Mass; and in some Masses the composer occasionally reworked musical material originally identified with

EXAMPLE 7–3. Nicolas Gombert, *Missa Beati omnes*, Kyrie I, mm. 1–32.

EXAMPLE 7–3. (*Continued*)

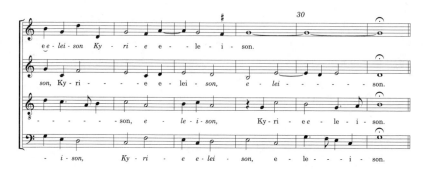

words that are related in one way or another to that particular passage of the
Mass text, thus creating a literary as well as a musical association between the
Mass and its model.

Some of the procedures composers had adopted in the fourteenth and
fifteenth centuries resembled parody, and yet the fully worked-out technique
of the sixteenth century reflects an entirely new attitude toward the task of basing a composition on pre-existing music; sixteenth-century parody technique
could come about only after the establishment of novel compositional methods.
We have seen that late-fifteenth-century composers began to enrich the textures
of their cantus-firmus compositions by bringing in from time to time other
voices from the polyphonic models they used. Parody technique simply
extended that practice.

The emergence of parody technique brought an important stage in the
history of the musical motive to its logical conclusion. Most important, full-
fledged parody technique depended on a simultaneous, harmonic conception
of all voices as interdependent and on the new practice of constructing music
from interlocked phrases in which each individual voice need not be a self-contained linear entity. Composers did not have to lay out their pieces beforehand
over a cantus firmus but worked with all strands of the polyphonic complex at
once, to create four or more equal and independent melodic lines. Individual
voices could drop in and out of the texture at will. Even though composers continued to write music over cantus firmi, they came to depend more and more on
the greater flexibility of parody procedures, better adapted to the new situation
in which *motives* constituted the basic building blocks of composition. The history of parody technique in the sixteenth century, and its changing conventions,
has yet to be written. It seems to have begun with the Mass and to have become
a central feature of sixteenth-century settings of that divine service, but it also
came to be applied to every other genre of music—madrigals, chansons, and
instrumental compositions, as well as motets.

ADRIAN WILLAERT

The sound of music by the composers of the post-Josquin generation was strongly affected by their increasing awareness of the rhetorical and expressive possibilities in writing music that fits exactly the words it sets and that can embody not merely their external form but also their intrinsic meaning. The music of Josquin, admired long after his death, was an important model in this respect. But the practice of composers working toward a closer union of poetry and music also was in keeping with the humanist linguistic reforms and literary trends that were so influential among intellectuals and writers in this period. This development took place in all genres of music, but in none so strikingly as the Italian madrigal. And few composers were as sensitive to the demands of poetry as Adrian Willaert (ca. 1490–1562), the Netherlandish chapel master at the basilica of St. Mark in Venice. During his early years in Italy he served at the court of Ferrara but also spent time in Rome and possibly Milan, before becoming *maestro* at St. Mark's in 1527. His mastery of musical declamation was recognized by his contemporaries; perhaps no one has explained his position in the history of text setting better than the German theorist Gaspar Stocker, who wrote in his treatise on text underlay (ca. 1570) that

> recently, Adrian Willaert seems to have begun, and happily so, a new music, in which he does away altogether with the liberties taken by the older composers. He so strictly observes well-defined rules that his compositions offer the singer greatest pleasure and no difficulties at all as far as the words are concerned. All modern composers follow him now. As Josquin appears to be the leader of the older school of music, so Adrianus stands out as the summit, the father, leader and creator of the new style which is now being generally imitated.

Stocker seems to be referring especially to Willaert's collection of motets and madrigals published in 1559 under the title *Musica Nova*. Like so many other sixteenth-century books of music, this was printed in partbooks, so that each voice part has its own small book to sing from. Combining the genres of motet and madrigal in one publication was unusual in the sixteenth century, and that fact itself singles *Musica Nova* out for special attention. Indirect evidence suggests that the music in the anthology had been assembled by the mid-1540s, and most of the compositions in the volume were probably written in the late 1530s and early 1540s, a conjecture that gives us an approximate idea of the date by which Willaert had achieved his art of joining poetry and music.

Willaert's *Musica Nova* contains thirty-three motets, many of them settings of Old Testament texts or liturgical sequences, and twenty-five madrigals, all but one of them set to sonnets by Petrarch. The madrigals have a seriousness of tone and an intricacy of technique that were more typically associated with motets than with the "light" genre of the madrigal; this new seriousness is another novel aspect of the collection, and it also started the fashion of grouping madrigal settings of sonnets together into cycles. The collection includes a few compositions for four or for seven voices, but most require five or six voices, numbers that were rapidly becoming standard. In keeping with the exalted tone of the poetry and the composer's own temperament, Willaert's expressiveness in these madrigals is usually quite restrained. A passage like that in Example 7–4, the beginning of *I piansi, hor canto,* is slightly exceptional in the clear way in which it depicts a typical Petrarchan antithesis, first weeping—*piansi* (by its slow tempo, long note values, relatively low register, and series of suspensions)—and then singing—*canto* (by its quicker note values, melismas, and high

EXAMPLE 7–4. Adrian Willaert, *I piansi, hor canto,* mm. 1–13.

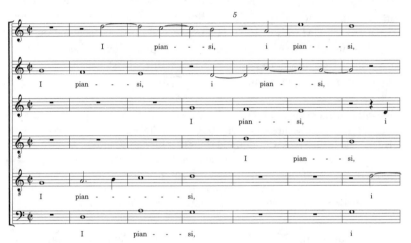

register)—in descriptive "madrigalisms" of the sort that only later came to be derided as naive. Nevertheless, the example demonstrates very well Willaert's intention to project the meaning of the text and to at the same time take care never to misaccentuate a word, but build into melodic lines the tonic accents of phrases and even of sentences. Often predominantly syllabic, with many repeated notes to which the poetry is simply declaimed, Willaert's melodic lines gain in word projection and emphasis what they lack in sweep and breadth (the latter being characteristics more clearly associated with his motets). The "new" element in Willaert's *Musica Nova*, then, consists in the first place in the careful way the composer treated the words, even in the midst of the quietly flowing rivers of sound that characterize so much of the music by composers of the post-Josquin generation.

The motets from this seminal publication are among Willaert's best. Among other things, they reveal the artistic tension that underlies much of the composer's sacred music, the unresolved conflict between freely composed music conceived entirely from the composer's imagination and based on interlocked phrases, and music built over strict cantus firmi, especially in motets combining that old-fashioned technique with Willaert's favorite device of canon. Willaert's setting of a part of the Beatitudes (Matt. 5:3–12), *Beati pauperes spiritu* (Example 7–5), exemplifies the newer style; it is free of borrowed material, and the composer took the greatest care to observe the natural text accents. It also typifies Willaert's style in general, with its relatively dark sonorities (the superius, for example, never rising above c″); its thick, seamless flow of sound; its fairly regular harmonic rhythm and chordally oriented counterpoint; and its floating, nonmetrical melodies that stress "downbeats" only at cadences or when the first beat of a "measure" coincides with a word accent.

In its treatment of thematic material the passage resembles many in Willaert's output; to call it an example of pervading imitation, though, would be an oversimplification. All voices take up the motive Willaert invented for "Beati pauperes," a motive that in various transformations permeates the series of parallel statements constituting the text of the entire motet ("Blessed are the poor in spirit ...," "Blessed are the meek ...," "Blessed are those who mourn ...," and so on). On the other hand, the remainder of the first phrase, "quoniam ipsorum est regnum caelorum" ("for theirs is the kingdom of heaven"), is scarcely imitated at all beyond a few entries on "quoniam" that exhibit the same general shape, and a tendency to write repeated notes for "ipsorum." In this motet and in many others, Willaert preferred a steady, unbroken flow of polyphony rather than clearly separated sections, each identified by differentiated themes. Willaert gave *Beati pauperes* a discernible shape by repeating the motive that sets "Beati" and by shifting into a chordal texture in triple meter, at the end of the motet, for the final exclamation: "gaudete et exsultate, quoniam merces vestra copiosa est in caelis" ("rejoice and be glad, for your reward is great in heaven").

Willaert's brilliant setting of *Alma redemptoris mater* is no more obsessively imitative than *Beati pauperes*, even though all parts share the themes of

EXAMPLE 7–5. Adrian Willaert, *Beati pauperes*, mm. 1–21.

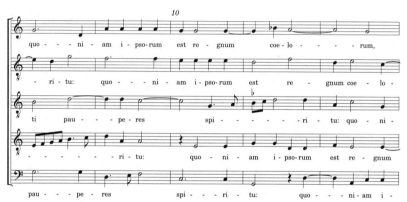

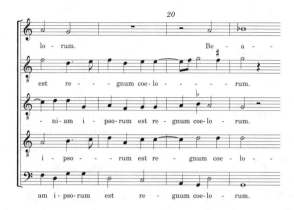

the paraphrased Marian antiphon, which appears in canon between the next-to-top and next-to-bottom voices. The music of this motet pours out with a continuity, ease, and homogeneity of sound that belies the presence of the old-fashioned "Netherlandish artifice" on which the work is based; but the scaffolding technique gives firm anchorage to the melodic lines that float above, beneath, and between the two canonic voices.

Willaert's career and his music demonstrate how fruitfully Netherlandish and Italian cultures interacted in the sixteenth century. Willaert had studied with Jean Mouton in Paris, where he gave up law studies in favor of music, and so he transmitted directly the heritage of Josquin and his circle to the Italian peninsula. But without the influence of Italian humanism and the poetic revival proposed by Pietro Bembo, whose theories informed his work and that of some colleagues, Willaert might not have involved himself so deeply in the quest for a perfect marriage between poetry and melody. Without Willaert the history of music in sixteenth-century Italy would certainly be much different, for he was the most influential of the three great Franco-Flemish composers of the post-Josquin generation. His official position as chapel master at St. Mark's in Venice and his unofficial position as teacher to Italy's most talented younger musicians allowed him to gather together an international circle of friends, students, and admirers whose influence on the Italian music of the time can scarcely be overestimated—figures such as Cipriano de Rore, Andrea Gabrieli, Gioseffo Zarlino, Annibale Padovano, Jachet Brumel, Jacques Buus, Marc'Antonio Cavazzoni, Gioseffo Guami, Claudio Merulo, Girolamo Parabosco, and Nicola Vicentino.

As a composer Willaert reflects the universality, elegance, and cosmopolitan sophistication so admired during the Renaissance. He excelled in every genre. His parody Masses, and even more his motets, are among the finest of their kind. His madrigals show him to be extraordinarily sensitive to the natural accents of the words he set and deeply involved with the new search for musical expression. His chansons display the contrapuntal inventiveness and complexity of the best Netherlandish masters. His ricercars and fantasias for instrumental ensemble weave a virtually seamless web of pervading imitation. His arrangements for solo voice and lute of Verdelot's madrigals furnish important evidence of the differing ways in which apparently *a cappella* polyphonic music could be performed.

Willaert's famous chromatic puzzle "duo," *Quid non ebrietas* (probably composed around 1518 but not published until 1530), which Lowinsky revealed to be a quartet, explores the possibilities of chromaticism and modulation through the hexachordal system and thus shows him to be fully cognizant of the avant-garde tendencies of his time. By applying the traditional rules of musica ficta to *Quid non ebrietas* and following Willaert's own hints in carrying his signed accidentals as far as $G^\flat$ and $C^\flat$, the musician bold enough to add $F^\flat$'s, $B^{\flat\flat}$'s, $E^{\flat\flat}$'s, and $A^{\flat\flat}$'s to the written music will proceed around the complete cycle of fifths, a voyage that is necessary to land finally on an octave instead of the seventh that the notation most improbably seems to suggest. This setting of an epistle by Horace identifies Willaert, then, as a musician alive to the new humanistic currents in Italy, and it attests to the fascination of musicians there with controversial problems in musical theory and with their classical heritage.

Finally, Willaert's psalm settings for double choirs (so-called *cori spezzati*), published in 1550 (some are collaborative settings composed with Jacquet of Mantua), are important landmarks in the history of this technique of antiphonal singing. Even though they are not the first examples of psalms set for double chorus, they began a trend of printing such collections of Vesper psalms that became a Venetian tradition. Though polychoral singing is now known to have been widespread in northern Italy from the end of the fifteenth century, the practice of *cori spezzati* came to be associated especially closely with Venetian church music. The musical grandeur of the double-choir psalms was heard only on special feast days at St. Mark's, when the traditional liturgy of the basilica dictated that the treasured *pala d'oro*, or golden altarpiece, was to be opened.

CLEMENS NON PAPA AND OTHERS

Whereas Willaert and Gombert were both famous men, working in centers of artistic activity that brought them to the attention of musicians everywhere in western Europe, the third great Netherlandish composer of the post-Josquin generation, Jacob Clemens non Papa (Jacob Clement, ca. 1510–ca. 1556), led a relatively obscure life as a church musician in his native country. An enormously prolific composer, Clemens wrote 15 parody Masses (plus a Requiem Mass based on Gregorian melodies), 15 Magnificats, more than 230 motets (the majority for four or five voices), 159 *Souterliedekens,* and about 90 chansons. He composed in a wide range of styles; at one extreme are the *Souterliedekens* (1556), based on tunes published in 1540. Models of unpretentious simplicity, these were the first polyphonic settings of the complete psalter in Dutch. Clemens presented folk or popular tunes in the tenor or the superius of the three-voice texture, in simple settings intended to be sung in the home or at social gatherings.

With such a large output in several musical genres with different social functions, it is no surprise that Clemens's music was influential in his day and after. That his works are as yet little studied and performed is probably due to the tension between two conflicting views of his Latin-text music, which has tended to blur the larger picture. On the one hand, Clemens has been presented as exemplary of conservative, strict Netherlandish counterpoint, and his music has been neglected as inexpressive or uninteresting. On the other hand, some of his most expressive motets have been studied as examples of extremely radical music—a "secret chromatic art," in Edward Lowinsky's phrase, of the Netherlands motet.

In a group of six motets, Clemens departed from his usual diatonic harmonic style, and for these pieces Lowinsky put forth the theory that the motets may reveal the composer's hidden sympathies with the religious reformers of his time: Clemens, the composer-publisher Hubert Waelrant, and a few other Netherlandish composers expressed their unorthodox beliefs by means of "secret chromaticism." In a passage such as that shown in Example 7–6 from Clemens's motet on the resurrection of Lazarus, *Fremuit spiritu Jesu,* initiated singers could, by following the rules of musica ficta, produce a beautiful and daringly chromatic reading of the music. (Omitting the accidentals will result in a conventionally diatonic if somewhat awkward but perfectly acceptable version.) Such an obscure and enigmatic practice accords well with the mystical and arcane tendencies in Netherlandish art and thought in both the fifteenth and the sixteenth centuries. As Lowinsky wrote, this secret chromatic art expressed the "idea pervading all manifestations of the time—literary, artistic, philosophical—that the world offers two faces to man: one esoteric, full of significance and profound truth, accessible only to the initiate; the other exoteric, moving on a level of common understanding, open to the many, the vulgar." Lowinsky's interpretation has been a matter of considerable debate. But even if these motets were not governed by secret chromatic modulation, Lowinsky was right to point out that they reveal Clemens to be a composer fully aware of music's power to interpret and express a text. Pushing against the limits of the musical language of his generation, Clemens employed extraordinary musical means to express the words (or the thoughts behind them) and to convey highly charged affective moments. The musical rhetoric employed by Clemens, especially in these motets, was effected through the application of dissonances, surprising changes in melodic patterns, changes in texture and in mode, mixture of modes, insistent sequences, and the alteration of expected cadential patterns.

Beyond these unusual pieces, Clemens's other motets deserve further attention for their musical rhetoric, their treatment of text and motive. A fluent exponent of the style of pervading imitation, Clemens often extended to great lengths motets based on short biblical texts by repeating the principal thematic

EXAMPLE 7–6. Jacob Clemens, *Fremuit spiritu Jesu*, mm. 1–14.

material over and over, or by writing long ostinati or chains of melodic sequences. In motets such as *Sancta Maria succurre miseris* (Example 7–7), a prayer to the Virgin, Clemens employed a subtle but nevertheless effective rhetorical strategy to bring out the text. The motet is freely constructed, except that the motive that is the basis for the opening point of imitation refers to a chant melody. As the motet proceeds, the sense of the text is revealed to the listener only very gradually, as the composer uses points of imitation to set very few words of text, with each voice repeating individual words in the midst of brief sections of tightly knit polyphony. Within a continuous flow of music, repetition is crafted to emphasize particular words or phrases. The first obvious rhetorical gesture in *Sancta Maria succurre miseris* is an emphasis on the name "Maria" in the opening point of imitation through extension and melisma in every voice. Clemens sets only two words, "Sancta Maria," in the first nine or so measures, and in the next ten or so measures treats only two more words, "succurre miseris." It takes eighteen measures—two complete points of imitation— to get through the opening line of the text. At the close of this section, the plea "succurre miseris" is emphasized through a distinctive repeated figure in the bass voice (mm. 12–14 and 15–18). The plea is made more urgent in mm. 15–18, where two statements of the bass figure setting "succurre miseris" are run together in steady quarter notes; and it is dramatized at the close of this section by the use of homorhythm between alto and bass parts in mm. 15–17 for the penultimate statement of "succurre miseris," followed by a homorhythmic treatment of the final statement, in which both tenor parts reinforce the bass pattern in mm. 17–18.

In spite of all that is going on within the music to emphasize the text, the overall sonority of such passages as the opening of this motet leaves an impression of densely integrated, continuous polyphony. This makes Clemens's music seem somewhat ponderous and uniform in comparison, for example, with motets by Josquin, which make greater use of textural contrast and in which the text is declaimed more rapidly, with fewer repetitions.

Willaert, Gombert, and Clemens non Papa were the greatest of the Netherlandish composers of the post-Josquin generation, but they were by no means the only ones whose works deserve to be studied and performed today. A second group of three men stands out for the brilliance of their music, the eminence of their reputations among their contemporaries, and the distinction of their careers: Thomas Créquillon (died ca. 1557), Gombert's colleague and successor at the court of the Emperor Charles V; Jean Richafort (ca. 1480–1547/48), sometime composer to the French king; and Pierre de Manchicourt (ca. 1510–1564), who died in Madrid while serving King Philip II. In varying ways the Masses, motets, and chansons of these composers reflect their musical inheritance from Josquin and their dedication to the new manner of pervading imitation. Other northern musicians, French as well as Flemish, followed the example of their predecessors by seeking employment in Italy, where they spent most of their lives and ended by completely assimilating themselves into the foreign culture. Indeed, some of them were instrumental in

EXAMPLE 7–7. Jacob Clemens, *Sancta Maria succurre miseris,* mm. 1–22.

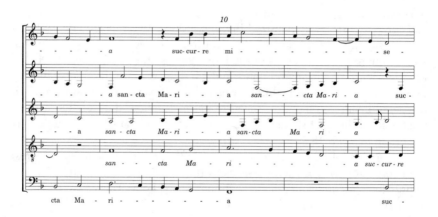

establishing a specifically Italian style of composition, especially in the madrigal. Notable among them were Jacques Arcadelt (ca. 1504–after 1567); the Frenchman Philippe Deslouges, called Verdelot (ca. 1470–before 1552); and Jacques Buus (d. ca. 1564). Besides these major figures of the post-Josquin generation, numerous minor masters helped keep alive the Franco-Flemish musical traditions everywhere in western Europe.

BIBLIOGRAPHICAL NOTES

Some important aspects of the music of this period are considered in Iain Fenlon, ed., *Music in Medieval and Early Modern Europe: Patronage, Sources and Texts* (Cambridge, 1981), and Howard Mayer Brown, "Emulation, Competition, and Homage: Imitation and Theories of Imitation in the Renaissance," *JAMS* 35 (1982): 1–48. On parody technique, see René Lenaerts, "The 16th-Century Parody Mass in the Netherlands," *MQ* 36 (1950); Lewis Lockwood, "'Parody' as Term and Concept in 16th-Century Music," in *Aspects of Medieval and Renaissance Music,* ed. Jan La Rue (New York, 1966); and Lockwood, "A View of the Early Sixteenth-Century Parody Mass," *Twenty-fifth Anniversary Festschrift (1937–1962)* (Queens College of the City University of New York, Department of Music, 1964). On matters related to compositional methods, see Jessie Ann Owens, *Composers at Work* (Oxford, 1997), and her "The Milan Partbooks: Evidence of Cipriano de Rore's Compositional Process," *JAMS* 37 (1984): 270–98.

Willaert's complete works, edited by Hermann Zenck and Walter Gerstenberg, are in progress by the American Institute of Musicology (CMM 3). A fine overview of Venice at the time of Willaert is Iain Fenlon's "Venice: Theatre of the World," chap. 3 in *The Renaissance from the 1470s to the End of the Sixteenth Century,* ed. Fenlon (Englewood Cliffs, N.J., 1989), 102–32; it is enriched by Giulio Ongaro's "Sixteenth-Century Patronage at St Mark's, Venice," *EMH* 8 (1988): 81–115.

In addition to the bibliography compiled by Lewis Lockwood and Jessie Ann Owens for the article on Willaert in *TNG*, see Lockwood, "Adrian Willaert and Cardinal Ippolito I d'Este: New Light on Willaert's Early Career in Italy, 1515-1521," *EMH* 5 (1985): 85–112; Anthony Newcomb, "Editions of Willaert's *Musica nova:* New Evidence, New Speculations," *JAMS* 26 (1973): 132–45; David S. Butchart, "'La Pecorina' at Mantua, *Music Nova* at Florence," *EM* 13 (1985): 359–66; and Jessie Ann Owens and Richard J. Agee, "La stampa della *Musica nova* di Willaert," *RIM* 24 (1989): 219–305. Michele Fromson, "Themes of Exile in Willaert's *Musica nova,*" *JAMS* 47 (1994): 442–87, offers new hypotheses.

On Willaert's madrigals, see also the Bibliographical Notes to Chapter 8. Edward E. Lowinsky's classic article on Willaert's *Quid non ebrietas,* "Adrian Willaert's Chromatic 'Duo' Reexamined," originally published in 1956, has been reprinted with additional commentary in *Music in the Culture of the Renaissance and Other Essays,* ed. Bonnie J. Blackburn, vol. 2 (Chicago, 1989), 681–98, together with a companion article, "Echoes of Adrian Willaert's Chromatic 'Duo' in Sixteenth- and Seventeenth-Century Compositions," 699–729.

Concerning double-choir psalms, see Anthony F. Carver, *Cori Spezzati: The Development of Sacred Polychoral Music to the Time of Schütz,* 2 vols. (Cambridge, 1988), as well as G. D'Alessi, "Precursors of Adriano Willaert in the Practice of *Coro spezzato,*" *JAMS* 5 (1950): 187–210; Carver, "The Psalms of Willaert and his Northern Italian Contemporaries," *AcM* 47 (1975): 27–83; David Bryant, "The *Cori spezzati* of St Mark's: Myth and Reality," *EMH* 1 (1981): 165–86; and James H. Moore, "The Vespro delli cinque laudate and the Role of salmi spezzati at St Mark's," *JAMS* 34 (1981): 249–78.

Nicolas Gombert's complete works, ed. Joseph Schmidt-Görg, are in progress (CMM 6). The principal studies of Gombert and his music are listed in the bibliography to the article on Gombert by George Nugent in *TNG*. See also Jerome Roche, "Gombert's motet *Aspice Domine,*" in *Chormusik und Analyse* 1, ed. Heinrich Poos (Mainz, 1983), 77–85, which offers a careful analysis and a succinct statement concerning Gombert's style.

Clemens non Papa's complete works, edited by Karel Ph. Bernet Kempers, have been published by the American Institute of Musicology (CMM series 4). As with Gombert, the principal studies of Clemens non Papa and his music are included in the bibliography to the article "Clemens non Papa," by Willem Elders, in *TNG*. Edward E. Lowinsky, *Secret Chromatic Art in the Netherlands Motet* (New York, 1946; reprint, 1967) is the controversial study of this aspect of Clemens's work; see also the summary of reactions to and reviews of this book in Lowinsky, "Secret Chromatic Art Re-examined" (1972), reprinted in Lowinsky, *Music in the Culture of the Renaissance and Other Essays,* ed. Bonnie J. Blackburn (Chicago, 1989): 754–78. Several refreshing analytic studies are Ellen S. Beebe, "Why Clemens non Papa did not need a 'Secret Chromatic Art,'" in *Musical Humanism and Its Legacy: Essays in Honor of Claude V. Palisca,* ed. Nancy Kovaleff Baker and Barbara Russano Hanning (New York, 1992), 213–40; Beebe, "Text and Mode as Generators of Musical Structure in Clemens non Papa's *Accesserunt ad Jesum,*" in *Music and Language,* Studies in the History of Music, 1 (New York, 1983), 79–94; Howard Mayer Brown, "Clemens non Papa, the Virgin Mary, and Rhetoric," in *Musicologia Humana: Studies in Honor of Warren and Ursula Kirkendale,* ed. Siegfried Gmeinwieser, David Hiley, and Jorg Riedlbauer (Florence, 1994), 139–56; and Brown, "Clemens and Claudin," in *Liber Amicorum Chris Maas: Essays in Musicology in Honour of Chris Maas on His 65th Anniversary,* ed. Rob Wegman and Eddie Vetter (Amsterdam, 1987), 245–66.

Among studies of musica ficta in the fifteenth and sixteenth centuries, Karol Berger, *Musica ficta: Theories of Accidental Inflections in Vocal Polyphony from Marchetto da Padova to Gioseffo Zarlino* (Cambridge, 1987), is the most complete.

On music printing in the sixteenth century and on the work of Pierre Attaingnant in particular, see Daniel Heartz, *Pierre Attaingnant, Royal Printer of Music* (Berkeley and Los Angeles, 1969). Bibliographies of the works printed by the following publishers are Nicolas du Chemin (in *AnnM*, vol. 1); Adrian Le Roy and Robert Ballard (by F. Lesure and G. Thibault) (Paris, 1955); Jacques Moderne (by S. Pogue) (Geneva, 1969); Tylman Susato (by U. Meissner) (Berlin, 1967); Pierre Phalèse (by H. Vanhulst) (Brussels, 1990); and Antonio Gardano (by Mary S. Lewis) (New York, 1988). See also the Bibliographical Notes to Chapter 8. Most of the motets published by Attaingnant between 1534 and 1539 have been edited by Albert Smijers and A. Tillman Merritt as *Treize livres de motets parus chez Pierre Attaingnant en 1534 et 1535* (Monaco, 1934–63); Merritt has also edited the *Quatorzième Livre de motets composés par Pierre de Manchicourt, parus chez Pierre Attaingnant (1539)* (Monaco, 1964). The complete works of Pierre de Manchicourt, ed. John D. Wicks, are published in CMM 55, and those of Johannes Richafort, ed. Harry Elzinga, as CMM 81. *Twenty-nine Chansons* by Manchicourt, ed. Margery Anthea Baird, are published as vol. 11 in RRMR.

EIGHT

SIXTEENTH-CENTURY GENRES AND TRADITIONS

The decades just before and after 1500 proved remarkably fertile for music. Because the growth of princely establishments created a demand for musical personnel, musicians—primarily singers and composers—traveled widely in the service of their patrons or in search of new employment. Courtly patronage for music was important in this period, but the Catholic Church, with its pan-European network of several kinds of churches, cathedrals, monasteries, convents, and other places of religious devotion, provided the greatest employment source of all. Musicians could travel all over Europe and still be employed within the church's network, and this facilitated to some degree the musical integration of Europe. Though it is convenient to describe musical Europe in this period as having a center and a periphery, we should bear in mind that repertories of several kinds coexisted; the new music did not simply replace the old, and, in most places, regional or local traditions and musical tendencies were combined with techniques adopted from the mainstream.

Most of the musicians we have studied were employed primarily or ostensibly as church musicians whose works with Latin texts could be performed both in court chapels and in urban churches, but most of them composed secular music as well. Obviously, the Mass and the motet were the most international musical genres (though even these could be shaped by regional conditions, preferences, or religious practices), but during the sixteenth century two genres of secular music in particular grew to new international prominence: the chanson and the madrigal.

THE PARISIAN CHANSON

Though composers from several parts of Europe composed chansons, a new sort of chanson was shaped especially by composers in the Parisian orbit; it more clearly embodied Renaissance humanist ideals of text expression and rhetorical elegance than did its predecessor, the fifteenth-century chanson. Given the close ties between the French and Burgundian courts in the fifteenth century, it is impossible to speak of a distinctively French as opposed to a Franco-Flemish or Netherlandish style of music much before the second decade of the sixteenth century. But in the late 1520s the Parisian music publisher Pierre Attaingnant began to issue vast quantities of music written mostly by composers living and working in and around Paris and cast in a style markedly different from that of music by the post-Josquin Netherlanders, with its complex imitative polyphony. Between 1528 and 1549 Attaingnant's presses issued almost two thousand chansons, most of them designed for the tastes prevalent at the court of Francis I (r. 1515–47) but also appealing to a segment of French society outside court circles. Because these chansons were published in Paris and the genre was cultivated by composers living in Paris or associated with the royal court, they are called "Parisian" chansons.

Beyond France, Attaingnant's prints were collected in German-speaking areas, in England, and on the Iberian peninsula; his competitors soon included the firm of Moderne in Lyons (where the city's mercantile ties to Italy aided musical distribution) and the other Parisian firms of Du Chemin and of Le Roy & Ballard, whose collections were also widely distributed. In Italy, Petrucci, Valerio Dorico, and Antico included French music in the collections they published. Chansons by French composers appeared next to their Netherlands counterparts even in anthologies published by Phalèse in Louvain and Susato in Antwerp. The "Parisian" chanson enjoyed a spectacular international vogue and was anything but a "local" genre.

Beyond its geography, musical style in the new chanson was shaped by a number of factors, especially the form, meter, and content of its texts. Fashionable for its elegant simplicity and clarity, the chanson was influenced by the French *rhétoriciens* and their humanist interest in the revival of classical ideals. The poetry of Clément Marot (1496–1544) was the favorite inspiration for chanson settings, above all in works by the two greatest French composers of the early sixteenth century, Claudin de Sermisy (ca. 1490–1562) and Clément Janequin (ca. 1485–ca. 1560). Many of Claudin's chansons are graceful but quite straightforward lyrical miniatures with charming melodies that closely follow the rhythms of their texts. Claudin harmonized his polished soprano lines

with simple chords or placed them in a polyphonically animated homophony, or
else he elaborated the important melodic material by means of relaxed bits of
imitation that make the texture varied and interesting. But it is the very simplicity of a song like Claudin's *Tant que vivray* (Example 8–1), to a poem by
Marot, that makes its greatness so elusive. Both the poem and the chanson
seem to have been based on an earlier popular song; Claudin's setting is actually
a polyphonic arrangement of a humble pre-existent tune. It certainly reaches
no great expressive heights, although its charm is immediately evident. As in so
many of Claudin's chansons, the words seem to control the flow of the music.
They are set for the most part syllabically, with short melismas occurring only
toward the ends of phrases, with a purely decorative function. The structure of
each musical phrase exactly matches the formal details of the poetry. The pause
on the fourth note of each of the first three phrases, for example, marks the
caesura in the middle of the poetic line, and the characteristic opening rhythm,
♩ ♪ ♪, repeated at the beginning of each phrase, mirrors the long-short-short
dactyls of the poem. In spite of its imitative second half (not shown in Example
8–1), *Tant que vivray* is unusually homorhythmic; in most Parisian chansons the
texture is enlivened by more actively moving and independent inner parts.

EXAMPLE 8–1. Claudin de Sermisy, *Tant que vivray*, mm. 1–12.

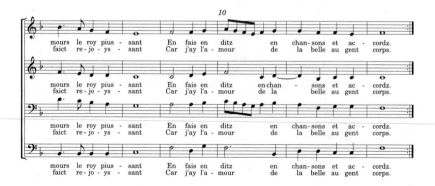

Moreover, most chansons in this repertory reveal more clearly than *Tant que vivray* that their counterpoint is based on a self-sufficient duet between superius and tenor, to which a harmonic bass and a complementary (and sometimes extraneous) altus have been added. Parisian composers, in other words, continued the older fifteenth-century Franco-Flemish traditions in the way they related individual lines to one another, even in these new compositions with their strikingly chordal textures; in *Tant que vivray,* though, Claudin did little more to emphasize this superius-tenor relationship than to move these voices much of the time in parallel sixths.

Parisian composers in the second quarter of the sixteenth century no longer set their music to poems that followed the rigid formal and thematic conventions of the fifteenth-century *rhétoriqueurs.* Old-fashioned *formes fixes* such as rondeaux, ballades, and virelais, for example, virtually never appear in any of the anthologies published by Attaingnant. Instead, the poems on which Parisian chansons are based follow no fixed rhyme scheme, although they are often strophic, and their patterned repetitions are usually immediately intelligible. Often, as in *Tant que vivray,* the first several phrases of music are repeated to new text, and the last phrase or two of both words and music is also repeated, rounding off the composition convincingly. Many Parisian chansons are organized according to the scheme AABCC, but that is only one of several similar ground plans commonly adopted.

The subject matter and diction of the poems chosen by Parisian composers also reflect a new freedom and a release from the strictness of late-medieval traditions. The subject matter was more varied; it encompassed fulfilled as well as unrequited love and comic as well as serious aspects of the amorous predicament. Many poems mix popular with courtly elements. Marot, the leading chanson poet of the time, even edited anthologies of the song texts that were presumably those most frequently heard in the streets of Paris. Poetic diction, less strained and artificial than in fifteenth-century chansons, took on a more relaxed, natural, sincere, and individual tone.

How different these Parisian chansons of the 1530s are from their Netherlandish counterparts can be seen immediately in comparing *Tant que vivray* with Clemens non Papa's five-voice *Las ie languis et si ne scay pourquoy* (Example 8–2), a chanson typical of those by Clemens, Gombert, Willaert, Richafort, and Créquillon and favored by Flemish printers of the mid–sixteenth century. Without its words, *Las ie languis* could well be mistaken for a motet, so pervading is its imitation and so dense its texture once all the voices have entered. In purely musical terms its secular nature can be discerned only in matters of detail and emphasis: it is shorter, less serious, and somewhat more tuneful than many motets; its phrases are concise and clearly defined, its rhythms short-winded and inclined to regular emphasis.

French composers also wrote narrative chansons, many of them humorous and some as wittily indecent as Marot's tale of an amorous priest, *Frère Thibault,* whose plans are foiled when his young lady friend gets stuck halfway

EXAMPLE 8–2. Jacob Clemens, *Las ie languis et si ne scay pourquoy,* mm. 1–12.

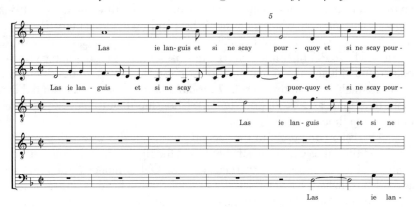

in the latticework while attempting to enter his bedchamber. Marot's poem was set by Pierre Certon (died 1572), somewhat younger than Claudin de Sermisy and Janequin. Like most narrative chansons, Certon's *Frère Thibault* alternates points of imitation based on short, precise motives with simple chordal passages that occasionally break into triple meter, changes of texture designed to project the words and to underline their wit. Such procedures bear at least a slight family resemblance to those used in earlier chansons, such as Compère's *Nous sommes de l'ordre de saint Babouin,* that also include *parlando*-style declamation and exploit imitation as the language of wit rather than of solemnity.

Claudin and Janequin between them wrote more than four hundred chansons of various sorts—lyrical or narrative, relentlessly imitative, simply chordal, or in some in-between style of polyphonically animated homophony. Claudin excelled at composing delicate and sophisticated love songs, whereas Janequin's most characteristic works are vivacious or irreverent. Quite literally extraordinary and in a class by themselves are Janequin's long descriptive chansons, for which he is best known today. In them—*La guerre, La chasse, Le chant des oiseaux, Les cris de Paris, Le caquet des femmes,* and others—he took up themes, such as battle, hunting, birdsongs, street cries, and ladies' gossip, that allowed him to make a virtuoso display of their onomatopoeic possibilities. The harmonically static *La guerre,* for example, probably written to commemorate King Francis I's victory at the battle of Marignano in 1515, imitates trumpet fanfares, calls to arms, battle cries, cannon fire, and other warlike sounds. It became one of the best-known pieces of the entire century, copied by many other composers and arranged for keyboard or lute solo and for all varieties of instrumental ensemble. *Le chant des oiseaux* includes a veritable ornithological garden of natural sounds. When the birdsongs first appear in it, the harmonic rhythm slows down and the "counterpoint" becomes simpler; the series of slowly moving chords merely furnishes an unobtrusive frame for the rich jangle of fancifully elaborated birdsong noises that constitute the main point of this brilliantly amusing work.

In spite of the artificial charm and musical simplicity of many of its individual pieces, the sixteenth-century chanson is a genre richly complex in its themes and geography and in the questions it raises concerning the place of music in society. What is the heritage of the Parisian chanson and how did its style come about? Scholars are divided on these issues. Some have maintained that one kind of the new chanson—the homophonic, four-part arrangement setting narrative poetry—originated in Italy and was first cultivated by French composers who worked or traveled there between approximately 1480 and 1515. Indeed, the superficial resemblance between frottole and such chansons, and the chordal textures common to both, are highly suggestive. But for the most part a direct relationship between the two genres seems highly unlikely, since they grew up in such different ways: the frottola from a tradition of declaiming poetry over improvised, conventional chord progressions, and the chanson from a simplification of the complex superius/tenor–oriented polyphony of the fifteenth century. Italian influence on the chanson may have come only indirectly, by way of its effect on the music of an earlier generation of northern musicians who worked in Italy: Josquin des Prez and his contemporaries. Relatively few sources of the chanson survive for the years between Petrucci's *Odhecaton* (1501), *Canti B* (1502), and *Canti C* (1504) and Attaingnant's publications of the 1530s and 1540s. But a handful of manuscripts and printed books do preserve a repertory of chansons by composers of this middle generation, musicians such as Ninot le Petit, Antoine Bruhier, Mouton, and Févin. This repertory suggests that there was a continuous tradition, from the late fifteenth to the second quarter of the sixteenth century, into which the Parisian chanson fits convincingly. The vogue for popular songs among the courtiers of Louis XII greatly influenced the character of secular music at his court. Composers there made many polyphonic arrangements of popular tunes, for three or four voices, either by putting the borrowed melody in the tenor and weaving imitative counterpoint around it, or by using the tunes as a source for freer points of imitation and chordal passages; and they wrote some chansons

EXAMPLE 8–3. Ninot le Petit, *Et la la la,* mm. 1–12.

apparently free of borrowed material but resembling popular arrangements in their alternation of witty counterpoint and simple chords. It matters not whether Ninot le Petit's *Et la la la* (Example 8–3) is based on a borrowed popular melody. Such a chanson furnishes a link between the cantus-firmus chansons of the preceding generation and the narrative Parisian chanson, just as some of the love songs by Mouton and Févin prefigure Claudin de Sermisy's most lyrical effusions, both in their simplicity and in their delicate beauty.

Claudin, Janequin, and Certon were not the only composers whose chansons were printed by Pierre Attaingnant. Along with works by these major figures, he published chansons by a host of minor masters as well—as did, after mid-century, the other two great Parisian publishing firms of Du Chemin and Le Roy & Ballard. During the first half of the century there also grew up in France a school of provincial composers centered in Lyons, where Moderne published not only the works of Parisian composers but also compositions by local musicians.

French composers of the second quarter of the sixteenth century developed a distinctive new style and cultivated other genres beyond the chanson, although most features of the chanson were transferred directly to sacred music. Motets and Masses came to be written in France in the same simple manner as songs. Collections of French sacred music of this period include seven volumes of Masses (1532) and thirteen of motets (1534–35) published by

Attaingnant. In addition, the so-called Medici Codex—a manuscript anthology of motets prepared in 1518 for the wedding of Lorenzo de' Medici, duke of Urbino, and Madeleine de la Tour d'Auvergne, daughter of one of Francis I's relatives—contains French motets in addition to other kinds of pieces. All these collections contain a miscellany of works by Frenchmen, Netherlanders, northerners active in Italy, and even some Italians—in short, motets and Masses from the musical mainstream and from its various tributaries. But if one isolates those compositions written by the Parisian chanson composers—Claudin's seventy-odd motets and thirteen Masses, for example—it will be seen that they cultivated a kind of sacred music quite different in its stylistic profile from the mainstream. French Masses, for example, built over Gregorian chants or parodying chansons, are generally brief and contrapuntally simple; their concise melodies usually set the text in declamatory style, with frequently faulty accentuation of words, without many melismas and without ever reaching great heights of expression. Claudin occasionally used structural canons in his motets, and in some (as in motets by other Parisian composers of the time) he developed the melodic material by means of extended and elaborate counterpoint. But in general, Parisian motets, of which there are many of great charm and beauty, are distinguished for the condensation of their form, their easy, pleasing melodies, and the simplicity of their manner—just those features, in fact, that separate Parisian chansons from their Netherlandish counterparts.

THE ITALIAN MADRIGAL

Like the French chanson, the sixteenth-century Italian madrigal can be viewed as a regional dialect of the pan-European musical language of the sixteenth century, yet the madrigal also quickly became an international genre. Like the earlier *frottola,* the term *madrigal* has both a generic and a specific meaning. Most narrowly it refers to a poetic form new in the sixteenth century (though named for its fourteenth-century predecessor), a form distinguished by its irregularity and its freedoms. The most concise definition—that the madrigal is a canzone of one strophe—is accurate as far as it goes; indeed, it is difficult to be much more precise. Usually each line of verse has either seven or eleven syllables; strophes mix the two lengths in irregular combinations. The rhyme scheme is not fixed, although some madrigals end with a couplet, and there can be as few as six or as many as sixteen lines, although most madrigals have from ten to twelve. With reference to the music, the term *madrigal* in the sixteenth century encompasses settings of various forms of verse, especially those with relatively irregular structures—madrigals proper and canzone stanzas—but also sonnets, sestina stanzas, and even ballate. The poems are mostly of high literary quality, and composers worked hard to fit the music carefully to them, in more or less rich polyphonic textures, allowing themselves the freedom to use simple chordal textures as well as imitative polyphony. They set the words in ways ranging from straightforward syllabic declamation to extended melismas; their choice of texture and technique depended more on the content of the poem than on its form, and more on rhetorical effect than on abstract formal principle. Since it is unlikely that music conceived for one set of words can with equal appropriateness fit a second set as well, madrigals are in principle through-composed. Certainly each stanza of a multistanza work invariably received new music, although composers frequently repeated individual musical phrases in different verses to give their compositions an easily intelligible form.

Whereas the typical frottola consisted of schematic musical formulae that were repeated to subsequent stanzas of text, madrigals are through-composed. In spite of this, some of the same kinds of poems were set as madrigals and as frottole. In particular, the poems of Petrarch show up in both genres. When composers set canzoni and verses similarly irregular in length as frottole, they had to modify the stereotyped and formulaic character of their music, as is evident in Example 4–5, Tromboncino's setting of Petrarch's *Sì è debile il filo.* How different is Example 8–4, the beginning of Bernardo Pisano's imitative, almost motetlike version of the same poem, which he included in his volume of *Musica ... sopra le canzone del Petrarcha,* published by Petrucci in 1520. Pisano's setting is almost a madrigal and yet not quite, for he apparently intended the same music to be repeated for each stanza of the canzone. But the application of imitative polyphony to the poems of Petrarch certainly constitutes a link between the frottola (and other simple, strophic forms) and the early madrigal.

EXAMPLE 8–4. Bernardo Pisano, *Sì è debile il filo,* mm. 1–12.

To claim that the madrigal was born as a result of the application of Franco-Flemish polyphonic techniques to the native Italian frottola, however, would be overly simple. The madrigal was not invented as an improvement upon the frottola, nor did it immediately replace it in musical collections. The first madrigalists were all deeply committed from the very beginning to the proposition that music should intensify the poetry it sets; they were therefore attempting to invent a music that enhanced poetry and revealed its inner meanings, and, naturally, they drew first upon the potentially expressive techniques of familiar musical genres (frottola, chanson, motet). The impulse to the madrigal seems also to have come from poetic as well as musical circles. Pietro Bembo (1470–1547)—poet, Venetian nobleman, scholar, papal secretary in Rome from 1512 to 1520, and cardinal from 1539—was one of the most important influences in this movement. Bembo was much admired; he was the leading authority on Petrarch and had prepared the 1501 edition of Petrarch's *Canzoniere.* By praising and imitating the written Tuscan of Petrarch, Boccaccio, and Dante, he did more than anyone else to establish Italian as a literary language (Latin had been preferred by Italian humanist writers throughout much of the fifteenth century). In his analysis of Petrarch, Bembo stressed not only the poet's mastery of poetic technique and the propriety of his imagery but also the way he matched the sounds of words (as opposed to their meanings) with their effect on the reader. Bembo singled out two qualities that the sounds and rhythms of words can create: *piacevolezza* (roughly akin to "sweetness" or "grace") and *gravità* ("majesty" or "dignity"). His analysis opened the way for composers to illustrate each word in a poem by *word painting*—that is, by writing fast notes to set words like *running* or *flying,* close imitation for *fleeing,* pauses for *sighing* or *dying,* and so on—or to devise music that abstracted literary concepts to a greater extent; thus, hard, harsh, or cruel words were set to music filled with minor chords, dissonances, suspensions, appoggiaturas, and unexpected harmonies, and merry, happy, serene, or contented words were set to major chords and consonant or sweet sounds. Moreover, by manipulating the rhythms and phrase structure of a madrigal, composers could emphasize individual words or sentences, declaiming some sections simply and extending others at great length, to interpret the content rather than the form of the poem.

The early madrigal was a synthesis of elements, and, though it owed a great deal to the Italian tradition of secular song, the best of the earliest composers who wrote and published Italian madrigals, with one exception, were foreigners: Philippe Verdelot, Jacques Arcadelt, and Adrian Willaert. The exception was Costanzo Festa (d. 1545), the first Italian musician of the century to command the techniques of imitative polyphony as masterfully as did the foreigners. These composers' mix of international elements was the result of aesthetic ideals akin to those of the Petrarchist poets, and their search was for a suitably elevated musical language as rich, varied, and nuanced as the imitative polyphony setting Latin motet texts and as elegantly clear and responsive to metrical patterns as the "Parisian" chanson. Festa, Verdelot, Arcadelt, and Willaert shaped the musical style of the madrigal and brought it to its first peak of achievement. Several other native-born composers of madrigals may be included in their circle: Francesco Corteccia (d. 1571), Domenico Maria Ferrabosco (1513–74), Girolamo Parabosco (d. 1557), and Alfonso dalla Viola (ca. 1508–ca. 1573) of Ferrara.

Madrigals were written for a variety of reasons. Some were commissioned by noblemen who wanted music to honor the ladies they loved. Some were composed for specific entertainments, banquets, weddings, plays, and other festivities. After about 1540, Italian literary academies (small groups of poets, musicians, artists, and amateurs who met regularly to discuss intellectual and artistic subjects, to hear one another's works, and to witness musical performances) had madrigals written especially for them; the Accademia Filarmonica of Verona, founded in 1543, was the first academy to have well-developed musical interests. The madrigals composed for such groups were usually the most serious and intellectual. Some madrigals were doubtless composed for performance by professional groups at a prince's court; some were probably composed more as performer's music than as listener's music, to be sung by courtiers for their own amusement. Normally, madrigals were performed with one singer to a part, either *a cappella* or, as many contemporary documents show, with the participation of various instruments, either substituting for voices or doubling them.

The discussions about the nature of music and poetry that led to the madrigal must have taken place in Rome, Venice, and Florence in the 1510s and 1520s, and madrigals were circulating in manuscript copies as early as the 1520s, although the term *madrigal* did not appear on a musical title page until *Madrigali de diversi musici: libro primo de la Serena* (Rome, 1530), a mixed anthology including some chansons and lighter Italian pieces as well. The first printed book devoted exclusively to the madrigal was Verdelot's *Primo libro* (Venice, 1533) of four-voice madrigals. These early pieces of Verdelot, like many of the earliest madrigals (from about 1530 until Festa's death in 1545) are simple and chordal, punctuated by clear cadences to delineate phrases of the poetic text. They are through-composed and only slightly more complex polyphonically than frottole, and they do not display any very new techniques for embodying in music the meaning of the poetry. Verdelot's *O dolce notte,* for instance, never departs from the lightly decorated homophonic texture with which it opens; in part this is because it was written to be performed during Act 5 of Machiavelli's play *La Mandragola,* and the homophonic texture nicely projects the words.

Costanzo Festa's slightly more complex *Cosi suav'è'l foco* (Example 8–5) shows more clearly than many madrigals the integration and interaction of diverse elements within a single madrigal. It opens with a Josquin-like duet for "Cosi suav'è'l foco" ("So sweet is the fire") and continues with the superius singing in the manner of a frottola the phrase "et dolce il nodo" ("and pleasant the noose") while the lower and faster-moving voices function as accompaniment; the second line of the poem, "Con che m'incendi amor" ("with which love inflames me"), begins with a full-fledged point of imitation for all four voices.

EXAMPLE 8–5. Costanzo Festa, *Cosi suav'è'l foco*, mm. 1–12.

Arcadelt's madrigals tend to be written in a style not very different from that of the French chanson, a genre in which he was also expert. They are apt, for example, to be formally clear, since Arcadelt often repeated musical phrases, and their bland diatonic harmonies, attractive melodies, simple suave polyphony, and transparent textures make them immediately appealing.

It was Willaert, among the early generation of madrigalists, who first achieved a perfect union between words and music, although he avoided syllabically set chordal passages on the one hand and extravagant rhetorical flourishes on the other. On occasion he could portray Petrarchan antitheses vividly, as we have seen in *I piansi, hor canto* (Example 7–4), even to the extent of violating melodic decorum. The superius of its opening, for instance, fragmentary and containing an abrupt change of pace, makes no sense as a self-sufficient and autonomous melodic line; but once the words it sets are taken into account, its aptness is self-evident. More typically, Willaert's restraint in devising melodic lines that support and illuminate the verses prevents him from depicting the poetic imagery with literal or vivid word painting or from breaking the even flow of sound. His setting of Petrarch's *Giunto m'ha Amor* is more characteristic than *I piansi, hor canto* of his madrigals in *Musica nova*, not only for the dense web of imitations and near imitations within the lush harmonic framework, but also because it exemplifies the convention that Willaert established of setting sonnets in two formal sections (*partes*), the first for the octave of the poem, the second for the sestet. He did not project the meaning of *Giunto m'ha Amor* in any obviously dramatic way—the counterpoint is too thick for that—but his diction is so painstaking that the individual melodic lines virtually sing themselves. The music has a shape that follows the sense rather than the form of the text: the points of articulation are often planned according to the meanings of the verses and not merely where the lines end. Willaert's madrigals do not dazzle the ears; they are sober, decorous, and highly refined interpretations of great poetry.

Willaert, Festa, and the other early madrigalists wrote some compositions in a notation that began to appear from about 1540 onward in which smaller note values were used, with the common-time signature (c) replacing the more usual alla breve (¢). These madrigals, called *madrigali a note nere* or *madrigali a misura di breve*, are filled with lively rhythms and syncopations. They are also sometimes known as *madrigali cromatici*, not because they require many accidentals, but because they are written with many *crome*, or flagged semiminims (transcribed in modern editions as sixteenth notes or smaller). Semiminims, heretofore used only in melismas, now often appeared with single syllables. From 1540, "black-note" madrigals appeared in both separate collections and anthologies together with "normal" madrigals with alla breve time signatures.

By the second generation of sixteenth-century madrigalists—reaching their maturity in the 1540s and 1550s—the diverse elements of madrigal style had been completely amalgamated into a sensitive and expressive vehicle for enhancing fine poems. By 1560 native musicians predominated. Although the most brilliant madrigalist of the generation, Willaert's pupil Cipriano de Rore (1516–65), came from beyond the Alps, the classical madrigal style of the mid-century and later is chiefly associated with men such as Andrea Gabrieli (1510/20–86), Annibale Padovano (1527–75), Costanzo Porta (ca. 1529–1601), Francesco Portinaro (ca. 1520–after 1578), Vincenzo Ruffo (1510–87), and Nicola Vicentino (1511–72).

Unlike his teacher, Cipriano de Rore did not shun extroverted rhetorical devices. Indeed, he made of the madrigal a passionate and personal vehicle capable of bringing out every nuance of the expressive content of the texts. Rore is thus known today primarily for his contributions as a madrigalist, although he also composed sacred music, especially motets. His early madrigals share some of the same features as those by Willaert: above all, impeccable diction, but also a penchant for relatively thick, continuous counterpoint, intensive if inexact imitation, and overlapped cadences. Rore followed Willaert's example in composing Petrarchan sonnets in two *partes;* even more ambitiously, he set as early as 1548 all the stanzas of Petrarch's canzone *Vergine bella* as a cycle of eleven madrigals, beginning a fashion for similar cycles. Rore deserves his place of honor in the history of the madrigal, however, less for his formal ambitiousness and ingenuity or for his contrapuntal mastery (though that is very impressive) than for his profound skill in capturing and reflecting the changing moods of serious poetry—his mastery of rhetoric. Whereas most of his predecessors set

EXAMPLE 8–6. Cipriano de Rore, *O sonno*, mm. 1–11.

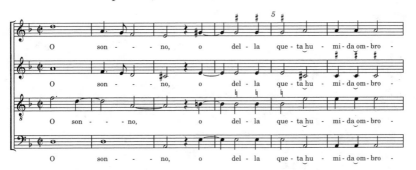

the verse line by line, accommodating musical phrases to poetic lines, Rore composed according to the grammatical sense of the text, observing enjambment when it occurs so that musical phrases preserve grammatical units but contradict the bare structure of the poem.

An illustration of this is the way that the musical phrase continues past the new poetic line begun with the word "Notte" in *O sonno* (see m. 7 of Example 8–6). Rore's polyphonic cunning notwithstanding, he could choose to compose a work such as *O sonno* almost entirely in homophonic textures. Rore makes palpable the image of sleep as the "placid son of humid shadowy night" by chord spacing, control of range, and especially sensitive use of harmonic color. Even though he generally stayed within the bounds of the diatonic modal system, Rore could also use extreme chromaticism with stunning effect, as in the passage from *Da le belle contrade* shown in Example 8–7. The excerpt is remarkable not so much for the realism of the exclamation "T'en vai, haimè!" ("You go, alas!") or for the graphic (and literal) depiction of "Sola mi lasci!" ("You are leaving me alone!"), set for one voice only, as for the series of striking chromatic sideslips: the C minor triad, for example, poignant and unexpected immediately following A major—a progression that makes the lover's cry "Ahi crudo amor" ("Oh, cruel love") sound tangibly heartfelt and touching—or the incredible sweetness of the D-flat major triad on "dolcezze."

EXAMPLE 8–7. Cipriano de Rore, *Da le belle contrade*, mm. 30–51.

In short, Rore exploited a wide range of techniques, from the strictest imitation to the plainest homophony, from bland diatonic to startlingly chromatic and "distant" harmonies, and from simple syllabic declamation to florid melismatic display. But all these devices were subservient to his central aim: to express the meaning of individual words and hence of the poem as a whole. This was the aspect of his musical personality that led writers on music later in the century to identify him as the inventor of a "second practice" in contradistinction to the strict and musically autonomous polyphony of the Netherlands and the sonorous purity of the Counter-Reformation music of Roman composers such as Palestrina. Rore proved to be the model whom the great virtuoso madrigalists of the late sixteenth century followed—the composers who made up a third generation of madrigalists—northerners such as Philippe de Monte, Giaches de Wert, and Orlando Lasso as well as a trio of famous Italians: Luca Marenzio, Carlo Gesualdo, and Claudio Monteverdi.

Italian musicians throughout the sixteenth century also cultivated lighter kinds of music in addition to serious madrigals. Roughly akin to present-day popular songs, *villanelle* (or *canzoni villanesche alla napoletana,* as they were first called) were presumably intended for the enjoyment of a wide spectrum of social classes in the various Italian cities. These lively but unpretentious pieces cannot be considered genuine folk art; for one thing, some of their composers also wrote refined madrigals. Villanelle, or villanesche—the two terms seem to be used almost interchangeably in sixteenth-century sources—are generally quite simple three-part settings of popular verse in strophic forms, either in bare chordal style (so humble, in fact, that parallel fifths were readily tolerated) or in only slightly elaborated homophony. Thomas Morley somewhat rudely but not inaccurately described them as "a clownish musick to a clownish matter." Their Neapolitan origin, implied in their being first characterized as "alla napoletana," is confirmed by the volumes of canzoni villanesche issued in the 1530s, 1540s, and 1550s by Neapolitan composers such as Giovanni Thomaso di Maio, Giovanni Domenico da Nola, and Thomaso Cimello. Many of the poems are

quite irreverent, and some follow the tradition of canti carnascialeschi by immediately identifying the characters singing as old ladies, blind beggars, German
soldiers, stuttering Venetian noblemen, local citizens speaking in dialect, or
members of some other group who can illuminate the human comedy. Other
poems, like *Madonna io non lo so,* set by Giovanni Domenico da Nola, are
slightly more refined lovers' laments. The fashion for villanelle soon spread
from Naples northward, and was taken up by composers as serious as Willaert
(whose four-part arrangements of some of Nola's compositions, including
Madonna io non lo so, place the Neapolitan's melody in the tenor), Baldissera
Donato, and, somewhat later, Luca Marenzio.

Some of the variants of the villanella exploit local dialects or customs,
such as the *greghesca* (in a mixture of Venetian and Greek), the *giustiniana* (in
Venetian dialect; unrelated to the fifteenth-century poems of Leonardo
Giustiniani), the *moresca* (incorporating Moorish elements), the *todesca* (in
which a German accent is written into the poetry), and the *bergamasca* (in the
dialect of Bergamo). Some, like the *mascherate* sung at masked balls and in processions, were presumably written for special occasions. Sixteenth-century title
pages sometimes call similar pieces *villotte,* but the term *villotta* should probably be reserved for the late fifteenth- and early sixteenth-century polyphonic
arrangements in four parts of actual street songs and popular tunes, such as
Compère's version of *Che fa la ramacina* or *Scaramella va alla guerra.* Similarly, a distinction should be made between the villanella and the late-sixteenth-
century canzonetta, a slightly more "respectable" if equally lighthearted genre
cultivated by composers such as Giovanni Ferretti, Girolamo Conversi, and
Giuseppe Caimo. (Given sacred words, the *canzonetta spirituale* was used in
the service of the Counter-Reformation late in the century.) One should also
distinguish between villanelle and *balletti,* the dance songs written by Giovanni
Giacomo Gastoldi. Beginning in the last quarter of the sixteenth century, these
lighter forms had a great impact on music outside Italy. Gastoldi's balletti were
imitated in England, for example, and composers such as Hans Leo Hassler and
Johann Hermann Schein brought the villanella style to Germany in the late sixteenth and early seventeenth centuries.

THE COEXISTENCE OF INTERNATIONAL AND REGIONAL GENRES

Germany

Musical evidence from the German-speaking countries in the late Middle Ages tells us more about their traditions of monophonic song than about the
cultivation of polyphony. It would appear that music in German-speaking lands
followed a course somewhat detached from that of the mainstream of western
Europe, and we know almost nothing about the work of German composers in
the European tradition before the late fifteenth century. Much of the music is

anonymous in manuscript anthologies (such as the Trent Codices) and awaits scholarly investigation, but signs are emerging that music in south Germany (including present-day Austria) was more broadly European than has been assumed before now.

In the late fifteenth and early sixteenth centuries Germany brought forth a distinctive polyphonic genre of secular music consistent with its strong monophonic tradition. Even though German composers about 1500 borrowed elements from Franco-Flemish music, they wrote songs, or *lieder,* essentially independent of secular genres in other countries. In *Tenorlieder* the tenor states the principal melodic line, a simple but elegant tune addressed either to courtly circles (in the so-called *Hofweisen,* which tend to be polyphonic arrangements of the "courtly tenors," or *Hofweisentenores*) or more broadly to the educated classes (in the *Gesellschaftslieder,* or "community songs"). The history of German lieder in the Renaissance divides neatly into four periods according to the groups of sources that preserve the songs: (1) several chansonniers from the second half of the fifteenth century, which include a number of mostly anonymous lieder along with chansons, song-motets, and instrumental music; (2) a group of printed anthologies and manuscripts from the second decade of the sixteenth century, which contain songs written by Heinrich Isaac and his contemporaries; (3) anthologies published between 1534 and the mid-1550s, in which appear lieder by these men as well as composers of the following generation, of whom Ludwig Senfl was the most distinguished; and (4) after the mid-1560s, collections that began to include German songs deeply influenced by foreign music, notably by Italian madrigals and villanelle.

The three best-known of the late-fifteenth-century chansonniers are the Lochamer Liederbuch (now in Berlin), assembled in or near Nuremberg between 1455 and 1460 and containing for the most part monophonic melodies, some of them parts of polyphonic compositions; the Schedelsches Liederbuch (now in Munich), written by Hartmann Schedel, a doctor and historian, during his student days in the 1460s in Leipzig, Padua, and possibly Nuremberg; and the Glogauer Liederbuch (now in Kraków, Biblioteka Jagiellónska), containing about 290 pieces. The three volumes of the Glogauer Liederbuch were prepared between 1475 and 1480 and are therefore the earliest example of a collection of music gathered together as a set of partbooks. These manuscripts offer a selection of most of the kinds of music prevalent in Germany at the time.

The Glogauer Liederbuch includes, besides its 70 lieder, 158 pieces with Latin text or incipit, 61 without text, 3 quodlibets, and 1 Italian and 1 Slavic song. This is an international repertory—a somewhat old-fashioned one, given the musical style of its pieces and the fact that so few of its secular pieces are for four voices. Many of the Latin and textless compositions are Franco-Flemish chansons by Dufay, Binchois, Ockeghem, Busnoys, and their contemporaries; some of the Latin pieces are settings of hymns, sequences, responsories, and antiphons; and some of the textless pieces are very probably instrumental in conception. Among the last-named group appears a series of compositions with such fanciful titles as *Das yeger horn* ("The hunter's horn"), *Der fochss schwantcz* ("The fox's tail"), *Der kranch schnabil* ("The crane's beak"), *Der pfawin schwancz* ("The peacock's tail"), *Der ratten schwancz* ("The rat's tail"), *Dy ezels crone* ("The ass's crown"), *Dy Katczen pfothe* ("The cat's paw"), and *Dy krebis schere* ("The crab's claw"). Some of these were originally songs or motets, and others may well be dances, descriptive music, or at the very least compositions written for instrumental ensembles without any relationship to a text.

The most distinctively German of the pieces in these anthologies are the lieder, such as the anonymous *In feuers hitz* from the Glogauer Liederbuch (Example 8–8), in which the simple songlike melody in the tenor is accompanied by three other parts—two slightly faster-moving discants above it and a stable harmonic bass beneath it. Like many German lieder of the time, *In feuers hitz* uses the same music for each of its first two couplets and new music for the second quatrain, in a scheme known as *bar* form (consisting of two *Stollen* and an *Abgesang*—that is, AAB—for each strophe), one of the favorite formal designs of the earlier Minnesinger. The slightly awkward charm of the song depends partly on the way the composer has juxtaposed contrasting rhythms at different levels of perception—not only the four-square duple meter of the tune with the triple meter of the other voices but also the faster-moving altus, with unexpected triplet figures, in lively rhythmic counterpoint to the main melody.

In the first decade of the sixteenth century, humanism made its influence felt on German music through the efforts of the poet and scholar Konrad Celtes (1459–1508). In 1507 he encouraged his pupil Peter Treibenreif (or

EXAMPLE 8–8. Anonymous, *In feuers hitz,* mm. 1–5.

Petrus Tritonius, the Latin name he used in humanistic circles) to publish specimen settings of the odes and epodes of Horace to help students learn the metrical patterns of classical Latin. Tritonius composed music for these Latin poems in simple four-part chords and metrically irregular rhythms that carefully make a distinction between long and short syllables. Interesting and important as they are in the history of attempts by Renaissance musicians to incorporate precepts from the ancient world in their own work, Tritonius's settings are too plain and bare to be significant artistically, and they had no great part in determining the character of later German music. Such odes were regularly performed, however, in Latin school dramas throughout Germany during the sixteenth century, and several important composers, including Hofhaimer and Senfl, experimented similarly with classical meters, even borrowing some of Tritonius's melodies.

In addition to humanistic settings of classical Latin poetry, monophonic song also flourished in Germany during the early sixteenth century through the activities of the Meistersingers, self-conscious and pedantic groups of middle-class amateur musicians who modeled themselves on the noble medieval Minnesingers. They maintained organizations for the cultivation of singing and composing from about 1450 until about 1600 and devised elaborate rules for composing the rather stilted songs, many in *bar* form and based on biblical texts, that they sang to each other at contests held in their singing schools. The most famous of the Meistersingers, Hans Sachs (1494–1576), a cobbler in Nuremberg, wrote more than six thousand such songs, mostly set in notes of equal length and syllabically declaimed except for the rather elaborate melismas, or *Blumen,* that decorate the beginnings of lines and important points of articulation.

After the Glogauer Liederbuch was completed about 1480, no major collection of German polyphonic songs appeared until the second decade of the sixteenth century, when several anthologies were issued by various printers. Erhard Öglin of Augsburg published a collection of songs in partbooks in 1512, the first in Germany to be printed by movable type and the first to contain music entirely for four voices; a second volume, without date or publisher's name, may also have come from his shop. Peter Schöffer, son of one of Gutenberg's assistants, also issued two volumes of lieder, one in 1513 and a second perhaps a few years later. Arnt von Aich's Liederbuch, printed in Cologne, probably appeared toward 1520. These collections contain music by a host of minor composers, such as Jörg Brack, Heinrich Eytelwein, Malchinger, Adam Rener, Jörg Schönfelder, and Sebastian Virdung, as well as songs by two of the most important lieder composers of the period, Heinrich Isaac and Paul Hofhaimer (1459–1537). A third great song writer, Heinrich Finck (1447–1527), is represented in contemporary manuscripts, only later in printed sources.

This generation of composers can be said to have consolidated a later Renaissance style for German music, following the models established in the late-fifteenth-century manuscripts. While not abandoning the framework of the Tenorlied, these composers joined to it the technical features of music of the

Josquin generation. Tenorlieder came to be written regularly in four rather than three parts; they included considerable imitation, especially at the beginning of each song and often at the beginning of each of the very clearly differentiated phrases, underlining the greater equality of the voices (even though the altus was still often only a harmonic filler); and the superius often enjoyed a melodic line almost as finely and carefully shaped as the tenor.

Within their closely defined stylistic limits, German songs of this period use a variety of musical techniques and set poetry with a wide range of subject matter. The music of Isaac's famous *Innsbruck ich muss dich lassen,* for example, as nostalgic and touching as the poem it sets, is written in as simple a style as can be found among these compositions; its elegant melodies are combined to make a series of chord progressions only lightly animated by rhythmic interplay. Some of the comic songs, on the other hand, such as Isaac's *Es het ein Baur ein Töchterlein* or Hofhaimer's *Greyner zanner,* are filled with coarse peasant humor as well as considerable contrapuntal artifice, including extensive imitation. Many German lieder are love songs, like Hofhaimer's *Ich klag und rew,* which combines chordal and imitative textures and admirably demonstrates the superb craftsmanship of these composers.

Some fifteen or twenty years elapsed between the appearance of the Öglin, Schöffer, and Arnt von Aich songbooks and the publication of the next important German songbooks, those with music by the generation of composers following Isaac, Hofhaimer, and Finck—a period that saw some of the most decisive events of the Reformation in Germany. Johannes Ott, a Nuremberg book dealer and bibliophile (at one time he owned the Lochamer Liederbuch), gave a new impulse to the dissemination of secular music in Germany by editing *121 neue Lieder,* published by Hieronymus Formschneider in 1534; Ott prepared a second volume of 115 songs in 1544. Meanwhile, various other publishers and editors had begun to issue important collections, notably the six volumes of *Gassenhawerlin, Reutterliedlein, Graszliedlein,* and so on, printed by Christian Egenolff in Frankfurt am Main in and about 1535; the five volumes of Georg Forster's *Frische teutsche Lieder,* published by Johannes Petreius of Nuremberg between 1539 and 1560; the 65 *teutscher Lieder,* printed by Peter Schöffer and Matthias Apiarius in Strasbourg about 1536; and a volume, published in the same year by Formschneider, devoted chiefly to music by Heinrich Finck. These anthologies include music by earlier composers like Finck and works with French, Latin, and Italian texts, in addition to lieder by the newest composers. The sources preserve many works by the best composer of German lieder during the second quarter of the sixteenth century: Ludwig Senfl (ca. 1486–1542/43), a Swiss who served Maximilian I until the emperor's death in 1519 and then worked in Munich for Duke Wilhelm IV of Bavaria from around 1523 to his own death.

Although German songs from the late fifteenth century to about 1560 have come down to us in neatly divided chronological groups of sources, the character of the compositions changed only gradually; before 1560 there are no abrupt transformations of the style of lieder. Composers of the early sixteenth century incorporated the new musical techniques they had learned from Josquin and his contemporaries, and Senfl carried on in the tradition of his most important predecessors: Isaac, Hofhaimer, and Finck. Some of Senfl's songs are virtually indistinguishable in style from those by the earlier composers. Others, like *Ich stuend an einem morgen* (Example 8–9), one of several settings Senfl made of the same melody, do reflect new attitudes and techniques. It differs from the version by Isaac chiefly in its greater length and expansiveness and its greater floridness and complexity of counterpoint. At the same time, Senfl's individual lines are combined so as to create a more dynamic and predictable harmonic direction.

Senfl's secular music opened a new path in the history of German music of the Renaissance, but its influence soon died out as the rage for the international musical styles and genres reached the German-speaking lands. From the mid-1560s to the end of the century, a number of composers including the two great masters of the lied, Orlando Lasso and Hans Leo Hassler, published collections of songs in which musical works of international status and popularity, especially Italian madrigals and villanelle, began to crowd out the native German contributions. Without their words, many late-sixteenth-century lieder could be mistaken for Italian compositions, although the best works, such as Hassler's *Ach Schatz, ich thu dir klagen,* achieved a synthesis of the two styles. Like Thomas Morley, who played an analogous role in English music, Hassler was especially attracted to the lighter Italian forms, and his balletti, modeled on those by Gastoldi, are filled with catchy tunes and lively dance rhythms. One of Hassler's songs, *Mein G'müt ist mir verwirret,* a song with an amorous text from 1601, was adapted with new words for a published anthology of 1613, and then adapted yet again by Johann Crüger in 1647 to set another text appropriate for Passiontide, "O Haupt voll Blut und Wunden" (its most famous chorale setting being that in J. S. Bach's *St. Matthew Passion*).

Composers of sacred music in the Germanic countries during the fifteenth and sixteenth centuries did not cultivate as distinctively separate a musical style as did the composers of secular song, except in the congregational songs and other compositions that grew within the Protestant Reformation (see Chapter 10). Musically speaking, parts of Germany remained provincial outposts of western Europe throughout much of the fifteenth century: there even exist some examples of late-fifteenth-century German organum, in a style centuries out of date; and there are also large manuscript anthologies of sacred music, such as that prepared for Magister Nikolaus Apel of Leipzig (Leipzig, University Library, MS 1494), that contain quantities of Franco-Flemish music, as well as native German music written in a style not far different from the mainstream. By the turn of the century some German composers, such as Hofhaimer and Finck, were garnering the sort of recognition enjoyed by major composers in western Europe; and, as suggested, Isaac's *Choralis Constantinus,* composed for the German liturgy, was one of the great monuments of its time.

The connections between religious orthodoxy, liturgy, and musical style and genre during this richly textured period of Western musical history are by

EXAMPLE 8–9. Ludwig Senfl, *Ich stuend an einem Morgen*, mm. 1–15.

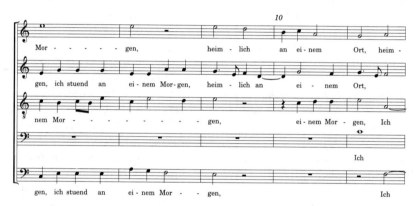

no means fully understood. During the second quarter of the sixteenth century, Geman musicians were faced with the necessity of declaring their religious sympathies; their decision did not necessarily, however, affect the style of their compositions. Many Protestant composers, such as Sixt Dietrich, Benedictus Ducis, Adam Rener, and Balthasar Resinarius, supplied florid polyphony for the Catholic liturgy, and their music does not differ along sectarian lines from that by their Catholic contemporaries such as Arnold von Bruck, Stephan Mahu, Senfl (who had Protestant sympathies), or Thomas Stoltzer, much of whose magnificent music was composed for the Hungarian royal court.

Though not altogether surprising in light of Martin Luther's advocacy of polyphonic music in worship, the publication in Germany of anthologies of sacred music originally composed for the Catholic liturgy, by Josquin and other great masters, raises a number of questions. One such publication, the *Novum et insigne opus musicum, sex, quinque, et quatuor vocum, cuius in Germania hactenus nihil simile usquam est eidtum,* in two volumes, edited by Hans Ott and issued by the press of Formschneider in Nuremberg in 1537 and 1538, contains one hundred motets. A landmark in the history of German music in the Renaissance, it tells us that there was an important market for the kind of sacred music it contains, and that the works of composers in the western European mainstream were known and eagerly received in Germany. No earlier collection contained so large a group of sacred compositions from every part of Europe. But as an anthology of the motet, it is decidedly limited: Ott, the editor, included only settings of texts that could have been accepted into Protestant worship. Motets in praise of saints were excluded altogether, and though a few motets were included whose texts originally praised the Virgin Mary, they were altered to honor Christ instead.

Spain and Her American Dominions

By the end of the fifteenth century, Spain was a participant in the musical mainstream and yet showed clear signs of independence. Franco-Flemish polyphony was widely performed in Spain, and many Flemish, French, and German musicians sang alongside native performers in Spanish cathedrals and chapels. Italy had close ties with Spain, especially with the kingdom of Aragon after Alfonso V of Aragon was declared king of Naples in 1442. It is no wonder, then, that Italian music was known in Spain or that some Spanish musicians lived and worked in Italy. Juan Cornago, for example, served both Alfonso and his son Ferrante in Naples, and he may have composed there his *Missa de la mapa mundi,* based on an Italian cantus firmus that refers to a map of the world. But a musical style with strongly identifiable characteristics seems to have grown up in Spain, as in other western European countries, only at the end of the fifteenth century, especially in the music written during the reign of the so-called Catholic Monarchs, Ferdinand of Aragon and Isabella of Castile. Their marriage in 1469 created a dynastic alliance between the kingdoms of Castile and Aragon, and ushered in an age of prosperity and political stability, sustained through careful economic, political, and social controls. Spain's wealth and power grew immensely as a result of its vast empire in the New World, which Spain acquired because Ferdinand and Isabella rather fortuitously if unenthusiastically supported Christopher Columbus's voyages of exploration and discovery.

As befitted the defenders of Catholic orthodoxy, Ferdinand and Isabella encouraged sacred music at their court. Their royal chapels grew to include a large group of composers, and the court became a center for sacred polyphony performed by the excellent singers from both the Castilian and the Aragonese royal chapels. Because of their prestige and the new political power invested in the monarchs, the two royal chapels were ever in contact with the mainstream centers of European music, yet they also cultivated strong ties to other Spanish musical establishments (at cathedrals, in monasteries, and in other noble households). Ferdinand and Isabella sought to emulate and even outdo the splendor of the Burgundian court chapel, but their investment in sacred music also expressed their devotion to the Catholic faith. Within Spain, such a large musical establishment devoted to serving the faith was as important to the promotion of Spanish music as was its high standard of musical excellence, which affected Spanish musicians employed elsewhere on the peninsula. Because they were staffed primarily by Spanish singers trained at the cathedral schools, the royal chapels were in close contact with other Spanish musical institutions.

The many composers who worked for the Castilian and Aragonese chapels were well paid. Among them Juan de Anchieta (1462–1523), Francisco de Peñalosa (ca. 1470–1528), and Pedro de Escobar (1465–1535?) were perhaps the best of the composers of Masses and motets, but other musicians demonstrated a high level of musical activity and accomplishment, among them Alonso de Alva, Juan Escribano, Juan Ponce, and Martín de Rivaflecha. A manuscript collection of sacred music now at Tarazona cathedral (Tarazona 2/3) is the most important repository of sacred music by Spanish composers in this period. Although it was probably not compiled for the monarchs themselves, a large manuscript miscellany at Segovia cathedral (called the Cancionero de Segovia) is our oldest source for sacred polyphony from the royal chapels in this period. Prepared around the turn of the sixteenth century, it is an important source for both Spanish and non-Spanish music, with pieces by composers such as Peñalosa and Anchieta alongside pieces by Franco-Flemish composers (such as Brumel, Compère, Isaac, Josquin, Obrecht, and Pipelare).

Among the sacred pieces in the Segovia manuscript, the motets in particular demonstrate that a distinctive Spanish dialect of the pan-European musical language indeed existed about 1500, especially when Spanish composers set texts associated with Holy Week and Christ's Passion or intended for use on feasts of local significance. This distinctive Spanish sound is more chordal, its strongly harmonic character resulting from chord progressions driven by the relationship between bass and superius parts, rather than the tenor-superius scaffold essential to mainstream modal polyphony. The words are projected with a clarity and directness unclouded by florid ornamentation or imitation, giving the music a stunning affective immediacy. The opening of one of the

Anchieta motets included in the Segovia manuscript, *Domine Jesu Christe qui hora diei ultima* (Example 8–10), exemplifies how the simplest chordal, declamatory texture could be used to project the text and dramatize the devotional character of a Passion motet. Its juxtaposition of harmonies seems, though, to demonstrate a concern for expression that goes beyond mere declamation.

Together with pieces in this unadorned but highly effective style, there are others in the Segovia manuscript (as in other Spanish sources from this period) that exemplify a fusion of mainstream musical techniques with local preferences, textures, and expressive tendencies. Like their northern counterparts, Spanish composers tailored their compositions to satisfy the requirements of locally important religious feasts, special liturgies, and local customs, but also cultivated the international style. Thus, Spanish sacred music offers an ideal opportunity for studying the dynamic relationship between center and periphery in this era of musical integration.

The largest and most characteristically Spanish repertory of music to survive from the age of Ferdinand and Isabella consists of secular songs, chiefly *romances* and *villancicos*. Many more song texts than musical settings have survived, in part because many music manuscripts have been lost, but also because the flowering of Spanish Renaissance secular song was essentially linguistic and literary in motivation. In their humanist promotion of the "arts of peace" and by dignification of Castilian as an elegant literary and courtly language, the Catholic monarchs pursued the renovation of elite Spanish culture after the courtly Burgundian model. Their courts became centers of learned discourse and humanist investigation, sparking a number of important publications. With Isabella's patronage, Antonio de Nebrija published a *Gramática sobre la lengua castellana* (Salamanca, 1492), the first Spanish vernacular grammar (and the first for any modern European vernacular); and the poet-musician Juan del Encina published his *Cancionero* (Salamanca, 1496), the first published "collected works" of a Spanish poet (and one of the first monographic publications in any European language).

The wealth of manuscript and printed evidence of the literary culture of the period is not matched by a similar wealth of musical sources. Five great manuscript cancioneros from the late fifteenth and early sixteenth centuries and one later printed anthology are our only sources for musical settings of romances and villancicos. The largest source of all, the Cancionero musical de palacio, now in the library of the royal palace in Madrid, preserves in some 458 items the music performed in the household of the Duke of Alba, one of Spain's most powerful grandees. The bibliophile Ferdinand Columbus, son of the explorer, acquired the Cancionero musical de la biblioteca Colombina for his library in Seville. It was copied out at the end of the fifteenth century and includes the earliest compositions to be found in this group of sources. The Cancioneiro musical d'Elvas (also known as the Cancioneiro musical e poético da Biblioteca Pública Hortênsia), copied in the sixteenth century and now kept at the municipal library in Elvas, Portugal, contains Spanish and Portuguese songs exclusively; they are all anonymous in the manuscript, but some are known to

EXAMPLE 8–10. Juan de Anchieta, *Domine Jesu Christe qui hora diei ultima,* mm. 1–23.

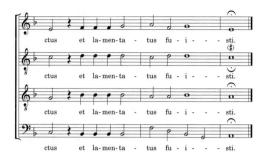

have been written by Juan del Encina and Pedro de Escobar. The fourth great manuscript cancionero (Barcelona, Biblioteca de Catalunya, M. 454), on the other hand, mixes Spanish secular music with sacred works by foreign and native-born composers, and the Cancionero de Segovia at the Segovia cathedral also contains villancicos in addition to Latin sacred music. The Cancionero de Uppsala (*Villancicos de diversos autores*) published in Venice in 1556, also belongs with this group of manuscript anthologies: despite its late date, some of its villancicos in two, three, four, and five parts (including one by Nicolas Gombert, the only composer named in the collection) were doubtless composed many years earlier, and all fall squarely into the earlier tradition, even if some display an amount of imitation that argues for a later date of composition.

Most of the Spanish songbooks, then, like their counterparts in other countries—French chansonniers and German Liederbücher—include various kinds of music and not simply Spanish secular songs; compositions with Latin, French, and Italian texts by foreign composers such as Fogliano, Josquin, Robert Morton, Ockeghem, Tromboncino, and the Fleming Johannes Wrrede (known as Urreda or Urrede in Spain) appear in these sources beside works with Castilian texts by native-born Spaniards—Alonso de Alva, Anchieta, Cornago, Escobar, Peñalosa, Ponce, and others. The best, and the best-represented, composer in the cancioneros is Juan del Encina (1468/69–ca. 1529), all of whose secular music seems to have been written when he was a young man in the service of the Duke of Alba. Although Encina later spent many years in Rome, and his religious commitment led him to undertake a pilgrimage to the Holy Land in 1519, he never published any liturgical music; at least, none survives today. He returned to Spain, where he served as prior at León during the last decade of his life.

The musical style and social status of the villancico and the romance are comparable to those of other vernacular genres we have studied. In spite of the frankly popular origins of many of the texts and tunes, the villancico was a courtly genre, yet its transparent musical style is quite distinct from the exquisite complexity of the contemporaneous Burgundian chanson. The villancico closely resembles the Italian frottola in musical structure and the Parisian chanson in declamation; its fixed and conventional repetition scheme is very similar to the French virelai or the Italian ballata. The music for one strophe of a villancico normally observes the following pattern:

Estribillo (Refrain)   *Copla* (Stanza)

Mudanza   *Vuelta*

A   B   B   A

To be more precise, villancicos often follow the formula aB cd cd aB, in which each letter represents a single line of verse or a couplet, and the capital letter indicates a repetition of the same text as well as the same music—that is, a refrain—though the refrain that ends both the *estribillo* and the *vuelta* (the B of aB) does not invariably appear. As in the frottola, the principal melody of a villancico, usually relatively simple and even tuneful, appears in the top voice. The bass provides solid harmonic support, and the one or two inner voices often seem to be little more than written-out realizations of harmonies implied by the bass. Escobar's *Coraçón triste, sofrid* displays the typical form and texture of the three-part villancico on a condensed scale, with a three-line estribillo and two couplets for the mudanza; Example 8–11 shows the music for the first two lines of the estribillo. Much of the effect of this relatively simple piece depends on the composer's surprisingly sophisticated handling of rhythm, not only his careful balancing of long against short notes and introduction of a disconcerting near-sequence at the end of the estribillo, but also his delightfully irregular phrase lengths.

Some villancicos have a more pronounced tonal (or at least chordal) focus than others; some, in fact, are nothing more than arrangements of one of

EXAMPLE 8–11. Pedro de Escobar, *Coraçón triste, sofrid*, mm. 1–11.

those standard chord patterns, such as the Passamezzo Antico or the Folia, that underlay so much music for dancing and entertainment in both Spain and Italy during the sixteenth century. For instance, Encina's *Hoy comamos y bebamos* is based on the Folia, a sequence of chords used by countless composers and improvisers for all sorts of pieces in the sixteenth and seventeenth centuries.

The way in which the bass lines rather than the tenors support and control the polyphony of the villancicos reminds us of the bass orientation of the frottola; and both genres use harmonic patterns and progressions of chords in a tonally logical manner, belying the traditional view that fifteenth- and sixteenth-century harmony consists exclusively of more-or-less fortuitous coincidences of melodic lines. But there are also significant differences between the two genres. The villancico has a far greater range of expressive possibilities than the frottola. The patterned dance rhythms of so many frottole are rare in their Spanish counterparts, with their more diversified and subtle rhythms. In addition, many villancicos establish a pathetic, contemplative, serious, or lyrical mood quite foreign to the frottola.

The overwhelming majority of Spanish songs in the early cancioneros are villancicos, but composers also set a substantial number of *romances,* long narrative poems of many strophes. Since the strophes are almost always quatrains, settings of romances usually consist of four phrases of music, presumably intended to be repeated over and over or as the basis for elaborate variations or *glosas.* The character of music and text in the romances suggests an earlier and now lost unwritten tradition of singing, but the preserved examples are idealized versions of each song, to be fully nuanced and realized by the performers in performance. The romances copied into the cancioneros were surely blueprints for sophisticated, courtly music; and though they have "harmonic" basses, like the villancico and the frottola, they also have supporting tenors, like the fifteenth-century chanson. Not surprisingly, Spanish composers were expert at writing sets of variations, in view of the multistrophic romances on the one hand and villancicos based on traditional patterns of chords on the other.

Juan del Encina's romances and villancicos establish their moods more sharply and succinctly than those by his contemporaries; they are more charming, more moving, or more tuneful. His romance *Triste España sin ventura,* for instance, probably written to lament the death of Queen Isabella or her son, Prince Juan, is touching despite its utter simplicity. *Gasajémonos de husía,* with its changes of texture and meter slightly more ambitious musically than others, compellingly invites the listener to abandon all cares and enjoy. Both it and *Hoy comamos y bebamos* were composed (probably in 1496 and 1494, respectively) for theatrical entertainments—*representaciones* or *églogas*—that Encina provided for the household of the Duke of Alba. Encina wrote the plays, composed the music, supervised the productions at carnival and other times, and sometimes even acted in them.

The villancico and the romance were still the principal genres of Spanish secular song in the later sixteenth century, after the deaths of Ferdinand and

Isabella and into the reigns of Charles V and Philip II, but in addition, Spanish musicians cultivated the art of the Italian madrigal and composed madrigal-like settings of Spanish poems. Between about 1530 and 1560, concurrent with an increasing vogue for romances, Italianate poetry at once erudite and lyrical was very much in fashion in Spain, and this, too, affected secular music. For example, in the Cancionero de Medinaceli (now in the private library of Bartolomé March in Palma), compiled about 1560, about half the manuscript is devoted to settings of madrigal-like texts—in Spanish, but in Italian poetic meters. The themes, poetic style, and poetic and musical content of these songs differ considerably from those of the villancicos and romances; the tone is grave and the themes are deeply serious, expressed through elegant but reserved musical means. The handful of Spanish composers who took up the challenge of setting the new Petrarchan poetry by writers such as Garcilaso de la Vega, Juan Boscán, Gutierre de Cetina, and Jorge de Montemayor responded quite differently to it than they did to the more traditional romance and villancico texts. Juan Vásquez (ca. 1500–ca. 1560) wrote expertly in both the Spanish and the Italianate genres; his collection of *Villancicos y canciones* for three, four, and five voices was published in 1551, his *Recopilación de sonetos y villancicos a quatro y a cinco* in 1560. Mateo Flecha the Younger (ca. 1530–1604) published a book of Italian madrigals in Venice in 1558, and his compatriot Sebastián Rabal published two books of madrigals (Venice, 1593; Rome, 1595), but the madrigal was especially prominent in a few collections published in Barcelona. Joan Brudieu (ca. 1520–91), a Frenchman, composed madrigals with texts both in Castilian and in Catalan that can stand comparison with those by the major Italian and Franco-Flemish musicians of his time; his book of *Madrigales* was published at Barcelona in 1585. Pere Alberch Vila published two books of *Odas* (odes) also in Barcelona (1560 and 1561), the first containing settings *a 4* of poems in Italian, Castilian, and Catalan.

The sixteenth-century *ensalada,* with its through-composed form and attention to text painting, might seem a likely offspring of the madrigal in Spain, but in fact it developed entirely as an Iberian genre. Ensaladas have textual quodlibets filled with fragments of popular music, street songs, dramatic exchanges, bits of satire, and quotations from scripture, the liturgy, and classical authors; they are a clever and amusing reflection of the everyday life of their times. Among the earliest known ensalada texts are those found in the works of the Portuguese poet Gil Vicente beginning about 1510, and pieces of the ensalada type by Peñalosa and Garcimuñoz are preserved in the Cancionero musical de palacio. The genre is defined in Juan Díaz Rengifo's *Arte poética española* (Salamanca, 1592), and the most characteristic examples are those by Mateo Flecha "el viejo" ("the elder," ca. 1481–ca. 1553), published in Prague (1581) in a collection prepared by his nephew, Mateo Flecha the younger. They include a number of witty masterpieces comparable to Janequin's descriptive chansons.

Whereas it is clear that royal patronage of music had an important effect on Spanish musical life at the court and beyond it in the late fifteenth and early sixteenth centuries, the extent to which subsequent monarchs Charles V and

Philip II actually affected the course of musical history in Spain is less easily judged. Individual monarchs—indeed, whole royal families—were "prisoners of ceremony," such that historians take into account the restrictive structures and political philosophies that manufactured the public image of the monarchy. From the time of Charles V, Spanish court administration and ceremonial were bound to a double inheritance from Castile and Burgundy. Musicians were hired, governed, and paid not through a single administrative unit but by various units, each with its own regulations, forms of payment, and (often conflicting) administrators. The character of the chapel was determined by this bureaucracy and by the Burgundian protocols that Charles V maintained. Even the assumptions behind the choice of music for royal occasions were largely a matter of tradition and ancestral emulation. Although the procedures and ceremonies of the administration known as the Casa de Castilla contrasted with those of the Casa de Borgoña (inherited by Charles V), the royal chapel and most of the musical posts at court, including that of *maestro de capilla,* belonged, in fact, to the Casa de Borgoña and were governed by the Burgundian protocols. The royal chapel, with its large group of Flemish singers classified for administrative purposes as the *capilla flamenca* and small group of Spaniards known as the *capilla española,* was directed by Flemish *maestros de capilla* until the last of this succession retired in 1634. Through the sixteenth century, the Spanish chapel recruited its singers in Flanders—surprising in light of the fact that Spanish singers were valued elsewhere, especially in Italy, and that quite a number of them sang in the choir of the papal chapel in Rome, but perhaps less so in light of the Burgundian inheritance that governed the chapel's musical activities.

Both Charles V and Philip II were extremely pious men, and they lavished great care on their choral establishments. Under Philip II, such eminent musicians during the 1540s and 1550s as Juan García de Basurto, Pedro de Pastrana, Francisco de Soto, and the great blind organist Antonio de Cabezón served in the royal chapel. A number of outstanding composers directed the choir during the second half of the sixteenth century: Nicolas Payen, Pierre de Manchicourt, George de la Hèle, and Philippe Rogier. Under their leadership, the repertory performed in the royal chapel itself preserved tradition through both the continued use of older music and the performance of newly composed music in the venerated Franco-Flemish style until well into the seventeenth century.

It is difficult to know how much the Spanish court affected the course of music elsewhere in Spain in the sixteenth century. The greatest Spanish composers before Tomás Luis de Victoria never were in royal service. Cristóbal de Morales (ca. 1500–53) spent all of his career in the service of the church, as did his most distinguished pupil, Francisco Guerrero (1527/28–99).

Born and educated in Seville, a distinguished center for music and of humanist erudition, Morales served as *maestro de capilla* in the cathedrals of Ávila and Plasencia before going to Rome to sing in the papal chapel for ten years (1535–45). By 1538 his reputation was such that the pope commissioned his motet *Jubilate Deo omnis terra* for the signing of a peace treaty at Nice between Charles V and Francis I; in the next year a pair of his motets was published in an anthology by Moderne in Lyons. Although his tenure as a member of the papal choir was highly successful, Morales seems to have desired a more prestigious and lucrative position. He probably offered his services to Emperor Charles V when the latter visited Genoa in 1543 and to Duke Cosimo de' Medici in Florence, to whom he dedicated two books of Masses in 1544. In 1545 Morales returned to Spain and took the job of *maestro de capilla* at the Toledo cathedral, only to find himself disappointed financially two years later. He seems then to have returned south, serving as maestro first to the Duke of Arcos at Marchena (near Seville) and then at the cathedral in Málaga, where he died in 1553. Apparently an unusually pious man, Morales left very little secular music. His fame and distinction rest entirely on his sacred music: twenty-two Masses (more than any other major composer of the post-Josquin generation); sixteen Magnificats, which enjoyed unprecedented fame during his lifetime and afterward; a set of Lamentations published posthumously; and more than eighty motets.

In his *Declaración de instrumentos musicales* (Osuna, 1555), the theorist Juan Bermudo described Morales as "the light of Spain in music" and wrote also of the "foreign music that today comes from the excellent Cristóbal de Morales, the profound Gombert, and other outsiders"—acknowledgment that one of his Spanish contemporaries considered Morales a composer who carried on the traditions of Franco-Flemish polyphony, perhaps with an Italian accent derived from his years in Rome. Bermudo's assessment comes close to the mark. Even if Morales did not meet or work with Gombert when he was a young man in Seville, his music reveals certain affinities with that of the northern master. Especially his two volumes of Masses, published at his own expense and under his personal supervision, show that Morales belonged in the mainstream of sixteenth-century polyphony. These and others of his Masses include works using all the compositional techniques prevalent at the time: parodies of Franco-Flemish motets, paraphrases and old-fashioned cantus-firmus arrangements of French and Spanish songs and Gregorian chants, and even one cycle of canons, a device used very little by Spanish composers before him but often employed by Morales in Masses and motets.

Morales is one of the major figures of the post-Josquin generation, the equal in every way of Gombert, Clemens, and Willaert. Like them he valued continuity and a compact dense texture over clearly articulated formal divisions and transparent sonorities; he tended to introduce imitation wherever he found an opportunity; he seldom interrupted the flow of polyphony for declamatory chordal passages; and his polyphony is shaped and controlled by a strong sense of harmonic direction and logical chordal progressions. If in his Masses he reveals himself to be a devout if reserved polyphonist, in some of his motets he shows a dramatic flair and a penchant for pungent, movingly expressive effects. The telling suspensions, for example, at the beginning of one of his most famous motets, *Lamentabatur Jacob*, make the sense of the text palpable in a way more characteristic of Josquin than of the more discreet and diffident Gombert. If the texture of his well-known *Emendemus in melius* is almost unrelievedly continuous, the ostinato (one of his favorite devices) on "Memento homo quia pulvis es et in pulverem reverteris" ("Remember, man, that thou art dust, and unto dust shalt thou return") sets up a dramatic tension between the insistent and forbidding threat of judgment in the tenor and the appeal for mercy sung by the other voices. Like Josquin, but also like some of his Spanish predecessors, Morales was committed not only to clarity of musical rhetoric and structure but to vivid text expression as well.

After Morales, who, as we have seen, worked primarily outside the Spanish territory, the best-known Spanish composer of the later sixteenth century was Francisco Guerrero. In Guerrero's music two streams of Renaissance musical technique converge, for he was heir to both the style and the practice typical of Spanish cathedral music in his youth and the mainstream of northern Renaissance polyphony brought to Spain especially in the works of Josquin and Gombert and through the works and tutelage of Morales. Guerrero first studied with his brother, Pedro Guerrero, an accomplished composer, and then with Morales sometime about 1545. The influence of Morales's teachings is seen already in Guerrero's first published works (Seville, 1555), and it was Morales who recommended him enthusiastically for his first job as *maestro de capilla* at the cathedral in Jaén (1546). Only a few years later, in 1549, he accepted a post at the Seville cathedral, where in 1551 he became tenured as assistant to the maestro, Pedro Fernández, and then finally became *maestro de capilla* himself in 1574. For the rest of his life, Guerrero held this post at the Seville cathedral. But he was not in any sense merely a provincial figure: he participated in the heady intellectual life of Seville, published all but one of his collections abroad, traveled widely, and enjoyed international prestige. He presented a collection of motets to the Emperor Charles V at Yuste in 1555 and a copy of his first set of Masses to the King of Portugal in 1566, and he traveled in the royal retinue that welcomed the Hapsburg princess Anna when she came to marry Philip II in 1570. He spent time in Italy in 1581–82 and again in 1588–89, on his way to the Holy Land. In 1590 he published *El viaje de Jerusalén*, a book about his journey that was popular enough to require more than one edition.

Guerrero emphasized the genre of the motet, producing over one hundred and fifty motets and settings of Latin liturgical texts, in addition to about twenty Masses, a group of sacred songs in the vernacular (the *Canciones y villanescas espirituales* of 1589), and quite a number of secular songs. Guerrero's attention to the motet was most likely a result of his employment as director of music at a busy cathedral, for his books of motets are strictly organized according to liturgical season (Advent, Epiphany, Lent, etc.) and provide settings of texts for the entire liturgical year, most of them drawn from the gospel or the epistle for the day in the temporal cycle. Thus they are clearly service music to be sung at appropriate points in the Mass. Their music, however, is anything but routine; it shows every sign of having been crafted to heighten and explicate the texts. In his motets, as in his secular songs and spiritual madrigals, Guerre was a true musical humanist. While he was a master of counterpoint (and of parody technique in his Masses), his use of melodic motives, contrapuntal devices, and striking harmonies and shifts in harmonic color, and his bringing out specific words of the text or its larger meaning by special declamation go beyond those in motets by his predecessors. Some of Guerrero's motets were composed especially for local devotions or in association with religious traditions in Seville, even though they were published and widely circulated elsewhere.

Guerrero's music was particularly widespread and influential in Spain's New World colonies long after his death, and manuscript copies of his music survive at a number of cathedrals in Mexico and in Central and Latin America. Even before Guerrero was famous, however, the transmission of Iberian musical culture to the New World had already begun in the 1520s and 1530s, when missionary priests from the religious orders came and established churches and schools for the education and conversion of native children. Music was especially important in the missionaries' program, and their attempts to teach the indigenous musicians to play and sing European music were enormously successful. By the 1540s, polyphony was a regular part of sacred services at a number of cathedrals in Latin America, and the next several decades witnessed the rapid growth of their musical forces and musical collections. The manuscripts copied or used in the colonies in this period reinforce our impression that the "Spanish" musical culture transmitted to the New World in the sixteenth and early seventeenth centuries reflected the same coexistence of Spanish and European musics that characterized musical life on the Iberian peninsula. Thus, pieces by Josquin, Isaac, Mouton, Compère, and Sermisy are found in the earliest surviving manuscripts from the colonies, alongside works by Iberian composers such as Peñalosa, Anchieta, Escobar, and Morales. Slightly later sources include music by Morales, Guerrero, and Palestrina, alongside pieces by some of the first Spanish and Portuguese musicians who traveled to the colonies to fill new posts announced by the colonial cathedrals. Hernando Franco (1532–85) left Spain to become the chapel master at Guatemala cathedral and later moved on to Mexico City. Gutierre Fernández Hidalgo (1553–ca. 1620), from Andalusia, assumed the post of maestro at the cathedral at Bogotá in 1584 and later moved to Quito, Cuzco, and La Plata; another *andaluz*, Pedro Bermúdez (b. ca. 1560) from Granada, became maestro at Cuzco cathedral in 1597. The Portuguese Gaspar Fernandes (ca. 1565–1629) left his position as a singer at the prestigious cathedral in Évora, Portugal, sometime between 1590 and 1599, when he was hired as an organist at the Guatemala cathedral. He later served as chapel master at Guatemala and then as chapel master and organist at Puebla cathedral (from 1606). At Puebla, Fernandes worked with and was succeeded by Juan Gutiérrez Padilla, who had been trained in Málaga and had served as maestro at Cádiz cathedral before his trip to the New World. These were the first chapel masters of New Spain, and they brought with them the fruit of their disciplined musical training in Iberian cathedral schools, the craft of polyphonic composition as practiced at distinguished centers such as Cádiz, Évora,

Figure 5. The Mexican native Diego de Valadés was the first mestizo to become a friar. His *Rhetorica Christiana* (1579) was the first book by a Mexican to be published in Europe and reflects the evangelical utopianism of his training. Valadés described the splendor created by native musicians and their instruments in the celebration of Christian rites. Note the group of singers, or *cantores,* in his allegorical A. a sixteenth-century Franciscan mission in Mexico. A group of boys are listening to the Franciscan monk from Flanders known as Pedro de Gante (ca. 1480–1572), who had been Valadés's teacher. Gante learned Náhuatl and was beloved for "teaching his native pupils every art known among us." Music was central to his method of imparting Christian doctrine while preserving indigenous customs and ritual. (Photo courtesy of the Edward E. Ayer Collection, The Newberry Library, Chicago)

Granada, Málaga, and Seville, and a knowledge of mainstream European musical techniques and repertories.

This is not to say that the indigenous peoples in the so-called New World lacked musical culture and traditions. We know about their music primarily from the documents concerning the Spanish clergy's attempts to control and regulate its performance, as well as the very successful compaign to teach the native musicians to play European instruments and sing sacred polyphony. Indeed, the first piece of vocal polyphony printed in he New World, *Hanacpachap cussicuinin,* carries a text in the Inca language, Quechua, and was "composed in music for four voices so that the [native] singers sing it as they enter the church in processions." It was published in the *Ritual formulario* of Juan Pérez Bocanegra, an instruction book for priests printed in Lima in 1631. All the sources, from the intricate and beautifully decorated Aztec codices to the letters, prose diaries, and reports of Spanish monks, priests, and administrators, indicate that the indigenous cultures were richly musical. Perhaps the most

Figure 6.   Depiction of an Aztec musician from the Codex Ixtlilxochitl (ca. 1600), a pictorial account of Aztec ritual life with inscriptions in Náhuatl and Spanish. The Spanish inscription explains that for this festival young boys in costume pull a cart lined with corn-stalk leaves (*hojas de caña de maiz*) in which a devil rides, dressed as a parrot and carrying a sceptor made of feathers. The cart is announced by musicians playing flutes (at the top right of the drawing). (Cliché Bibliothèque nationale de France, Paris)

important record of indigenous life in Peru from the period following the Spanish conquest is the *Nueva crónica y buen gobierno* written and illustrated in the first years of the seventeenth century by Guamán Poma de Ayala, a native who describes the customs of the Incas and other groups and their interactions with the Spaniards in Peru. He describes the songs, dances, and instruments used in traditional celebrations and rituals of the Inca world, and his reports confirm what we know from other sources as well about the rich variety of dances in Incan culture. Although a great deal is as yet unknown about the musical culture of the first centuries of the Spanish colonial epoch, we know enough to recognize the myriad implications of the confrontation and coexistence of European Renaissance values and indigenous traditions in the New World.

England

Two factors help to explain why a national musical style developed differently in sixteenth-century England than in other countries. First, Franco-Flemish polyphony did not have the same impact on English music that it had on music elsewhere. Whereas English musicians exerted a strong and immensely fruitful influence on the formation of an early Renaissance musical style during the first half of the fifteenth century, composers such as Walter Frye and John Bedingham (active in the middle and late fifteenth century) wrote music that is virtually indistinguishable in style from that by their Franco-Flemish contemporaries. Nevertheless, continental influences appear not to have made many inroads at home, even though foreign musicians such as the Flemish lutenist Philip van Wilder and the Italian musicians Ambrose Lupo, a viol player, and Dionisio Memo, an organist, served at the English court from the time of Henry VIII on. When the pervadingly imitative music of the post-Josquin generation reached England, it did not immediately effect any large-scale or basic changes in the national style, at least until the era of Tallis and Byrd.

Second, a distinctively English style did not take place in secular music, unlike similar developments in other countries, if the evidence of the surviving sources can be trusted. (So few English songbooks survive from the sixteenth century, however, that they may not reveal the true situation.) Several large manuscripts in the British Library, among them the Fayrfax Book (MS Add. 5465), the Ritson Manuscript (MS Add. 5665), Royal Appendix MS 58, and King Henry VIII's Songbook (MS Add. 31922) preserve carols and court songs from the late fifteenth and early sixteenth centuries by Gilbert Banester, John Browne, William Cornysh the younger, Richard Davy, Robert Fayrfax, and others. The carols are written in a florid style quite unlike that of the earlier carols. A curious combination of monophony, imitative writing, syllabically declaimed lines of verse, and elaborately decorated melismas (or instrumental interludes) characterize this repertory. King Henry VIII's Songbook includes, in addition to continental music, instrumental pieces (some of them in the same florid style as the songs in the earlier anthology), English court songs, and carols in a lively, attractive, and apparently indigenous style, by Cornysh, Fayrfax, King Henry himself, and many other composers. Except for the incompletely preserved *XX*

Songes of 1530 (formerly believed to be the work of the distinguished publisher Wynkyn de Worde), which is the only printed collection of English polyphonic music from the first half of the sixteenth century, the four manuscripts listed above are the major sources of early sixteenth-century English secular music. After them and until the great vogue of madrigals and related pieces in the last quarter of the century, English songs were preserved only sporadically. The Oxford organist Thomas Mulliner arranged a few for keyboard and included them in the anthology (known as the Mulliner Book) he compiled after 1550. In 1571 the relatively minor composer Thomas Whythorne (author of a fascinating autobiography, the earliest in the English language) published a volume of his own songs. Other manuscripts are scattered throughout a number of libraries.

English church music gives a very clear picture of the growth of a national musical style, although in this sphere, too, the situation in Britain was more complex than in most other countries, for the effect of the Reformation on English music was more widespread and more profound. Harrison (in the *New Oxford History of Music,* vol. III) neatly summed up the position of English church music at the beginning of the sixteenth century when he wrote that "conservative design and florid style were the most characteristic features of English compositions from the death of Dunstable to the Reformation." In the several decades before and after 1500, large-scale choral music in England was generally written over a cantus firmus in highly decorative and ornate counterpoint, more often in five, six, or more parts than in four or fewer. The first section of John Browne's magnificent eight-part votive antiphon, *O Maria salvatoris Mater,* which opens the Eton Choirbook, furnishes an excellent sample of the rich tapestry of nonimitative counterpoint woven around a cantus firmus (in this case as yet unidentified) that typifies this repertory. Following the common practice of his time, Browne divided *O Maria* into clear-cut sections, many of them built up gradually from a few voices to a climactic passage for full choir. The contrasts in texture, especially between full choir and solo sections, serve to articulate the structure. The luxuriant polyphony is well controlled, not only by the placement of tuttis, but also by important cadences that mark major points of articulation, by the inexorable progress of the cantus firmus, and by the simple harmonic schemes that underlie the dense, complex interplay of voices. The elaboration of this lucid structure by an intricate filigree of melodic and rhythmic detail produces an effect of great sumptuousness that Harrison has aptly compared to English Perpendicular architecture.

English composers of the late fifteenth and early sixteenth centuries set only a limited number of types of sacred pieces, each of which had a clearly defined place within the rituals of the church. Votive antiphons—Browne's *O Maria,* for instance—are paraliturgical compositions, often addressed to the Virgin Mary, which were intended to be sung at services apart from the Mass and the Office, such as evening celebrations before the Virgin's image in the "Lady-chapel" (in large churches, a chapel dedicated to the worship of the Virgin Mary) or in some other votive chapel. Festal Masses, reserved for ceremonial occasions and roughly analogous to the Great Services of Anglican church music, were often based on cantus firmi appropriate to the liturgical occasion at which they were performed; like earlier English Masses, those from the sixteenth century often lack a polyphonic Kyrie, and sometimes portions of the Credo are also omitted. Most English Magnificats, which formed the musical high point of the Office of Vespers, were written to be performed in an *alternatim* manner. Besides votive antiphons, festal Masses, and Magnificats, English musicians also composed regular liturgical antiphons and simpler Mass settings (many of them intended for performance at Lady Mass) as well as music written to replace parts of the chant during the liturgy, such as responds, hymns, Prosas, Alleluias, Sequences, and Passions.

The largest source of English church music from the turn of the century is the Eton Choirbook (Eton College, MS 178). This contains votive antiphons and Magnificats but no complete Masses, and includes music by some of the finest composers of the late fifteenth century, such as John Browne, Richard Davy, William Horwood, Walter Lambe, and Robert Wylkynson, as well as compositions by slightly younger musicians such as William Cornysh (d. 1523) and Robert Fayrfax (1464–1521). Fayrfax, one of the best of all the early Tudor composers, wrote music that is slightly less florid than that by his older colleagues in the Eton Choirbook, and in which melodic imitation plays a greatly increased role. But typically, the imitation in the verse from Fayrfax's *Magnificat "Regale"* shown in Example 8–12 is not as consistent or important to the structure as in most compositions by Franco-Flemish musicians of Josquin's generation or just after; it is unmistakably English. Indeed, the style of this Magnificat verse resembles that of the main corpus of the Eton Choirbook because of its continuous full texture and its use of a cantus firmus (in this case a faburden to the Magnificat chant—that is, a melody that originated as a counterpoint to the plainsong). But Fayrfax made a greater effort than the older English composers to create a homogeneous texture by writing the same sorts of melodies and rhythms for each voice, and since his individual lines are less decorated with elaborate detail, his music has a plainer sound. Along with two Magnificats, about a dozen motets, and several secular songs, five of Fayrfax's Mass settings *a* 5 survive complete, and they too reflect the composer's allegiance to a native tradition (slightly modified by his own personality and temperament). Aside from the *Missa O bone Jesu,* which makes some use of parody technique, they are all based on plainsong cantus firmi, which are, however, used quite differently in each work. For example, in the *Missa O quam glorifica* the chant appears but once in each movement, and in the *Missa Regali ex progenie* twice, whereas the nine notes taken from an antiphon for the feast of St. Alban that form the scaffold of the *Missa Albanus* are repeated over and over in the manner of an ostinato.

Until the Reformation, whenever English composers based their music on chants they used Sarum chants, versions of plainsong adapted for the rituals of Salisbury cathedral (hence called *Sarum*). This rite differed in many respects from the Roman liturgy. It prevailed in Britain throughout the Middle Ages and the early Renaissance until it was abolished in 1547; thus the last composers to

EXAMPLE 8–12. Robert Fayrfax, *Magnificat "Regale,"* mm. 1–12.

use only these distinctively English chants were those younger contemporaries of Fayrfax and Cornysh who died about mid-century, men such as John Redford, the two Scottish priests Robert Carver and Robert Johnson, and Nicolas Ludford (ca. 1485–ca. 1557), whose most remarkable works are seven relatively short Lady Masses, one for each day of the week. These Masses, for three voices, include sections from the Proper as well as the Ordinary of the Mass; they are intended to be performed *alternatim;* and they are all based on a mysterious repertory of melodies called *squares,* a word whose exact meaning is unknown, although scholars now suppose that squares were originally counterpoints to earlier plainsong cantus firmi.

The greatest musician by far among Ludford's contemporaries, and arguably the greatest of all English pre-Reformation composers, was John Taverner (ca. 1495–1545), whose magnificent music can be said to sum up developments in England during the first forty years of the sixteenth century, for it embodies most of the achievements of his contemporaries. Perhaps the most important feature of Taverner's music is his obvious desire to impose a rational control on its texture without forgoing entirely the earlier richness of sound created by constantly moving rhythms and by the melodic independence of individual voices. Thus, in an apparent effort to achieve homogeneity of texture and clarity of structure, Taverner introduced into his larger and more elaborate music frequent imitations, melodic sequences, ostinatos, canons, and, in his shorter and simpler music, chordal passages and sections of antiphonal dialogue between parts of the choir. Yet he continued to write counterpoint in the florid English manner; indeed, much of his music is more florid than, say, the church music of Fayrfax. One verse of Taverner's *Magnificat in the Sixth Tone* for four voices (Example 8–13) illustrates the extent to which the composer sometimes

EXAMPLE 8–13. John Taverner, *Magnificat in the Sixth Tone*, mm. 37–47.

integrated his texture by means of imitation. Although the cantus firmus (in the tenor) does not share in the imitation at the beginning of the excerpt, by the end the other voices are almost entirely taken up with echoing the descending sequence stated by the tenor.

The complete regularity of both the imitation and the sequence in this example is slightly unusual in Taverner's work; more often he preferred to vary some of the intervals in the point of imitation or the pattern of the sequence, perhaps to veil slightly the clarity of his design, or merely to enjoy the pleasures of asymmetry. Like Fayrfax, Taverner made some use of parody in his *Missa Mater Christi,* but several of his Mass settings are built over cantus firmi, all but one derived from plainsong. The one exception, *The Western Wind Mass,* is the earliest English Mass setting based on a secular tune. (Actually, the only other English Masses based on secular melodies are the two by Tye and Shepherd that use *Western Wind* and the *L'homme armé* Mass by Robert Carver.) The tune recurs nine times (eight times complete and the ninth truncated) in each movement, and is sung by the treble (that is, superius), the tenor, or the bass part; thus, the Mass is, in effect, a gigantic set of variations.

The section of the Benedictus from Taverner's *Missa Gloria tibi trinitas* on the text "In nomine Domini" apparently seemed to some mid-sixteenth-century English musicians particularly appropriate to play independently on instruments. It appears, for example, in an organ arrangement in the Mulliner Book of about 1560–70. Composers wrote new voices around the plainchant fragment—sometimes they even alluded to Taverner's version—and a whole repertory of *In nomine* pieces for viols and other instruments came into being; newly composed *In nomine* settings are found until the late seventeenth century.

Scholars have yet to investigate fully the effect that political and social change had on musical style in England in this period, yet music was affected decisively by historical events. For example, Henry VIII, who made the definitive break with the Church in Rome in 1534 and suppressed the monasteries during the same decade, was conservative in liturgical matters and allowed florid Latin church music to flourish. On the other hand, Edward VI, who ruled from 1547 to 1553, came close to suppressing the English musical establishment altogether. During his years in power an English Prayer Book was approved that allowed few opportunities for elaborate polyphonic music; choral foundations and other important musical organizations were abolished; and many organs and liturgical books were destroyed. When Mary Tudor came to the throne in 1553, she restored the Roman rite with all its music, but neither she nor her Protestant half-sister, Elizabeth, who became queen in 1558 and who finally confirmed the establishment of the Anglican Church as the state religion, could undo completely the damage that had already been done. From the 1540s onward, church musicians were subject to numerous shifts of policy, and each change in doctrine dictated changes in musical style. At the Chapel Royal some degree of continuity was provided by the fact that the personnel of the chapel remained wholly English and did not change automatically with successive monarchs. English composers continued to set both Latin and English texts. During Mary's reign, there was a resurgence of interest in the Latin motet (and in continental models), and even after Elizabeth's accession Latin church music was permitted in Chapels Royal, colleges, and public schools; hence it continued to be written and performed during the late sixteenth century, alongside elaborate Anglican anthems and services and simpler music designed for congregational participation. The term *anthem,* applied generally to a polyphonic setting of a religious text in English, had been used in the fifteenth century for polyphonic settings of votive antiphons and other devotional texts in Latin, especially for feast days, but evidence from the mid–sixteenth century suggests that by the 1550s English anthems became a standard part of daily Anglican choral services. Composers drew the texts of their anthems from the Bible, the Psalms, the Prayer Book, and other religious sources.

The series of religious crises notwithstanding, a number of superb composers during the middle third of the century and slightly later managed to produce a very distinguished body of sacred music. This group included William Mundy (d. ca. 1591), Osbert Parsley (1511–85), Robert Parsons (d. 1571), John Shepherd (ca. 1520/25–ca. 63), Christopher Tye (ca. 1500–1573), Robert White (d. 1574), and Thomas Tallis (ca. 1505–85), Gentleman of the Chapel Royal and the best of them all. During the lives of these men the Sarum rite was abolished and the interest in large-scale cantus-firmus Masses dwindled, although elaborate votive antiphons continued to be written during the last years of the reign of Henry VIII and into that of Mary, and a tradition of sacred music in English, especially anthems and choral services, came to be established. With the end of the Sarum rite, composers set previously neglected sacred texts, such as psalms, and they turned to parts of the liturgy that had been only rarely cultivated before, such as responds, hymns, and Lamentations. The style of the English anthems of the later sixteenth century is based in simple note-against-note polyphony; whether laid out in a chordal declamation shaped by the word accents (as in Richard Farrant's prayer-like *Hide not thou thy face*) or through motet-like points of imitation, the style of the anthem allows for clarity of diction and expressive flexibility in bringing out the sense of the text. As Thomas Morley put it, the composer's goal was "to draw the hearer as it were in chains of gold by the ears to the consideration of holy things."

The career of Thomas Tallis was definitely shaped by the changes in religious policy that took place during his lifetime. Tallis sang in the Chapels Royal of four monarchs, from Henry VIII to Elizabeth, and composed in a bewildering variety of styles. As a young man he continued the earlier English tradition and composed florid music that preserved the independence of individual voices to a much greater extent than did contemporaneous continental music. These first works of his maturity include not only extended votive antiphons but also the *Missa Salve intemerata virgo,* which makes use of parody technique. His grand seven-voice festal Mass, based on the cantus firmus *Puer natus est nobis,* may have been written to celebrate Queen Mary's marriage to Philip II of Spain. During his middle years Tallis composed a number of strictly liturgical compositions in which, possibly for the first time, he used imitation as the chief structural principle. During the reign of Elizabeth he wrote several motets in which the technique of pervading imitation became allied with a greater concern to associate the musical design with the words. If Tallis never became quite so "expressive" in an extroverted way as some late-sixteenth-century continental composers (Lasso and Victoria, for example), he nevertheless took care to invent melodies that fit the syntax and the rhythms of the words, and he presented the points of imitation in an order that enabled their contrasting pace and shape to reflect something of the meaning of the text as a whole. The beginning of *Salvator mundi* (Example 8–14), a motet from the first book of Latin music printed in England, *Cantiones sacrae* (published by Tallis in 1575 in his old age, in collaboration with his much younger pupil, William Byrd), demonstrates his skill at handling imitative counterpoint in the "modern" European manner. The forty-voice motet *Spem in alium,* a spectacular tour de force possibly commissioned for a great state occasion, shows a command of contrapuntal technique that belies the charge sometimes leveled against Tallis that his part writing is wooden and awkward. Finally, his Anglican services and anthems

EXAMPLE 8–14. Thomas Tallis, *Salvator mundi,* mm. 1–12.

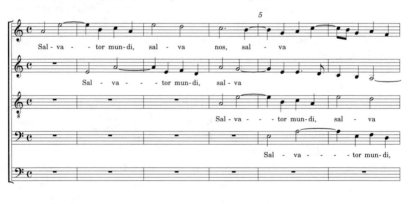

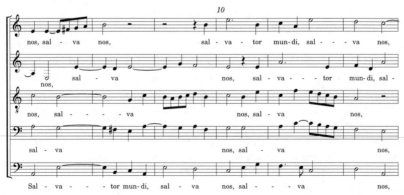

reflect dutifully the principles advocated by King Edward's musical advisers and other Protestants that the words should at all times be clearly audible. If an anthem like *O Lord, give thy Holy Spirit* mixes imitation and dialogue with its homophony, the music nevertheless preserves a simplicity of texture that ensures the clarity of the declamation.

Composers of church music in England responded very directly to their historical circumstances and, until late in the sixteenth century, stayed within the stylistic norms of the English tradition. Thus, in church music English composers remained at some distance from the technical developments of the Continental musical mainstream until late in our period. In the realm of secular music, however, the English madrigal is a case study in the adaptation of an international genre to regional tastes and circumstances.

The madrigal made its way to England in manuscripts that circulated there from the 1530s, probably because of the interest of amateur musicians who had social or business contacts on the Continent, and it was also known through the works of one of Queen Elizabeth's court musicians, Alfonso Ferrabosco. But the publication of Nicholas Yonge's *Musica transalpina* in 1588 is a landmark. Yonge's collection was published at a time when music printing was just becoming a busy industry in London, and this makes the collection's focus on the madrigal even more significant. In the preface to *Musica transalpina,* Yonge describes gatherings of musical amateurs, "gentlemen and merchants," who came to his house for the purpose of singing madrigals, and notes that his decision to publish *Musica transalpina* was prompted by a demand for "bookes of that kind" modeled on the printed madrigal collections issued in Italy. However, this and subsequent English collections did not present the absolute latest in madrigal fashion and radical experiment; in fact, the design and the content of *Musica transalpina* were based not on a representative Italian anthology but on *Musica divina* (1583), the first major collection of madrigals issued by Phalèse in Antwerp. The *Musica transalpina,* Thomas Watson's *Italian Madrigalls Englished* (1590), and several other anthologies are collections of madrigals with English translations or adaptations substituted for the Italian texts. This "Englished" manner of presentation made the genre accessible to English amateurs but also somewhat distorted the essential nature of the Italian madrigal; the close relationship between text and music is rendered more superficial through linguistic substitution.

It is hardly surprising, then, that in the 1590s, in the next stage of the madrigal's history in England, the composer Thomas Morley (1557–1602) brought forth his own madrigals in imitation of the lighter style of the pastoral Italian madrigal for three or four voices, and lively *balletts* and *canzonets* based on balletti by Gastoldi. Morley's published sets were popular enough to command more than one edition, and it was this uncomplicated style, setting English pastoral poetry in a rhythmically alive, Italianate manner, that established the genre in Britain. Example 8–15, *You that wont to my pipe's sound,* from Morley's *First Book of Balletts* (1595), is an example of this kind of piece, with

EXAMPLE 8–15. Thomas Morley, *You that wont to my pipe's sound,* mm. 1–17.

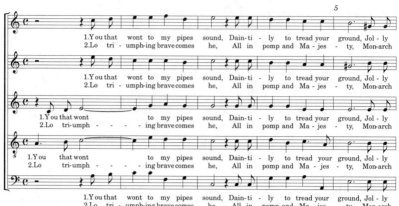

its strophic form, predominantly homophonic and homorhythmic texture, jaunty dancelike rhythms and consonant harmonies, and characteristic non-sense-word refrain. Here the refrain text "Lirum, lirum, lirum" is straight from Gastoldi—not surprising, given that Morley's ballett is an arrangement of *Vaghe Ninfe e voi pastor,* one of Gastoldi's *Balletti a cinque voci* of 1591 (Example 8–16). Morley's arrangement of the basic material from Gastoldi is slightly more contrapuntal; it is imbued with imitative entries at the opening, although the light counterpoint of Gastoldi's "lirum" refrain is left out altogether. The Morley piece has somewhat greater musical logic and complexity, and, in any case, Morley went well beyond merely providing English words to Gastoldi's music; from the balletto he derived primarily the homophonic, declamatory texture and the repeated rhythmic pattern.

Close to the turn of the century, a small group of younger composers ventured much further along the path Morley had cleared, composing original madrigals in a more serious style of contrapuntal polyphony, with a deeper affective range and greater attention to the words. Composers such as Thomas Weelkes (ca. 1575–1623) and John Wilbye (1574–1638) brought new depth to the genre, and with this a new spaciousness, a greater attention to musical structure, and a feeling of greater tonal solidity. Section *a* of Example 8–17 provides the opening of the first part of Weelkes's *O care, thou wilt despatch me,* one of his best-known madrigals, published in his *Madrigals of 5 and 6 parts* (1600). The affectively charged character of the music is wrought through a number of obvious devices (the agonizingly slow declamation of the text, sighing half-step figures in the melodic lines, carefully timed dissonances against the bass as suspensions, and a generally dejected feeling emphasized by the direct scalar descent in the soprano at mm. 7–13), all serving to provide a musical equivalent to the text's expression. The mood and the musical figures change for the next phrase ("if music do not match thee"), hinting at a lightness that never truly

EXAMPLE 8–16. Giovanni Giacomo Gastoldi, *Vaghe Ninfe e voi pastor,* mm. 1–21.

arrives, for the "Fa la" chorus here is ironic rather than carefree. The opening of the second section (*b*), "Hence Care; thou art too cruel," redoubles the melancholy with its return to slow declamation, descending lines, and the weeping semitones now turned to tortured chromaticism.

Like so many other composers in England and on the Continent, Weelkes made his living as a church musician. His madrigals appeared before he was established as choirmaster at Chichester cathedral, where he composed a great deal of music for the Anglican service, including almost fifty anthems. Many of these were probably too difficult for his choir to perform, and they display an approach to text setting very similar to that of his madrigals. Indeed, in pieces such as his *O Lord, arise* and in many anthems by his contemporaries (Morley's *Out of the deep* is another striking example), the musical logic and the use of musical figures or devices to "paint" words, images, feelings, or ideas in the text are overtly madrigalian, though the control of musical form and balance can justly be attributed as well not to the influence of the Italian madrigal but to the discipline of the long-standing English tradition of sacred music. Joseph Kerman has written that the English madrigal composers demonstrate a "preoccupation with purely musical devices, a reluctance to follow the Italians in splitting up compositions mercurially at the whim of the text." However problematic we may find Kerman's characterization of Italian madrigalists, this comment does get at a fundamental distinction between the English and the Italian approaches. Although English composers did imbue their madrigals and their vernacular sacred pieces with "madrigalisms" and other musical gestures and events expressive of their texts, they did not allow the quest for expressivity and affective depth to threaten their traditional values of structural clarity, integrity, and balance.

EXAMPLE 8–17. Thomas Weelkes, *O care, thou wilt despatch me.*

(a) First Part, mm 1–24

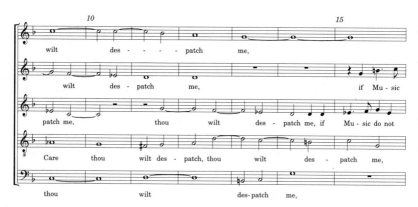

(b) Second Part, "Hence Care; thou art too cruel," mm 1–17

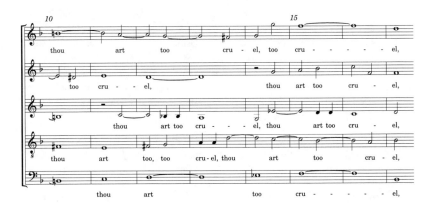

BIBLIOGRAPHICAL NOTES

Modern editions of chansons and other French music of the sixteenth century include Howard Mayer Brown, ed., *Theatrical Chansons of the Fifteenth and Early Sixteenth Centuries* (Cambridge, Mass., 1963); Charles Jacobs, ed., *Le Roy & Ballard's 1572 Mellange de Chansons* (University Park, Pa., 1982); Lawrence F. Bernstein, ed., *La Couronne et fleur des chansons à troys* (New York, 1984); Jane A. Bernstein, ed., *French Chansons of the Sixteenth Century* (University Park, Pa., 1985); and the 30 volumes of the series *The Sixteenth-Century Chanson: Previously Unpublished Full Scores of Chansons from the Ateliers of Le Roy, Ballard, Moderne, Waelrant, and de Laet,* ed. Jane Bernstein (New York, 1987–). Several volumes of RRMR, published by A-R Editions (Madison, Wis.) are devoted to sixteenth-century French chansons; see, in particular, vols. 36–37, *French Chansons for Three Voices* (ca. 1550), ed. Courtney Adams; vol. 38, *Thirty-six Chansons by French Provincial Composers (1529–1550),* ed. Leta E. Miller; and vol. 97, Jean de Castro, *Chansons, odes et sonetz de Pierre Ronsard,* ed. Jeanice Brooks. In the same series, the forthcoming *Responses and Repliques from Chanson Publications of Susato,* ed. Kristine K. Forney, will offer chansons by northern composers. A group of chansons by Jacques Arcadelt, ed. Everett Helm, is included in the *Smith College Music Archives,* vol. 5. There are complete editions of the chansons of Certon, ed. Henry Expert and Aimé Agnel (Paris, 1967); Claudin de Sermisy, ed. Gaston Allaire and Isabelle Cazeaux (CMM 52); and Clément Janequin, ed. François Lesure and A. Tillman Merritt (Monaco, 1965–66).

Many valuable earlier studies of the chanson are cited in the bibliography of the "Chanson" article in *TNG.* A central resource for studying the chanson at the court of Francis I is Daniel Heartz, *Pierre Attaingnant: Royal Printer of Music* (Berkeley and Los Angeles, 1969). The influence of royal musical patronage on sacred music at the French royal court is explored in John T. Brodbeck, "Musical Patronage in the Royal Chapel of France under Francis I (r. 1515–1547)," *JAMS* 48 (1995): 187–239. On the social context for the Parisian chanson, see Richard Freedman, "Paris and the French Court under François I," in *The Renaissance from the 1470s to the End of the 16th Century,* ed. Iain Fenlon (Englewood Cliffs, N.J., 1989), 174–96; and in the same volume, Frank Dobbins, "Lyons: Commercial and Cultural Metropolis," pp. 197–215. See also Dobbins, *Music in Renaissance Lyons* (Oxford, 1992), and Dobbins, ed., *The Oxford Book of Chansons* (Oxford, 1987). The collection *La chanson à la Renaissance,* ed. Jean-Michel Vaccaro (Tours, 1981), contains essays by specialist scholars on a number of issues surrounding the Parisian chanson (poetic theory and the relationship of words and music, the diffusion of the chanson to other countries, and the chanson and musical science, to name a few). See also Marie Egan-Buffet, *Les chansons de Claude Goudimel: analyses modales et stylistiques* (Ottawa, 1992).

Howard Mayer Brown's pathbreaking studies of the chanson include: "The Chanson rustique: Popular Elements in the 15th- and 16th-Century Chanson," *JAMS,* 12 (1959): 16–26; *Music in the French Secular Theater, 1400–1550* (Cambridge, Mass., 1963); "The Genesis of a Style: The Parisian Chanson, 1500–1530," *Chanson and Madrigal, 1480–1530,* ed. James Haar (Cambridge, Mass., 1964): 1–50; and, on the controversial origins of the Parisian chanson, "The Transformation of the Chanson at the End of the Fifteenth Century" (1970), reprinted in Ellen Rosand, ed., *Renaissance Music, part 1,* The Garland Library of the History of Western Music 3 (New York, 1985), 100–116. Brown's findings have been refined or contested in Lawrence F. Bernstein, "The 'Parisian Chanson': Problems of Style and Terminology," *JAMS* 31 (1978): 193–240, reprinted in Rosand, ed., *Renaissance Music, part 1,*

27–75; L. Bernstein, "Notes on the Origin of the Parisian Chanson," *JM* 1 (1982): 275–326; L. Bernstein, "Melodic Structure in the Parisian Chanson: A Preliminary Study in the Transmission of a Musical Style," in *Studies in Musical Sources and Style: Essays in Honor of Jan LaRue,* ed. Eugene K. Wolf and Edward Roesner (Madison, Wis., 1990), 121–90; Leeman L. Perkins, "Toward a Typology of the 'Renaissance Chanson,'" *JM* 6 (1988): 421–47; and Thomas D. Brothers, "Two Chansons Rustiques *a 4* by Claudin de Sermisy and Clément Janequin," *JAMS* 34 (1981): 305–24. See also Brown, "Theory and Practice in the Sixteenth Century: Preliminary Notes on Attaingnant's Modally Ordered Chansonniers," *Essays in Musicology: A Tribute to Alvin Johnson* (AIM, 1990), 75–100.

On important aspects of the relationship of text and music, see Kate Van Orden, "Sexual Discourse in the Parisian Chanson: A Libidinous Aviary," *JAMS* 48 (1995): 1–41; and Howard Mayer Brown, "*Ut musica poesis:* Music and Poetry in France in the Late Sixteenth Century," *EMH* 13 (1994): 1–63. The same volume of *EMH,* ed. Iain Fenlon, contains pathbreaking essays by Jeanice Brooks, Frank Dobbins, Richard Freedman, Isabelle His, Margaret M. McGowan, John O'Brien, Jean-Michel Vaccaro, and Philippe Vendrix on diverse aspects of the late-sixteenth-century chanson, all with citations to other writings.

The standard book on the sixteenth-century Italian madrigal remains Alfred Einstein's magnificent *The Italian Madrigal,* 3 vols. (Princeton, 1949), which includes well-chosen examples. A briefer introduction is Jerome Roche, *The Madrigal,* 2d ed. (Oxford, 1990). Harry B. Lincoln, *The Italian Madrigal and Related Repertories: Indexes to Printed Collections, 1500–1600* (New Haven, 1988), is an indispensable reference. On the business of music printing, see Suzanne G. Cusick, *Valerio Dorico: Music Printer in Sixteenth-Century Rome* (Ann Arbor, 1981); Donna G. Cardamone, "Madrigale a tre et arie napolitane: A Typographical and Repertorial Study," *JAMS* 35 (1982): 436–81; and Jane A. Bernstein, "Financial Arrangements and the Role of the Printer and Composer in Sixteenth-Century Italian Music Printing," *AcM* 63 (1991): 39–56.

On the madrigal in the early sixteenth century, see Walter Rubsamen, "From Frottola to Madrigal: The Changing Pattern of Secular Italian Vocal Music," in *Chanson and Madrigal, 1480–1530,* ed. James Haar, 51–87; Haar, "The Early Madrigal: A Re-appraisal of Its Sources and Its Character," in *Music in Medieval and Early Modern Europe,* ed. Iain Fenlon (Oxford, 1981), 163–92; Haar, "Towards a chronology of the Madrigals of Arcadelt," *JM* 5 (1987): 28–54; Richard Agee, "Ruberto Strozzi and the Early Madrigal," *JAMS* 36 (1983): 1–17, which offers evidence for the circulation in manuscript of early-sixteenth-century madrigals; and Iain Fenlon and James Haar, *The Italian Madrigal in the Early Sixteenth Century: Sources and Interpretation* (Cambridge, 1988). Chapters 3–5 of James Haar, *Essays on Italian Poetry and Music in the Renaissance, 1350–1600* (Berkeley and Los Angeles, 1986), focus on the madrigal in the sixteenth century. Haar, "Popularity in the Sixteenth-Century Madrigal: A Study of Two Instances," in *Studies in Musical Sources and Style: Essays in Honor of Jan LaRue,* ed. Eugene K. Wolf and Edward Roesner (Madison, Wis., 1990), 191–212, looks at two of the best-known works in the genre (by Arcadelt and Rore).

On the madrigal and literary influences in Venice, see Dean T. Mace, "Pietro Bembo and the Literary Origins of the Italian Madrigal," *MQ* 55 (1969): 65–86; Howard Mayer Brown, "Words and Music: Willaert, the Chanson, and the Madrigal about 1540," in *Florence and Venice, Comparison and Relations,* ed. Sergio Bertelli et al. (Florence, 1980), 2: 217–66; Martha Feldman, "The Composer as Exegete: Interpretations of Petrarchan Syntax in the Venetian Madrigal," *SM* 18 (1989): 203–37; and Feldman, *City Culture and the Madrigal at*

Venice (Berkeley and Los Angeles, 1995). On Rore's madrigals in particular, see Feldman, "Rore's 'selva selvaggia': The 'Primo libro' of 1542," *JAMS* 42 (1989): 547–603; and Jessie Ann Owens, "Mode in the Madrigals of Cipriano de Rore," in *Altro Polo. Essays in Italian Music of the Cinquecento,* ed. Richard Charteris (Sydney, 1990), 1–15.

Among studies of the late-sixteenth-century madrigal, see especially Howard Mayer Brown, "A Typology of Francesco Corteccia's Madrigals," *The Well Enchanting Skill: Music, Poetry, and Drama in the Culture of the Renaissance. Essays in Honour of F. W. Sternfeld,* ed. John Caldwell et al. (Oxford, 1990), 3–28; Ruth I. DeFord, "The Evolution of Rhythmic Style in Italian Secular Music of the the Late 16th Century," *SM* 10 (1981): 43–74; and Tim Carter, "Music Printing in Late 16th- and early 17th-Century Florence: Cristofano Marescotti and Zanobi Pignoni," *EMH* 9 (1990): 27–72. On the madrigal and other secular genres, see Ruth I. DeFord, "Musical Relationships Between the Italian Madrigal and Light Genres in the Sixteenth Century," *MD* 39 (1985): 107–68; and DeFord, "The Influence of the Madrigal on Canzonetta Texts of the Late 16th Century," *AcM* 39 (1987): 127–51. See as well Donna G. Cardamone, *The Canzone villanesca alla Napolitana and Related Forms 1537–1570* (Ann Arbor, 1981). An interesting glimpse into sixteenth-century music in Italy is offered by Cathy A. Elias, "Musical Performance in 16th-Century Italian Literature: Straparola's *Le piacevoli notti,*" *EM* 17 (1989): 161–73.

Garland Publishing's series *The Sixteenth-Century Madrigal,* under the general editorship of Jessie Ann Owens, is a 30-volume set with editions of an important cross-section of the madrigal repertory; in addition to pieces by lesser-known composers, a selection of madrigals by Verdelot makes up volumes 28–30. Editions of the works of the following important madrigal composers have been published by the American Institute of Musicology: Jacob Arcadelt, ed. Albert Seay (CMM 31); Costanzo Festa, ed. Alexander Main (CMM 25); Cipriano de Rore, ed. Bernhard Meier (CMM 14); Philippe Verdelot, ed. Anne-Marie Bragard (CMM 28); and Adrian Willaert, ed. Hermann Zenck and Walter Gerstenberg (CMM 3). Those of Domenico Ferrabosco are also available, ed. Richard Charteris (CMM 104); and madrigals and other works by Pisano, Coppini, Layolle, Corteccia, and others are edited in Frank A. D'Accone, ed., *Music of the Florentine Renaissance* (CMM 32). *Canzone villanesche alla napolitana and Villote* of Willaert and his circle in Venice, ed. Donna G. Cardamone, constitute volume 30 of RRMR; volumes 41–52 contain the complete madrigals of Andrea Gabrieli, ed. A. Tillman Merritt.

Other collections of madrigals include Alfred Einstein, ed., *The Golden Age of the Madrigal* (New York, 1942); Gertrude P. Smith, ed., *The Madrigals of Cipriano de Rore for 3 and 4 Voices,* Smith College Music Archives, vol. 6 (Northampton, Mass., 1943); Luigi Torchi, *L'Arte musicale in Italia,* 7 vols. (Milan, 1897–1908); and H. Colin Slim, *A Gift of Madrigals and Motets,* 2 vols. (Chicago, 1972). A selection of villanelle appears in *Das Chorwerk,* vol. 8. Gastoldi's balletti for three voices are published by W. Hermann (Berlin, 1927); those for five voices have been published by Michel Sanvoisin (Paris, 1968). The theatrical madrigals composed for intermedii in Florence in 1539 are published in Andrew C. Minor and B. Mitchell, *A Renaissance Entertainment: Festivities for the Marriage of Cosimo I, Duke of Florence, in 1539* (Columbia, Mo., 1968). Those for the Florentine intermedii of 1589 appear in D. P. Walker, ed., *Les Fêtes du mariage de Ferdinand de Médicis et de Christine de Lorraine, Florence 1589* (Paris, 1963).

The most comprehensive books on German secular music in the fifteenth and sixteenth centuries are written in German; among them are Ernst Bücken, *Das deutsche Lied* (Hamburg,

1939); Hermann Kretzschmar, *Geschichte des neuen deutschen Liedes* (Leipzig, 1911); Günther Müller, *Geschichte des deutschen Liedes* (Munich, 1925); and Helmuth Osthoff, *Die Niederländer und das deutsche Lied (1400–1640)* (Berlin, 1938). Among studies in English, Reinhard Strohm, *The Rise of European Music 1380–1500* (Cambridge, 1993), gives special attention to music in German-speaking lands; for the period 1450–1500, see especially the section devoted to "Central Europe: Masters and Apprentices," pp. 489–539. See also Strohm, "Native and Foreign Polyphony in Late Medieval Austria," *MD* 38 (1984): 205–30, concerning foreign music in German sources. The essays in John Kmetz, ed., *Music in the German Renaissance: Sources, Styles, and Contexts* (Cambridge, 1994), make a substantial contribution toward filling the lacuna in English-language studies on German music.

The Lochamer Liederbuch is published in a facsimile edition by Konrad Ameln (Kassel, 1925; new ed., 1972), and in modern editions by F. W. Arnold (*Jahrbuch für musikalische Wissenschaft*, 2, 1867), Konrad Ameln (the polyphonic music, Augsburg, 1929), E. Rohloff (the monophonic music, Halle, 1953), and Walter Salmen (Denkmäler der Tonkunst in Bayern, New Series, Sonderband 2, Wiesbaden, 1972). The secular music in the Schedelsches Liederbuch is included in Robert Eitner, *Das deutsche Lied des XV. und XVI. Jahrhunderts*, 2 vols. (Berlin, 1876–80). The Glogauer Liederbuch is available in a facsimile edition, ed. Howard Mayer Brown, Frank A. D'Accone, and Jessie Ann Owens, RMF, vol. 6 (New York, 1986), and in a modern edition in EDM, vols. 4, 8, 85, and 86 (1936–81). The Horatian odes of Tritonius and others were published by Rochus von Lilieneron, "Die Horazischen Metren in deutschen Kompositionen des 16. Jahrhunderts," *Vierteljahrsschrift für Musikwissenschaft*, 3 (1887). Some of Hans Sachs's Meistersinger melodies are in Georg Münser, *Das Singbuch des Adam Puschman, nebst den Originalmelodien des M. Behaim und Hans Sachs* (Leipzig, 1907).

The Öglin Liederbuch of 1512 is published in *Publikation älterer praktischer und theoretischer Musikwerke*, vol. 9 (Berlin, 1880); the Peter Schöffer Liederbuch of 1513 in facsimile (Berlin, 1908), and a selection from it in modern edition in *Das Chorwerk*, vol. 29; and the Arnt von Aich Liederbuch in H. J. Moser and E. Bernoulli, eds., *Das Liederbuch des Arnt von Aich* (Kassel, 1930). The Liederbücher of the 1530s, 1540s, and 1550s have been partially published in modern editions in various volumes of *Das Erbe deutscher Musik* and *Publikation älterer praktischer und theoretischer Musikwerke*. See also the facsimile edition of *Gassenhawerlin* und *Reutterliedlin (1535)*, ed. H. J. Moser (Augsburg and Cologne, 1927), and various volumes of Denkmäler der Tonkunst in Bayern and Denkmäler der Tonkunst in Oesterreich. The Codex of Nikolaus Apel is published in *Das Erbe deutscher Musik*, vols. 32 and 33 (Kassel, 1956–60).

Heinrich Isaac's German music is published in DTÖ vols. 18 and 32; Hofhaimer's music in H. J. Moser, *Paul Hofhaimer* (Stuttgart and Berlin, 1929); and a selection of music by Heinrich Finck in *Publikation älterer praktischer und theoretischer Musikwerke*, vol. 8. The complete works of Ludwig Senfl, ed. E. Löhrer, O. Ursprung, and others, are published in the 10-volume *Sämtliche Werke* (Wolfenbüttel and Zürich, 1937–72).

For music of the Spanish Renaissance, the series Monumentos de la música española is an invaluable resource. It includes, among other things, the *Cancionero musical de palacio*, ed. Higinio Anglés (vols. 5 and 10); the *Cancionero musical de la casa de Medinaceli, siglo xvi*, ed. Miguel Querol Gavaldá (vol. 8); the *Cancionero musical de la Colombina* (vol. 33, Barcelona, 1971); and the complete works of Cristóbal de Morales, ed. Anglés (vols. 11, 13, 15, 17, 20, 21, and 24). The edition of the works of Francisco Guerrero begun in 1949 remains incomplete, but several volumes are included in MME.

The *Obras completas* of Rodrigo de Ceballos, ed. Robert J. Snow, are in the process of publication (Granada, 1995–). The *Opera Omnia* of Juan de Anchieta have been published, ed. Samuel Rubio (Guipúzcoa, 1980); those of Johannes Cornago, ed. Rebecca L. Gerber, in Recent Researches in the Music of the Middle Ages and Early Renaissance, vol. 15 (Madison, Wis., 1984); two volumes of the works of Francisco de Peñalosa have been published, ed. Dionisio Preciado (Madrid, 1986 and 1991); and Francisco de Peñalosa, *Twenty-Four Motets*, ed. with extensive commentary by Jane Morlet Hardie (Ottawa, 1994), is the first volume of another series of his works in progress. For Juan del Encina's poetry and song settings, see Juan del Encina, *Poesía lírica y Cancionero musical*, ed. R. O. Jones and Carolyn R. Lee (Madrid, 1975). *Cancionero de la Catedral de Segovia*, ed. Ramón Perales de la Cal (Segovia, 1977), is a facsimile edition; the *Cancionero de Uppsala* appears in an edition by R. Mitjana, J. Bal y Gay, and I. Pope (Mexico, 1944); the *Cancioneiro musical d'Elvas* has been issued in two editions by Manuel Morais in the series Portugaliae Musica (Lisbon, 1977 and 1992), and as *The Elvas Song Book*, ed. Gil Miranda in CMM 98 (1987); Portuguese and Spanish songs from three other cancioneros are brought together in *Vilancetes, Cantigas e Romances do século XVI*, ed. Manuel Morais, Portugaliae Musica 47 (Lisbon, 1986). The *Recopilación de sonetos y villancicos* of Juan Vásquez, ed. Higinio Anglés (Barcelona, 1946), is available in MME 4, as is the Anglés edition of *Las ensaladas* of Mateo Flecha [the elder] (Barcelona, 1955); in addition, María Carmen Gómez has edited *La viuda* by Mateo Flecha [the elder] (Barcelona, 1992); and *La feria* and *La cañas* by Fray Mateo Flecha [the younger] (Madrid, 1987), as well as his *Il primo libro de madrigali* (Madrid, 1985). The madrigals of Brudieu have long been available, ed. Higinio Anglés and Felipe Pedrell (Barcelona, 1921). A selection of Spanish madrigals, ed. Miguel Querol Gavaldá, is in *Madrigales españoles inéditos del siglo XVI*, MME 40 (Barcelona, 1981). The best study to date of the Spanish musical response to humanist poetry is Don M. Randel, "Sixteenth-Century Spanish Polyphony and the Poetry of Garcilaso," *MQ* 60 (1974): 61–79; and in *Estudios sobre lírica antigua* (Madrid, 1978), Margit Frenk Alatorre provides a number of unsurpassed essays on the Spanish vernacular tradition.

The two fundamental studies of Spanish music in this period are Robert Stevenson, *Spanish Music in the Age of Columbus* (The Hague, 1960), and Stevenson, *Spanish Cathedral Music in the Golden Age* (Berkeley and Los Angeles, 1961), although both are outdated. The introductory essays by Higinio Anglés to his edition of *La música en la corte de los Reyes Católicos* (MME 1, 4, 5, and 10) are to be used with caution, as is his introduction to MME 2, *La música en la corte de Carlos V*. These can be supplemented by studies on particular topics touched on in this chapter, such as Tess Knighton, "The Spanish Court of Ferdinand and Isabella," in *The Renaissance from the 1470s to the End of the Sixteenth Century*, ed. Iain Fenlon (Englewood Cliffs, N.J., 1989); Knighton, "Northern Influence on Cultural Developments in the Iberian Peninsula during the Fifteenth Century," *RS* 1 (1987): 221–37; Alejandro Planchart, "Music in the Christian Courts of Spain," in *Musical Repercussions of 1492: Encounters in Text and Performance*, ed. Carol E. Robertson (Washington, 1992), 149–66; Iain Fenlon, "An Imperial Repertory for Charles V," *SM* 13 (1984): 221–40; Richard Sherr, "The 'Spanish Nation' in the Papal Chapel, 1492–1521," *EM* 20 (1992): 601–9; Robert Stevenson, "Josquin in the Music of Spain and Portugal," in *Josquin des Prez*, ed. Edward E. Lowinsky and Bonnie J. Blackburn (London, 1976); Maricarmen Gómez, "The Ensalada and the Origins of the Lyric Theater in Spain," *Comparative Drama* 28 (1994): 367–93; Jo-Ann Reif, "Music and Grammar: Imitation and Analogy in Morales and the Spanish Humanists," *EMH* 6 (1986): 227–43; Owen Rees, "Guerrero's *L'Homme armé* Masses and their Models," *EMH* 12 (1993): 19–54; José Romeu Figueras, "Mateo Flecha el viejo, la corte literario-musical del duque de Calabria y el Cancionero llamado de Uppsala," *Anuario musical* 13 (1958): 25–101; Juan José Rey, *Danzas cantadas en el renacimiento español* (Madrid, 1978); Richard Hudson, "The Folia Melodies," *AcM* 45 (1973): 98–119; Jane Morlet Hardie, "The Motets of Francisco de Peñalosa and their Manuscript Sources," 2 vols., Ph.D. diss., University of Michigan, 1983; and essays by a number of scholars in *Musique des Pays-Bas anciens—Musique espagnole ancienne,* ed. Paul Becquart and Henri Vanhulst (Louvain, 1988).

The writings of Robert Stevenson are basic to any investigation into music in the Spanish colonies in the sixteenth century; see his *Music in Mexico* (New York, 1952); *The Music of Peru: Aboriginal and Viceroyal Epochs* (Washington, 1960); *Music in Aztec and Inca Territory* (Berkeley and Los Angeles, 1968); *Renaissance and Baroque Musical Sources in the Americas* (Washington, 1970); *Christmas Music from Baroque Mexico* (Berkeley and Los Angeles, 1974); and *Latin American Colonial Music Anthology* (Washington, 1975). Another valuable starting point is E. Thomas Stanford and Lincoln Spiess, *An Introduction to Certain Mexican Musical Archives,* Detroit Studies in Music Bibliography, vol. 15 (Detroit, 1969). Examples of music by Spanish composers in Latin America are included in Stevenson's publications, as well as in a number of volumes of his *Inter-American Music Review.* The sacred works of Gaspar Fernandes have appeared as Fernandes, *Obras sacras,* ed. Robert J. Snow, Portugaliae Musica 49 (Lisbon, 1990); Snow's introduction offers an excellent concise consideration of the transmission of music from the Iberian peninsula to the colonies in the sixteenth century, as does his extensive introduction in Snow, ed., *A New-World Collection of Polyphony for Holy Week and the Salve Service: Guatemala City, Cathedral Archive, Music MS 4,* MRM 9 (Chicago, 1995).

A very complete survey of English music in this period is given in the relevant chapters of John Caldwell, *The Oxford History of English Music,* vol. 1 (Oxford, 1991); its bibliography includes a valuable list of modern editions. Other important studies are Frank Ll. Harrison, *Music in Medieval Britain* (London, 1958); Denis Stevens, *Tudor Church Music* (London, 1961); Peter le Huray, *Music and the Reformation in England, 1549–1660* (London, 1967); and D. C. Price, *Patrons and Musicians of the English Renaissance* (Cambridge, 1980). On secular music at Henry VIII's court see John Stevens, *Music and Poetry in the Early Tudor Court* (London, 1961); a more general introduction to English song is Edward Doughtie's *English Renaissance Song* (Boston, 1986). On the madrigal's early years in England, see Lydia R. Hamessley, "The 'Tenbury' and 'Ellesmere' Partbooks: New Findings on Manuscript Compilation and Exchange, and the Reception of the Italian Madrigal in Elizabethan England," *ML* 73 (1992): 177–221. The standard book on the later madrigal in England is Joseph Kerman, *The Elizabethan Madrigal: A Comparative Study* (New York, 1962). A general picture of music during Elizabeth's reign is given in Craig Monson, "Elizabethan London," in *The Renaissance from the 1470s to the End of the 16th Century,* ed. Iain Fenlon (Englewood Cliffs, N.J., 1989). For individual English composers, see the composer entries in *TNG;* and Paul Doe, *Tallis* (London, 1968).

The series Musica Britannica includes modern editions of the Mulliner Book (ed. Denis Stevens), King Henry's Songbook (ed. John Stevens), and the Eton Choirbook (ed. Frank Ll. Harrison). The 10-volume series Tudor Church Music (London, 1922–29) contains music by Taverner, Byrd, Gibbons, White, Tallis, and others. The series Early English Church Music (London, 1962–   ) includes anthologies of Masses, Magnificats, and organ music, as well as volumes devoted to music by Mundy, Orlando Gibbons, Tomkins, Tallis, and others. A selection of representative examples of English church music appears in *Treasury of English Church Music,* vol. 1, ed. Denis Stevens, and vol. 2, ed. Peter le Huray (London, 1965). For music in the reign of Edward VI, consult *The Tudor Church Music of the Lumley Books,* ed. J. Blezzard, RRMR 65 (Madison, Wis., 1985). See also Peter Philips, ed., *English Sacred Music, 1549–1649* (Oxford, 1991). The most complete collection of English madrigals is still E. H. Fellowes, *The English Madrigalists,* 32 vols., rev. Thurston Dart et al. (London, 1956–79).

NINE

INSTRUMENTAL MUSIC

The emancipation of instrumental from vocal music is one of the most important features of the history of European music between 1400 and 1600. Though very little survives of fifteenth-century instrumental music, a great deal of music published in the sixteenth century was intended specifically for instruments, and even more is described as "apt for voices or instruments" on printed title pages. Moreover, a number of new instrumental forms were developed: the *toccata,* the *ricercar,* the *canzona,* the variation, various dance types, and others. Toward the end of the fifteenth century and through the sixteenth, new instruments transformed the standard instrumentarium and made possible new musical sounds.

Although instrumentalists were generally not as famous or as prized by their patrons as were their singer-composer colleagues, they were ubiquitous in the musical landscape of the Renaissance. We know much more about the ways musical instruments were used in the Renaissance than in the Middle Ages, and more about the sixteenth century than the fifteenth. Most of what we know about fifteenth-century instruments and their players comes from visual art (paintings, engravings, drawings, illuminations, etc.) and from historical documents and literary accounts. Instrumental music is discussed in a scant few musical treatises of the fifteenth century, but these represent a major change in attitude, given that instruments and instrumental music had been considered unfit for scholarly or philosophical discourse in the Middle Ages.

Bartolomeo Ramos de Pareia's *Musica practica* of 1482 seems to be the first general work on music to bring information on actual musical instruments into a theoretical context. The passages about instrumental music in Johannes Tinctoris's *De inventione et usu musicae*, from the last quarter of the fifteenth century, offer additional rare and important evidence about the practice of instrumental music and its social uses. The writings (ca. 1440) of Henri Arnault de Zwolle, a physician and astronomer to the Burgundian court, give us the earliest detailed specifications on the construction of certain instruments, among them the lute, harp, organ, and harpsichord. Ramos, Tinctoris, and Arnault are the first to make writing about practical matters (the construction of instruments and the nature and social function of instrumental music) fit for presentation in formal intellectual discourse. Their attitude, rare in the fifteenth century, becomes the norm in the sixteenth century, when an increase in technical writing on instruments and their playing techniques accompanies a sudden vogue for printed anthologies of instrumental music. By the sixteenth century, the practice of music was highly valued as a social accomplishment, and widespread enough to elicit a spate of books intended for a public of musically literate amateurs.

Because professional musicians belonged to a low level in the fifteenth-century social hierarchy, and their music was not a subject considered generally fit for serious consideration, they tend to have less presence as individuals in the historical record than do composers. Moreover, because instrumentalists performed almost exclusively without written music in the fifteenth century, only a few manuscript musical sources actually document their work. It is hard to establish a firm distinction between instrumental and vocal "styles" in fifteenth-century music because the designation "instrumental" can be applied with assurance only to music for keyboard and lute notated in tablatures for these instruments—and a great deal of this music is related to vocal models.

As was noted briefly at the beginning of Chapter 2, instrumental music in the fifteenth century was considered either *haut* (loud) or *basse* (soft), and instrumentalists worked for the same courtly, ecclesiastical, or municipal institutions that employed singers and composers. The courts called on their wind bands and trumpet corps for loud music for outdoor ceremonies, processions, dances, and entertainments. Civic organizations, cities, and churches also called on instrumentalists (players of crumhorns, shawms, sackbuts, cornetti, or trumpets, for example) for similar functions; thus the work of these performers was not only audible but also absolutely necessary to many events in the regular public life of the later Middle Ages and the Renaissance. The music of soft instruments—such as the fiddle, lute, harp, psaltery, or lira da braccio—was appropriate in more intimate settings and to accompany indoor activities, such as dance parties and banquets, and for private enjoyment. Because the very best players usually improvised and played without the aid of written music, our understanding of what they played is largely inferred from descriptions of musi-

Figure 7. The nine Muses playing loud and soft instruments, from a manuscript of Martin le Franc's *Le champion des dames*. Euterpe, Urania, Melpomene, Calliope, and Erato are playing loud wind instruments, organ, and percussion; Thalia sings from a scroll; and Polyhymnia, Terpsichore, and Clio play the softer recorder, harp, and fiddle. (Cliché Bibliothèque nationale de France, Paris)

cal performances and the scant comments of writers on music (such as Ramos and Tinctoris), and deduced, in light of what we know about slightly later music, through study of the few fifteenth-century musical sources that survive.

The relationship between written music and musical performance changed substantially in the sixteenth century, thanks in large part to advances in music printing. Though scholars are continuing to refine our understanding of how music printing related to musical performance and to the social and economic history of music in this period, it is safe to say that the explosion of printed instrumental music in the sixteenth century surely was fired by the existence of a large market of well-off, educated amateur musicians and by the incorporation of musical performance into the everyday life of the literate classes. The instruction books or instrumental tutors published all over Europe in the sixteenth century are important sources for our knowledge of Renaissance musical pedagogy and performance practice, but they were not meant to guide professional players, whose distinction and excellence were still proved through the art of improvisation.

Sixteenth-century writers tended to classify instrumental music according to its performance forces and its social function, though, for our purposes, it may be divided into seven categories, taking musical genre and technique into account as well: (1) vocal music played by instruments, including a sizable repertory of "intabulations" of chansons, madrigals, lieder, motets, and even Masses for solo keyboard or lute; (2) settings of pre-existing melodies, chiefly arrangements of plainchant for keyboard instruments; (3) variation sets, including pieces built on ground basses and recurring chord progressions; (4) ricercars, fantasias, and canzonas; (5) preludes, preambles, and toccatas for solo instruments, in a style that incorporated some idiomatic writing for the particular instrument involved; (6) dance music; and (7) songs composed specifically for lute (or other plucked instrument) and solo voice. These categories overlap to some extent and were interchangeable as to medium; they include compositions for "whole" consorts of like but different-size instruments (viols, recorders, flutes, and so on) and "broken" or mixed consorts of different instruments, as well as music for solo instruments, both keyboards and plucked strings.

All kinds of instrumental music were printed in the sixteenth century, especially in Italy, where music printing got a vigorous start and musical culture was particularly supportive of innovation. The earliest printed lute music, for example, was Italian: the volumes for solo lute, two lutes, and lute and voice by Francesco Spinacino, Joan Ambrosio Dalza, and Francesco Bossinensis published between 1507 and 1511. Eustachio Romano's collection of duos, issued in Rome in 1521, was the earliest printed book devoted entirely to music for instrumental ensemble. Though Andrea Antico's volumes of frottole arranged for keyboard (1517) and Marco Antonio Cavazzoni's *Recerchari, motetti, canzoni* of 1523 were not the first music for keyboard to be published—the German Arnolt Schlick's *Tabulaturen etlicher Lobgesang und Lidlein* (1512) preceded them by some years—they reveal the common performance practices of the period and show that Italians were in the forefront of new developments.

It was during the second quarter of the century that the market for instrumental music became especially busy in Italy. A great many Italian virtuoso lutenists published one or more collections of their own music, beginning with the greatest of them all, Francesco da Milano, whose first volume appeared in 1536, the same year as an anthology containing examples of music by him and by his distinguished contemporaries Pietro Paolo Borrono and Marco d'Aquila, among others. Also in 1536, Adrian Willaert published his arrangements for solo voice and lute of an entire volume of madrigals by Philippe Verdelot, a collection that furnishes valuable insights into the way one great composer worked with music by another. From 1546 onward, a veritable avalanche of anthologies of lute music began to be issued, by Julio Abondante, Giovanni Maria da Crema, Marcantonio del Pifaro, Perino Fiorentino, and many others, and two composers of keyboard music, Jacques Buus and Girolamo Cavazzoni, achieved prominence during the same period. Moreover, during the second quarter of the century, a number of composers—among them Willaert, Julio Segni, and Giuliano Tiburtino—published abstract instrumental music—ricercars, fantasias, and duos—in greater quantity than ever before.

In like fashion, the second half of the sixteenth century witnessed a bewildering amount of activity among instrumentalists and composers of instrumental music in Italy. The Gardane and Scotto families in Venice, rival publishing houses, issued many volumes of music for lutes, keyboard instruments, and instrumental ensembles. In the 1580s and 1590s, Simone Verovio in Rome and Giacomo Vincenti in Venice published several series of canzonette along with arrangements of them for both lute and keyboard. Among the leading lutenists of the second half of the century were Vincenzo Galilei, Joan Pacolini, and Giovanni Antonio Terzi; and Andrea Gabrieli, Claudio Merulo, and Annibale Padovano, among others, distinguished themselves as composers of keyboard music. Though the Italians were strangely reluctant to publish volumes of dances for instrumental ensemble—those by Francesco Bendusi in 1553 and Giorgio Mainerio in 1578 were the only ones issued in Italy during the century—a large number of composers wrote and published abstract instrumental music for consorts, among them Adriano Banchieri, Andrea Gabrieli, Gioseffo Guami, Fiorenzo Maschera, Vincenzo Ruffo, and Lodovico Viadana.

In France the publication of instrumental music got its start with the activities of Pierre Attaingnant, who issued in the late 1520s and 1530s an important series of editions of music for keyboard and for lute, and later, several sets of ensemble dance music. In the second half of the century, publication of instrumental music in France and Flanders was dominated by the firms of Pierre Phalèse in Louvain and Le Roy & Ballard in Paris, who both issued all manner of music for various plucked string instruments (lute, guitar, and cittern). Phalèse, along with Jacques Moderne of Lyons, Tielman Susato of Antwerp, and Nicolas du Chemin of Paris, also published sets of ensemble dances, a specialty of the French as much in the sixteenth as in later centuries. Their predilection for the dance explains why the major treatise on dancing in the century, Thoinot Arbeau's *Orchésographie* of 1588, is French. Aside from Attaingnant's series, keyboard music and abstract instrumental music (ricercars and fantasias, whether for lute or for ensembles) were hardly published in France. (This suggests that these kinds of music were rarer there than in other countries, but the printed sources do not give us the whole picture.) Important churches and cathedrals in France displayed huge organs and must have hired expert players to justify the outlay of funds that it took to build these instruments. Documents from the French court tell us that superb players of instruments had enough work to justify their salaries, and a number of distinguished lutenists were active in France and Flanders, most notably the great Italian virtuoso Alberto da Ripa (Albert de Rippe), who worked at the French royal court, and Adrian le Roy and Guillaume Morlaye, both of whom wrote guitar music in addition to lute music.

In Germany, the sources tell us that keyboard music flourished especially. Arnolt Schlick's *Spiegel der Orgelmacher* of 1511 is one of the very first instruction manuals for a specific instrument to be printed anywhere, and it includes information about both constructing and playing organs. After Schlick's tablature anthology of organ music of 1512, a number of manuscripts from the first half of the century include music by German organists and harpsichordists, especially within that circle of musicians who looked to Paul Hofhaimer for their inspiration: Johannes Buchner of Constance, Leonhard Kleber, Johannes Kotter, and Fridolin Sicher. In the second half of the century a group of composers for the keyboard—Elias Nicolaus Ammerbach, Jakob Paix, Bernhard

Schmid, and others—decorated their works so heavily with quick runs and passagework that they have become known as "colorists."

Lute music from the first half of the sixteenth century was published in Germany by Hans Judenkünig, Hans Gerle, and Hans Neusidler. A great many German lutenists had their music printed during the second half of the century, among them Melchior Neusidler, Sebastian Ochsenkun, and Matthaeus Waissel, and their lute books typically contain arrangements of madrigals, motets, and chansons spiced with varying amounts of passagework, or dances, such as the two three-movement suites composed of *passamezzo*, a related *saltarello*, and a *ripresa* in Neusidler's 1574 book. Dances and unremarkable arrangements of vocal pieces seem to have been what the market demanded, although abstract pieces such as fantasias and ricercars were also included.

Curiously, relatively little music for instrumental ensemble was published in Germany until the last decade or two of the sixteenth century, although depictions of musical ensembles are plentiful in visual art of the period. For the most part, Hieronymus Formschneider's *Trium vocum carmina* of 1538—instrumental "songs" (*carmina*) for three parts—contains vocal music with the text omitted. The vast collection of ensemble dances issued by Paul and Bartholomeus Hessen in 1555 is, regrettably, preserved only incompletely. Not until the very end of the century did abstract instrumental pieces and also dances for ensembles begin to appear in print, by Gregor Aichinger, Adam Gumpelzhaimer, and Valentin Hausmann, among others.

In Spain the popularity of the vihuela (a plucked instrument of the viol family much like an early guitar), both as a solo instrument and for accompanying singers, meant that most of the instrumental music printed in Spain is concentrated in the seven books of vihuela tablature published in the sixteenth century—those by Luis de Milán (1536), Luis de Narváez (1538), Alonso Mudarra (1546), Enríquez de Valderrábano (1547), Diego Pisador (1552), Miguel de Fuenllana (1554), and Esteban Daza (1576). Volumes of fairly virtuoso keyboard music, adaptable for performance on harp or vihuela, were prepared by Luis Venegas de Henestrosa (1557), Antonio Valente, a Spaniard who worked in Naples (1576), and Hernando Cabezón, who published the music of his father, the famed blind organist Antonio de Cabezón, in 1578.

Similarly scarce is English instrumental music before the great "golden age" that began in the last decades of the sixteenth century. A handful of manuscript sources, chief among them the Mulliner Book of about 1530–75, reveal that John Redford, Thomas Tallis, and John (not William) Blitheman were outstanding composers of music for the keyboard before William Byrd. But only toward the end of the sixteenth and the beginning of the seventeenth centuries did great quantities of instrumental music circulate widely in England—in the magnificent manuscript and printed anthologies of keyboard music (such as the Fitzwilliam Virginal Book, My Ladye Nevells Booke, and *Parthenia*), the collections of music for solo lute and for lute and voice (by John Dowland and his contemporaries), and music for consorts of viols and also broken consorts (such as the Consort Lessons of 1599 by Thomas Morley).

Figure 8. The humanist interest in bringing modern musical practice closer to that of antiquity is represented in this woodcut of the mythical singer Orpheus playing the vihuela instead of a classical lyre. The enchanting quality of Orpheus' song draws even the wild beasts and birds to him. The motto surrounding the illustration christianizes the pagan hero of the humanist musical quest. Luis de Milán, *El Maestro* (1536). (Courtesy of Biblioteca Nacional de España, Madrid)

INSTRUMENTAL PERFORMANCE OF VOCAL MUSIC

That most vocal music in the sixteenth century was said to be "apt for voices or instruments" continued an older tradition; the central repertory for all instruments consisted of arrangements of vocal music. Most sources offer no details of scoring, but in a few volumes specific instrumentations are suggested. In 1533, for example, Pierre Attaingnant published two volumes of chansons in which some are marked as good for consorts of flutes or recorders and others as better for one kind of instrument than for another. Treatises on ornamentation reveal that performances of polyphonic vocal compositions arranged for solo melody instrument (or voice) accompanied by lute (or keyboard) were common. By the end of the sixteenth century and the beginning of the seventeenth, composers such as Giovanni Gabrieli and Claudio Monteverdi were beginning more regularly to suggest instrumentation.

The largest repertory of vocal music arranged for instruments is found in the many extant volumes of intabulations of Masses, motets, and secular music for keyboard instruments, as well as lutes, vihuelas, guitars, citterns, and other plucked strings. The technique of intabulation remained essentially the same throughout the century. In an ideal arrangement, according to Adrian le Roy and Vincenzo Galilei, who both describe the process in treatises on lute playing, the performer takes over as much of the vocal music as the technique of his instrument allows, although in practice the arrangers sometimes omitted one voice or rearranged the part writing.

Virtually all sixteenth-century intabulators added ornamentation to the vocal models they arranged. They did so partly out of necessity—fast passage-work helped to sustain the fragile sounds of the lute, vihuela, and harpsichord—and partly from a love of decoration, but mainly because the application of ingenious "gloss" or decoration also showed off the true "art" of both skillful intabulators and instrumentalists. Most players relied on stereotypical figuration patterns: runs, turns, and trills. The anonymous editor of Attaingnant's keyboard books adopted this technique in decorating Claudin de Sermisy's *Tant que vivray,* for instance, as a comparison of Example 9–1 with Example 8–1, the vocal original, makes clear. Earlier in the century, lutenists such as Spinacino and Dalza maintained a steady eighth- or sixteenth-note motion in their

Example 9–1. Claudin de Sermisy, *Tant que vivray* (keyboard arrangement by Attaingnant), mm. 1–12.

intabulations, obscuring the contours of their models beneath an avalanche of endless and directionless scale fragments. Similarly, the German keyboard composers of the last thirty years of the sixteenth century (Ammerbach, Schmid, Paix, and the other so-called colorists) overwhelmed their models with mechanical decoration. Heavily ornamented intabulations from mid-century often restrict the number of stereotyped figuration patterns applied to any one section of a composition. Repeated wherever possible, these ornamental clichés form a superstructure, so to speak, over the given vocal piece, a network of motives completely independent of the original conception. Diego Ortíz employed this technique in his arrangements for viol and keyboard. Some of the greatest lute virtuosi of the century, such as the Hungarian Valentin Bakfark and Francesco da Milano, went further than lesser musicians in transforming the original composition into an idiomatic and virtuoso instrumental piece through a profusion of ever-varied runs, turns, and trills. Thus many levels of relationship were possible between instrumental pieces and their vocal models, from a very close one, in which the vocal piece is reproduced as exactly as possible in an instrumental version, to a more distant one, in which the instrumental piece consists of entirely new polyphony that is merely based on borrowed motivic material or inspired by some characteristic musical idea in the model.

SETTINGS OF PRE-EXISTENT MELODIES

A number of composers in the sixteenth century wrote counterpoints for melody instruments against a plainchant cantus firmus. A *Da pacem* for four-part consort by Girolamo Parabosco, for example, is included in the anthology *Musica nova ... per cantar et sonar,* published in 1540; and Fernando de Las Infantas published in 1579 a collection of one hundred two- to eight-part canons over the cantus firmus *Laudate Dominum omnes gentes.* Some composers based their abstract instrumental music on melodic material borrowed from chant or from secular music: Annibale Padovano published ricercars in 1556 based on chant melodies, and Vincenzo Ruffo's *Capricci* of 1564 incorporates music from madrigals and chansons. German keyboard players, such as Ammerbach in his *Orgel oder Instrument Tabulatur* of 1571, set Protestant chorales for the organ, a practice that retained its capacity for both technical and expressive innovation for generations to come.

The largest category by far of instrumental settings of pre-existent vocal melodies, however, consists of liturgical organ music, arrangements of plainchants for use as a part of the divine service. Organists set not only parts of the Office hours (hymns, antiphons, psalm tones, and Magnificats) and the Proper of the Mass (Introits, Sequences, and hymns), but also complete Mass Ordinaries and single movements. Most of these pieces were designed for *alternatim* performance in which sections for organ alone alternated with chant or polyphony sung by a chorus or soloists.

Many of these organ compositions doubtless reflect the practice of improvising keyboard movements based on chant during the service. Some of the published music, therefore, is didactic in intent, meant to teach the young organist the techniques necessary for his profession. But some of the pieces— by Girolamo Cavazzoni, Andrea Gabrieli, Antonio de Cabezón, and others—are of the highest artistic caliber, among the best instrumental music of the entire century. The simplest technique for incorporating chant involved placing the borrowed melody, virtually unchanged, in any one voice (superius, alto, tenor, or bass) and writing counterpoints around it. Alternatively, each phrase of the chant was treated as a point of imitation in the manner of vocal polyphony. But sixteenth-century composers also decorated the cantus firmus and enlivened it rhythmically, especially when it was placed in the top voice, using the paraphrase technique familiar from fifteenth-century hymn settings. Sometimes they transformed the chant by constructing a new melody based on its most characteristic features and then using the thematic material derived in this way for imitative entries and other contrapuntal manipulations.

The French organ music published by Attaingnant in 1531 relies mostly on cantus-firmus technique, whereas German composers such as Hofhaimer and Schlick were more adventurous in adapting imitative polyphony to their instruments. Girolamo Cavazzoni, whose music was issued in the 1540s, was one of the most skillful musicians in transforming chant into new melodic entities. His skill was matched by the later Italian keyboard composers—Andrea Gabrieli, Claudio Merulo, and their contemporaries—whose liturgical organ music includes a variety of techniques: strict cantus firmus, paraphrase, transformation, and imitation. Those techniques plus faburden also appear in the English organ music by John Redford, Thomas Preston, Thomas Tallis, John Blitheman, and other predecessors of the great William Byrd.

The Italians and their Spanish counterparts (Antonio Valente, Juan Bermudo, and especially Antonio Cabezón) developed a sophisticated and partly idiomatic keyboard style that is an important stage in the separation of instrumental from vocal styles of writing. Keyboard composers throughout the sixteenth century, especially those Italians and Spaniards who worked during its second half, began to take regular advantage of the freedom of a solo player to interrupt the polyphonic texture by adding or omitting notes, melodic lines, or chords at will; and this approach (derived from a long-standing practice of improvisation) sometimes extended to sections written in an altogether freer toccata-like texture in which polyphony, chords, and runs (in one hand or divided between both) alternate, independent of any strict contrapuntal framework. Moreover, at times ornamental figures do not merely decorate an underlying simpler melodic line but become in themselves the principal thematic material; and these complementary motives are sometimes used to weave an elaborate web around the liturgical cantus firmus.

VARIATION SETS

Arrangements of polyphonic vocal compositions for solo keyboard and lute in which the top voice is decorated with figuration patterns constitute, of course, variations of the original. Compositions based on ostinati are in effect sets of continuous variations on a given theme and rhythmic pattern. Settings of cantus firmi are, as it were, a single variation on a melody. These and other variation techniques were known during the Middle Ages. But full-fledged sets of variations, in which some elements of a relatively short, autonomous song or dance are preserved through a number of repetitions while other elements change, did not exist before the sixteenth century. Sets of variations began to be composed, apparently independently, in Italy and Spain at about the same time. In England the practice began in the early sixteenth century but really flourished only later; in Germany and France it never developed to the same extent as in the other western European countries.

Sixteenth-century composers treated the music to be varied in several different ways, sometimes changing from one to another technique from variation to variation. In some variations they preserved the original melody more or less intact, either in the top voice or in one of the lower voices, and changed the counterpoints or chords around the *cantus prius factus*. In some, the process of variation consisted of ornamenting the melody itself with figuration patterns, and in others, the original melody disappeared and only its harmony and structure were preserved.

Some sixteenth-century sets of variations for lute or keyboard use figuration patterns either to embellish a given melody or to form motives that permeate the texture; a combination of the two techniques creates a more-or-less free texture adapted to the exigencies of solo playing. Many sixteenth-century sets of variations are continuous—that is, they are based on a simple melodic formula, harmonic progression, or repeating bass, and no complete stop separates one statement from the next. The ground basses especially cultivated by the English fall into this category, as do the Italian song and dance formulae— the passamezzo basses, the romanesca, the Ruggiero, the folia, and so on. Other sets of variations, on the other hand, differentiated one unit from the next more clearly by pausing at the end of each segment, as in the English variations on popular songs, such as William Byrd's on *Carman's Whistle, John Come Kiss Me Now, Walsingham,* or *The Woods so Wild* (excerpted in example 11-13). Finally, variation technique in the sixteenth century included the practices of varying the repetitions of dance-music strains and of grouping dance pieces in suites that were effectively variation sets. The former practice is exemplified by the English habit of writing out the repeated (but varied) strains of pavanes and galliards (thus: A A' B B' C C'). The latter practice consists in its simplest form of a dance in duple meter followed by an "after-dance" based on the same melodic material but reworked in triple meter; eventually, longer sequences of dances were all unified by being based on the same thematic material.

The earliest printed variation sets are those in Joan Ambrosio Dalza's book of lute music, the *Intabolatura de lauto libro quarto* published by Petrucci (Venice, 1508). These sets of variations are dances based on harmonic patterns, and they are all of the continuous sort. Other Italian lutenists did not begin to publish similar sets until the 1540s. Abondante (1546), Bianchini (1546), Gorzanis (1561), and others included dance pieces with varied sections, especially passamezzos, in their anthologies, and some wrote suites of dances in which each movement is built on the same melodic material.

Though many of the melodies and dances on which sets of variations were based were Italian in origin, they were pan-European in practice, linking the musical and social pastimes of the aristocracy and the well-off middle classes in different courts, cities, and regions. Thus the German composer Melchior Neusidler (1531–90) achieved great success in composing, among other things, Italian dances such as the passamezzo and the saltarello as variation pieces intended for performance by amateurs who could afford to buy musical collections. Neusidler was internationally known, thanks primarily to his music's being published in Italy, Germany, and The Netherlands. His *Intabolatura di liuto,* first published in the notation known as Italian lute tablature (Venice, 1566), was later issued as a book of German tablature (Frankfurt, 1573), and pieces from it were later also published in anthologies in French tablature by Phalèse of Louvain (1571 and 1574). Neusidler's *Pass'e mezo antico,* the opening piece in the 1566 *Intabolatura,* given here as Example 9–2, illustrates a typical short set of variations on a standard Italian dance bass pattern. A version of the passamezzo antico melody is heard clearly in the bass part of the piece in largely unadorned presentation. The first statement of the passamezzo comprises mm. 1–16, with the bass notes C B♭ C D G E♭ B♭ C G C. For this first variation, the figuration in the other "voices" of the texture is largely devoted to filling out the harmonies with short scale figures in a steady stream of eighth notes. This first section of the piece lays out the passamezzo and sets the pace of the dance. The second and third variations (mm. 17–32 and 33–48 of the piece, not shown) present slightly more inventive and challenging figurations for the lutenist, with passagework in smaller note values, but even these cannot rightly be termed "virtuoso." Though Neusidler's passamezzo is not among the most innovative or ingenious of sixteenth-century variation sets, it does exemplify the simple dance pieces that were published in great numbers in the later sixteenth century.

From the 1570s onward, German keyboard players, too, began publishing passamezzo settings: Ammerbach (1571), Schmid (1577), Paix (1583), and others. The French, by contrast, restricted their use of variation technique to writing out repetitions of dance sections with added ornamentation, as in the keyboard dances published by Attaingnant in 1531.

Spanish musicians and writers on music made an essential and widely recognized contribution to the practice and pedagogy of variation sets. Luis

Example 9–2. Melchior Neusidler, *Pass'e mezo antico,* mm. 1–32.

Example 9–2. (*Continued*)

de Milán ornamented repeated strains in the pavanes of his *El Maestro* (1536), but the Spanish tradition of published variation sets for vihuela, harp, and keyboard did not begin until 1538, when Luis de Narváez included variations (called *diferencias*) on Gregorian hymns, villancicos, and romances in his *Delphín de música*. Narváez was followed by the vihuelists Mudarra (1546) and Valderrábano (1547) and the keyboard composer Antonio de Cabezón (1578), whose variety of approach and richness of invention made him one of the outstanding masters of the genre. The Spanish viol player Diego Ortíz, maestro of the viceregal chapel in Naples, was author of the first printed manual on ornamentation for players of bowed string instruments. His *Trattado de glosas* (1553) includes instructions on the art of diminution for the solo viol as well as variations, or *glosas,* on various Italian grounds (passamezzo, la Spagna, folia, romanesca, Ruggiero) and ricercars based on other tunes, arranged for viol and keyboard or other accompanying instrument, such as the harp.

In England ground basses, including several "dumps" (perhaps implying "laments") and Hugh Aston's dance-based *Hornepype* (where the ground is actually in the tenor), were composed during the first half of the century; and passamezzo sets, such as those in the Dublin Virginal Book, and variations on chants, such as those in the Mulliner Book, showed that English composers were keeping abreast of continental developments. But it was not until the second half of the century that the variation flowered in England. Italian dance basses, varied repetitions in single and paired dances, cantus-firmus settings of chants, and variation sets based on popular tunes all appear in great profusion in the virginal books of the late sixteenth and early seventeenth centuries, the largest and most famous of which is the Fitzwilliam Virginal Book. Composers such as John Bull, Giles Farnaby, Orlando Gibbons, and, above all, William Byrd, carried the genre to its highest peak of perfection.

RICERCARS, FANTASIAS, AND CANZONAS

The terms *ricercar, fantasia,* and (in Spanish) *tiento* seem to have been used more or less interchangeably for an instrumental composition based neither on borrowed melodic material nor on a dance rhythm or a preformed scheme of any kind. By the middle of the sixteenth century, ricercars and fantasias came to be built on successive points of imitation, but they were not always imitative, and the terms do not presuppose any rigid formal plan. Canzonas, on the other hand, are compositions written in direct imitation of the intabulations of French chansons so common during the period; they are, therefore, more unified stylistically as a genre, even though composers during the seventeenth century transformed their character completely.

With the exception of France, where the evidence suggests that abstract instrumental music was not much cultivated during the sixteenth century, the genre comprising ricercars and fantasias was pan-European, but its nature changed drastically in the course of the century. The earliest sixteenth-century ricercars, those by Spinacino, Dalza, Francesco Bossinensis, and Vincenzo Capirola for lute, and Marco Antonio Cavazzoni for keyboard, are improvisatory in character. They mix sections that exploit the idiomatic performance styles of lute or keyboard—their penchant for runs, figuration patterns, and textures of varying density—with clichés borrowed from late fifteenth- and early-sixteenth-century vocal music.

Formal symmetry—balanced phrases, paired imitative motives repeated in various octaves, cadential extensions, and short imitative sections—characterize the ricercars and fantasias by composers writing between about 1530 and 1545, especially the lutenists Francesco da Milano and Marco d'Aquila and the keyboard player Giacomo Fogliano, composers whose technique seems to have been influenced most decisively by the works of Josquin des Prez and his contemporaries.

From about 1540 onward, ricercars and fantasias were more often than not based on a consistent use of points of imitation. This technique derived from the vocal style of the post-Josquin generation, especially that of the motet, even though ricercars and fantasias often concentrate on a smaller number of motives than do motets and some are even monothematic. The new technique appears to have reached print for the first time in the *Musica nova ... per cantar et sonar* of 1540, a collection containing ensemble pieces by Adrian Willaert, Giulio Segni, Girolamo Parabosco, and others. But it soon dominated instrumental writing in Italy—by Girolamo Cavazzoni, Jacques Buus, Annibale Padovano, Andrea Gabrieli, Claudio Merulo, and many others—and in other countries: Spain (Cabezón, Bermudo, and others), Germany and eastern Europe (Bakfark, Drusina, Melchior Neusidler, and others), and eventually England (fantasias by Byrd, Bull, Gibbons, and others). Indeed, the imitative ricercar is precisely the kind of composition Thomas Morley described (in his *Plaine and Easie Introduction to Practicall Musicke* of 1597) with his famous definition of a fantasia as "the most principall and chiefest kind of musicke which is made without a dittie ... that is, when a musician taketh a point at his pleasure, and wresteth and turneth it as he list, making either much or little of it according as shall seem best in his own conceit."

The canzona as an independent instrumental genre developed later than the ricercar. The earliest canzonas for keyboard—those by Marco Antonio Cavazzoni (1523) and his son Girolamo (1542)—all seem to be based on thematic material actually drawn from French chansons. Models have not been found, however, for all the *canzoni francesi* published in the lute anthologies by Barberiis (1546 and 1547) and Rotta (1546), and so it is not clear whether they are intabulations of vocal pieces or compositions conceived for lute in imitation of chansons. It was not until the 1570s that the instrumental canzona was regularly cultivated, first by Nicola Vicentino and Marc'Antonio Ingegnieri and later by Fiorenzo Maschera, Claudio Merulo, and Giovanni Gabrieli (writing for instrumental ensemble) and by Andrea Gabrieli, Merulo, Pellegrini, and others (for keyboard).

Instrumental canzonas, like the vocal models on which they were originally based, are generally divided into clearly articulated sections, with strongly metrical themes (often beginning with the rhythm ♩ ♪ ♪). The sections are often contrasting (for example, an imitative section followed by a more chordal one, or a section in duple meter followed by one in triple), and canzonas are sometimes built on a simple repetition scheme (ABA, ABB, AABC, or the like).

PRELUDES, PREAMBLES, TOCCATAS, AND INTONATIONS

Early-sixteenth-century ricercars, as we have seen, were often improvisatory pieces, apparently used to introduce performances of longer and weightier arrangements of vocal music (or perhaps vocal compositions themselves). They thus resembled the preludes and preambles that appeared in early-sixteenth-century lute books—those by Dalza (1508), Judenkünig (1523), Attaingnant (1529), and Gerle (1532 and 1533), for example. But whereas the ricercar came to be increasingly imitative and "learned," preludes preserved their improvisatory character. Filled with abrupt changes of texture, fast scale passages, and sections exploiting the idioms of lute or keyboard, they were the true successors of the fifteenth-century German keyboard preludes found in the Buxheim Organ Book and other manuscript sources.

In the second half of the sixteenth century, Italian and Spanish composers excelled in composing in these free forms. Andrea and Giovanni Gabrieli's brief *intonazioni* mix chordal sections with those in which fast passagework is accompanied by chords. The longer and more elaborate toccatas by Andrea and Giovanni Gabrieli, Annibale Padovano, and Claudio Merulo introduce imitative sections as well as passages in which figuration patterns are treated motivically in the midst of freer, more improvisatory textures. From the earliest years of the sixteenth century, these "free forms" for polyphonic instruments (lute, vihuela, harp, keyboards) were truly instrumental in style: they exploited techniques possible only on the instruments for which they were conceived and were incapable of being adapted for voices because they were not written in a consistent polyphonic texture.

The famous *Fantasía que contrahaze la harpa en la manera de Luduvico*, Example 9–3, from Alonso Mudarra's *Tres libros de música en cifra para vihuela* (1546), is a brilliant example of an instrumental piece whose musical ideas are derived exclusively from virtuoso improvisatory techniques idiomatic to instruments. This *Fantasía* is meant to sound like a free improvisation. It is a "fantasy" invented for vihuela but based on the playing techniques of the famous late-fifteenth-century Spanish harp player Luduvico (or Ludovico). In particular, this piece captures his special ability to play trills and accidentals or chromatic notes on the harp, and to punctuate his improvisations with unexpected cadences and chords on notes that fall outside the usual cadential points for the mode. Mudarra's fantasia in some ways resembles a prelude or a toccata. It begins slowly and delicately with a simple chordal gesture that is intensified through repetition. The texture becomes rhythmically animated as it proceeds, especially if the performer takes advantage of the free approach to tempo and rhythm that was conventional in sixteenth-century practice. The piece is really only "about" what the performer does to it, though Mudarra provided a focus for interest and excitement at its center by notating syncopations and daring harmonies—some of these being *falsas* or cross-relations, such as the F♯ against the F♮ after m. 125—and juxtaposing chordal passages (both strummed chords and plucked arpeggios on the vihuela) with trills and scales. Though composed for the vihuela and notated in tablature for six-course vihuela, this fantasia could also be played on the harp or keyboard, of course, but it could never be mistaken for a piece based on a vocal model, a dance rhythm, or a systematically applied contrapuntal subject.

DANCE MUSIC

In the sixteenth century a vast quantity of dance music was published, much of it consisting of relatively straightforward harmonizations of simple tunes or continuous variations on a set of chords or on a bass or soprano formula. Single dances included *basse-dances, tourdions, branles* of various kinds, *allemandes, courantes, pavanes, galliards,* and *passamezzos.* Pavanes and galliards were often combined into related pairs, as were allemandes and courantes, allemandes and saltarellos, passamezzos and galliards, and passamezzos and saltarellos. There were also groupings of three or more dances into suites, although there seems to have been no conventional ordering of

Example 9–3. Alonso Mudarra, *Fantasía que contrahaze la harpa en la manera de Luduvico.*

dance types; thus, the suites by Antonio Rotta of 1546 combined a passamezzo with a galliard and a pavane; Phalèse in 1570 published suites consisting of a passamezzo, a pavane, and a galliard; and Dominico Bianchini in 1546 followed a passamezzo with a pavane and a saltarello.

It is difficult to know the purpose for which published dance music was intended in the sixteenth century, whether for actual social dancing, for home entertainment, or as stylized artistic versions of more or less popular melodies. If the professional dance musician of the time had developed his ability to extemporize on tunes from a current repertory—to invent spontaneous sets of variations in the manner of today's jazz musicians—he would not have needed the elaborate polyphonic versions or the decorated arrangements for lute and keyboard that the printed books provided. At most an *aide mémoire* would

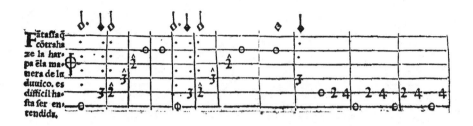

Figure 9. "Fantasía que contrahaze la harpa en la manera de Ludovico," opening line and concluding pages, showing vihuela tablature with rubrics, from Alonso Mudarra's *Tres libros de música en cifra para vihuela* (1546). Even the spacing of the numbers within the tablature suggests a certain degree of rhythmic freedom to the performer. The first rubric (fol. 13) identifies the piece and notes that "it is difficult until it is understood"; the second rubric (fol. 14v and 15) warns "from here until near the end there are some *falsas* [but] if they are played well they will not seem so harsh." (Courtesy of Biblioteca Nacional de España, Madrid)

Figure 9. *(Continued)*

have sufficed. Perhaps, then, the printed dance music of the time was intended for amateurs to play at home, or as "neutral" versions to enlarge the professional's repertory. Some dances—notably those by the English keyboard composers—were artistic, highly refined, and stylized; they were never intended for the ballroom.

Whatever the purpose, dance music was published for every medium—for lute, keyboard, and ensemble—and in every country of western Europe. In France and Flanders the flow of dance music from the presses was especially copious. Pierre Attaingnant, Nicolas du Chemin, and the firm of Le Roy & Ballard (all of Paris), Jacques Moderne of Lyons, Tielman Susato of Antwerp, and Pierre Phalèse of Louvain published dances for every conceivable combination. Many Italian and German anthologies of lute and keyboard music contain at least one or two dances, but arrangements for instrumental ensembles were relatively rare in those countries. The voluminous, though incompletely preserved, collections of almost five hundred ensemble dances made by Paul and Bartholomeus Hessen in 1555 partly make up for our ignorance about German ensemble dances from the early sixteenth century. These anthologies were in fact the earliest collections of ensemble dance music to be published in Germany. The first such collection printed in Italy—the *Opera nova de balli* by Francesco Bendusi—had appeared only two years earlier, in 1553. The artistic highpoint of the century, though, was reached in the magnificent dances for keyboard by the English virginalists, above all those by John Bull, Orlando Gibbons, and William Byrd.

Dancing was an important social activity in the life of sixteenth-century courts, and a number of different kinds of sources (works of visual art, letters, diaries, literary fiction, texts of plays, descriptions of important celebrations and entertainments) provide a context for the extant dance music. Aristocratic men and women, and even those members of the middle class who could afford it, took dancing lessons and danced both at intimate parties and at large balls that their dancing masters helped them organize and choreograph. The art of dancing was important to courtly etiquette, as a vehicle for flirtation and for the expression of both feminine and masculine virtue. It is no surprise that, by the close of the sixteenth century, a number of treatises on dancing had been published. These manuals contain instructions on how to participate in and execute the steps of late Renaissance courtly dances, along with pieces of actual dance music. Though the core of the repertory of courtly dances was pan-European (the same dances could be performed at courts in differing countries and regions, although often with important differences), all the dance treatises were published in Italy and France. All three of the large-scale Italian treatises—*Il ballarino* (Venice, 1581) and *Nobiltà di dame* (Venice, 1600) by Fabritio Caroso, and *Le gratie d'amore* (Milan, 1602) by Cesare Negri—and the most important of the French treatises, Thoinot Arbeau's *Orchésographie* of 1589, provide choreographic notations, pieces of dance music (in lute tablature and in mensural notation), and prose instructions and advice that reflect musical and social traditions and dance techniques current for decades before and after their dates of publication.

LUTE SONGS

Compositions for solo voice and lute or other plucked stringed instruments during the sixteenth century were, for the most part, arrangements of vocal pieces—frottole (those by Bossinensis, for example), lieder (Schlick), chansons (Attaingnant), madrigals (those by Verdelot arranged by Willaert), psalms (Morlaye), the lighter Italian forms (canzonette by Antonelli, Fallamero, and Verovio, for example), and even, perhaps, English ayres (Dowland and Cavendish). (Most ayres, however, were probably conceived in the first instance for solo voice and lute.) Some volumes contain music for one or more voices and one or more lutes (Adriansen's *Pratum musicum* of 1584, for example), others for voice and keyboard (Verovio's *Diletto spirituale* of 1586). But at least one volume published in the sixteenth century (and there were probably more) contains music apparently conceived directly for lute and voice, or for lute alone. Adrian le Roy's third book of lute music (1552) contains arrangements of psalm tunes for which polyphonic originals have never been found. They may never have existed, for the music seems to have been conceived for only two real parts, melody and bass. Le Roy apparently added a bass beneath each tune, which he had taken from the 1549 Lyons edition of *Pseaulmes cinquante de David, mis en vers français par Clément Marot*. He then filled out the texture, not with two other polyphonic voices, but with chords, planned for their harmonic effect; with divisions including a good many stereotyped figuration patterns; and with various formulas for ornamenting a given interval, for cadencing, and for arpeggiating or prolonging a triad. These lute songs, then, mix elements of vocal counterpoint with features that are specifically instrumental.

BIBLIOGRAPHICAL NOTES

Instrumental music printed in the sixteenth century is listed and described in Howard Mayer Brown, *Instrumental Music Printed Before 1600, A Bibliography* (Cambridge, Mass., 1965), which also includes a bibliography of editions to 1965. Jean Jacquot, ed., *La musique instrumentale de la Renaissance* (Paris, 1955), contains essays on various aspects of sixteenth-century instrumental music. Brown's essay on "Instruments" in *Performance Practice: Music Before 1600,* ed. Brown and Stanley Sadie (New York and London, 1989), is a superb overview of the repertory that also surveys the kinds of information that can be culled from both musical sources and Renaissance writings on performance. The 30-volume series *Italian Instrumental Music of the Sixteenth and Early Seventeenth Centuries,* ed. James Ladewig (New York, 1994), offers in modern edition music by some of the important composers or from the most influential printed collections.

On keyboard music in general, see Willi Apel, *The History of Keyboard Music to 1700*, trans. Hans Tischler (Bloomington, Ind., 1972); and Alexander Silbiger, ed., *Keyboard Music Before 1700* (New York, 1995). On lute music, see Jean Jacquot, ed., *Le luth et sa musique* (Paris, 1958); Jean-Michael Vaccaro, ed., *Le luth et sa musique 2* (Paris, 1984); Jean-Michael Vaccaro, *La musique de luth en France au XVIe siècle* (Paris, 1981); and John Ward, *Music for Elizabethan Lutes,* 2 vols. (Oxford, 1991). The essays in *Une fantaisie de la Renaissance: Compositional Process in the Renaissance Fantasia. Essays for Howard Mayer Brown, in memoriam,* ed. Victor Coelho and John Griffiths, in *JLSA* 23 (1990), are reflective of important new approaches. On Mudarra's *fantasía,* see John Griffiths, "La *Fantasía que contrahaze la harpa* de Alonso Mudarra; estudio histórico-analítico," *Revista de musicología* 9 (1986): 29–40. As a guide to the extensive literature on Renaissance music for plucked string instruments, especially that found in journals such as the *JLSA* and *EM,* D. H. Smith and L. Eagleson, *Guitar and Lute Music in Periodicals: An Index* (Berkeley, 1990), is useful, as are David B. Lyons, *Lute, Vihuela, Guitar to 1800: A Bibliography* (Detroit, 1978), and Meredith McCutcheon, *Guitar and Vihuela: An Annotated Bibliography of the Literature on Their History* (New York, 1985).

Ensemble music is discussed in Dietrich Kämper, *Studien zur instrumentalen Ensemblemusik des 16. Jahrhunderts in Italien* (Cologne, 1970; Italian trans. Torino, 1977). On German instrumental music and performing ensembles, see Keith Polk, *German Instrumental Music in the Late Middle Ages: Players, Patrons, and Performance Practice* (Cambridge, 1992), and numerous other articles by Polk listed there, but especially his "Voices and Instruments: Soloists and Ensembles in the 15th Century," *EM* 18 (1990): 179–98. On instrumentation and arranging vocal music for combinations of voices and instruments, see Howard Mayer Brown, *Sixteenth-Century Instrumentation: The Music for the Florentine Intermedii* (AIM, 1974).

The *TNG* articles by Ingrid Brainard and Julia Sutton on dance in the Renaissance (in the entry "Dance") are a good starting point and provide helpful bibliography, along with Meredith Little, "Recent Research in European Dance, 1400–1800," *EM* 14 (1986): 4–14. Other useful books or essays on dance include Daniel Heartz, "The Basse Dance," *AnnM* 6 (1958–63); Frederick Crane, *Materials for the Study of the Fifteenth-Century Basse Dance* (Brooklyn, 1968); Ingrid Brainard, "Bassedanse, Bassadanza and Ballo in the 15th Century," *Dance History Research: Perspectives from Related Arts and Disciplines* (New York, 1970); Barbara Sparti, "The Fifteenth-Century Balli Tunes: A New Look," *EM* 14 (1986): 346–57; Pamela Jones, "Spectacle in Milan: Cesare Negri's Torch Dances," *EM* 14 (1986): 182–96; and the essays in Walter Salmen, ed., *Musik und Tanz zur Zeit Kaiser Maximilian I* (Innsbruck, 1992). The important fifteenth-century treatise *De pratica seu arte tripudii* (*On the practice or art of dancing*) by Guglielmo Ebreo of Pesaro is available in a version edited, translated, and with an introduction by Barbara Sparti (Oxford, 1993). Other source materials are presented in *Fifteenth-Century Dance and Music*, 2 vols., trans. and ed. A. William Smith (Stuyvesant, N.Y., 1995). Thoinot Arbeau's treatise on dance, *Orchésographie* (Langres, 1588), is published in English translations by C. W. Beaumont (1925) and M. S. Evans (1948; reprint, 1967). Fabritio Caroso's *Il ballarino* is available in facsimile (New York, 1967), and his *Nobiltà di dame* in *Courtly Dance of the Renaissance*, trans. and ed. Julia Sutton (Oxford, 1986; rev. ed. New York, 1995). Examples from a number of dance treatises are included in Mabel Dolmetsch, *Dances of Spain and Italy from 1400 to 1600* (reprint, New York, 1975). See also Richard Hudson, *The Allemande, the Balletto, and the Tanz*, 2 vols. (Cambridge, 1986), an invaluable study with musical examples.

On musical instruments, see Anthony Baines, ed., *Musical Instruments Through the Ages*, and also several relevant chapters in *New Oxford History of Music*, vols. 3 (London, 1960) and 4 (London, 1968). See also entries for individual instruments in *The New Grove Dictionary of Musical Instruments*. On the viol, see Ian Woodfill, *The Early History of the Viol* (Cambridge, 1984); and on the early violin, see David Boyden, *The History of Violin Playing from Its Origins to 1761* (London, 1965). The most insightful study of the origins of the violin is Peter Holman, *Four and Twenty Fiddlers: The Violin at the English Court 1540–1690* (Oxford, 1995), 1–31.

TEN

THE MUSIC OF THE REFORMATION AND THE COUNCIL OF TRENT

The challenges to the authority of the Roman Catholic Church in Germany, France, and England were among the most important events of sixteenth-century history. These dramatic confrontations had important consequences for music. The form music took in the service of the new religions depended in large part on the temperaments and personalities of the leaders of the several Protestant movements and on their attitude toward Catholic ceremony and elaborate ritual. Whereas the puritanical John Calvin allowed only a restricted place for music in his city of God on earth, Martin Luther saw to it that the German countries under his spiritual leadership maintained a close connection with their rich musical past: a distinctively Protestant musical style evolved only very gradually in the Germanic countries. The effect on musical events of Martin Luther's successful battle with the Catholics is important not so much for what it accomplished in musical terms as for what it presaged for the future.

Martin Luther was very musical. He was a great admirer of Netherlandish polyphony and of the works of Josquin in particular; he played the lute and the transverse flute; he took a keen personal interest in the role of music in the new liturgical ceremonies; and he even composed some of the melodies intended for congregational singing, among them one of the best known and most rousing of all Protestant chorales, *Ein feste Burg ist unser Gott.* Luther had no desire to abandon the musical heritage of Catholic Europe. He did not intend that his vernacular liturgy, the *Deutsche Messe* of 1526, should completely replace Latin; and his enduring contribution to music—the encouragement of chorales, simple strophic hymns to be sung by the congregation—was prompted more by his desire that all the people should be exposed to the educational and ethical powers of music than by an attempt to drive elaborate polyphony out of the church.

From a variety of sources and using a variety of techniques, Luther and his musical advisers collected a large repertory of sacred songs in the vernacular simple and tuneful enough for the common people to sing. Some were Catholic hymns with translated or newly created texts; some were old poems set to new music or vice versa; some were new versions of older pre-Reformation German songs; and some melodies were composed especially to poems written for the purpose. Lutherans began publishing anthologies of sacred songs in the 1520s. In 1524 three collections with monophonic melodies appeared in print (the *Achtliederbuch* published by Jobst Gutknecht in Nuremberg and two volumes called *Enchiridion,* both printed in Erfurt), along with Johann Walter's *Geystliches gesangk Buchleyn,* which contains polyphonic arrangements of the Lutheran tunes. Walter, who was a singer in the chapel of Frederick the Wise of Saxony, then for many years municipal cantor in Torgau, and finally (after Luther's death) chapel master of the Elector of Saxony in Dresden, deserves his place in music history less for the greatness of his musical achievement, perhaps, than for his close association with Luther over a long period of time. In any case, there can be little doubt of his importance in shaping the new Lutheran music. Almost all his polyphonic sacred songs in the *Geystliches gesangk Buchleyn,* one or two of them in Latin but most in German, state the Lutheran melodies in the tenor. Some of his songs are simple note-against-note settings, the first attempts at the sort of German chorale so well known from the works of later composers and especially J. S. Bach. Others (such as Example 10–1) are more florid arrangements of the melodies, with free counterpoints woven around the tenor-voice cantus firmus and some imitations before and between statements of the borrowed melodies.

In the two or three decades after 1524, numerous collections of monophonic hymns were published that were similar in scope and purpose to the earliest anthologies. In 1526, Luther finished his proposals for the new German liturgy, the *Deutsche Messe,* based on the traditional service and partly adapting plainchant to the vernacular. In the 1530s and 1540s complete psalters, in German and with single-line melodies, began to appear; they were influenced by the tradition of congregational psalm singing at the cathedral of Strasbourg, for which Matthias Greiter, the principal singer there, had composed a number of melodies. Protestant German musicians also compiled some anthologies of polyphonic sacred songs, following the models established by Walter. Perhaps the most notable of these was the *Newe deudsche geistliche Gesenge ... für die gemeinen Schulen,* printed by Georg Rhau in Wittenberg in 1544 to give stu-

Example 10–1. Johann Walter, *Christ lag in Todesbanden,* mm. 1–10.

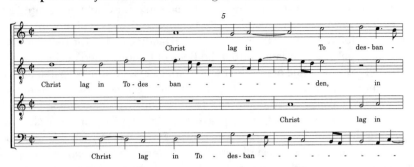

dents in German schools some understanding of church music and practice in performing it. The collection contains a cross-section of music in various German sacred song styles, by a wide variety of composers, among them Martin Agricola, Sixt Dietrich, Benedictus Ducis, Georg Forster, and Balthasar Resinarius, and even some Catholics, such as Arnold von Bruck, Lupus Hellinck, Heinrich Isaac, Ludwig Senfl, and Thomas Stoltzer.

In the 1560s and 1570s there seems to have been a reaction against congregational singing and simple German songs. Latin reasserted itself, and more complex polyphony came once more to be written by composers such as Jobst vom Brandt, Gallus Dressler, Matthaeus Le Maistre, and Jacob Meiland. In fact, throughout the latter half of the sixteenth century, Protestant composers continued to write music in Latin, and some Catholic composers did not disdain to set Protestant German texts. But by and large the later Protestant composers in Germany—such as Seth Calvisius, Johannes Eccard, and Leonhard Lechner—concentrated on German verses, although Hans Leo Hassler, the Protestant organist to the Catholic banker Octavian II Fugger of Augsburg before he became municipal chapel master in Nuremberg and then organist to the Elector of Saxony, wrote in all sacred genres, Catholic as well as Protestant, in both German and Latin.

Of all the Protestant reformers, John Calvin of Geneva was the most severe in his condemnation of Catholic liturgy and ceremonial, including music. He prohibited his congregation from singing in church any texts not found in the Bible, and he even discouraged his followers from singing at home any music except *chansons spirituelles,* sacred (and sometimes polemic) contrafacta of worldly French chansons. Since he disapproved of polyphony in church because he felt it detracted from a clear understanding of the words, the settings of rhymed metrical translations from the Book of Psalms issued in Geneva were restricted to a single line of music. (Psalm settings in four or more parts, most of them simple but some in elaborated polyphony, were nevertheless composed by French-speaking Protestant musicians in the course of the century, probably for domestic use.) In restricting the place of music in public worship, Calvin was following the example set by the earlier Swiss Protestant, Ulrich Zwingli, who, although a cultivated musician himself, was determined to keep music out of church services; Zwingli even sanctioned the destruction of Swiss organs.

When Calvin was banished from Geneva in 1538 he sought refuge in Strasbourg, and there he heard the congregational psalm singing led by Matthias Greiter. This inspired Calvin to take up his own earlier proposals in favor of the practice, and as early as 1539 Knobloch, in Strasbourg, published for him *Aulcuns pseaulmes et cantiques mys en chant,* a small collection of psalms in French translations, some by the French poet Clément Marot and some by Calvin himself, set to melodies partly derived from those composed by Greiter and his German colleagues in Strasbourg. Shortly after returning to Geneva in 1541, Calvin set to work to organize religious music in the community and, not surprisingly, placed much emphasis on the importance of congregational psalm singing.

It is ironic that the sober Calvin made such extensive use of psalm translations by the elegant and worldly poet Marot, who had originally prepared them for the Catholic court of Francis I. But after Marot escaped religious persecution in France by fleeing to Geneva, the council there was unwilling to support him while he completed his translations, and the job was taken over by Théodore de Bèze, whose complete psalter was not finished until 1562. An undistinguished musician, Guillaume Franc, who later published a psalter for the use of the Protestant church in Lausanne, began preparing the music for Marot's translations, but his job was soon taken over by Loys Bourgeois, the musician chiefly responsible for composing and arranging the melodies in the so-called Genevan Psalter. Bourgeois adapted chanson melodies, as well as plainchants and other earlier tunes, to the psalm translations, in which the originally irregular verse forms of the Bible had been turned into regularly recurring strophes so that they resembled hymns, in form if not in content. Even though Calvin disapproved of polyphonic settings of psalm tunes, Bourgeois published not only a collection of simple note-against-note settings, the *Pseaumes cinquante de David roy et prophète* (Lyons: Godefroy and Marcelin Beringen, 1547), but also more elaborate contrapuntal versions free of any borrowed melodic material. Of the many other polyphonic arrangements of the Marot-Bèze Psalter utilizing the tunes of Franc and Bourgeois, the most influential were those by the Frenchman Claude Goudimel. After his conversion to Protestantism in 1560, Goudimel set the entire collection twice. The two versions, one published in Paris in 1564 by Le Roy & Ballard and the other in Geneva in 1565, are both for four voices. Goudimel wrote the earlier collection in a slightly embellished chordal style, with the borrowed melodies mostly in the top voice, but in the later versions he returned to the earlier practice of placing the psalm tunes in the tenor, and he harmonized them with simple chords. Like the Dutch *Souterliedekens* (1540) that Clemens non Papa had composed and published more than twenty years earlier, Goudimel's psalm settings were intended for domestic use; in other words, they respected Calvin's strictures against polyphony within the church.

In England, policy with regard to church music was in an almost constant state of flux throughout much of the century after Henry VIII's break with Rome in 1534. Some Protestant extremists argued that music should be banned from church services, but the suggestion was never seriously followed. As in Germany, Latin motets and settings of liturgical texts continued to be written by some of the same musicians who composed anthems and services in the vernacular. Like Protestant communities in other countries, the Anglicans gradually developed a body of simple music fit for congregational singing. The first attempts at setting metrical psalm translations to music were made during Henry's reign. But Myles Coverdale's *Goostly Psalmes and Spirituall Songes* (ca. 1538), containing psalm translations and sacred songs supplied with monophonic tunes based on plainchant and German chorales, was suppressed by the king, who did not favor the Lutheran cause.

As a first step toward official liturgical reform, Archbishop Cranmer began to revise the service books for the Latin liturgy used in England. Cranmer's English version of the liturgy, *The Primer set forth by the King's Majesty and his clergy*, known as "the king's primer," was issued in 1545, for the express purpose of unifying and simplifying vernacular daily worship. This book does not contain musical notation, but the priests and choirs would probably have sung the English texts of the Office hymns in the 1545 *Primer* to melodies already familiar (indeed, known by memory) from the Latin service. A number of books with service music set to English texts were published about this time, however. In 1544 Cranmer's *A Letanie with suffrages to be said or sung*, with simplified music for use in processions and containing the traditional Sarum chants adapted to English words, was published in London. In 1549, only two years after Edward VI became king, the first *Book of Common Prayer* was prescribed for all services. In 1550 the Protestant musician John Marbeck (also Merbecke), organist at the collegiate church of St. George's, Windsor Castle, brought forth *The Booke of Common Praier Noted*, a service book in which he ingeniously arranged the traditional chants and composed new monophonic music in a mixture of measured time values and rhythmically free recitation to produce a collection of melodies that fit their English words very well indeed. But Merbecke's Anglican chant fell out of use as soon as a second *Book of Common Prayer* was introduced in 1552, a further step in the process of religious reform.

During Edward VI's reign the first translations of the Latin psalter by Thomas Sternhold and John Hopkins were published, without music. Some expatriate English Protestants, who had fled to the continent from their native country during the revival of Roman Catholicism under Mary, issued an Anglo-Genevan psalter in 1556 with music that was much indebted to the Calvinist melodies. But in spite of the various attempts in the 1540s and 1550s to set the psalms to music, the English psalter did not take its more or less definitive shape until the early years of Elizabeth's reign, when John Day of London published *The Whole Book of Psalms* in 1562; it was based on the Sternhold-Hopkins trans-lations and contained single-line melodies prepared by an unknown musician.

From the 1560s onward, psalters and collections of Protestant songs began to be issued for domestic and congregational use in ever greater num-bers. Among these were *Certaine notes set forthe in foure and three partes,* pub-lished by Day in 1560, which includes English contrafacta of Latin music written earlier in the century along with newly composed music for the Anglican service; and Archbishop Matthew Parker's *The Whole Psalter translated into English metre,* printed in 1567 or 1568 with nine settings for four voices by Thomas Tallis, which was never placed on sale. Among the other anthologies of simple Protestant music issued during the latter half of the sixteenth and the first half of the seventeenth centuries, several contain psalms intended to be sung either *a cappella* or with instrumental accompaniment. Richard Alison's *The Psalmes of David in Meter* (1599), for example, explains that the preexisting tune was "to be sung and plaide upon the Lute, Orpharyon, Citterne or Base Violl, severally or altogether, the singing part to be either Tenor or Treble to the Instrument, according to the nature of the voyce or for fowre voyces." That is, the tune alone could be sung either in the soprano or in the tenor octave, accompanied by an instrument (Alison supplies tablature for both lute and cit-tern); or his four-voice arrangements, with the tune in the soprano, could be sung *a cappella.*

Back on the Continent, Catholic reaction to attacks on the authority of the church and a genuine and long-standing desire to reform its abuses prompted the pope to call the Council of Trent, which met from 1545 to 1563. Toward the end of the cardinals' deliberations, which dealt with many aspects of the liturgy, they finally took up the role of music in sacred services. They dis-cussed it in 1562 and 1563 and appointed a commission consisting of eight car-dinals, of whom Carlo Borromeo and Vitellozzo Vitelli were the central figures, which met in Rome in 1564 and 1565 to study the problem further and to implement the suggestions of the Council within the papal organization in the city of Rome. At the beginning of their deliberations on music, Cardinal Otto von Truchsess von Waldburg, Bishop of Augsburg and Protector of Germany, had asked his private chapel master, Jacobus de Kerle, to compose settings of ten devotional Latin poems, the *Preces speciales pro salubri generalis concilii,* which were regularly performed at the Council's prayer sessions. Waldburg and the Italian prelates compared sacred music by the leading composers of their respective countries: Orlando di Lasso from Munich and Palestrina and Francesco Rosselli from Rome. The belief that the cardinals were saved from banning polyphony from the liturgy by the timely intervention of Emperor Ferdinand I is based on evidence that is highly ambiguous, to say the least; and the charming fable that church music was saved for all time by the performance before the cardinals of Palestrina's *Missa Papae Marcelli*, after angels had dictated it to him, has absolutely no foundation in fact.

The Council did not issue specific directives for practical reform but, rather, in keeping with the nature of an ecumenical council, formulated a general policy that the bishops were expected to implement at local levels. The consensus that emerged from the discussions of the Council centered on two important matters: the corruption of the liturgy caused by the introduction into it of secular elements, and the difficulty of understanding the words of sacred ritual if they were obscured by florid polyphony. The liturgy, which in the past had sometimes been neglected, should be maintained properly, according to the cardinals, and profane music (presumably including Masses built on secular compositions) should be banished from the services. Moreover, composers should make certain that the sacred texts they set polyphonically were clearly audible and therefore comprehensible to the congregation. To that end the Commission of Cardinals in 1565 tested various Masses for their intelligibility. Very probably they listened to a Mass especially written for the occasion by Vincenzo Ruffo and possibly also to a chromatic Mass by Nicola Vicentino. (Borromeo is known to have asked Vicentino to write such a work, but the composer's response is unknown and no Mass by him survives.) We do not know what else they heard. Their final rulings stressed once again how important it was that the sacred texts be understood even when enhanced by music; the commissioners encouraged the correct accentuation of Latin and warned against excessive melismas.

The deliberations of the Council of Trent and its subsequent Commission of Cardinals made explicit the ideals of the Counter-Reformation and gave strong support to the objections against florid polyphony that had been raised again and again over the years. Doubtless the reformers influenced the development of church music in succeeding generations, but they did not succeed in effecting basic or radical changes in musical style. Even after the Council, composers still often based their Masses on madrigals and chansons, and elaborate counterpoint continued to be written even by those late-sixteenth-century composers who paid lip service to the aims of the reformers in their title pages, prefaces, and dedications.

BIBLIOGRAPHICAL NOTES

Much of the scholarly writing on music and the Reformation is in German. Among studies in English, a fine overview of music and Reformation motivations and attitudes is the opening chapter, "The Reformation, Liturgical Change, and Hymnody," of Robin Leaver, *'Ghostly psalmes and spirituall songes,' English and Dutch Metrical Psalmes from Coverdale to Utenhove 1535–1566* (Oxford, 1991), although the book concentrates on English and Dutch music in the Reformation; see also Leaver's extensive bibliography. On three reformers and music, see Markus Jenny, *Luther, Zwingli, Calvin in ihren Liedern* (Zurich, 1983). On

Protestant music in Germany, see Konrad Ameln, *Luthers Kirchenlieder in Tonsätzen seiner Zeit* (Kassel, 1934); Ameln, Christhard Mahrenholz, and W. Thomas, eds., *Handbuch der deutschen evangelischen Kirchenmusik* (Göttigen, 1932–   ); Friedrich Blume, *Geschichte der evangelischen Kirchenmusik,* 2d ed. (Kassel, 1965); M. Jenny, ed., *Luthers Geistlicher Lieder und Kirchengesänge: Vollständige Neuedition* (Cologne, 1985); Christhard Mahrenholz, *Das evangelische Kirchengesangbuch* (Kassel, 1950); Mahrenholz, *Luther und die Kirchenmusik* (Kassel, 1937); H. J. Moser, *Die evangelische Kirchenmusik in Deutschland* (Berlin, 1954); Paul Nettl, *Luther and Music* (Philadelphia, 1948); Basil Smallman, *The Background of Passion Music* (London, 1957); Patrice Veit, *Das Kirchenlied in der Reformation Martin Luthers: eine thematische und semantische Untersuchung* (Stuttgart, 1986); and Johannes Zahn, *Die Melodien der deutschen evangelischen Kirchenlieder,* 3 vols. (Berlin, 1899–1910).

On Calvin and the French Huguenots, see H. P. Clive, "The Calvinist Attitude to Music, and Its Literary Aspects and Sources," *Bibliothèque d'humanisme et renaissance* 19 (1957) and 20 (1958); Orentin Douen, *Clément Marot et le psautier huguenot,* 2 vols. (Paris, 1878–79); Charles Garside, Jr., "Calvin's Preface to the Psalter: A Re-Appraisal," *MQ* 37 (1951); Garside, *Zwingli and the Arts* (New Haven, 1966); Théodore Gérold, *Psaumes de Clément Marot avec les mélodies* (Strasbourg, 1919); Gérold, *Les plus anciennes mélodies de l'Eglise Protestante de Strasbourg* (Paris, 1928); Pierre Pidoux, *Le Psautier huguenot du 16e siècle* (Kassel, 1962); Waldo S. Pratt, *The Music of the French Psalter of 1562* (New York, 1939); and R. R. Terry, *Calvin's First Psalter (1539)* (London, 1932).

On Protestant music in England, see E. H. Fellowes, *English Cathedral Music* (London, 1941); Percy Scholes, *The Puritans and Music in England and New England,* 2d ed. (New York, 1962); Peter le Huray, *Music and the Reformation in England, 1549–1660,* 2d ed. (London, 1978); Robert Illing, *The English Metrical Psalter: A Catalogue of Early Editions, an Index to their Contents, and a Comparative Study of the Melodies,* 3 vols. (Adelaide, Australia, 1983); and Robin Leaver, *'Ghoostly psalmes and spirituall songes,' English and Dutch Metrical Psalmes from Coverdale to Utenhove 1535–1566* (Oxford, 1991).

For a study of the role of music in the defense of Catholic orthodoxy before the Council of Trent, see George Nugent, "Anti-Protestant Music for Sixteenth-Century Ferrara," *JAMS* 43 (1990): 228–91. On the Council of Trent and the early Counter-Reformation, see Lewis H. Lockwood, "Vincenzo Ruffo and Musical Reform after the Council of Trent," *MQ* 43 (1957); Lockwood, *The Counter-Reformation and the Masses of Vincenzo Ruffo* (Venice, 1970); and Noel O'Regan, *Institutional Patronage in Post-Tridentine Rome* (London, 1995). See also Michele Fromson, "A Conjunction of Rhetoric and Music: Structural Modelling in the Italian Counter-Reformation Motet," *PRMA* 117 (1992): 208–46.

ELEVEN

PALESTRINA, LASSO, VICTORIA, AND BYRD

In his *Istitutioni harmoniche,* first published in 1558, the theorist Gioseffo Zarlino described his contemporaries, especially his teacher Adrian Willaert, as men who had brought music to a new state of perfection. In praise of their genius, Zarlino implied that musicians of his time summed up the achievements of their predecessors and that they could not go much further without challenging basic premises about the nature of musical style. Zarlino's views can be defended and even enlarged to take into account the successors of Willaert, Gombert, and Clemens non Papa—that is, the greatest figures of the late Renaissance: Palestrina, Lasso, Victoria, and Byrd. Their music is written in a style that refines to a state of perfection the techniques developed by composers during the first half of the sixteenth century.

Such a view, however, not only simplifies the character of these four great musicians but also distorts the distinguishing features of late-sixteenth-century music by placing too little emphasis on the variety of kinds of music written during that time. The intense concern of musicians for text expression, especially in the madrigal, led to the dissolution of the kind of polyphonic fabric that had been regarded as an ideal during most of the sixteenth century. Mid-sixteenth-century investigations into the nature of music in the ancient world helped to bring about the invention of monody and opera in Italy and produced *musique mesurée à l'antique* in France. We have already seen that some musicians by the late sixteenth century had become specialists in composing instrumental music; that is, they concentrated on constructing autonomous forms in sound of a sort not heard before in western Europe. And even in perfecting the "classical" style of the Renaissance without dramatically stressing music's ability to express human emotions, Palestrina inspired a whole school of Roman composers whose sobriety and decorum can be contrasted with the extravagances of some of their more flamboyant contemporaries.

In short, it is not so easy to perceive a mainstream of music during the late sixteenth century as it is for the earlier part of the Renaissance, partly because so much more music survives from the later period, but also because so many conflicting styles coexisted and composers expressed such different attitudes and points of view.

From about 1560 to 1600, Italy continued to be the country where most of the significant innovations took place. Whereas foreigners, especially Netherlanders, held almost all the important musical positions in Italy during the first half of the century, by the second half Italian musicians trained by Adrian Willaert and his contemporaries had taken over the direction of musical life in most Italian cities. Andrea and Giovanni Gabrieli, Baldassare Donato, Francesco and Gioseffo Guami, Claudio Merulo, Annibale Padovano, and eventually Claudio Monteverdi all lived and worked in Venice, and Giovanni Matteo Asola and Costanzo Porta were in nearby cities in the Veneto (the area around Venice). In Rome, besides Palestrina and the superb madrigalist Luca Marenzio, the roster included Felice and Giovanni Francesco Anerio, Giovanni Animuccia, Paolo Bellasio, Ruggiero Giovanelli, Cristofano Malvezzi, Giovanni Maria Nanino, and Paolo Quagliati. In Naples, Carlo Gesualdo, prince of Venosa, and Pomponio Nenna were among the foremost composers, along with a northerner, Giovanni de Macque. Alhough a Netherlander, Giaches de Wert, brought fame and brilliance to the courts of Mantua and Ferrara, a number of distinguished Italians also took an active part in those cities, among them Giovanni Giacomo Gastoldi, Luzzasco Luzzaschi, Benedetto Pallavicino, and Salamone Rossi. Vincenzo Galilei worked in Florence, Alessandro Striggio in Mantua and Florence, Vincenzo Ruffo in Milan, Adriano Banchieri in Bologna, Orazio Vecchi in Modena, Marc'Antonio Ingegneri in Cremona. Some of the greatest non-Italian composers of the time, including Lasso, Victoria, Giaches de Wert, and Philippe de Monte, had much of their education or their earliest musical experiences in Italy, or else they spent much of their later life there. Even William Byrd, who never left England, could not escape the influence of the Italians. Moreover, as we have seen, German musicians of the late sixteenth century wrote in a highly Italianate style, as did such seventeenth-century German composers as Schütz, Scheidt, and Schein.

To single out, among all these composers, only four as the most important of their time may seem an intolerably arbitrary procedure. To be sure, if it suggests that the quartet of virtuoso madrigalists—Gesualdo, Marenzio, Monteverdi, and Wert—were not magnificent composers of great historical importance, or that figures such as Philippe de Monte and Francesco Guerrero were not musicians of the first rank, to focus attention on so few may mislead the unwary. Yet Palestrina, Lasso, Victoria, and Byrd, perhaps to a greater extent than any of their contemporaries except the madrigalists, wrote music that transcends the limitations of their age; moreover, they conveniently illustrate the diversity of temperament and approach so characteristic of their time.

That Palestrina should be included among the great composers of the late Renaissance hardly needs justification, since his music has been regarded for generations as the quintessence of the period. If today, with our greater historical perspective, we have modified that opinion somewhat, his music nevertheless embodies the *ars perfecta* more convincingly than that by anyone else. Victoria, who may have been Palestrina's student, brought to his Roman training a passionate religiosity. Lasso, the Franco-Flemish composer who passed much of his youth in Italy before spending most of his mature years at the Bavarian court in Munich, was the virtuoso of the four. He was the master of every style, genre, and technique, as befitted his cosmopolitan career; and his music shows off the brilliant, expressive, and even experimental sides of the late Renaissance. William Byrd shared with Lasso an astounding fluency to command every technique and genre of his time, but he differs from his great contemporaries in at least two important ways: his music reflects the English independence from developments on the Continent, and he, more obviously than the others, stands at the beginning as well as the end of a period of history: he not only incorporated into his own music the achievements of his predecessors but also ushered in the most brilliant musical era his country had ever known, during the later years of Elizabeth I and the reigns of James I and Charles I.

GIOVANNI PIERLUIGI DA PALESTRINA

Giovanni Pierluigi (ca. 1525–94), called Palestrina after the town of his birth, was a man of his time insofar as his music reflects the ideals of the Counter-Reformation and, especially, the desire of the reformers to encourage a spiritual quality completely detached from secular concerns. But our perception of Palestrina's place in music history, and ultimately even our conception of his music, has been highly colored by his reputation in later times. He passed on to his students and followers in Rome techniques of writing superbly well controlled and transparent counterpoint and ideals of serenity and balance. In turn, music by him and his pupils served church musicians everywhere in western Europe during the seventeenth, eighteenth, and nineteenth centuries as models for their own compositions written in a *stile antico* that still seems intrinsically "sacred" to many people. Even by the time Monteverdi was called upon to defend his stylistic innovations in the foreword to his fifth book of madrigals, printed in 1607, he understood the sort of music written by Palestrina to be different from his own; it was a *prima prattica*, a "first practice" of "pure" counterpoint, more fit for the church than his own *seconda prattica*, which was more emotional, more expressive, and altogether freer of contrapuntal restrictions, and therefore more appropriate for secular music and the theater. By the eighteenth century the Viennese composer Johann Joseph Fux had distilled Palestrina's style and written rigid rules for imitating it in his treatise *Gradus ad Parnassum,* which generations of students have learned to regard as the book containing the sacred tenets of sixteenth-century counterpoint. After Giuseppe Baini's pioneering biography of Palestrina, first published in 1828, many musicians in the nineteenth and twentieth centuries have considered Palestrina the greatest musician of the Renaissance, whose music offers the clearest examples of modal counterpoint, uncontaminated by harmonic planning.

If some of these views can be shown to be naive or overly simple—Palestrina's counterpoint is in fact carefully regulated by harmonic progressions, for example, and Fux's rules give a distorted picture of standard sixteenth-century practice—the popular image of Palestrina nevertheless contains more than a little truth. His musical style is a refinement to the utmost of techniques used by earlier composers, and thus it can be said to reflect a state of perfection, but the "spiritual" quality so often noted in his music seems to derive mainly from his overriding concern for balance and moderation. His compositions invariably take into account the proper accentuation of words, and often even their meaning, but without heightening their rhetoric so emphatically that the continuous flow of polyphony is broken. To ensure that the stream of counterpoint remained even and uninterrupted, he controlled dissonances rigorously and invented melodies that introduce neither abrupt or disturbing leaps nor sudden changes of direction or pace. In addition, the clarity of his textures is always maintained by the care with which he worked out imitative entries and antiphonal dialogues, leaving plenty of air and space and never producing the thick, almost impenetrable tangle of polyphony sometimes found in works by the northern composers of the post-Josquin generation. Palestrina's modernity is heard, however, not only in clear textures, sensitive text declamation, and smooth counterpoint; his large number of works for double choir also show him leaving the well-trodden path of intricate, through-composed contrapuntal polyphony to work with chordal textures and harmonies, exploiting in a thoroughly up-to-date way (for his time, of course) the sonic grandeur of blocks of sound in a fashionable "modern" polychoral idiom.

Unlike many composers of the Renaissance, Palestrina never left his homeland, Rome and its environs. He was educated as a choirboy at Santa Maria Maggiore in Rome, but at about nineteen, in 1544, he returned to the town of his birth, Palestrina, some forty-five miles away, to take up his first position as organist and singer at the cathedral there. The bishop of Palestrina at the time was Cardinal Giovanni Maria del Monte, who was elected pope and took the name Julius III in 1551; shortly thereafter he called the young composer back to Rome to become master of the Julian Chapel (the Cappella Giulia), which sang at services in St. Peter's. For the rest of his life Palestrina worked for one or another church or institution in Rome—the papal chapel (the Cappella Sistina), St. John Lateran, Santa Maria Maggiore, or the Roman Seminary, founded after the Council of Trent to educate young men for the priesthood. During several brief periods he was in charge of concerts given at the villa of Cardinal Ippolito d'Este in Tivoli. At least twice he was tempted to leave Rome: both the Duke of Mantua and Emperor Maximilian II of Vienna tried to lure him away, but Palestrina asked such a high salary that the invitations came to nothing.

Palestrina was not a priest but a family man, trying always to enhance his earnings and better his family's situation. Indeed, his period of service at the Sistine Chapel ended because he was married, contrary to the rules of the organization. (These had been ignored by Julius III in his eagerness to promote his young protégé, but Pope Paul IV insisted that Palestrina and the other married members of the chapel resign, albeit with a pension.) So far as we know, Palestrina was only once tempted to become a priest, when he was in his mid-fifties and shortly after his wife, two sons, and two brothers died in the plagues of the late 1570s that almost killed him as well. In 1581, after his first wife's death, he took minor orders, although not vows of celibacy; but he had a sudden change of heart and married the widow of a furrier. For at least a decade after his second marriage, he assisted his wife in managing her fur business, in addition to fulfilling his responsibilities as a church musician and composer. In short, he was a very practical man, and the spirituality of his music should not mislead us into romantic notions about his life.

Although Palestrina became known as the official papal composer after 1585, it is important to remember that during the early years of his career in Rome, he was an innovator, accustomed to swimming upstream. Before the Council of Trent, the musical establishments of churches in mid-sixteenth-century Rome were still dedicated to the performance of conservative Franco-Flemish polyphony (the music of Josquin, Morales, and Mouton, for example) under the direction of French or Flemish chapel masters. (Palestrina and Giovanni and Paolo Animuccia were among the very few exceptions.) This tradition began to dissolve when the Council of Trent completed its work. Pius V issued a reformed Breviary in 1568, followed by a new Missal in 1570, and Palestrina and Annibale Zoilo were commissioned to revise the chants of the Gradual and Antiphoner (a task they never completed). Although the Council's provisions did not constitute a wholesale liturgical reform, some aspects of the liturgy were changed and a number of texts were revised. Composers were suddenly called on for appropriate new liturgical music to replace some of the older repertory in use at many churches but now found to be inadequate or liturgically obsolete. Contemporary composers were thus newly important, and they responded as well to the Council of Trent's guidelines concerning musical reform, issued in 1562. These specified that profane material was to be excluded altogether from the sacred rite, and they called for a sort of musical repose or aural "tranquility" to enhance religious observance. Sacred music should be composed "not to give empty pleasure to the ear, but in such a way that the words may be clearly understood by all, and thus the hearts of the listeners be drawn to the desire of heavenly harmonies and in the contemplation of the joys of the blessed."

Post-Tridentine religious orthodoxy did not smother the creativity of musicians within the church; on the contrary, it prompted the composition of new religious music and reinvigorated musical life in late-sixteenth-century Rome. The new requirements directly influenced the way that composers approached sacred texts for musical setting and stimulated the production of new settings in which the sacred words could be easily appreciated. Palestrina was in the first generation of Roman musicians to benefit from this opening up of Rome's sacred-musical life. Beginning in 1571, when he once again became maestro of the Cappella Giulia, he composed a great deal of new music for its choir; through his position there and the influence of his many published collections, he was a leader in the formulation of an orthodox Roman musical style.

Although it has long been commonplace to generalize about a "Palestrina style" with a regular set of compositional procedures, in fact because he was so prolific, composed in a number of genres, and indeed varied his style over time it is as inaccurate to describe Palestrina's music as conforming to a single style as it is to do so for any other great sixteenth-century composer. Palestrina did produce a refined polyphonic fabric, purified of harsh or abrupt interruptions—but one highly expressive through exploitation of rhythm, harmony, phrase structure, and dissonance. When working with special kinds of texts—especially the Holy Week Lamentations and the Song of Solomon—Palestrina was as adept as any of his contemporaries in composing what he himself defended in a dedication of 1584 as "a kind of music somewhat livelier than I have been accustomed to use in ecclesiastical melodies," but which "I felt that the subject itself demanded"—in other words, a musical language filled with expressive musical rhetoric and explicit musical imagery.

To commemorate the four hundredth anniversary of Palestrina's birth-date, Knud Jeppesen published a thorough, systematic, and long-influential study of Palestrina's counterpoint (*The Style of Palestrina and the Dissonance*, 1927; 2d ed. 1946). Although to accept all of Jeppesen's results is to accept a distorted view of Palestrina's music, his points about the nature of Palestrina's melodic lines can serve as a useful starting place. He describes Palestrina's typically long-breathed melodies, formed of gentle arches in which "the ascending and descending movements counterbalance each other with almost mathematical exactness." Palestrina's elegant curves of sound, in which nothing disturbs the even flow of the line, consist mostly of stepwise motion with relatively few repeated notes and no large or unusual leaps. Indeed, except for minor sixths and octaves, he virtually never wrote melodic skips of more than a fifth, and he almost invariably reversed the direction of the line immediately after intervals larger than a third. In compositions like the sparsely texted movements of Masses—the Kyrie, Sanctus, and Agnus Dei sections—these melodic lines often attain great length and freedom from obtrusive metrical regularity, since they are built from rhythmic units of changing length. On the other hand, in Mass movements with a greater density of text—the Glorias and the Credos—and in many motets, Palestrina often wrote relatively short motives that alternate with long flowing lines and short declamatory passages.

In the Agnus Dei of Palestrina's *Missa Aeterna Christi munera* (Example 11–1b), a Mass that paraphrases an Office hymn, all melodic intervals larger than a third are carefully "recovered" (by a reverse of direction), and where series of thirds all move in the same direction, as in mm. 9–10 in the inner voices, the direction of the melody soon reverses itself to maintain the music's typically placid sense of balance. The initial gentle curve of melody in the superius and the extended second phrase (mm. 11–21) are both inspired by the chant on which the polyphony is based (Example 11–1a), but to say that Palestrina modeled his melodic style on chant would be an exaggeration; it was Palestrina who, together with Zoilo, took on the creative challenge of rewriting those passages in the chant books that to a cultivated sixteenth-century ear seemed barbaric, and improving the chants' text setting, according to the prevailing humanistic views of the late Renaissance.

The Agnus Dei of Example 11–1b illustrates, too, another of the most striking features of Palestrina's music: the careful preparation and resolution of dissonances. The longer the note values, the more careful and discreet was Palestrina's preparation. Dissonant notes never have a value greater than a minim in the original notation (transcribed here as a quarter note but in some modern editions as a half note), and they are never preceded by a note smaller in value. Palestrina introduced many of the long dissonances as consonant notes and then suspended them against a change of harmony, so that the dissonance and its resolution form 4–3 or 7–6 intervals with one of the lower voices (as in mm. 5, 9, 12, 15, 18, 21, and 22 of Example 11–1b). Dissonances also appear as passing notes on "weak" beats (that is, the second or fourth minim—quarter note—of a larger metrical unit). He treated smaller note values a bit more freely, although shorter dissonances usually occur either as passing notes or in one of a limited number of ornamental figures, such as turns ("cambiatas"). Except for suspensions, then, dissonances are almost entirely limited to normally unstressed beats. This well-regulated metrical plan increases the impression that a constant pulse underlies Palestrina's compositions, even though it is precisely the rhythmic irregularity of the details that brings the surface of his music to life and gives to his melodic lines their delicate vitality. While banishing harsh or unexpected clashes, he included just enough dissonance to avoid a saccharine sameness and to keep the motion flowing steadily forward.

Palestrina's counterpoint is controlled not only by the shape of his elegant melodic lines and careful handling of dissonance but also by his manner of using imitative techniques and by shrewd harmonic planning. He often built up his compositions by repeating entire passages, simply or with variants, or by adding new voices to the original material; and he used other rational devices, such as invertible counterpoint or the transposition of whole points of imitation. The Agnus Dei in Example 11–1b, for instance, opens with a clear-cut point of imitation, constructed by transposing the initial duet up a fourth for the third and fourth entries (mm. 4–8) while giving the original two voices new material. In spite of the imitations at the beginning of the second phrase (mm. 9–10), the "second theme" in the superius is subsequently treated like a cantus firmus

EXAMPLE 11–1. Giovanni Pierluigi da Palestrina, *Missa Aeterna Christi munera.*

(*a*) The chant on which the Mass is based

Ae-ter-na   Chri-sti mu - - - ne-ra,   A- po-sto-lo-rum   glo-ri-am,

(*b*) Agnus Dei, mm 1–23

mus than a point to be imitated; it appears first in the bass (mm. 13–16), then overlapped in the tenor (mm. 16–18), and finally truncated in the bass (mm. 19–22)—each time with new counterpoints written over or around it. The treatment of the melodic material—the initial transposition and the reiteration of the second theme—plays an important role in creating the clear tonal outlines of the movement. The first theme moves from V to I and its answer from I to IV (mm. 1–5), making an easy transition to the transposed entries, which explore the subdominant area (mm. 6–9). The second theme returns to the tonic (mm. 9ff), even though it quickly moves up to V, and Palestrina cadences on the dominant in m. 22. The third phrase (after the excerpt quoted) is once again taken up with music centered around the tonic. Thus the overall plan, I–IV–I–V–I, is clearly organized and clearly tonal (though with a pattern different from later tonal schemes); even the vocabulary of chords, different as it is in many particulars from seventeenth- and eighteenth-century music, includes a surprisingly high percentage of progressions based on "tonal" scale degrees— that is, I, IV, and V in the tonic, subdominant, and dominant "keys." For a presumably modal piece, this Mass section, like most of Palestrina's work, is remarkably susceptible to explanation in tonal terms.

The beginning of the Sanctus from Palestrina's magnificent *Missa Assumpta est Maria* (Example 11–2), a Mass that parodies one of his own motets, shows in a slightly more complex way how clearly his forms unfold. The first section (mm. 1–12) begins with a statement in four-part counterpoint of two principal motives (mm. 1–4); this is then transposed down a fifth and slightly rewritten (mm. 5–8). The section continues with a shorter phrase (mm. 9–12) made up of the initial two motives in stretto, leading to a cadence on the fourth scale degree that ends the threefold invocation "Sanctus, sanctus, sanctus." "Dominus Deus Sabaoth" is set as a declamatory passage that broadens out to a cadence (mm. 12–16); it is transposed down a fifth and rewritten (mm. 16–20), and Palestrina continued to work with the same material beyond the excerpt quoted in the example.

Many of Palestrina's compositions resemble these two fragments in growing from a short section of counterpoint that is then repeated, transposed, slightly revised, or recomposed, always in a way that enhances the tonal organization of the entire work and that helps the listener follow the musical thought as it occurs. From these two excerpts it is also clear that Palestrina did not always write points of imitation of the sort associated with Josquin and his immediate successors. Instead, he invented passages that introduce several motives simultaneously or play one or two voices off against the others, and he frequently wrote chordal sections, often with antiphonal dialogue between sections of the choir. He was a master at manipulating sonorities and in grouping, spacing, and doubling chords; and his expertise produced polyphonic textures that sound clear and clean in performance.

EXAMPLE 11–2. Giovanni Pierluigi da Palestrina, *Missa Assumpta est Maria*, Sanctus, mm. 1–21.

Like most composers of the late sixteenth century, Palestrina scrupu-
lously respected the syntax and accent patterns of the texts he set. He planned
every voice within his polyphonic textures so that literary and musical accents
coincide with a naturalness that is the hallmark of a great composer. In highly
contrapuntal music, to be sure, the words are not always clearly audible, and a
work such as the *Missa Papae Marcelli*—evidently conceived in the spirit of
those Catholic reformers who urged that listeners be able to follow the words
easily—is unusual in the amount of chordal declamation it contains. Example
11–3, the beginning of Palestrina's setting of *Surgam et circuibo civitatem,* from
the Song of Songs, is more typical in showing the care with which he matched
his musical motives to the words in a polyphonic texture; the passage is slightly
unusual, however, in that the opening ascending scale fragment seems to illus-

EXAMPLE 11–3. Giovanni Pierluigi da Palestrina, *Surgam et circuibo civitatem,* mm. 1–5.

trate the sense of the text ("I will rise now and go about the city"). To be sure, discreet word painting had long since become a standard part of every composer's expressive arsenal; but Palestrina seldom went to greater lengths than this to illustrate the meanings of individual words, and he did not disturb the continuous stream of music in any dramatic way—by abrupt changes of pace or texture, for example—to insist on the priority of text over music. If some of his motets seem to fit the mood of their words beautifully—*Super flumina Babylonis* is melancholy, the eight-part *Jubilate Deo* joyous, and the sustained chords at the beginning of *O magnum mysterium* suggestive of awe and wonder—the reason is to be found less in the particular musical techniques used than in a number of intangible things (not least, perhaps, the subjective reaction of the modern listener). It is precisely Palestrina's reticence to disturb the placid surface of his works that has created the impression that his music is impersonal and imbued with spiritual qualities.

Palestrina may have been self-conscious about his role as a Roman church musician and the example he thought to set as papal composer; this perhaps explains why he wrote so few madrigals and why, when he published a collection of Song of Songs motets in 1584, the dedication to Pope Gregory XIII contained a curious apology for having written secular music (just two years before the second of his two volumes of four-voice madrigals was to appear in print). The first volume, published in 1555, had revealed him to be a fine madrigalist in the tradition of Festa and Arcadelt but hardly a pathbreaker. His two volumes of sacred madrigals (*madrigali spirituali*) in five voices, printed in 1581 and 1594, were doubtless more acceptable to the authorities in the reform-minded Rome of his time. Even though Palestrina did not write in the intense and personal manner of some of his contemporaries—his settings of Italian poems are by and large as sober and moderate in their expression as his motets—he nevertheless composed some fine madrigals, among them the unusually brilliant *Alla riva del Tebro* and one of the best-known and most-often-arranged madrigals of the entire half century, *Vestiva i colli.*

Palestrina's motets contain superb music and reveal the breadth and variety of his expressive palette and technique, although some critics have maintained that they do not show him at his best, and that his 105 settings of the Mass Ordinary, with their ceremonial abstraction and reservation, form the principal core of his work. He composed more than 250 motets, preserved both in manuscript and in printed sources. During his lifetime there appeared in print two volumes of four-voice motets, five volumes for five or more voices (including the 1584 collection devoted entirely to settings from the Song of Songs), and several volumes containing music for particular liturgical functions (Lamentations for Holy Week, hymns, Magnificats, Offertories, and litanies).

Palestrina wrote most of his motets on themes of his own invention, without recourse to borrowed chants or other strict constructive devices, a procedure that left him free to plan each work according to a purely musical design or the dictates of the text or both. The sequence of musical events, the particular techniques he employed, and the formal proportions vary so much from motet to motet that it is impossible to generalize about his procedures, beyond pointing out that almost all the motets are based on imitative techniques modified in the various ways we have seen, with ample contrast furnished by more or less chordal passages. In general, each unit of text generates its own thematic material, and the successive points of imitation—with declamatory passages judiciously placed to set them off—are arranged so that a listener can follow the process of musical thought clearly and easily. But within these limits Palestrina elaborated each motet in a new and different way. In his magnificent *Dum complerentur,* for example, he exploited opportunities to set the various parts of a six-voice choir against one another in antiphonal dialogue largely made up of declamatory passages; in his equally splendid seven-voice *Tu es Petrus,* by contrast, the even polyphonic flow is never interrupted by all the voices singing together in the same rhythm. The first part of his well-known *Sicut cervus* is taken up with a spacious exposition of three groups of themes, whereas the second part sets more lines of text and thus includes more, and more varied, melodic material and is altogether more condensed and faster paced. In *Super flumina Babylonis,* where Palestrina exercised his penchant for repeating points of imitation with variants and revisions, the motet consists of a series of double expositions. In short, his vast repertory of freely composed motets exhibits an incredible diversity of forms and approaches; individual works repay close study, for each is unique and most are masterpieces.

Some of the texts Palestrina set must have suggested their own repetition schemes. His responsories, for example, such as *Assumpta est Maria* and *Sancta et immaculata virginitatis,* both *a 6,* and *Fuit homo* and *Ascendo ad Patrem meum, a 5,* follow the liturgical pattern aBcB. Some of his settings of sequences, such as the famous *Stabat mater,* ignore the double versicle structure of the sacred text, whereas others follow it more or less closely. In many of his motets, Palestrina did base his thematic material on chant; in *Veni Sancte Spiritus,* for example, he paraphrased the monophonic melody, distributing it among all the voices without stating it complete in any one, and thus merely borrowing melodic ideas without influencing the details of the polyphonic structure. Some of his motets—for example, the six-voice *Columna es immobilis* and *Cum ortus fuerit*—are built around canons, usually with extensive imitation between the scaffolding voices and the others, welding the whole into a homogeneous texture.

The smaller liturgical works by Palestrina tend to be in a somewhat simpler style than his Masses and motets; they were evidently meant for everyday use in the service or, as in the case of the Lamentations, which were regularly sung in the papal chapel during Holy Week, for occasions when more florid polyphony was not appropriate. Palestrina's litanies as well as the Lamentations are set for the most part in simple chords or slightly animated homophony. Except for the melismas that adorn the Hebrew letters beginning each section of the Lamentations, they resemble *falsobordoni,* the completely chordal harmonizations of psalm-tone formulas and other liturgical recitations found especially in Spanish and Italian sources of the sixteenth century. Palestrina's Offertories are important historically, since they and Lasso's similar collection are the earliest written in free motet style, without the use of borrowed chant. Though not so simple as the litanies and Lamentations, they reveal Palestrina at his most austere. Both the settings of hymns for the whole church year, the *Hymnius totius anni,* and the series of Magnificats in each mode were intended for *alternatim* performance. Because Palestrina paraphrased the Gregorian tunes, each stanza is based on the same melodic material; thus the hymn settings afford an unusually convenient opportunity to study the variety of his techniques and approaches.

Palestrina's Masses contain some of his finest music and are as varied as his motets. They include some works built over cantus firmi; some that paraphrase chants; some built on canonic cycles; some that parody polyphonic motets, madrigals, or chansons; and some that are entirely free of borrowed material or constructive devices. Moreover, the Masses show the gradual perfection of Palestrina's contrapuntal technique and the simplification and greater homophony of his late works. Most of the Masses were published in thirteen volumes that appeared in print between 1554 and 1601, the last seven after his death. The works in them were not necessarily printed in the order in which they were composed; at best, the volumes present a very approximate chronological sequence, and their posthumous publication may have gathered together works written at various times during the composer's long lifetime.

The *Missa Ecce sacerdos magnus* is surely an early work, for it opens Palestrina's first published collection, the *Missarum Liber Primus* (Rome: Dorico, 1554). It is an appropriate composition for such a place of honor, for it was almost certainly written to celebrate the elevation of the composer's patron, Julius III, to the pontificate; moreover, since each movement is based on a cantus firmus taken from a Gregorian antiphon for a pope-confessor, it looks back toward the past. Indeed, the work is so retrospective that Palestrina even combined voice parts in three different mensuration signs for the last Agnus Dei, a technical trick more commonly found in music by much earlier composers. In this Mass the borrowed melody appears in long notes in one of the inner voices except in several sections where the superius sings it; the other voices mostly weave independent imitations around it, although occasionally, as at the beginning of the Credo, the point to be imitated is derived from the scaffolding voice. Though Palestrina could already write characteristically elegant arches of melody, which combine to form suave counterpoint, in this Mass the phrases are short-winded; hence, the longer movements tend to sound more disjointed than in most of the composer's later works; control of architectonic features came with maturity. Palestrina built most of his other seven cantus-firmus Masses on plainsong tenors, except for one based on the *L'homme armé* tune and another on the hexachord formula *Ut re mi fa sol la.*

Palestrina based a second Mass on the *L'homme armé* tune, but in that work as well as in many of his Masses derived from plainchant (about a third of his total output in the genre), he applied paraphrase technique. In forging a subject suitable for imitation from a plainsong, Palestrina usually stuck remarkably close to his model. Often, in fact, he retained all or almost all the pitches of the chant, merely omitting a note or two of the original to make his theme more concise as he cast it in a distinctive rhythmic form; less often he embellished the original. We have already seen from his *Missa Aeterna Christi munera* (Example 11–1) how close the relationship between model and paraphrase could be. Moreover, in that Mass, as in many of Palestrina's paraphrased works, the model was deployed in a way that enhances the structure of the new composition. The Gregorian hymn *Aeterna Christi munera* consists of four phrases, the last of which repeats the first. Palestrina invariably used the melodic material in the order in which it appears in the hymn. He based the three sections of the Kyrie, for example, on successive phrases of the hymn. In the Sanctus he created the following refrain form:

Sanctus	phrases 1 and 2 of the model
Pleni	phrase 3 of the model
Osanna I	phrase 4 (= 1) of the model
Benedictus	phrases 2 and 3 of the model
Osanna II	phrase 4 (= 1) of the model

In some of his other paraphrase Masses, such as the *Missa Sanctorum meritis*, Palestrina chose to elaborate only one or two phrases from the borrowed melody, allowing them to permeate the whole work. In his nine Mantuan Masses—so called because they use versions of chant as sung at the church of Santa Barbara in Mantua—he set only the alternate verses in the Gloria and Credo movements; the remaining verses are to be sung in plainchant.

Five of Palestrina's Masses are constructed as cycles of canons. Each movement of the *Missa Ad fugam*, for example, consists entirely of double canons, two two-part canons superimposed one on the other, except for the Pleni and Benedictus (each a three-part canon) and the last Agnus (a three-part over a two-part canon). To relate the movements even more closely to one another, Palestrina based some of the canons on the same or similar thematic material.

Of Palestrina's six apparently free Masses, the *Missa Papae Marcelli,* designed to make the text as intelligible as possible, is by far the best known, though in its simpler way the *Missa Brevis,* a short work intended for everyday use in the service, is an equally attractive composition.

Almost half of Palestrina's Masses parody a polyphonic model, either one of his own motets or a madrigal, motet, or chanson by some earlier composer whom he admired or wished to emulate or better; among these are Domenico Maria Ferrabosco, Lupus Hellinck, Jachet of Mantua, Josquin, L'Héritier, Morales, Moulu, Richafort, Rore, and Verdelot. Palestrina's parody Masses are among his best works, and those based on his own works (the six-voice *Missa Assumpta est Maria* and the *Missa Tu es Petrus,* for instance) top the list. In his *Missa Ascendo ad Patrem,* the composer's technique of adapting the music of his own motet to new textual and formal circumstances is unusually sophisticated. The beginning of the first Kyrie duplicates the beginning of the motet almost exactly, whereas its second half is less obviously modeled on Palestrina's setting of a second phrase of text, in which the head of the motive has been changed and the music recomposed. The Christe elaborates motives from the middle of the motet's first part, and the second Kyrie quite conventionally takes up themes from the beginning of the second part. Through much of the Gloria, Palestrina did not duplicate music from the motet literally, although its derivation from the motet's opening motives is ultimately clear. But neither his technique of parody, its great skill notwithstanding, nor the exquisite detail of his counterpoint completely explains Palestrina's genius, which resides as well in the impressive way he built individual phrases into gigantic structures of sound. His Masses especially are best studied in their entirety as architectonic wholes.

ORLANDO DI LASSO

In many ways Orlando di Lasso (1532–94) was very different from Palestrina, with whom he is often linked. Both Lasso's career and his music contrast strongly with those of the Italian composer. Whereas Palestrina spent his entire life in and around Rome, Lasso traveled widely; he was truly cosmopolitan. One of the last of the great Netherlanders (along with Philippe de Monte and Giaches de Wert), Lasso received much of his education in Italy, and Italian musicians played a decisive role in shaping his musical personality, although from his mid-twenties he lived and worked in Germany. Whereas Palestrina concentrated his attention almost exclusively on sacred music, Lasso displayed a dazzling virtuosity in every style and genre of his time. His motets are often singled out by modern musicians as the most important segment of his oeuvre, but he was equally skillful at writing Italian madrigals, French chansons, German lieder, and settings of the Mass Ordinary. Whereas Palestrina wrote a counterpoint distinguished for its sobriety and decorum, Lasso's passionate commitment to the idea that music should heighten, enhance, and even embody textual meaning elicited a boldness and directness that sets him apart. Though this taste for vivid expression distinguishes him from Palestrina and some other contemporaries, it constituted one of the main preoccupations of many composers in the late sixteenth century; for them Lasso's music served as model and inspiration.

Lasso was born in Mons in the province of Hainaut (in southern Belgium) and may have begun his musical career as a choirboy at the church of St. Nicholas there. For a decade during his formative years—from the age of twelve to about twenty-two or twenty-three—he lived and worked in Italy. In the service of Ferrante Gonzaga, viceroy of Sicily, the young composer traveled to Mantua and Milan; he lived in Naples from 1549 to 1551, visited Palermo, and became, at the incredibly early age of twenty-one, chapel master of St. John Lateran in Rome, a position he took over from Giovanni Animuccia but left a scant year and a half later for personal reasons. Palestrina, whom he must have known during his service in Rome, succeeded him. In 1554 or 1555, at the age of twenty-two or twenty-three, Lasso returned from Italy to Antwerp, where he lived for several years and where he published his first important works: a collection of seventeen motets printed by Jan Laet (the so-called Antwerp Motet Book, 1556), and an anthology printed by Tielman Susato in 1555 that contains madrigals, villanesche, and chansons as well as motets, and includes the highly chromatic *Alma nemes* and the work on which it was modeled, Cipriano de Rore's *Calami sonum ferentes.*

In 1556, soon after his return to the Netherlands, Lasso was called to Munich to serve at the court of Albrecht V, Duke of Bavaria, a court with a distinguished and cosmopolitan musical tradition, established by Isaac and continued by Senfl and others. Lasso stayed there for the rest of his life, eventually becoming not only chapel master but also the respected and honored official court composer and friend to the ducal family. He was granted a patent of nobility by Emperor Maximilian II and made a Knight of the Golden Spur by Pope Gregory XIII. Duke Albrecht valued Lasso's music so highly that he had the composer's settings of the penitential psalms (*Psalmi Davidis penitentiales*) copied into magnificent choirbooks elegantly decorated by the court painter, Hans Mielich, with illustrations that include several portraying Lasso with his court musicians. Duke Albrecht's son, who became Duke Wilhelm V after his father's death in 1579, encouraged the Munich printer Adam Berg to publish the *Patrocinium musices* (twelve volumes, 1573–98), a sumptuously produced collection of sacred music, seven volumes of which were devoted entirely to music by Lasso. A number of letters by the composer survive, almost all of them addressed to Wilhelm. Written in an amusing mixture of Italian, Latin, French, and German, they reveal Lasso to have been a man of strong temperament, quick and witty, and with a lively sense of humor occasionally

Figure 10.   Lassus and the Bavarian court chapel performing festive music. The musicians play and sing from part-books, in a late Renaissance ensemble that includes both loud and soft instruments. The harpsichord, lutes, and viols in the foreground most likely provided a bass line and polyphonic or chordal accompaniments. Duke Albrecht V is standing at the far left, at the foot of a column. Miniature by Hans Mielich from the Mielich Codex. (Courtesy of Bayerische Staatsbibliothek, Munich)

darkened by moodiness. During the last several years of his life, this moodiness gave way to a deep depression that found expression in his final collection of spiritual madrigals, the *Lagrime di San Pietro,* posthumously published by Berg. After Lasso's death his two sons, Rudolph and Ferdinand, brought out the *Magnum opus musicum* (1604), a vast retrospective collection of his motets—516 of them, for from two to twelve voices. (This collection unfortunately served as a basis for the incomplete modern edition of the composer's works: Lasso's sons did not always reproduce the best readings; they sometimes replaced the words Lasso set with others; and they adopted an ordering by number of voices, thus obscuring the chronology of the motets and hence an easy view of the composer's development.)

By the age of twenty-three, at the time the Antwerp Motet Book was published, Lasso had already formed a fully mature and personal musical style, related both to older Netherlandish practices and to the new freedoms of Italian musicians. But if his desire to create a music generated by the words may be considered the most distinctive feature of the Antwerp motets, their great variety—equally a hallmark of Lasso's work—should not be overlooked. The composer did not restrict himself to one compositional procedure or to a single approach to problems of form, style, and technique. *Creator omnium Deus,* for example, is built around a canon derived in part from Willaert's setting of the same text; an ostinato serves as scaffolding in *Fremuit spiritu Jesu,* a work that imitates some features of Clemens non Papa's motet on this text; and the final motet in the volume, *Da pacem Domine,* merely alludes to the Gregorian melody associated with this prayer for peace without presenting it complete in any one voice or paraphrasing each of its phrases. Most of the motets in the collection eschew borrowed material and constructive devices to leave the composer free to mold the music according to the shape and meaning of the text. Moreover, Lasso chose his texts from a number of different sources. Some of the Antwerp motets are taken from psalms, some from other parts of the Bible or from a liturgical service book. Some set secular texts: *Stet quicumque volet potens* is from Seneca's tragedy *Thyestes* and celebrates the virtues of the quiet life; and there are three works honoring individuals: the opening motet, *Delitiae Phoebi,* addressed to Antonio Perenotto, bishop of Arras, to whom Lasso dedicated the collection; *Te spectant,* celebrating the English cardinal Reginald Pole; and *Heroum soboles,* praising Emperor Charles V. Most of the compositions in the Antwerp Motet Book make some use of imitative techniques, albeit in a way markedly different from the earlier Netherlanders (e.g., Gombert, Willaert, and Clemens non Papa) and from Palestrina. But Lasso's dependence on imitation as a formal procedure can easily be exaggerated, and some of these early motets, such as *Heroum soboles,* consist largely of music in homophonic textures.

No single work, then, can be considered completely representative of Lasso's Antwerp Motet Book, and yet a closer study of such a composition as *Gustate et videte* reveals at least some of the most important features of his style. This motet, which sets several verses from Psalm 34, achieved great fame in Lasso's own lifetime, though not for purely musical reasons. Rain and thunder threatened to curtail the Corpus Christi procession in Munich in 1584, but as Lasso and his musicians began to sing *Gustate et videte*, the sun came out. Every year from then on Lasso's motet was performed during the procession, to ensure that the weather would be fine.

The motet opens (Example 11–4) with a point of imitation on "Gustate et videte" ("O taste and see") that resembles earlier Netherlandish counterpoint in its general layout and style, although Lasso's theme—with its obvious division into two motives, its clear rhythmic shape, and the easy natural way it fits the words—is more memorable than many by musicians of the post-Josquin generation. Continuing without a break, the music for "quoniam suavis est Dominus" ("that the Lord is good") consists of a passage without any imitations beyond the dotted rhythmic motive that sets the first word; instead, the contrapuntally animated chords work around to a B♭ major triad that beautifully embodies the sense of "suavis." After the important cadence in m. 20, the next section, on "Beatus vir qui sperat in eo" ("Happy is the man who takes refuge in him"), centered on a simple motive that fills in a fourth by stepwise motion, gradually works up from the initial syncopated imitation between bass and tenor II to the high point of the composition immediately preceding the cadence in m. 32, which divides the *prima pars* of *Gustate et videte* into two halves. The second part relaxes and gradually subsides in a series of phrases involving relatively little imitation.

Working within a continuing northern European tradition in *Gustate et videte* and the other compositions of the Antwerp Motet Book, Lasso nevertheless departed in significant ways from the style of his predecessors. The degree to which his music is informed and controlled by the words can scarcely be exaggerated. Almost every page reveals particular compositional decisions made to heighten, illustrate, or embody a literary meaning. Short motives, suggested by the words and hence more often syllabic than melismatic, generate many of the thematic events in his motets, and these epigrammatic ideas, expanded and manipulated, take the place of the long gentle arches of melody so often found in Palestrina's music. Moreover, within any one work the sections vary widely in length, density, and style; their character is usually determined either by the literary context—the way each phrase fits the meaning and rhetoric of the entire text—or by Lasso's conception of overall musical design. The latter consideration, for example, undoubtedly determined the unusually clear sectionalism of *Gustate et videte*.

In building individual phrases Lasso relied less on imitation as a structural device than did many of his contemporaries. In its place he generally preferred textures that depend for their effect on varied and imaginative choral groupings (one voice part against three or more, semi-chorus against semi-chorus, or one group echoed by another); or he wrote a kind of nonimitative counterpoint that retains its clarity because of the careful shape of individual melodic lines; or he animated an essentially chordal texture by rhythmic imitations and other allusions of one voice to another. The importance of harmonic

EXAMPLE 11–4. Orlando di Lasso, *Gustate et videte*, mm. 1–32.

progressions directed toward tonal goals must also be considered in assessing Lasso's style. Neither Lasso nor his contemporaries had a technical vocabulary capable of explaining in detail the way each chord within a mode relates to its tonic, and we have still not devised a completely satisfactory method of dealing with the "tonal" implications of "modal" music. Yet Lasso's works plainly exhibit a sophisticated network of tonal relationships, including a highly developed sense of movement within a key and even modulation away from and back to a central point.

In at least one of his early works (*Prophetiae sibyllarum,* the series of twelve motets on Latin humanist texts that invoke the Sibyls who in ancient times prophesied the coming of Christ), Lasso even made use of extreme chromaticism. In their radical use of accidentals, the Sibylline compositions go even further than *Alma nemes,* which, as mentioned earlier, appeared in Lasso's first published collection. The opening nine measures of the introduction to the *Prophetiae* (Example 11–5), for instance, introduce all twelve chromatic semitones, and the chords of which they form a part stray so far from the G-Mixolydian mode in which the movement ends that the listener loses all sense of tonal orientation. This remarkable cycle can only have come about as a result of Lasso's contact with the music of the Italian avant-garde, works by composers such as Nicola Vicentino, Rore, and others, whose chromaticism—evocative of

EXAMPLE 11–5. Orlando di Lasso, *Prophetiae sibyllarum,* "Carmina Chromatico," mm. 1–9.

ancient Greece's chromatic and enharmonic tunings—was sanctioned by classical authority within the fashionable humanist thought of the time. Lasso never again went so far in exploring chromatic musical space; these works of his youth remained isolated experiments.

Lasso was astonishingly productive after his arrival in Munich in 1556. During his first dozen or so years there, he wrote almost a third of his more than five hundred motets. For many of them he chose texts that allowed him scope for personal expression: passages from the Psalms and the Song of Songs, for example, and biblical excerpts that present tragic figures (Job, the Prodigal Son, Rachel). His motets cover a wide spectrum of moods, styles, and techniques. The antiphonal eight-voice motets, such as *Omnes de Saba venient, Confitebor tibi Domine, In convertendo Dominus,* and *Laudate Dominum* (all published in vol. 21 of his *Complete Works*) are as splendid and brilliant as any Venetian motets of the time. Some of the secular Latin compositions, among them *Jam lucis orto sidere* (*Works,* XXI) and *Quod licet id libeat* (*Works,* XI), reveal the composer's robust sense of humor; others—for example, his largely homophonic setting of Dido's lament from the *Aeneid, Dulces exuviae* (*Works, XI*)— show his more serious side. A few motets are built over cantus firmi. Lasso was especially fond of weaving elaborate polyphony around an ostinato; in *Congregati sunt* (*Works,* IX), for example, the superius sings "Dissipa gentes quae bella volunt" five times, each time a tone lower, and then repeats the sequence; and in *Libera me, Domine* (*Works,* XV), the tenor sings "Respice finem" at various pitches and, in the latter section, in halved note values. For the most part, however, Lasso avoided borrowed material and scaffolding devices and instead conveyed the mood or the meaning of the text by adroitly inventing well-defined motives of contrasting character, sometimes but not always placed in imitative entries; by skillfully planning his compositions so that the rhythmic character and pace varies from section to section to reflect and enhance the rhetoric of the text; and by alternating and combining in a masterly and imaginative way imitative, nonimitative, homophonic, and antiphonal textures.

Lasso's settings of the seven penitential psalms are among the best (and most famous) motets from the composer's first decade in Munich. In the commentary written by Samuel Quickelberg—physician, humanist, and member of the Bavarian court—which appears in the magnificent manuscript containing the psalm settings, Lasso's music is praised precisely for the beautifully apt way it enhances the somber texts. "One cannot know whether the sweetness of the emotions more adorns the plaintive melodies or the plaintive melodies the sweetness of the emotions," wrote Quickelberg. He called the sequence of compositions an excellent example of *musica reservata,* a somewhat mysterious term, the exact meaning of which scholars have debated ever since; it probably refers to music that expresses its text, as Quickelberg's statement seems to suggest, though it may also refer to music intended for connoisseurs rather than a wider public, a definition that would also fit Lasso's psalms. His settings of these are all composed of many relatively short, self-contained sections. *De profundis cla-*

EXAMPLE 11–6. Orlando di Lasso, *De profundis*, mm. 1–13.

mavi, for example, consists of ten *partes* scored for from three to six voices. In some ways the most impressive of the lot dramatically in spite of its austerity, *De profundis* is exceptional in being built over a declamatory psalm tone used as cantus firmus. Even within this relatively restrained work, however, Lasso was able to achieve a wide range of effects. The opening section (Example 11–6), for instance, exhibits one of Lasso's typical textures—word-generated melodic lines in which rhythmic imitation plays a greater role than pitch identity, and in which the nearly imitative counterpoint is controlled by a clearly focused series of harmonic progressions. The later trio on "Quia apud Dominum" is a model of how to add two contrapuntal parts to a cantus firmus. Several sections set the cantus firmus in canon, either simply or in contrary motion. The "Gloria Patri" begins with a classical point of imitation derived from the scaffolding voice, and its final section, "Sicut erat in principio," begins with half-chorus pitted against half-chorus but ends with all voices joined together for an appropriately impressive close.

Just as the trio in *De profundis clamavi* sets a contrapuntal standard worth emulating, so the twelve duos, or *bicinia*, six with moralizing Latin texts and six without text (they were also called *fantasie* or *ricercari* in the original editions), which Lasso published in 1577 and which were reprinted many times in later years, can serve today in the same way they served students in the sixteenth century: as models and exercises to be played and studied by young musicians learning counterpoint and also by aspiring instrumentalists and singers. Lasso's *bicinia* differ from others in the century chiefly by being better; neither schoolmasterly nor pedantic, they contain some first-rate music.

During his last years, in the 1580s and the early 1590s, Lasso seems to have restricted his emotional range somewhat and emphasized the serious and even melancholy side of his musical personality. He drew the texts of many of his late motets from the liturgy, a practice he did not cultivate as much in his earlier years. His *Sacrae cantiones* of 1585, for example, consist chiefly of short Offertories, among the best he wrote. His last motets, the *Cantiones sacrae sex vocum* (Graz: Georg Widmanstätter, 1594), published during the year of his death, do not restrict themselves exclusively to items from the sacred service; they, too, lack the fire and brilliance of much of his earlier work, replacing those qualities with a sobriety and austerity reminiscent in some ways of earlier Netherlandish music—that is, the mainstream tradition of Lasso's youth. Some of the *Cantiones*, however, such as *Heu quis armorum furor* (*Works*, XIX), which conjures up the day of the Last Judgment using largely homophonic textures in antiphonal combinations, seem just as emotive and vivid as the motets of the early and middle periods; and some, such as *Lauda anima mea* (*Works*, XVII), include sections where the top two voices dominate the others to an extent that seems to prefigure early-seventeenth-century monody. Nevertheless, most of these motets resemble the opening section of *Musica Dei donum*, the composer's panegyric to the art of music, in which short motives relatively lacking in contrast are woven into a thick and fairly seamless contrapuntal web. Lasso's motets of 1594 are the noble and dignified last testament of a serious old man who has put away the frivolities of his youth even while rediscovering his musical patrimony.

In addition to his magnificent motets, Lasso also wrote several compositions intended for special occasions during the liturgical year. His *Lectiones matutinae de nativitate Christi* (1575), meant to be sung at matins on Christmas morning, and his two sets of *lectiones* drawn from the book of Job (the first published in 1565, the second in 1582) are among his most beautiful and impressive works, as are his settings of the Lamentations of Jeremiah (1585), performed during Holy Week. The Lamentations and the passages from Job are comparable in general mood and musical achievement to Lasso's settings of the penitential psalms, the prevailing homophony of the later set of *lectiones* notwithstanding. Lasso left us some one hundred settings of the Magnificat (by far a greater number than any other sixteenth-century composer); these were published in their entirety posthumously in the *Magnum opus musicum* and include some superb music. About half of the Magnificats are based on Gregorian chant, and most of the others parody chansons, madrigals, or motets by Lasso himself, Rore, and others. Some are complete settings in polyphony of the entire canticle of the Blessed Virgin, whereas others follow the traditional pattern of alternation between verses composed polyphonically and others to be performed either as monophonic chant or as organ versets.

Lasso used parody technique much more often in his Masses than in his Magnificats. Almost all his more than fifty Masses derive in one way or another from some pre-existent chanson, madrigal, or motet. Lasso appears not to have been stimulated, however, to ingenious feats by the challenge of recomposing older material, and for the most part he confined himself to extensive literal quotation only in the Kyrie, merely alluding in the other movements to his model at the beginning, possibly at the end, and sometimes at a few structurally important passages in the middle. Some of his Masses, especially the simpler ones of the *Missa brevis* variety, seem to have been tossed off in the line of duty. They are perfunctory workaday compositions that were probably intended for unimportant daily services. But others of his Masses, such as those on Sandrin's chanson *Doulce memoire*, Palestrina's madrigal *Io son ferito*, and Lasso's own motets *In te Domine speravi* and *Dixit Joseph*, are filled with felicitous details of counterpoint and text setting and display the composer's sure command in organizing large musical forms.

Lasso was so astonishingly productive that his approximately 150 chansons seem an insignificant part of his entire output. But they were influential in his day, even though Lasso never lived in Paris, that center of chanson composition, and they include some of the best works of the entire century in this genre. Stylistically, many of them resemble earlier French or Netherlandish chansons, or at least use those traditions as a point of departure—yet another indication of Lasso's impressive ability to assimilate diverse elements into his own musical language. His many light, witty, and even licentious songs are especially close to the chanson tradition of the early sixteenth century. *Quand mon mary vient de dehors* (*Works*, XII), for instance, with its initial paired duets and its incisive homophony, is not very different from many of the chansons published by Pierre Attaingnant in the 1530s and 1540s, nor is the bawdy *Il estoit une religieuse* (*Works*, XII), with its blasphemous joke associating "Pater noster" and "Ave Maria" underlined by mock-pompous counterpoint and long melismas. What differences there are between the two repertories, early and late, can be explained by Lasso's greater harmonic focus and motivic concentration and the sensitive way in which his music reveals both the form and the meaning of the poems it sets. Lasso built on earlier styles, too, for his more serious songs, working out his musical material with a finesse and imagination that produced a series of unique masterpieces. His famous *Susanne un jour* (*Works*, XIV)—one of the most widely distributed songs of the late sixteenth century and far better known than the earlier setting by Didier Lupi on which it is based—clothes the borrowed material in rich Netherlandish counterpoint. Lasso's equally well-known setting of Ronsard's *Bon jour mon coeur* (*Works*, XII), on the other hand, maintains a deceptively simple chordal texture almost throughout; but no Parisian composers of earlier times ever enhanced the rhetoric of a poem as directly as Lasso did here, varying the rhythmic pace, determining the lengths of the phrases, and shaping the melodies according to the emphasis he wished to place on various words or phrases. In some compositions Lasso set French poetry in a musical style that combines rich harmonic effects, contrasting sections of counterpoint, word painting, and a constant insistence on expression and atmosphere—a style, in short, that recalls the Italian madrigal and represents a genuinely new contribution to the history of the chanson. Even the opening few bars of *La nuict froide et sombre* (Example 11–7), one of the best of his Italianate French songs, suffice to show how far such music is from the emotional neutrality of many chansons.

Similarly, some of Lasso's ninety-odd German lieder exhibit madrigalian traits, whereas others continue the older tenor-song tradition (even to the extent of using either a pre-existent or a newly invented cantus firmus), make extensive

EXAMPLE 11–7. Orlando di Lasso, *La nuict froide et sombre,* mm. 1–15.

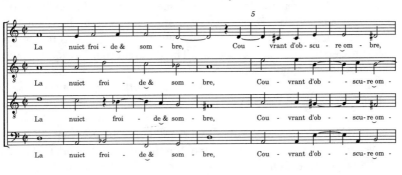

use of motetlike imitation, or borrow from the chanson the technique of fast syllabic declamation. Some lieder repeat themes or phrases according to the sense of the text, some contain no repetitions at all, and in others entire sections are repeated literally. In short, the lieder show even more stylistic and formal variety than Lasso's works in other genres. Even the texts he chose to set differ widely in type one from another: lieder with sacred words are mixed with drinking songs, bawdy songs, comic narratives in several sections, and lyrical love songs.

The strain of slightly raucous humor, even licentiousness, that runs through Lasso's chansons and lieder appears also in some of his settings of Italian poetry. As late as 1581 he published a volume of villanelle, moresche, and other light pieces in which characters from the Neapolitan streets and the commedia dell'arte figure prominently (Giorgia, Lucia, Pantaleone, Zanni, and others). The collection contains, too, the well-known echo song for double chorus, *O la, o che bon eccho* (*Works*, X), as well as *Matona mia cara*, the villanella (or more properly *tedesca*) with a text in a heavily accented Italian as though sung by one of the emperor's German soldiers. The Bavarian court obviously enjoyed these playful, quasi-popular songs.

By and large, Lasso's serious side came to the fore in his almost 150 madrigals, especially as he got older. The extroverted polyphony or animated homophony of his earlier madrigals—the first of which were published in 1555—gradually gave way to a more sober and dense counterpoint. The opening of *Nessun visse giamai* (Example 11–8), for instance, a late work first printed in 1584, does not immediately engage the listener by obvious madrigalisms or striking thematic material. Rather, each of the two phrases expands in full, chordally determined polyphony from the same simple rhythmic motive on one repeated pitch, which conveys so effectively a mood of sadness and resignation. Petrarch, whose works were associated in the sixteenth century with more serious madrigal settings, seems to have remained Lasso's favorite poet throughout his life. Lasso came increasingly to prefer those of Petrarch's poems written, like *Nessun visse giamai*, after the death of his beloved Laura; earlier, he chose more often Petrarch's sonnets "in vita di Madonna Laura." Besides poems by Petrarch, including several complete sestinas, Lasso also composed madrigals on poems by Ariosto, Tasso, Bembo, Sannazaro, and others. He neglected the new pastoral poems of Guarini in favor of sacred texts by the religious Petrarchists Gabriele Fiamma and Luigi Tansillo. Tansillo wrote the words for Lasso's cycle of twenty seven-voice *madrigali spirituali*, the *Lagrime di San Pietro*, on morbidly religious texts of almost Baroque fervor. Like Lasso's last motets, these were written in an austere polyphony that seldom allows a place for elaborate melismas and yet draws on a lifetime's experience to bring out the poetry's meaning by relatively simple but inexhaustibly subtle and inventive means.

It is virtually impossible to characterize succinctly Lasso's work as a whole. His mastery and the range of his capabilities were so great that his music is still not completely understood. To be sure, much of his polyphony is very difficult to control in performance; it is no easy task to bring out the subtlety

EXAMPLE 11–8. Orlando di Lasso, *Nessun visse giamai*, mm. 1–8.

and shapeliness of individual melodic lines within the typically dense mass of counterpoint. Unlike Palestrina's music, Lasso's does not virtually sing itself, for it lacks the transparency of texture and grace so important to the Roman composer. But Lasso's compositions gain thereby in energy and "rugged power" (Gustave Reese's phrase). If one characteristic feature should be emphasized more than any other, it is his deriving inspiration chiefly from the words he set, allowing them to generate most of the musical details in his works. More than any of the other great composers of the late sixteenth century except the virtuoso madrigalists, Lasso believed that the words were to be master of the music.

TOMÁS LUIS DE VICTORIA

Tomás Luis de Victoria (ca. 1548–1611), like Cristóbal de Morales before him, spent many years in Rome, and his music reflects the contact he had with Palestrina and his circle. Born in Ávila, Victoria received his early education as a choirboy at the cathedral there under Gerónimo de Espinar and Bernardino de Ribera—the latter one of the most respected Spanish composers of the day. At about the age of seventeen he was sent to pursue his studies in Rome and enrolled in the Collegio Germanico (a Jesuit college founded to counteract Lutheran tendencies among German youth), which was under Spanish direction at the time. Palestrina served as chapel master at its sister institution, the Seminario Romano, during those years, and the young Spaniard may have learned from him. In 1575 Victoria was ordained as a priest and worked as singer, organist, and chaplain at several Roman churches; he also became chapel master at the Collegio Germanico but kept the position for only two years, from 1575 to 1577.

In spite of his musical abilities, Victoria evidently did not desire work as director of music at a high-ranking institution and did not seek a place of honor and distinction in Rome's musical life. He carried out his pastoral work and devoted himself to acts of charity and to musical composition (he published eight books of sacred music before 1585).

In his last years in Rome, Victoria's finances were improved by income from the Spanish benefices conferred on him by the pope. He developed strong ties to the Castilian community in Rome through his work for the Spanish Confraternity of the Resurrection, and in the dedication to King Philip II of his second book of Masses (1583) he wrote that he wanted only to return to Spain and a life of religious service there. Perhaps in answer to Victoria's homage, and certainly in recognition of his standing as a composer and musician, Philip II appointed him chaplain to his sister the Dowager Empress Maria, widow of Maximilian II, who had retired to the convent of the Descalzas Reales in Madrid in 1584. From 1587 Victoria remained with her, and he worked at the convent until his death in 1611. Although it housed a strictly cloistered community of nuns, the Descalzas Reales convent was extremely well endowed; its chapel was one of the royal chapels of Spain, and its services were often attended by the royal household and Spanish noble families. The chapel choir was expected to meet the highest standards in the quality of its voices and performance, and there is evidence suggesting that Victoria had relatively free rein in adjusting or adding to the musical forces of the chapel as his music required. Thus, Victoria's move back to Spain not only gave him the prestige and perks of royal service but also provided an ideal experimental laboratory for the performance of his music.

As we have seen, Spain had a rich and flourishing musical culture during the sixteenth century and could boast a number of excellent composers. Of them all, however, only Victoria can be compared to Palestrina, Lasso, and Byrd in the stature of his achievement, even though the Spaniard was neither very prolific (at least not by comparison with the others, each of whom composed a strikingly large number of masterpieces) nor very wide-ranging in his outlook. His complete works comprise about twenty Masses, about forty-five motets, and a number of other compositions with specific liturgical functions—Magnificats, Offices for the Dead and for Holy Week (including superb Lamentations and two dramatic Passions), and a series of hymns for the complete church year. He wrote no madrigals or other secular music of any kind, and this restriction of genre provides a key to his musical personality. His music is devout, pious, and intense. "He had no other aim," Higinio Anglés wrote (*New Oxford History of Music,* vol. 4, 1968) "than to sing of the Cross and the mysteries of the Redemption, using means uncontaminated by profane art."

Actually, however, Victoria's compositions *are* "contaminated" by techniques associated with secular music to the extent that these techniques support and enhance the deeply felt views expressed in the sacred texts he chose to set. He never composed a sacred work on a secular cantus firmus (although one of his Masses parodies Janequin's *La Guerre*). Though his motets are imbued with the notion that music must reveal and intensify textual meaning, an idea supported by the engineers of the Counter-Reformation, that notion derived at least in part from the fashionable musical humanism so important in sixteenth-century Italian musical and intellectual circles and was worked out first and most enthusiastically in the madrigal. In his concern with text expression Victoria resembles Lasso, although the Spaniard's style is closer to Palestrina's. Like Palestrina, Victoria wrote a music distinguished for its clarity and internal logic. But Victoria was willing to disturb the even flow of counterpoint: to emphasize a word or a phrase he would, for example, tolerate an "ungraceful" leap of a major sixth (which Palestrina avoided), or he would allow a strong melodic line to proceed on its way without immediately reversing its direction to preserve a sense of careful balance. In fact, it is no exaggeration to say that Victoria showed a genuinely dramatic flair in the way he set sacred texts.

Victoria's motets are all so finely made and so perfectly fitted to their words that it is difficult to know which of them represent him at his best or most typical. Many choice passages come immediately to mind. The beautifully balanced chordal opening of *O quam gloriosum,* for example, soon rises to its high point before sinking down to the cadence; the passage vividly conveys the sense of the words, "O how glorious is the kingdom where all the Saints rejoice with Christ." In the same motet, stunning bursts of imitative rising scale passages erupt beneath the sustained line of the superius at the word "gaudent" ("they rejoice"). The spacious opening imitation of the Christmas motet *O magnum mysterium* (Example 11–9) is skillfully fitted together so that none of the joins show; the new music sung by the upper two voices at the entrance of the lower two forms a perfect foil for the last member of the phrase, the partially sequential cadencing material (mm. 15ff) derived from the second part of the opening melody. Victoria varied the rhythmic pace and texture of *O magnum mysterium* to bring out the rhetoric of the words; the reverent chordal salutation to the Virgin, "O beata Virgine," for example, contrasts very effectively with the preceding imitative counterpoint and with the conventional but nevertheless impressive shift to triple meter on "Alleluia" that follows almost immediately afterwards. In the five-voice *Resplenduit facies ejus* (and several other five-voice motets), Victoria showed off his contrapuntal skill in constructing a canon between the two top voices. And he made symbolism palpable in *Iste Sanctus* when he introduced a Gregorian cantus firmus in long notes at the words "for he was founded upon a sure rock."

EXAMPLE 11–9. Tomás Luis de Victoria, *O magnum mysterium*, mm. 1–19.

Victoria's art consists of more than striking passages in isolation and demonstrations of contrapuntal skill. Individual phrases fit into their proper place within a larger context, and technical feats are subordinated to the composer's expressive intent. *O vos omnes* (Example 11–10), a relatively short and contrapuntally uncomplicated motet of great emotional impact and intensity, serves well to demonstrate Victoria's mastery at shaping entire movements. To be sure, the formal outlines of the composition are quite conventional: since the text is a responsory—taken from the Lamentations of Jeremiah: "All ye that pass by, behold and see if there be any sorrow like unto my sorrow"—the music is shaped according to the scheme aBcB. The motet seems to grow from the single pitch D, sung first by the tenor and then doubled by the altus. The voices

EXAMPLE 11–10. Tomás Luis de Victoria, *O vos omnes*, mm. 1–24, 34–51.

(*a*) mm. 1–24

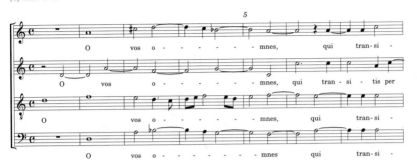

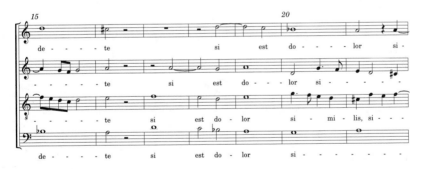

EXAMPLE 11–10. (*Continued*)

(*b*) mm. 34–51

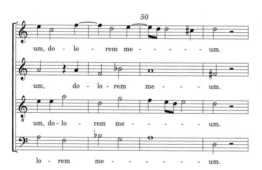

enter one by one without imitating each other (see Example 11–10a), yet we sense the multiplicity of the "All ye" of the opening words. This opening text is set relatively neutrally as two balanced phrases, the first ending on a chord other than the tonic (III in D-Dorian), the second cadencing (with a VII⁶–I formula) on the tonic.

Some of the affective power of the work comes from its superb details, especially those in the refrain. The descending tetrachord on "si est dolor" (a motive already suggested in the first phrase of the motet) calls forth suspensions, and their frequency and level of dissonance increase sharply on "similis" (Example 11–10a mm. 20–24). Indeed, the train of suspensions starting in m. 21 with the pungent interplay between the "forbidden" interval C$^\sharp$ to F, takes no fewer than three measures to resolve. The declamatory motive on "sicut dolor meus," rising a minor second and then falling back to its original pitch, is extraordinarily poignant despite its simplicity and adherence to convention. Victoria frequently expressed sorrow by motives similarly involving a minor second. Here introduced by empty fifths, this motive is stated three times, each time being reworked with different harmonies.

Even more striking than these details, though, is the effect Victoria achieved by recomposing the phrase "attendite et videte" ("behold and see") the second time it appears. The first time, he began the phrase with a straightforward declamatory motive on "attendite," mostly on one pitch and scored as a dialogue between a trio of voices and the solo superius, followed by a tutti on "et videte" (mm. 11–15). When the phrase reappears (Example 11–10b), it is recomposed in a higher range (at the beginning the roles of the voices are reversed, the solo superius being answered by a trio) and extended; and the music for "dolorem meum" reworks—one might almost say "develops"—material from the first phrase. The effect of these changes gives the second exhortation much greater intensity, if not greater urgency, and makes the refrain that follows more than the last member of a conventional repetition scheme; it is a moving dénouement, made necessary by the previous buildup.

In *O vos omnes*, Victoria gave musical coherence to the structure not merely by following a traditional formal pattern, by concentrating his attention on the few central motives that permeate the entire motet, or by carefully balancing each phrase against the others (a procedure in which the role of harmony should not be underestimated). Though he did all those things, the most important element in the coherence of the motet is its dramatic credibility.

In addition to his relatively small but very fine corpus of motets for from four to six voices, Victoria also wrote a series of sacred works for two or three antiphonal choirs, including several Masses, Magnificats, Marian antiphons, psalms, and sequences. These double- and triple-choir pieces remind us that, whatever his personal humility, his musical profile is striking. His pieces for two or more choirs, moreover, are among the first in what would soon become a fast-growing repertory of Roman music for multiple choirs; indeed, his psalm setting *Laetatus sum* for twelve parts in three choirs was the first piece of Roman triple-choir music ever published (in his *Motecta* of 1583). Neither so concentrated nor so intensely expressive as his motets for single choir, Victoria's antiphonal compositions generally proceed in a fairly relaxed imitative polyphony frequently interspersed with purely chordal passages—a style similar to that of most polychoral music of the late sixteenth century. Victoria's antiphonal works are solemn and ceremonial: if he did not strive for great depth of feeling in them, neither did he attempt the spectacular and colorful effects achieved by the Venetian composers of the time. The *Missa pro victoria*, based on Janequin's *La Guerre*, is exceptional not only in being his sole work built on a secular model but also in its exploration of a *concertante* style, with many repeated notes and short time values, more characteristic of the virtuoso northern Italian musicians (even then in the process of forging a new, Baroque style) than of the sober Roman circle of composers around Palestrina.

When they were first published, many of these antiphonal works were supplied with an organ part that duplicates all the voices of the first chorus as literally as the limitations of the instrument permit; when the other choruses sing, the organ remains silent. Perhaps Victoria intended precisely the particular sonority that the published music indicates. More likely the existence of the printed organ accompaniment reflects a widespread performing convention of the time. If organists had the option to double singers whenever they wished, they would have needed to prepare such parts for themselves; the printed version saved them time and trouble and ensured them an accompaniment free from errors. It may even be that Victoria's organ parts for Chorus I imply instrumental support or doubling for Choruses II and III as well.

Victoria's twenty Masses include some that paraphrase plainchant (such as the *Missa Ave maris stella* and the *Missa De Beata Virgine*) and some that parody motets by other great composers of the time (among them those on Guerrero's *Simile est regnum coelorum* and Palestrina's *Surge propera,* and the *Missa Gaudeamus,* based on Morales's *Jubilate Deo*). But more than half of the composer's Masses parody his own motets—*Ascendens Christus, O magnum mysterium, O quam gloriosum, Quam pulchri sunt, Trahe me post te,* and others. In reworking his own music for use in a new context, Victoria seems neither to have followed a single set of rules mechanically nor to have developed a fixed convention that he applied to all his parodies. Instead, he chose passages from his motets that seemed to him most appropriate for recomposition (or for a particular section of the new work); sometimes he quoted them quite literally, whereas at other times he reworked them almost beyond recognition. Nowhere in his *Missa O quam gloriosum,* for example, does he quote the splendid opening phrase of his own motet on which the Mass is based; he focused his attention on the subsequent points of imitation in the model and especially on the three that dominate the three sections of the Kyrie movement. The "Christe" section duplicates the final phrase of the motet; Victoria preserved his original polyphony except for minor adjustments and the addition at the very beginning of a new imitative line in the altus. The same musical material appears again at the end of the first half of the Credo and at the end of the first section of the Sanctus, as well as during the opening section of the Gloria, where it comes into and goes out of focus, as it were, barely recognizable and embedded in newly written polyphony. Victoria's technique of parodying pre-existent music, in short, is highly sophisticated, reflecting the refinement and change that any procedure undergoes after a half century or more of common use.

Victoria seldom set the words of the Mass dramatically. His tendency toward restraint and concision in the Mass Ordinary is illustrated in the opening of his Mass *O quam gloriosum*: perhaps he chose not to cite the magnificent opening phrase of his motet because he felt the passage to be too highly charged, expressive, or vivid, or merely too intimately connected with its original text to serve appropriately as a part of the solemn and traditional ritual of the Mass Ordinary. In his Mass settings he introduced madrigalisms only occasionally, and frequently gave special attention to the passages traditionally singled out for emphasis (such as "Et incarnatus est," "Crucifixus," and "Et resurrexit" in the Credo) only by setting them in contrasting textures. In general, his Masses, with their impeccable diction and reserved and sober counterpoint, show off his conservative, Palestrinian side. If they are not filled with as many sweeping melismas or long gentle arches of melody as those by the Roman composer, they are often marked by a concision in declamatory and imitative passages that allows neither for extensive elaboration of the musical material nor for illustrating the words. A fervent, intensely focused musician, Victoria showed in his Masses that he, like Palestrina, understood the virtue of economy of means. His Masses show him to have been one of the great masters of the "strict" contrapuntal style of the late Renaissance, and they demonstrate, too, the strong association between severely refined counterpoint and sacred texts that shaped a great deal of religious music in the seventeenth century, especially in Spain, Portugal, and the Hispanic New World.

WILLIAM BYRD

Rather than concentrating his efforts on a single style or on one kind of music, William Byrd (1543–1623), like Orlando di Lasso, displayed a multifaceted musical personality. The range and versatility of Byrd's achievement, as well as the superb quality of individual compositions, distinguish him from his contemporaries. He excelled in almost every genre cultivated in the England of his time: Latin Masses and motets, English anthems and services, songs and madrigal-like compositions, and music for viol consort and for keyboard instruments. It is not only the character of Byrd's work but also his chronological position that makes him a pivotal figure in the history of English music. He was both the last great composer in the rich tradition of Catholic polyphony in Britain and the first of that "golden age of music" which began in the middle years of Elizabeth I's reign. His Latin church music embodies the final perfect union between the native tradition and the contrapuntal techniques that flourished in Italy and the Netherlands earlier in the century. His English church music, including his verse anthems (a genre that he did much to shape), ushers in a period of great creativity during the seventeenth century by musicians like Orlando Gibbons, Henry and William Lawes, William Child, and Matthew Locke. Elements from an older English song tradition combine in his consort songs and other polyphonic songs and madrigals with new techniques introduced into England from Italy; his secular works make a unique contribution to a repertory that underwent amazing development during the reigns of Elizabeth I and James I and that produced many fine madrigals and related compositions by Thomas Morley (one of Byrd's pupils), Thomas Weelkes, and John

Wilbye, among others, and lute ayres by musicians such as John Dowland, Thomas Campion, Philip Rosseter, and John Danyel. Byrd's fantasias for viol consort and his pavans, galliards, and sets of variations for virginals and other keyboard instruments have an honored place in the rich repertory of Elizabethan and Jacobean instrumental music. They herald an astonishing burst of activity, in the late sixteenth and seventeenth centuries, that brought forth compositions for lute, cittern, bandora, and other plucked stringed instruments by Anthony Holborne, John Dowland, Francis Cutting, Francis Pilkington, Robert Johnson, and many others; for viol consort by composers such as Alfonso Ferrabosco the younger and other members of his family, Thomas Lupo, Richard Deering, John Cooper (or Giovanni Coperario, as he preferred to call himself), John Jenkins, and Orlando Gibbons; and for keyboard instruments by John Bull, Orlando Gibbons, and a host of only slightly less important virginalists, among them Thomas Tomkins, Giles Farnaby, and Peter Philips.

Byrd spent most of his professional life as organist for the Chapel Royal. He was appointed to it in 1570 (though he may not actually have joined it until 1572) as a young man in his late twenties, after having worked as organist at Lincoln cathedral for almost ten years, and he continued to serve the court until he died more than fifty years later in 1623. To judge from the texts he chose to set—many of them grave, penitential, or supplicatory—he was a sober and pious man. He remained a Catholic throughout his life in a Protestant country hostile to his religion. Byrd was in some sense a religious activist: despite difficulties with the authorities from time to time about his deeply held beliefs, he nevertheless composed and published a great deal of music for the Catholic liturgy. Yet his religious views did not prevent him from holding an important position in the Anglican church or from providing compositions for its services.

One early commentator wrote that Byrd was "bred up to music under Tallis," although just when or where the young Byrd could have studied with the older master is unclear. Certainly the two shared the position as organist in the Chapel Royal; and until Tallis's death in 1585 they shared, too, a monopoly to print music in England, a privilege that turned out to be not quite so profitable as the two musicians might have hoped, and one that Byrd eventually assigned to Thomas East of London. The first volume that the two composers published under their license was the *Cantiones, quae ab argumento sacrae vocantur* of 1575, to which each of them contributed seventeen motets. (Denis Stevens has made the ingenious suggestion that this number was chosen because the collection appeared in the seventeenth year of Elizabeth's reign.) These thirty-four motets were the first Latin church music to be printed in England and the earliest of the two composers' works to be published.

Tallis seems to have included in the 1575 *Cantiones sacrae* some works that he had written a number of years earlier. It is not surprising, then, that his choice of texts and his treatment of imitation reflect slightly older practices. His contribution to the anthology, however, includes some of his best works, such as the highly expressive *In jejunio* and the adroitly canonic *Miserere nostri*. By and large, however, the music in this collection, especially the compositions by the thirty-two-year-old Byrd, must have astonished musicians in London, who would have appreciated the new subtlety and flexibility displayed in the handling of imitative techniques and in the manipulation of texture, the new expressiveness of the melodies, and the new freedom Byrd enjoyed in choosing texts.

Early English composers who made extensive use of imitative techniques tended to lay out their points in perfectly symmetrical patterns. In the 1575 *Cantiones sacrae*, Byrd adopted a more flexible procedure and introduced successive voices irregularly so that he could spin out his contrapuntal lines in a complex and interesting manner. In *Domine secundum actum meum* (Example 11–11), Byrd's setting of a respond from the Office of the Dead, the initial exposition takes up two sharply defined motives: the declamatory "Domine" and another, separated from the first by rests, on "secundum actum meum" involv-

EXAMPLE 11–11. William Byrd, *Domine secundum actum meum*, mm. 1–10.

ing an upper-neighbor note. The shape of both themes is clearly suggested by the words. To develop them independently, a process that continues throughout the typically expansive thirty-two-measure opening section, Byrd staggered the entrances of the voices in asymmetrical sequence. That he derived his plan for doing so from a similar motet by Alfonso Ferrabosco the elder (*Domine, non secundum peccata mea*) does not, as Joseph Kerman has convincingly shown, challenge the notion that Byrd broadened the horizons of English music in the 1570s by developing freer and more flexible methods of writing imitative counterpoint than had previously been heard. Many of his motets, for example, are unusually long, allowing him full scope to work over his themes and show them off in various combinations; and a number of his works proceed as a series of expositions with two, or occasionally even three, subjects. One or two of the 1575 motets employ canon in a systematic way, and one, *Diliges Dominum*, is written for eight voices in two choirs (although some of the six-voice compositions exploit antiphonal effects more fully). But in spite of Byrd's preoccupation with contrapuntal technique, the most important voices in his motets—those that most clearly reveal the underlying structure as the music proceeds—are apt to be the soprano and the bass. The polarity of voices is of course especially evident in those works written almost entirely in a homophonic texture, like *Emendemus in melius*, one of the finest motets in the whole collection.

For a few of the motets in the 1575 *Cantiones sacrae*, Byrd chose texts of a traditional kind, which he treated in a traditional way: there is one respond, *Libera me*, built over a cantus firmus, for example, and one canonic antiphon, *Miserere mihi Domine*, with cantus firmus; one motet, *Laudate, pueri*, is nothing more than a previously composed fantasia for viols to which selected psalm verses have been added. Many of the texts in the anthology do not have a regular place in the liturgy, and most of the responds are handled freely, without borrowed material, in imitative polyphony. As we have seen, continental composers earlier in the century had begun to choose motet texts for reasons other than strictly liturgical ones, but Byrd departed radically from English practice in doing so. It may be that his choices reflect his Catholic sympathies or were shaped by the devotional activities of the Catholic community. Whatever the case, Byrd's motets are striking for their directness and expressive power. He crafted his music to support and enhance the texts he selected, whether they were from Scripture, hymns, prayers, or parts of the liturgy. He made his attitude explicit in the preface to his *Gradualia* of 1605, where he wrote, "In sacred words ... there is such a profound and hidden power that to one thinking upon things divine and diligently and earnestly pondering them, all the fittest numbers occur as if of themselves." Eschewing madrigalisms and other extroverted sorts of word illustration, Byrd invented themes and musical structures tied as closely to their words and as expressive in their musical rhetoric as any devised by the other great exponents of text expression in the late sixteenth century— Lasso, Victoria, or the virtuoso madrigalists of Italy.

Byrd published two further volumes of *Cantiones sacrae*, one in 1589 for five voices and the other in 1591 for five and six voices. These later sets of motets, as long and expansive as those in the 1575 collection, contain even fewer strictly liturgical works. Kerman has even convincingly argued that the large number of motets from the 1589 and 1591 *Cantiones sacrae* that deal with the Babylonian captivity or the coming of God, or that beg not for mercy but for liberty, reflect the composer's deep concern for the plight of the recusant (Catholic) community in Protestant England. Byrd's response to the motets' texts, captured in powerfully direct and expressive music, is even more apparent in the later than the earlier collections. His later motets also span a wider range of textures and styles; Byrd makes greater use of chromaticism and antiphonal effects, for example, and he writes livelier and more varied rhythms.

Whereas the *Cantiones sacrae* are largely independent of the liturgy, Byrd's two volumes of *Gradualia* (first published in 1605 and 1607 and both reissued in 1610) contain the most important collection of Mass and Office Propers since Isaac's *Choralis Constantinus*. In the *Gradualia*, which Byrd himself described as his "swan song" (although he was only in his early sixties when the volume was published, and he was to live almost twenty years longer), the composer included more than one hundred motets, mostly settings of Introits, Graduals, Alleluias, Offertories, and Communions for the principal feasts of the Catholic church year. As befits music used within the ritual, the motets in the *Gradualia* are relatively short and concise; the service does not allow time for the elaborate and leisurely contrapuntal developments of which Byrd was so fond in the *Cantiones sacrae*. But the music in the *Gradualia* is not less fine because it is more succinct; on the contrary, the composer maintained a consistently high standard of excellence throughout the volume.

That the pieces in the *Gradualia* are so concise may reflect not simply Byrd's maturity as a composer and his talent for directness of expression but also the devotional context for which the collection was written. Public celebration of the Catholic Mass was forbidden under both Elizabeth and James—at least one person was arrested for owning the *Gradualia* in 1605. The two volumes of the *Gradualia* contain music intended for the Roman Catholic liturgy, a liturgy that in England was celebrated in secret and in which we can imagine that clandestine Masses were celebrated perhaps with some haste. Byrd's three settings of the Mass Ordinary were surely performed in secret Catholic services, and they survive only in copies with their title pages missing, perhaps significantly; we do not know the year they were published (though a case can be made for supposing they came out between about 1592 and 1595). These Masses—for three, four, and five voices, respectively—are all free of borrowed material or any scaffolding devices, although they do make limited use of head motives. He built up these magnificent structures from imitative polyphony handled freely and flexibly in his finest mature manner. They are also unique, for no continental composers invented a textural complexity quite the same as that characterizing Byrd's music as English, and no other English composers of his generation wrote polyphonic settings of the Ordinary of the Mass.

In spite of his deeply held religious beliefs, Byrd wrote some of his finest music for the Anglican Church, including two complete Services—settings of the morning and evening canticles (in Byrd's time the Venite, Te Deum, Bene-dictus, Magnificat, and Nunc Dimittis) and the Communion Service (Kyrie, Creed, and sometimes Sanctus), which together form the central ritual of the English church. Byrd's services are the Anglican counterparts of his Catholic Masses. The Short Service, like all English "short" services, is written largely in the note-against-note counterpoint that Archbishop Cranmer recommended to Henry VIII as the only appropriate style for church music; in Byrd's setting the two sides of the choir, *decani* and *cantoris,* answer each other without overlap-ping. On the other hand, his Great Service ("great" because written in elabo-rated florid counterpoint) fully explores all possible combinations of its two five-voice choirs. The rich density of its frequently imitative texture helps explain why this is one of the greatest works in the Anglican tradition.

Byrd also composed anthems—in effect, English motets. Whereas some of them appeared only in manuscripts, many were printed in three miscella-neous collections issued during his lifetime: *Psalmes, Sonets and Songs* (1588), *Songs of Sundrie Natures* (1589), and *Psalmes, Songs and Sonets* (1611). As their titles imply, these anthologies contain a variety of types of music by Byrd: settings of psalms, full and verse anthems, secular and sacred songs for solo voice accompanied by a consort of viols (so-called consort songs), one or two genuine madrigals along with a greater number of works that are better called simply "polyphonic songs," two instrumental fantasias, and even one setting in Italian of a stanza by Ariosto.

Byrd gave equal importance to all the lines in the three- and four-voice compositions in his miscellany of 1589; they are classical examples of late Renaissance imitative polyphony, some with simultaneous expositions of two subjects and other contrapuntal artifice. But most of the works for five and six voices in the volumes from 1588 and 1589 (and some of the six-voice composi-tions of 1611) were conceived for a single singer (or sometimes two), whose rel-atively simple melodies are contrasted with a complex contrapuntal web of melodic lines originally intended to be played by a consort of viols, even though they are supplied with texts in the printed volumes (probably to take advantage of the new market for madrigals). As Byrd wrote in the epistle to the reader in the 1588 collection, "Heere are divers songs, which being originally made for Instruments to expresse the harmonie, and one voyce to pronounce the dittie, are now framed in all parts for voyces to sing the same." These consort songs, which include metrical psalms as well as moral and courtly poems (many of them cast in strophic form), are not written as solos with subordinated accom-paniment. Instead, the voice shares the musical interest with the viols; it is as though a sung cantus firmus were imposed on a fantasia for viols. The beginning of *Susanna fair* (Example 11–12), its text a translation of the chanson *Susanne un jour* so popular with continental composers, shows the typical stylistic fea-tures of the composer's consort songs. The well-shaped vocal line, with its impeccable diction and carefully planned climax, does not assertively express the meaning of the text; the emotionally neutral cast of the melody enabled Byrd with greater ease to repeat it literally to set subsequent stanzas of the

EXAMPLE 11–12. William Byrd, *Susanna fair*, mm. 1–16.

poem, and the composition proceeds in uninterrupted flowing counterpoint with no abrupt changes or contrasts. In his consort songs Byrd concentrated on elements of musical design and formal structure, giving less attention to rhetorical display or vivid text expression.

Byrd was the chief composer to carry forward the tradition of instrumentally accompanied solo songs that had existed in England at least since the choirboy plays and court entertainments of the 1550s and 1560s. The lute ayres of Dowland and Campion share some of the traits of the consort songs, at least in their strophic orientation, though the textures of the two genres are totally different. In addition, the small repertory of seventeenth-century "cries" by Thomas Weelkes, Orlando Gibbons, and others—extended viol fantasias on which a collection of street cries and songs of itinerant vendors is superimposed more or less at random—constitute a special subcategory of music derived in style from consort songs. Byrd evidently resisted the well-nigh overwhelming tide of madrigal writing that swept England after the *Musica Transalpina* of 1588. He continued to cultivate his intricate, finely wrought, continuous counterpoint in which an uninterrupted flow is more important than a dramatic presentation of the text. Only very occasionally, as in *This sweet and merry month of May,* did Byrd ever approach the madrigalian attitude as expressed, for example, in the works of Thomas Morley, Thomas Weelkes, and John Wilbye.

Many of the metrical psalms in Byrd's three miscellaneous volumes were conceived for solo voice and viols in the manner of consort songs. Two carols in the 1589 collection, *From Virgin's womb* and *An earthly tree,* contrast a verse for solo voice (or duet) and viols with a burden for full choir. The 1589 anthology includes an Easter anthem, *Christ rising again,* in which sections— "verses"—for two solo singers and viols alternate with sections for full choir. Each of the three volumes contains, as well, some anthems for unaccompanied choir ("full" as opposed to "verse" anthems such as *Christ rising again*); some of these in the 1611 collection, such as *Retire my soul* and *Arise, Lord, into thy rest,* are superb examples of Byrd's contrapuntal and expressive skill and are among his finest works.

Byrd's instrumental music, which set new artistic standards for his contemporaries, consists for the most part of fantasias, dances, variation sets, and cantus-firmus settings (including *In nomines*), for solo keyboard (harpsichord, virginals, or organ) or for instrumental ensemble (chiefly consorts of viols but presumably also groups of recorders or other appropriate instruments). The viol music is preserved mostly in manuscript miscellanies of textless part music (though some of the pieces in these anthologies may be motets and secular vocal pieces without their words), the virginal music in a number of important keyboard collections, the most famous of which is the enormous Fitzwilliam Virginal Book, containing nearly three hundred pieces copied out by a Catholic, Francis Tregian, while he was in prison for his religious (and political) beliefs from 1609 to 1619. Other keyboard sources include the elegantly written My Ladye Nevell's Booke, dated 1591 and containing exclusively works by Byrd; a number of other manuscript books copied out by or for private individuals; and one important printed anthology, *Parthenia, or the Maydenhead of the First Musicke that ever was printed for the Virginalls,* published in 1612 or 1613. (The title involves a pun on the Greek word for "virgin," *parthenos,* which was repeated and carried further in a companion volume from about 1614, *Parthenia Inviolata,* containing songs and dances for virginals with bass viol.) *Parthenia* offers music by three of the most distinguished virginalists—Byrd, John Bull, and Orlando Gibbons.

Almost half of Byrd's viol music is made up of cantus-firmus settings in three, four, and five voices, apparently mostly early works, in which the composer added suave imitative counterpoint around a simple statement of a plainsong hymn or Miserere, or the *In nomine* melody so beloved of English composers of the sixteenth and early seventeenth centuries. Byrd's few dances for viols—a five-voice pavan and a six-voice pavan-and-galliard that are thematically linked—show how skillfully he could work out an intricate texture in music that is structurally simple (consisting normally of three short strains, each repeated) and basically homophonic; and his two grounds for viol consort, one of them the well-known five-voice *Browning* (on a tune also known as *The leaves be greene*), display his ingenuity in devising constantly renewed counterpoints against the same repeated melody. Byrd's viol fantasias are written in the rich and rather dense imitative texture of much of his other music; we have seen that one could be transformed into a motet with very little adjustment. Byrd sometimes divides his fantasias into clearly articulated sections, and several include passages of dancelike music.

In Byrd's keyboard music, which was written largely in the same forms as his viol music, fantasias and other abstract musical forms are far outweighed by dance movements (especially the magisterial pavan-galliard pairs that he stylized and brought into the realm of high-art music) and long, brilliantly developed sets of variations (many of them based on simple folk or popular tunes such as *Go from my window, Gypsies' Round,* and *John come kiss me now*). An alignment of the first two bars from several variations on *The Woods so Wild* (Example 11–13) demonstrates Byrd's inventiveness in devising figuration patterns to fit within the melodic and harmonic framework suggested by the tune, but such excerpts cannot illustrate the expert way he formed complete pieces from disparate units by controlling the pace of each voice and building to an impressive climax. Perhaps the greatest pleasure in hearing Byrd's keyboard music (indeed, music by any of the English virginalists) comes from perceiving the sumptuous and imaginative ways he put together a rich texture and then varied it, often by applying and manipulating a different figuration pattern for each unit of the structure. It is a kind of music to be savored in its details.

Byrd did not write every kind of instrumental music cultivated in England in his time. He left us no music composed especially for lute, no ayres, and no music for the favorite English combination of lute, pandora, cittern, two viols, and flute—the "broken consort" that Thomas Morley, for example, exploited in his *Consort Lessons* of 1599. Nevertheless, few composers of the late Renaissance were as broad in their interests and achievements as William Byrd. He would have been memorable for his Latin or English church music alone or for his consort songs or virginal music. As it is, his extraordinary accomplishments in virtually every genre earned for him a place of distinction even during England's golden age of music.

EXAMPLE 11–13. William Byrd, *The Woods so Wild,* mm. 1–2 of variations 1, 5, 7, 9, 10.

BIBLIOGRAPHICAL NOTES

Palestrina's complete works are available in two editions, the earlier made by F. X. Haberl, F. Espagne, and others and published in 33 volumes (Leipzig, 1862–1907), the second made by R. Casimiri, L. Virgili, K. Jeppesen, and L. Bianchi, in 35 volumes (Rome, 1935–87; one vol. forthcoming). Palestrina's *Pope Marcellus Mass* is available as a Norton Critical Score, edited and with a scholarly introduction by Lewis Lockwood (New York, 1975). For further examples of music composed in the spirit of Catholic Church reform, see Vincenzo Ruffo, *Seven Masses,* ed. Lewis Lockwood, RRMR 32–33 (1979).

The best-known study of Palestrina in English is Knud Jeppesen, *The Style of Palestrina and the Dissonance* (London, 1946; reprint 1970); see also Jerome Roche, *Palestrina* (London, 1971). Jeffrey Dean, "The Repertory of the Cappella Giulia in the 1560s," *JAMS* 41 (1988): 465–90, gives evidence for the Franco-Flemish polyphony performed at this institution at mid-century, as does Richard Sherr, "From the Diary of a 16th-Century Papal Singer," *Current Musicology* 25 (1978): 83–98. Although it concentrates on a slightly earlier period, Christopher Reynolds, "Rome: a City of Rich Contrast," in *The Renaissance from the 1470s to the End of the 16th Century*, ed. Iain Fenlon (London, 1989), 63–101, is an extremely informative look at Roman musical life and institutions. Recent studies of Roman documents and of Palestrina's music include Noel O'Regan, "Palestrina and the oratory of SS. Trinità dei Pellegrini," *Atti del secondo convegno internazionale di studi palestriniani* (Palestrina, 1991); Noel O'Regan, "Palestrina, a Musician and Composer in the Market-place," *EM* 22 (1994): 551–72; and Peter Phillips, "Reconsidering Palestrina," *EM* 22 (1994): 575–85.

On Palestrina's compositional methods, see Quentin Quereau, "Aspects of Palestrina's Parody Procedure," *JM* 1 (1982): 198–216. Works by Palestrina and Lassus are the focus of several studies of sixteenth-century modality by Harold S. Powers, including "The Modality of 'Vestiva i colli,'" *Studies in Renaissance and Baroque Music in Honor of Arthur Mendel* (Kassel, 1974), 31–46; "Modal Representation in Polyphonic Offertories," *EMH* 2 (1982): 43–86; and "Tonal Types and Modal Categories in Renaissance Polyphony," *JAMS* 34 (1981): 428–70.

The incomplete edition of Lasso's works, *Orlando di Lasso Sämtliche Werke*, 21 vols., ed. F. X. Haberl and A. Sandberger (Leipzig, 1894–1927), is being issued in a revised second edition, ed. Horst Leuchtmann (Wiesbaden, 1968–); the works by Lasso not included in this series appear in *Orlando di Lasso Sämtliche Werke neue Reihe*, a continuation begun by Wolfgang Boetticher and edited by Siegfried Hermelink, Kurt von Fischer, James Erb, and others (Kassel, 1956–). RRMR includes Lasso, *Two Motet Cycles for Matins for the Dead*, ed. Peter Bergquist, RRMR 55 (1983); *Canzoni villanesche and villanelle*, ed. Donna G. Cardamone, RRMR 82–83 (1990); and *Seven Penitential Psalms and Laudate Dominum de caelis*, ed. Peter Bergquist, RRMR 86–87 (1990). A modern edition of all the Lassus chansons published by Le Roy & Ballard is Orlande de Lassus, *Chansons from the Atelier of Le Roy and Ballard*, vols. 11–14 of *The Sixteenth-Century Chanson*, ed. Jane Bernstein (New York, 1987).

Most of the scholarly writings on Lasso are in German, and the most recent definitive study is Horst Leuchtmann, *Orlando di Lasso*, 2 vols. (Wiesbaden, 1976). Wolfgang Boetticher, *Orlando di Lasso und seine Zeit* (Kassel, 1958), is an exemplary biography but is now outdated and should be used only in light of more recent specialized studies; see also Boetticher, *Aus Orlando di Lassos Wirkungskreis* (Kassel, 1963). Of writings in English, the best introductions are the especially fine Lassus article by James Haar in *TNG*; Clive Wearing, "Orlandus Lassus (1532–1594) and the Munich Kapelle," *EM* 10 (1982): 147–53; and Jerome Roche, *Lassus* (London, 1982), a useful short overview. David Crook, *Orlando di Lasso's Imitation Magnificats for Counter-Reformation Munich* (Princeton, 1994), considers a single genre and its cultural context. *Orlando di Lasso, A Guide to Research* by James Erb (New York, 1990) is useful and carefully annotated, with lists of works, editions, and documents; an English translation of a 1982 essay by Horst Leuchtmann, "Orlando di Lasso or Inspired Madness: Humanistic Music In and Out of Season," xxi–xxxiv, serves as a thoughtful introduction. Some classic studies of Lasso's music are Kenneth Levy, "Susanne un jour, The History of a 16th-Century Chanson," *AnnM*, 1 (1953): 375–408; Edward E. Lowinsky, "Orlando di Lasso's Antwerp Motet Book and Its Relationship to the Contemporary Netherlandish Motet," in *Music in the Culture of the Renaissance and Other Essays*, ed. Bonnie J. Blackburn, vol. 1 (Chicago, 1989), 385–431; and Claude V. Palisca, "*Ut oratoria musica*: The Rhetorical Basis of Musical Mannerism"; in Palisca, *Studies in the History of Italian*

Music and Music Theory (Oxford, 1994), 282–309. The last-named considers Lasso's musical rhetoric and its analysis by his contemporary Joachim Burmeister. Other informative studies of Lasso's music include Denis Arnold, "The Grand Motets of Orlandus Lassus," *EM* 6 (1978): 170–81, on Lasso's double-choir music; Noel O'Regan, "The Early Polychoral Music of Orlando di Lasso. New Light from Roman Sources," *AcM* 56 (1984): 234–51; and James Haar, "The Early Madrigals of Lasso," *RBM* 39–40 (1985–86): 17–32. The same volume of *RBM* contains specialized but accessible studies of Lasso's music, such as Kristine K. Forney, "Orlando di Lasso's Opus 1: The Making and Marketing of a Renaissance Music Book," and Frank Dobbins, "Lassus—Borrower or Lender: The Chansons."

The complete works of Victoria were published by Felipe Pedrell in 8 volumes (Leipzig, 1902–13; reprint, 1965); and issued in a separate but incomplete edition within MME (vols. 25, 26, 30, 31), ed. Higinio Anglés (Barcelona, 1965–68). A separate edition of some of his motets was published by Samuel Rubio (Madrid, 1964), who also edited Victoria's monumental collection of music for Holy Week, the *Officium Hebdomadae Sanctae* (Cuenca, 1977). Another edition of the *Officium Hebdomadae Sanctae* is that of E. C. Cramer for the Institute of Mediaeval Music (Henryville, Pa., 1982). On Victoria's life and works, see Raffaele Casimiri, *Il Vittoria: nuovi documenti per una biografia sincera di Tommaso Ludovico de Victoria* (Rome, 1934); Hans von May, *Die Kompositionstechnik T. L. de Victorias* (Berne, 1943); Felipe Pedrell, *Tomás Luis de Victoria Abulense* (Valencia, 1918); and Robert Stevenson, *Spanish Cathedral Music in the Golden Age* (Berkeley and Los Angeles, 1961). Victoria's music has not received the scholarly attention it merits; in addition to the article by Robert Stevenson in *TNG*, a fine overview is his "Tomás Luis de Victoria (ca. 1548–1611): Unique Spanish Genius," *Inter-American Music Review* 12 (1991): 1–100. On Victoria in Rome, see especially Noel O'Regan, "Victoria, Soto and the Spanish Archconfraternity of the Resurrection in Rome," *EM* 22 (1994): 279–95.

Edmund H. Fellowes, *William Byrd* (London, 1936), remains the standard monograph on the composer, although it is by now out of date in a number of details and in its approach to Byrd's Catholicism. Fellowes's pioneering work also led him to edit *The Collected Works of William Byrd,* 20 vols. (London, 1937–50), an edition that is now being reissued with revisions (some volumes completely reedited) by Thurston Dart, Philip Brett, and others. A new edition, *The Byrd Edition,* under the general editorship of Philip Brett, is also in progress (London, 1970–   ). Byrd's keyboard music has been edited by Alan Brown, MB vols. 27–28 (and vol. 28 reprint, 1985). For a study of Byrd's instrumental music see Oliver Neighbour, *The Consort and Keyboard Music of William Byrd* (London, 1978). H. K. Andrews, *The Technique of Byrd's Vocal Polyphony* (London, 1966), is a detailed investigation of the composer's compositional technique, but the most scholarly and critical approach to Byrd's sacred music is Joseph Kerman, *The Masses and Motets of William Byrd* (London, 1981), subsuming his many earlier articles listed in the bibliography of his entry on Byrd in *TNG*. Joseph Kerman's *Write All These Down: Essays on Music* (Berkeley and Los Angeles, 1994) contains updated versions of several of his essays on Byrd's music; "William Byrd and Elizabethan Catholicism," 77–89, is especially important. *Byrd Studies,* ed. Alan Brown and Richard Turbet (Cambridge, 1991), contains a dozen essays by specialist scholars; see especially Peter Le Huray, "Some Thoughts about Cantus Firmus Composition; and a Plea for Byrd's *Christus resurgens,*" 1–23; Owen Rees, "The English Background to Byrd's Motets: Textual and Stylistic Models for *Infelix ego,*" 24–50; and Craig Monson, "'Throughout All Generations': Intimations of Influence in the Short Service Styles of Tallis, Byrd and Morley," 83–111. Craig Monson, *Voices and Viols in England 1600–1650: The Sources and the*

Music (Ann Arbor, 1982), sheds light on the dissemination of some of Byrd's music during his last years and beyond. On other aspects of the composer's work, see Philip Brett, "The English Consort Song, 1570–1625," *PRMA* 88 (1961–62); Brett, "Word-Setting in the Songs of Byrd," *PRMA* 98 (1971–72); Brett, "Homage to Taverner in Byrd's Masses," *EM* 9 (1981): 169–76; Craig Monson, "The Preces, Psalms and Litanies of Byrd and Tallis: Another 'Virtuous Contention in Love'," *MR* 40 (1979): 257–71; Monson, "Authenticity and Chronology in Byrd's Church Anthems," *JAMS* 35 (1982): 280–305; and other studies listed in Richard Turbet, *William Byrd: A Guide to Research* (New York, 1987).

Some general studies of English music during the period include Morrison C. Boyd, *Elizabethan Music and Musical Criticism,* 2d ed. (Philadelphia, 1962); Bruce Pattison, *Music and Poetry of the English Renaissance* (London, 1948); Walter L. Woodfill, *Musicians in English Society* (Princeton, 1953); and the appropriate chapters of John Caldwell, *The Oxford History of English Music,* vol. 1 (Oxford, 1991). Both the Fitzwilliam Virginal Book and My Lady Nevell's Booke have been issued in facsimile by Dover Publications, New York.

TWELVE
THE END OF THE RENAISSANCE

No matter how great the achievement of Palestrina, Lasso, Victoria, and Byrd, their work did not reflect everything that went on in Western music between 1560 and 1600, nor can it explain the radical change in style that took place at the turn into the seventeenth century. It is in Italy, especially in the madrigal and the lyric genres that grew out of it, that the shift away from older techniques and aesthetic norms can be seen most clearly. But even within Italy the situation was complex, and elements of continuity and change existed side by side at the end of the sixteenth century. For example, in addition to highly expressive settings of lyric poetry in a genuinely new style requiring the services of virtuoso singers to do them full justice, some composers wrote madrigals that scarcely differ in aesthetic outlook from those of the preceding generation; others put together sequences of simple, tuneful pieces to form narrative or quasi-dramatic *madrigal comedies,* or composed light and entertaining canzonette, balletti, balli, and the like. Some composers of sacred music took Palestrina or Victoria as their model and continued to write carefully regulated and expressively restrained counterpoint in a *stile antico* well into the seventeenth century and beyond. In Venice, Andrea and Giovanni Gabrieli and their contemporaries refined the technique of combining voices and instruments into splendid polychoral works known as "concertos."

ARMONIA.
Come dipinta in Firenze dal gran Duca Ferdinando.

V N A vaga, & bella donna, con vna lira doppia di quindici corde in mano, in capo hauerà vna corona con sette gioie tutte vguali, il vestimento è di sette colori, guarnito d'oro, & di diuerse gioie.

Figure 11. The allegorical figure of harmony is here shown "as she was depicted in Florence for the Grand Duke Ferdinand ... a beautiful woman holding a double lyre (a *lirone*) of 15 courses of strings; on her head she has a crown with seven jewels ... her dress is of seven colors, decorated with gold and diverse gems." The word for "jewels" is also that for "joys." The emblem, from Cesare Ripa, *Iconologia* (Rome, 1603), equates the richness of musical harmony with earthly concord and shows a realistic depiction of a relatively new instrument designed to produce a simple bowed chordal accompaniment of the very sort that Renaissance humanists imagined to have been used in ancient performances. (Courtesy of Kunsthistorisches Institute, Florence)

Among the many important intellectual developments of the sixteenth century, one facet of the more general humanism was a fascination with music of the ancient world. In Italy, discussion about ancient Greek music led on the one hand to various experiments in tuning and temperament and on the other toward the invention of monody and opera. In France, similar discussions inspired the foundation of Jean-Antoine de Baïf's Académie de poésie et de musique and created a new style, *musique mesurée à l'antique,* which had a great influence on French music of the early seventeenth century. As early as

the first decade of the sixteenth century, as we have seen, the German composer Tritonius, under the influence of the humanist Konrad Celtes, had published settings of Horace designed to help students learn classical meters. But
more general and widespread study of the music of the ancients did not take
place until later in the century. The nature of classical studies in music was different from studies in other fields, since very few specimens of actual Greek
music were known, and they could not be accurately deciphered. Scholars were
forced to speculate about the true nature of Greek music on the basis of theoretical treatises, some of which began to be generally known only toward the
middle of the sixteenth century.

Interest in Greek musical thought was of such currency in the Renaissance that it became almost universal. Aspects of humanist thought had influenced poets and composers in the fifteenth century, and most sixteenth-century
treatises pay at least lip service to the Greeks. Many writers made a serious
attempt to understand the character of Greek music. Surprisingly enough, in
spite of the lack of practical music sources, all the sixteenth-century scholars
arrived at very much the same general conception of ancient music, though
there were important details about which they differed. They were, however, in
basic disagreement about the extent to which modern music ought to be
reformed according to ancient precepts. The humanists Franchino Gafori, Giovanni Artusi, Francisco Salinas, and Pietro Cerone took a purely scholarly interest in Greek music. Others, such as Pontus de Tyard, Vincenzo Galilei,
Girolamo Mei, and Giovanni Battista Doni, imagined modern music to be vastly
inferior to the ancient and wished to change it radically. Still others, including
Gioseffo Zarlino, Heinrich Glareanus, Nicola Vicentino, and perhaps most of
the more humanistically inclined composers, took a middle position: sixteenth-
century music, they thought, had reached a new state of perfection, but it could
be improved still more, since it was in certain ways inferior to that of the Greeks.

A great deal of sixteenth-century speculation and discussion about
ancient music centered on theoretical problems: the nature of the scales and
modes from which Greek melodies had been constructed (including the characteristics of the diatonic, chromatic, and enharmonic *genera* and of the various
tuning systems proposed by ancient theorists); and the way quantitative Greek
and Latin meters could best be adapted to the accentual prosody of French,
Spanish, and Italian poetry. Nicola Vicentino, for example, described the Greek
genera in his treatise *L'antica musica ridotta alla moderna prattica* (published
in 1555, partly as a result of his defeat in a public debate on the subject), and he
explained how to demonstrate them on his invention, the *arcicembalo*, a harpsichord with six manuals capable of dividing the octave into thirty-one parts.
Vicentino also furnished specimens of his own compositions, including some
that illustrate the enharmonic genus and use microtones (indicated by dots over
the notes). Andrea Gabrieli wrote choruses for the first performance in Italian
of a Greek tragedy, Sophocles' *Oedipus rex*, translated by Orsatto Giustiniano
on the occasion of the opening of the neoclassical Teatro Olimpico in Vicenza in
1585. In his music Gabrieli tried to match the ancient meters exactly. However

important historically, the task defeated him artistically. In the long run, such experiments with prosody and speculation about genera, modes, meters, and tuning systems had only an indirect influence on the mainstream of music. Some stylistic innovations, like the increased use of chromaticism in the sixteenth-century madrigal, can be linked to humanistic study (see, for example, Lasso's *Prophetiae sibyllarum* or even the highly chromatic works in Vicentino's fifth book of five-voice madrigals, published in 1572), but the more historically oriented experiments, like those reported in Vicentino's treatise, had no far-reaching practical consequences.

From the beginning of discussions about Greek music, the avenue of approach that proved most fruitful to composers was the exploration of means for connecting the music more closely with the text to which it was set. Many mid-sixteenth-century theorists were concerned that their music could not produce the powerful psychological and sometimes even miraculous effects on listeners that Greek music was supposed to have been capable of producing. Writers on music described the miracles said to have been worked by Orpheus (see Figure 8, page 255), Amphion, Arion (see cover photo and Figure 12), Timotheus, and various other Greek musicians. Zarlino, for example, noted that although ancient music was imperfect, the ancient musicians were able to arouse in the human soul many different kinds of emotions. They could move the soul to anger and then change that anger to gentleness and docility. They could also induce sadness, joy, and other similar passions. Their ability to *move* people, he wrote, was all the more amazing, since modern music was incapable of producing such effects.

Vincenzo Galilei, Florentine lutenist and father of the famous scientist, was extreme in his condemnation of modern music and in his support of Greek music, especially because the ancient musicians appeared to have acknowledged fully the power of words. The noblest and most important part of music is the conception of the soul expressed by means of words, Galilei wrote, and modern musicians had made reason a slave of their appetites in pretending that the way in which all the parts of a polyphonic composition come together is more important than expression. His treatise *Dialogo della musica antica et della moderna*, published in 1581, apparently sets down the sentiments of the circle of musicians, poets, and scholars around Count Giovanni de' Bardi in Florence, who met from the late 1570s to the early 1590s to discuss, among many other things, music in ancient Greek culture. The radical stance of this Camerata, as Giulio Caccini called this informal group of intellectuals, and especially their insistence that the words be declaimed in order to convey their emotion, and that emotional power could be gained only by abandoning elaborate polyphony and returning to some sort of texture reminiscent of Greek monody, contributed to the development of monody in the decades around 1600. Caccini, the professional singer in the group, and Jacopo Peri, who may also have attended the Camerata's meetings, both explored ways of composing songs that communicated the feelings, or "affects," expressed in the text immediately and directly to the listener. Although the new monody certainly drew on exist-

Figure 12. In this engraving by Balthasar Küchler from *Repraesentatio der fürstlichen Auffzug und Ritterspiel* (Stuttgart, 1611), a scene from a pageant in honor of princely wedding festivities shows Arion playing a harp and riding to safety on a dolphin's back. In this late Renaissance depiction, a hero of classical antiquity represents the power of music within the elaborate humanist iconography surrounding a strictly Lutheran wedding. (New Haven, Beinecke Rare Book and Manuscript Library, Yale University)

ing kinds of popular song for some of its inspiration, especially in its style of a soloist's performance with simple instrumental accompaniment, it was the most radical response of the late sixteenth and early seventeenth centuries to the challenge of writing a persuasive music that would affect the listener's emotions, the "affetto dell'anima."

   In France, literary figures led the discussions about music in the ancient world to a much greater extent than in Italy. Interest in the subject centered on the group of poets known as the Pléiade, with Pierre de Ronsard their greatest representative. Ronsard's colleague, Joachim du Bellay, outlined the group's aims in his important treatise *La Deffence et illustration de la langue françoyse* (1549), in which he urged poets to imitate classical forms and meters. As a model of collaboration between the arts, Ronsard included in his *Amours* of 1552 an appendix with ten musical settings by some of the best musicians of the time—Clément Janequin, Pierre Certon, and Claude Goudimel—as well as the lesser-known humanist composer Marc-Antoine de Muret. The ten chansons were so conceived that all 150-odd sonnets in the collection could be sung to one or another of them. In Ronsard's preface to his *Mellanges de chansons* (1560) and in his *Abrégé de l'art poétique françoys* (1565), the poet set out his vision of a new union of poetry and music that was intended to revive the ideal state of the arts in ancient times. Ronsard's ideas, many of them derived from Plato, stressed the ethical and moral quality of music. Whether or not he and his collaborating poets and musicians really succeeded in bringing the arts closer together is questionable—the issue is still being debated by scholars—but it is clear that Ronsard succeeded in creating a mystique about the arts in the ancient world, a climate of opinion that welcomed neoclassical postures without imposing any specific technical prescriptions on composers; and most of the best French musicians of the time set Ronsard's poetry to music in a variety of styles, among them Guillaume Costeley, Pierre Cléreau, Anthoine de Bertrand, and Claude Le Jeune, as well as the great Orlando di Lasso.

One of the members of the Pléiade was Jean-Antoine de Baïf, who in co-operation with an obscure musician named Joachim Thibaut de Courville, *joueur de lyre du roi*, went further than anyone else in attempting to establish a firm connection between music and poetry and to rediscover the effects of ancient music, by devising both "vers et musique mesurés à l'antique." They worked out an accentual version in French of the metrical patterns of Greek and Latin poetry and invented a kind of music in which long syllables were set by long notes and short syllables by short notes. Baïf's Académie de poésie et de musique, founded in 1570 partly with the support of King Charles IX, had an elaborate set of statutes. The chief function of the Académie was to give concerts of musique mesurée at Baïf's house and to educate young musicians as well as listeners in the new art. Baïf's secrecy—neither the *auditeurs* who paid for the concerts nor the *musiciens* who played in them were to reveal what went on—prevents us from knowing in detail precisely what these performances were like (although much of the music was eventually published, albeit some years after the event). Baïf obviously wished to impose his views about music, especially about its ethical power and good prosody, on the intellectual elite of France. The Académie in its original form did not survive for more than a year or two, but the influence of its work continued to make itself felt for many decades to come; it extended even to the strophic *airs de cour* of the early seventeenth century.

The most distinguished musician associated with Baïf's enterprise was Claude Le Jeune (ca. 1525/30–1600), a superb composer whose works are unjustly neglected today. A Protestant, Le Jeune took so active a part in the religious debate in France that he had to flee Paris in 1590, and his works were saved from destruction only through the efforts of his good friend and collaborator in Baïf's circle, the important composer Jacques Mauduit (1557–1627). The best-known example of *musique mesurée* is probably Le Jeune's setting of *Revecy venir le printemps* (Example 12–1), in which the stark chordal texture is skillfully enlivened with brief melismas. Like most compositions in this style, Le Jeune's chanson alternates between refrain (called *rechant*) and stanzas (called

Example 12–1. Claude Le Jeune, *Revecy venir du printemps*, rechant and beginning of chant.

Rechant

Chant

chants). The close relationship between poetic meter and musical rhythm gives the composition its most distinctive feature and explains why barlines cannot be added regularly without distorting the music's character. But Le Jeune also composed more conventional polyphonic chansons, such as his exquisite setting of Ronsard's *Rossignol mon mignon*. His activity as a composer also led him to collaborate with Nicholas de la Grotte, Henry III's organist, on the occasion of the marriage in 1581 of the Duc de Joyeuse, one of the king's favorites, to the queen's half-sister. It was on the same occasion that the *Balet comique de la Royne* was performed—the first *ballet de cour* and the first time in France that drama, music, and dancing had been combined. That Baïf was not called on to contribute to this entertainment, organized by the court violinist Balthasar de Beaujoyeux, can probably be explained by court intrigue; Baïf was certainly interested in extending his ideas to take in dance and drama, and as early as 1573 he supposedly had ready a ballet with music by Courville and Le Jeune in which even the dancing was *mesuré à l'antique*.

THE VIRTUOSO MADRIGALISTS

Vast quantities of Italian madrigals were composed and published during the second half of the sixteenth century, in a variety of styles. Musicians set epic, lyric, pastoral, dramatic, erotic, and even moral or philosophical poetry to music for performances by virtuosi at courts, dilettanti in academies, and amateurs at home, or for splendidly festive occasions such as princely weddings and banquets. Poetry by Petrarch continued to be set throughout the second half of the century, along with excerpts from Lodovico Ariosto's semiheroic, semicomic, very humane epic *Orlando Furioso,* and from the gentle Arcadian verses of Jacopo Sannazaro. But more and more composers were attracted to the gloomier, more mannered and emotional work of Torquato Tasso, including excerpts from his pastoral play *Aminta* and his epic *Gerusalemme liberata,* and to the poetry of Tasso's fellow writer in Ferrara Giambattista Guarini, whose brilliantly artificial pastoral *Il Pastor fido* became the literary rage of the decades around 1600.

The small city-states of Italy vied with one another to procure the best available musicians, and musical courtiers and critics alike valued novelty highly; fashions changed rapidly in the madrigal. To some extent, then, it is within sixteenth-century criteria to select four composers—Giaches de Wert, Luca Marenzio, Carlo Gesualdo, and Claudio Monteverdi—as representatives of their time, because they wrote the newest and best madrigals, even though many other musicians during the same period were also composing excellent music. Their works reveal most clearly the changes in style that gradually took place during the last decades of the sixteenth century and the new aesthetic attitudes and techniques that characterize late Renaissance musical practice.

The changes in musical style and aesthetic in Italian music of this period were nourished and supported by social, intellectual, and cultural changes that affected the world of music in various ways. One phenomenon that exemplifies the close bonds between social and musical practices is the rise of professional women singers. Beginning at the court of the Este family of Ferrara in 1580, a group of virtuoso sopranos—Anna Guarini, Livia d'Arco, Tarquinia Molza, and Laura Peverara—was established as the *concerto di donne* for the pleasure of the duke and his court. Their novel performances in Ferrara for almost twenty years brought them fame throughout all of Italy and inspired a number of composers to write madrigals for them. Wert, Marenzio, Luzzasco Luzzaschi, and even Gesualdo, among many others, created some works in which two, three, or four high parts, clearly intended for this group of "singing ladies" of Ferrara, are set off in one way or another from two or more lower voices. Singers such as those in Ferrara were professional virtuosos, although they came from the noble class. Their presence in the musical life of the courts of northern Italy not only made possible the performance of certain kinds of madrigals but also signaled an important change in attitude toward professional musical employment for female musicians. Of course, as females these singers could not be hired into the ranks of the official musical establishment of the chapel, even at a progressive place such as Ferrara in the 1580s. They were hired to perform the private chamber music known as the *musica secreta* or *musica privata* of the sovereign's household. They were paid lavishly for their service and were called on to sing almost daily for the court and its invited guests. Once established at the court of Ferrara, the fashion for madrigals performed by virtuoso female singers spread quickly as well to other musical centers (Mantua, Venice, and Florence, and later Rome), such that it became not only possible but to some extent socially acceptable for women to have professional careers as singers. This phenomenon had a decisive impact on the composition of secular music in the decades before and after 1600, beginning with the madrigal in Ferrera and Mantua but later affecting the new genres of accompanied monody and opera in important ways as well.

Given the influence of professional female singers on performance practice and compositional style in late-sixteenth-century madrigals, it is hardly surprising that the madrigal was also the genre most cultivated by women composers. Indeed, the social changes that permitted the rise of professional female performers also facilitated, to a very limited extent, the emergence of women composers in this period in greater numbers than ever before or since. The first pieces composed by a woman to be published were four madrigals by Maddalena Casulana (1566–83) included in an anthology, *Il Desiderio* (1566), published by Scotto in Venice. Between 1566 and 1600 madrigals by a handful of other women composers were published in Venice, Ferrara, and Milan, and in succeeding decades more and more pieces by women, primarily madrigals and accompanied solo songs, appeared in print. This is not to say that the status of women composers in the culture of late Renaissance Italy was unproblematic, that women claimed a prominent share of the market in printed music, or that they posed a challenge to the dominant male point of view. Women could not be hired as musicians by the largest employer in the period (the church), and, even beyond the church, virtually the only musical career open to women was that of court or theatrical singer. The social conventions of the period discouraged women of noble birth (and their emulators in the educated middle class) from competing in public with men or, indeed, from pursuing occupations that would give them a voice in the public arena, even in print. In short, even though women composers emerged in print with a great vitality during this period, they remained a distinct minority.

At the height of her career, one of the virtuoso madrigal singers, Tarquinia Molza of Ferrara, was virtually ruined by her involvement with a famous composer, Giaches de Wert (1535–96), who was the oldest of the "virtuoso madrigalists" and the only Netherlander among them. Wert spent most of his mature working life at Mantua, in the service of the Gonzaga family, where he was also in close contact with the musical circles at the Este court in Ferrara; Mantua and Ferrara formed an axis around which many of the most significant events in the history of the late-sixteenth-century madrigal turned. Indeed, Wert's connection with Ferrara was very close, for, after his wife had cuckolded him and deserted him, he fell in love with Tarquinia Molza and she returned his love. Their affair became known and Molza was banished to Modena (though Wert was only temporarily disgraced).

Wert's secular music—eleven books of madrigals for five voices, one volume for four, a collection of light *canzone villanelle,* and a handful of madrigals printed in various miscellaneous collections—makes up the largest part of his output. The first three books of five-voice madrigals contain youthful compositions, written before he came to Mantua. Books 4–6, published in 1567, 1571, and 1577, during his first twenty-odd years at the Gonzaga court, reveal him in his maturity as a composer of madrigals similar in many ways to those by Cipriano de Rore, his fellow Netherlander who had worked in Ferrara until a few years before Wert's arrival in Mantua in 1565. In Wert's compositions, as in Rore's, technical artifice was by and large subservient to text expression. Dense imitative counterpoint, homophony, splendid polychoral dialogue, choral declamation, simple diatonic or highly chromatic melodic lines—these as well as various other textures and styles were all brought into play following the sense of text rather than any abstract musical design.

In Wert's last five books of five-voice madrigals, published between 1581 and 1595, he showed a markedly increased willingness to underscore literary meaning at the expense of polyphonic decorum: lyric, dramatic, and pathetic texts all receive highly individual settings that sometimes threaten the stability of the polyphonic fabric. This change in his style during the 1580s and 1590s partly reflected a shift in Wert's taste for poetry, away from his earlier favorites (Petrarch, Ariosto, and the mid-sixteenth-century Petrarchist Luigi Tansillo) and toward the greater emotionalism and sensuality of his colleagues in Ferrara, Torquato Tasso and Giambattista Guarini. Wert was the first composer to set stanzas from Tasso's epic *Gerusalemme liberata*—he may even have done so at the poet's request—and they demonstrate Wert's new manner very well. For example, in *Giunto alla tomba* (Example 12–2)—Tancredi's lament at the tomb of Clorinda—the low-pitched, gloomy declamation of the opening (in the parlando style Wert came more and more to use for narrative passages) contrasts so strikingly with the melismatic madrigalism of "al fin sgorgando un lagrimoso rivo" ("finally gushing forth a river of tears") that the continuity is threatened; and the affective leaps downward on "in un languido oimè" ("with a languishing 'alas'") violate older ideals of melodic elegance as thoroughly as they embody the meaning of the words. Changes of pace like that between the first and second phrases of *Giunto alla tomba* occur in various other madrigals from Wert's seventh book, either to enhance the drama or merely to illustrate a word or a clause. His setting of Petrarch's sonnet *Solo e pensoso,* for example, moves at the beginning in generally slow notes that aptly fit the opening lines, "Alone and thoughtful, I pace the most deserted fields with slow and dragging steps," but the music soon picks up speed and never returns to its first tempo. The expressive—one is tempted to say expressionistic—nature of Wert's music for *Solo e pensoso* is evident, too, from the character of the opening melodic line (Example 12–3), which covers a range of almost two octaves. Beside this intense, artfully distorted theme—this parody of a classically proportioned Renaissance melody—the gentle arches of a Palestrina seem tame indeed.

Wert's eighth book of five-voice madrigals (1586) is filled with compositions that offer unusually good opportunities for virtuoso display; the volume

Example 12–2. Giaches de Wert, *Giunto alla tomba*, mm. 1–26.

Prima parte

was dedicated to the Duke and Duchess of Ferrara, and much of it was apparently written for the superb performers at their court. Book 9 (1588) opens with *Hor si rallegri il cielo,* a madrigal composed for the coronation of Vincenzo Gonzaga as fourth duke of Mantua; the volume contains other examples as well of Wert's splendid official manner, most of them intended for the duke's singers

Example 12–2. (*Continued*)

Example 12–3. Giaches de Wert, *Solo e pensoso*, bass, mm. 1–12.

in Mantua. Book 10 (1591) was dedicated to the duke's mistress, and many of the madrigals in it may be settings of poems written by her and her circle of friends and sung by them at her residence, the Palazzo del Tè on the outskirts of Mantua. Both the poetry and its courtly music are slightly lighter in tone than most of Wert's other works; the composer evoked the atmosphere of the canzonetta and the balletto while using the more elaborate techniques of the madrigal. Nearly half of Book 11 (1595) is devoted to compositions originally conceived for theatrical performances, a genre Wert had had to cultivate assiduously during his career at the Mantuan court. It opens with *Ah, dolente partita* (Example 12–4), on a passage from Guarini's *Il pastor fido;* Einstein has described it as an "aria in advance of its time," doubtless because the top line carries much of the burden of presenting the principal melodic material; since it was intended for the theater, it may well have been performed the first time by a solo singer accompanied by instruments.

In all four of his last madrigal books, Wert favored pastoral rather more than dramatic or pathetic poetry, and by the second half of the 1580s he had all but abandoned complex imitative counterpoint as his normal texture. Passages

Example 12–4. Giaches de Wert, *Ah, dolente partita*, mm. 1–22.

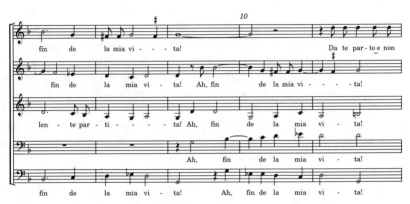

Example 12–4. (*Continued*)

in imitation still occur, but they are often quite short and they seldom predominate. Instead, Wert more often pitted duos, trios, or other sections of the ensemble against one another in dialogue, or wrote chordal passages in which the top voice naturally stands out. His constantly changing textures, his sensitive use of harmonic progressions for expressive purposes, and his melodic lines filled with written-out *passaggi* (ornamental runs and turns) make these late madrigals exciting, highly colorful compositions. As Einstein wrote, "The later Wert is no longer Rore's successor; he is the contemporary of Marenzio, Gesualdo, and the young Monteverdi and one of the forerunners and founders of the music of the seventeenth century."

The second of the four virtuoso madrigalists, Luca Marenzio (1553–99), spent most of his life in Rome. He went there from his native village near Brescia when he was in his mid-twenties, if not before, but during the course of his life he had contact with various other centers of music in Italy, notably Ferrara and Mantua (through his patron, Cardinal Luigi d'Este) and Florence (where he collaborated with Cristofano Malvezzi, Alessandro Striggio, and others in composing music to celebrate the wedding of Grand Duke Ferdinand I de' Medici to Christine of Lorraine in 1589), and he worked for King Sigismund III in Poland for several years.

Just as Wert excelled throughout much of his life at the dramatic and pathetic madrigal, so Marenzio must be considered the genius of the lyrical and pastoral manners. It might even be argued that Marenzio wrote the most refined and elegant madrigals of the entire century. His earliest works—brilliant, playful and sensuous—were (and are) his best known. They are better known now than his later works because his first three books for five voices have been available in a modern edition for some time; they were better known then because he burst upon the Roman scene in 1580 with astonishing success, a success that may be partly explained by the fact that he had no real competition as a madrigalist in Rome and partly because his works filled a genuine need in

Roman society for music that could be sung by cultivated amateurs (as opposed to the professional virtuosi for whom many of the northern Italian musicians composed). But his fame was more than merely local; his madrigal books were reissued again and again—his first book *a 5*, for example, was reprinted at least nine times by 1610—and his works quickly spread throughout all of Europe. A number of his compositions even appeared in English translations in Yonge's *Musica Transalpina* of 1588, and they had an important influence on the development of the English madrigal.

Marenzio was extraordinarily prolific. Besides a single book of madrigals for four voices (rather an anachronism by 1585), he published nine books for five voices (ten including his *madrigali spirituali* of 1584), six books for six voices, one of serious madrigals for four, five, and six voices (printed in 1588 and composed in a manner very different from his former style, to paraphrase his dedication of the volume), and five books of villanelle for three voices, as well as a number of individual works in miscellaneous collections. His first publication, *Il primo libro de madrigali a cinque voci*, was printed in Venice by Angelo Gardano in 1580. Within five years, Marenzio had published twelve volumes in all and had become perhaps the best-known madrigalist of his time.

Like all the late-sixteenth-century madrigalists, Marenzio adapted his compositional techniques to fit the sense of the particular poem he was setting; thus each work is individual to a high degree, making generalizations unusually unreliable. Still, two characteristics of his style should be emphasized in considering his earlier works: his brevity and conciseness and his penchant for depicting graphically as many of the concrete details of a poem as he could, qualities that do not explain the polish and effectiveness of his music but help to distinguish his madrigals from those by his contemporaries. The first trait is evident even in the first several phrases of his setting of Petrarch's sonnet *Zefiro torna* (Example 12–5a). Within twenty measures, four different textures appear: the initial dialogue among the voices on the simple descending motive for "Zefiro torna" ("The west wind returns"); the homophony of "e'l bel tempo rimena" ("and brings back the beautiful weather"); the imitation, or rather the repetition at different pitches, of a brief motive (consisting of an ornamented ascending second) over a sequential descending scale in the bass, on the words "e i fiori e l'erbe" ("and the flowers and the grass"); and the animated homophony, harmonizing a continuation of the sequential bass pattern that leads to a cadence on "sua dolce famiglia" ("his sweet family"). Each half-line gets its separate treatment, and even though the first line is repeated with some variants and the two halves of the second line are related by the bass pattern, there is no lengthy discourse or extensive thematic manipulation. Each literary conceit is given a characterization that is as economical as it is telling and vivid, and then the composer moves on.

The poem contrasts the life and vitality of nature in the spring with the lover's bitter sense of loneliness at being deprived of his beloved. The turning point is depicted in an instant by a few bold strokes (Example 12–5b). The

Example 12–5. Luca Marenzio, *Zefiro torna*, mm. 1–22, 74–90.

(*a*) mm. 1–22

(b) mm. 74–90

series of suspensions on "Ma per me, lasso, tornano i più gravi sospiri" ("but for me, alas, the deepest sighs return") includes no unusually harsh dissonances (and for once the word *sospiri*—"sighs"—is not realistically illustrated by a rest before it begins). Nevertheless, Marenzio immediately captured the essence of the text by his abrupt change in pace and texture. The result, of course, is a composition broken up into small segments, a work that violates the earlier madrigalists' concern to maintain an uninterrupted flow of polyphony. Marenzio pushed almost to its breaking point the ideal of a continuous polyphonic fabric that had guided musicians throughout the fifteenth and sixteenth centuries.

Marenzio's habit of musical word painting, of graphically illustrating individual words or clauses, followed naturally from his desire to be brief and to the point and to characterize instantly and vividly the mood or meaning of the text. Example 12–6 furnishes an unusually clear sample of the lengths to which he was prepared to go. The passage comes from *Dolorosi martir*, which, together with *Liquide perle* and *Tirsi morir volea* (an erotic dialogue by Guarini and a favorite text of late-sixteenth- and early-seventeenth-century composers), is perhaps the most stunning and most modern of the compositions in Marenzio's first book of madrigals for five voices. In the Elizabethan translation in *Musica Transalpina,* the first lines of *Dolorosi martir* read:

Example 12–6. Luca Marenzio, *Dolorosi martir*, mm. 14–25.

Dolorous mournful cares, ruthless tormenting,
Hateful gyves, cursed bondage, sharpest endurance
Wherein both nights and days my heart ever venting,
Wretch, I bewail my lost delight and pleasure.

Example 12–6 includes the music for the last clause of the second line and all of the third and fourth lines. Marenzio not only heightened the sentiment "Wretch, I bewail" by writing a poignantly chromatic progression; he also depicted at least four words and phrases literally by means of "madrigalisms." "Aspre catene" (literally, "harsh chains" rather than the "sharpest endurance" of the translation) is set to an inordinately long chain of suspensions. "Night" is set by two blackened notes (the triplet in m. 19 in modern notation), an example of so-called *Augenmusik* ("eye music"), in which the notation suggests text painting that is not audible (such as blackened notes for grief or night, two white semibreves, o o, for "eyes," and so on). In a famous passage from another madrigal, Petrarch's *O voi che sospirate*, Marenzio illustrated the line "muti una volta quel suo antico stile" ("change once his ancient style") by means of a somewhat less literal madrigalism: because "ancient style" suggested to the composer the recent researches into the diatonic, chromatic, and enharmonic genera of the Greeks, he set the line with a strikingly chromatic series of chords involving enharmonic equivalents (and therefore, by the way, implying equal temperament). Marenzio's extravagant pictorialism may well be as naive as some critics claim, but it is an integral part of the style of these delightful, playful, voluptuous compositions, which are highly sophisticated evocations of extraordinarily subtle, refined poetry.

Lest Marenzio be seen, however, only as the most brilliant, if slightly superficial, member of the quartet of virtuoso madrigalists, his late works should also be considered. He wrote of the change in his style that took place during the last decade or so of his life in the dedication of his *Madrigali a quattro, cinque, et sei voci* of 1588, explaining that the compositions included in the volume were "composed in a manner very different from my former one in that through the imitation of the words and the propriety of the style I have sought a sort of melancholy gravity [*mesta gravità*] that will perhaps be prized the more highly by connoisseurs." It may be that he underwent a spiritual crisis (possibly influenced by the ideas of the Counter-Reformation), a reaction against the frivolities of his youth; certainly he began to prefer texts expressing hopelessness and melancholy and even longing for death. Or perhaps the change resulted from a more purely musical response to the artistic climate of his time, an answer to Tasso's complaint that modern music was decadent: Tasso called for precisely that quality of *gravità* that Marenzio claims in his dedication. Whatever the cause, the result was a repertory of works more austere in their contrapuntal orientation and less immediately charming and pictorial, more chromatic and with better-integrated excursions into distant harmonic areas, more continuous and less fragmented in their structure, and altogether more intense than any of his earlier works. Madrigals such as *Fiere silvestre* and *O fere stelle* from his 1588 *Madrigali* (modern edition by Steven Ledbetter, 1977) reveal a new and magnificent gravity that pervades even such pieces as the five canzone set as a cycle in five sections beginning *Baci soavi e cari* from his *Quinto Libro de Madrigali a sei Voci* of 1591 (*Opera Omnia 6*, ed. Meier), in which an exquisite musical eroticism is enveloped in the gravity of the overtly serious style.

Carlo Gesualdo, Prince of Venosa (ca. 1560–1613), in some of his madrigals went even further than Wert and Marenzio in transforming Renaissance polyphony into something strange and new for the sake of text expression. The melancholy and temperamental Gesualdo was a man of excess, a member of the high Neapolitan nobility and the central figure in one of the most notorious scandals in sixteenth-century music history. (He murdered his wife and her lover.) Most important, he was a distinguished musician, although even his reputation as a composer has fluctuated wildly over the centuries, from the scathing denunciation by Burney in the eighteenth century to his adulation as a cult figure by Aldous Huxley and Stravinsky in the twentieth. Gesualdo's influence was neither wide nor lasting—his work affected most directly a small group of Neapolitans (who may have influenced him as much as he influenced them), among them Giovanni de Macque, Scipione Dentice, and his presumed teacher Pomponio Nenna; and he made a striking impression in Ferrarese musical circles in the 1590s. Nevertheless, his music exemplifies in extreme form that body of late-sixteenth-century works in which the older styles and ideals of the Renaissance were rapidly breaking down; he can be neither dismissed as a mere aberration nor patronized as a noble dabbler in the arts.

Always a gloomy, eccentric, and rather willful man, Gesualdo seems to have increased in emotional instability after his double murder of 1590. In 1594 he married again. His new wife, Leonora d'Este, niece of Alfonso II, duke of Ferrara, brought the Neapolitan prince into contact with the brilliant Ferrarese court. He lived in Ferrara for several years and had particularly close ties there with Luzzasco Luzzaschi, a composer most famous for his madrigals for one, two, and three sopranos with written-out keyboard accompaniment, the first such compositions in the history of music. Gesualdo and Luzzaschi may have laid plans for an ambitious aesthetic program to renew the Ferrarese madrigal—Luzzaschi's preface to his sixth book of five-voice madrigals (1596) is clearly intended to be a manifesto of the composer's musical hopes for the future. In 1596, however, after traveling for a time, Gesualdo returned to the small town of Gesualdo near Naples and never again paid an extended visit to the north.

Gesualdo's first two books of five-voice madrigals, published in Ferrara in 1594 but written before he arrived there, show him to have been a gifted if rather conventional composer as a young man. Books 3 and 4 (published in 1595 and 1596) reflect the influence of the Ferrarese musicians. In them he began to reveal his mature musical personality and to demonstrate how far he was to go in fragmenting textures, juxtaposing drastically contrasting elements within a very short space of time, and increasing the harmonic and melodic intensity of his music by means of strikingly chromatic progressions. All this he

did in his search for heightened expression. The individual brief sections of
Ecco morirò dunque (Example 12–7), from his fourth book, for instance, are
fragmented: "Ecco" is separated by rests from "morirò dunque" and "Ne fia"
from "che pur rimire." The harmonic surprises of the first few measures, created by chromaticisms, are, however, perhaps no more startling than the unconventional chords, chord spacings, and part writing of the subsequent measures
of the example.

Many of the poems Gesualdo set are undistinguished as literature; he
took relatively few texts from the major poets favored by other late-sixteenth-
century composers, although he did write some madrigals on poems by Guarini
and quite a few on texts given him by his friend and fellow neurotic, the Ferrarese poet Torquato Tasso. *Ecco morirò dunque* illustrates Gesualdo's para-
doxical attitude toward the poems he chose. Example 12–7 reproduces only half
of the first part of the madrigal; the second half repeats the same text with the
same music recomposed, rescored to include the bass (which had been silent
for the entire first statement), and extended at the end. Gesualdo, like his contemporaries, was intent on devising a music derived from the words; in this
spirit he reshaped the poems he set by repeating clauses or whole lines of verse

Example 12–7. Carlo Gesualdo, *Ecco morirò dunque*, mm. 1–7.

at will. That is why in general he preferred brief poems that could be reworked. Gesualdo's mutilation of poetic structure is yet another sign of the transformation of the madrigal genre by the late masters; earlier madrigalists never permitted themselves such license.

Within a period of ten years at the end of his life, five volumes of Gesualdo's music appeared: two volumes of motets (the *Sacrae Cantiones* of 1603), responsories for Holy Week, and Books 5 and 6 of five-voice madrigals, all printed at Gesualdo in 1611 under the direct supervision of the composer. A single collection of six-voice madrigals, unfortunately incompletely preserved, was published posthumously in 1626. Gesualdo's sacred music is somewhat more traditional than his madrigals—the polyphony is less chromatic and flows more continuously—but the motets are deeply felt and highly expressive, and the responsories are imbued with techniques worked out first in his secular compositions.

The last two volumes of five-voice madrigals, Books 5 and 6, contain the music that has established Gesualdo's reputation for waywardness and disequilibrium. Example 12–8, the beginning of his most famous work, *Moro lasso,* from Book 6, reveals why. The extreme chromaticism and fairly slow pace of the first and third phrases, with their progressions of only distantly related chords, contrast drastically with the faster pace and the diatonic close imitation of the second phrase, with its melodic material partly consisting of written-out ornamental figures. As in *Ecco morirò dunque,* Gesualdo proceeded to repeat the entire first section of *Moro lasso* before going on, recomposing it by rearranging the same musical elements at different pitches and by writing new points of imitation. He managed, barely, to keep his polyphonic structures from disintegrating completely into separate and unrelated clauses and to give his harmonic progressions, with their sudden juxtapositions, coherence and direction. But it is difficult to see how anyone could have extended or developed his techniques or carried them further.

Marenzio, and to a lesser extent Wert and Gesualdo, often worked with short, well-defined motives rather than building up long arches of melody; and all three composers, instead of restricting themselves to evenly paced, smoothly flowing lines, gave to some of their voices the sorts of highly decorated runs and trills that had become a part of the improvisational arsenal of virtuoso singers. Gesualdo, and sometimes Wert and Marenzio, occasionally came close to harmonic chaos because they overloaded some of their music with so many chromatic notes, chords, and progressions. All three composers disrupted the continuous flow of polyphony by juxtaposing short sections in contrasting textures and styles in an effort to increase the immediate emotional impact of their madrigals on the listener, but they all maintained at all times at least a semblance of the traditional polyphonic fabric.

It was Claudio Monteverdi (1567–1643) who added an obligatory *basso continuo* part for keyboard or *chitarrone* (a large bass lute) as accompaniment to six of the madrigals in his fifth book (1605), as well as an optional *basso*

Example 12–8. Carlo Gesualdo, *Moro lasso,* mm. 1–15.

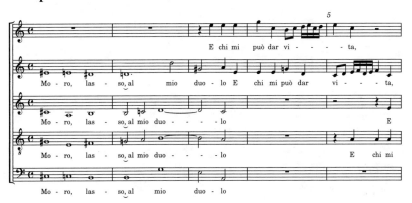

Example 12–8. (*Continued*)

seguente (a bass line "following"—that is, doubling—the lowest-sounding vocal notes, regardless of the voice part assigned them) to the rest of the compositions in that volume. Doubtless the chordal instrument was intended to hold together even the most fragmented texture, but that was surely not the sole reason for the innovation. The consistent requirement of a basso continuo (from the sixth book of 1614 onward) was also one symptom that Monteverdi, the youngest of the virtuoso madrigalists, was among those composers and performers who were in the process of forging an essentially new style and aesthetic that would transform the genre from within.

Monteverdi's first book of five-voice madrigals was published in 1587, when he was twenty years old and still living in his native Cremona; it is filled with passages that remind the listener of canzonette in their playfulness, their frequent three-part textures, and their evocation of pastoral moods (hardly surprising in view of the fact that Monteverdi had published an entire volume of the lighter canzonette three years previously). In many of their details these earliest madrigals by Monteverdi resemble those by Wert, Marenzio, contemporary Venetians like Andrea Gabrieli, and other northern Italian masters. Books 2 and 3, issued in 1590 and 1592, came out during Monteverdi's first three years in Mantua, long before he had become *maestro di cappella;* Wert was still the leading musician there, and Monteverdi sang and played the viol under his direction. Even these early madrigal books of Monteverdi's include some superb music, such as the atmospheric, naturalistic, and justly famous *Ecco mormorar l'onde;* the magnificent settings of Tasso's poetry that make up almost half of Book 2; and the brilliant virtuoso settings in Book 3, most likely intended for performance by Mantua's *concerto delle donne.* Monteverdi's fourth and fifth books, published in 1603 and 1605 after he had lived in Mantua for some years and had absorbed the influence of the brilliant musical life there and in neighboring Ferrara, contain examples of the most fully mature and individual manner the composer developed for the polyphonic madrigal (leaving the later concerted and continuo madrigals in another category). The madrigals in Books

4 and 5 give us the clearest impression of Monteverdi's strengths as a madrigalist of the late Renaissance and the currency of his work in this genre.

Examples 12–9 and 12–10, the first sections of the madrigals that open Books 4 and 5 (both based on poems by Guarini), *Ah, dolente partita* (compare Wert's version of the same passage in Example 12–4) and *Cruda Amarilli*, can furnish us with at least a preliminary notion of Monteverdi's approach. By 1603, attenuated textures in polyphonic music and a central concern for text expression can surely be taken for granted. In these examples, as in many of the compositions in the first five madrigal books, Monteverdi worked with small, well-defined motives. Some, like the motive setting "Ah, fin de la mia vita" in Example 12–9, closely resemble those used by Marenzio and the other virtuoso madrigalists. Some, like that setting "ahi lasso" in Example 12–10, incorporate written-out ornamental turns, runs, or trills within the very nature of the motive, a device that became an important feature of baroque melodic style. Some motives are starkly declamatory, like that setting "Ah dolente partita" in Example 12–9: an extraordinarily effective yet simple passage, it is nothing more, really, than a recitation formula on two notes, depending for its immensely telling effect on the obvious and easy device of two suspensions. There are a number of similarly declamatory phrases in Monteverdi's first five books, from the chanted passages of *Sfogava con le stelle* of Book 4, in which the words are set beneath a single chord and meant to be sung in unmeasured speech rhythm, to the declaimed narrative or dramatic passages in almost every one of the works in Book 5.

One of the things genuinely new in Monteverdi's works is the constructive and combinative way he worked with brief motives. In a number of madrigals Monteverdi superimposed various parts of the poem (and the motives associated with them) to make a complex and rather dense texture, different from the dense imitative polyphony of earlier generations. The opening of *Ah, dolente partita* is an example of such a rich *simultaneous* mixture of diverse poetic lines. Musically it presents four ideas or motives to be repeated and carefully combined: the declamatory two-voice "Ah, dolente partita," which recurs four times (all but once with both voices intact); the simple descending motive on "Ah, fin de la mia vita"; and the two different declamatory motives on "Da te part'e non moro?" and "E pur io provo la pena de la morte."

In *Cruda Amarilli* (Example 12–10), Monteverdi's setting of a famous speech from Guarini's *Il pastor fido*, characteristic musical motives or figures are assigned to successive sections of the text, such that its contrasting images and states of emotion are made musically audible as the madrigal unfolds. The suspensions and intense dissonances produced by the movement of the voices against each other establish the severity and sensual anguish of the opening exclamation, for example, while the tiny melismatic runs in the lower voices at the words "ahi lasso" lend a quite different quality to that exclamation. Controlled repetition of whole blocks or units of music and text (note the higher-pitched repetition of the opening measures, for example) is important not only

Example 12–9. Claudio Monteverdi, *Ah, dolente partita,* mm. 1–31.

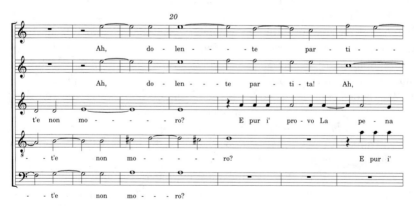

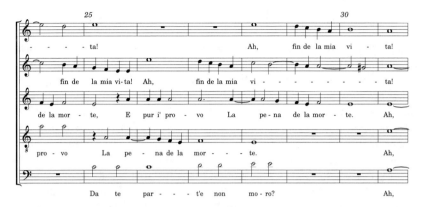

Example 12–10. Claudio Monteverdi, *Cruda Amarilli*, mm. 1–14.

to the basic structure of this madrigal but also to Monteverdi's interpretation and projection of its text. The first five books of madrigals include many similar examples, as well as passages in invertible counterpoint, expositions with two subjects, varied transpositions, and other such devices for achieving textural and structural coherence in a highly volatile context.

Harmony, as well as melody and counterpoint, is treated in a distinctive way in Monteverdi's madrigals. In *Cruda Amarilli,* unconventional voice leading, unprepared dissonances, and delayed or unorthodox resolutions of dissonance make the texture so unstable that consonant triads, concordant homophony, and smooth counterpoint are themselves special expressive devices, rather than basic norms to be taken for granted. In Example 12–10 note especially the bass moving to a dissonance against the superius in m. 2 and m. 6, and the superius entering after a rest on an unprepared dissonance, then leaping to another dissonance in m. 13. The section of *Cruda Amarilli* shown here is one famous passage that elicited such vehement protest from the conservative Bolognese theorist Giovanni Maria Artusi that Monteverdi felt he had to reply and promised, in a short preface to Book 5, that he would write a treatise to be called "Second Practice, or Perfection of Modern Music." He never had time to finish his written defense, but his brother, Giulio Cesare Monteverdi, expanded on his few remarks in a slightly more informative foreword to Claudio's *Scherzi musicali* of 1607. In it, Monteverdi makes clear his distinction between "first practice" and "second practice."

First practice "considers the harmony not commanded, but commanding, not the servant, but the mistress of the words." He goes on to explain that such compositions, in which purely musical principles predominate over text expression, had been written by Ockeghem, Josquin, Pierre de la Rue, Mouton, Créquillon, Clemens non Papa, Gombert, and others; this practice had been perfected "with actual composition" by Willaert and "with most judicious rules" by Zarlino—and he might have added Palestrina and his Roman followers (Giovanni Bernardino and Giovanni Maria Nanino, Felice and Giovanni Francesco Anerio, Ruggiero Giovanelli, and Giovanni Animuccia) as well as the composers who continued to write "Renaissance polyphony" (in the *stile antico*) well into the seventeenth century.

With this style of composition Monteverdi contrasts the second practice, which "considers harmony not commanding, but commanded, and makes the words the mistress of the harmony." This famous slogan of those who put expression above contrapuntal rules—*l'oratione sia padrona del armonia e non serva*—was hardly a new sentiment in 1607. Cipriano de Rore, fifty years before, would surely have subscribed to it, even though Rore never went to the extremes in rending the polyphonic fabric that Monteverdi and his colleagues and contemporaries were prepared to tolerate. Indeed, Monteverdi names Rore as the first exponent of the second practice; as followers he lists Ingegneri, Marenzio, Wert, Luzzaschi, Peri, Caccini, and a "Heroic School" of gentleman composers including Gesualdo.

After Book 5 there was a gap of almost ten years before Monteverdi published another volume of madrigals. By the time Book 6 appeared in 1614, Monteverdi was already maestro di cappella at the basilica of St. Mark in Venice, and he had composed his Mantuan operas *L'Orfeo* (performed in 1607 and published in 1609) and *L'Arianna* (performed in 1608; only Ariadne's lament survives, separately and also in an arrangement for five voices in Book 6 of the madrigals). These works, as well as his Venetian madrigals, published in Books 7 (1619), 8 (1638), and, posthumously, 9 (1651); his Venetian operas *Il Ritorno d'Ulisse in patria* (performed in 1641) and his great masterpiece, *L'Incoronazione di Poppea* (performed in 1642); and his gorgeous sacred music, composed both in Mantua and in Venice, belong outside the subject of this book. By the time Monteverdi died in 1643, even the first stages of the baroque era had already come to a close.

Wert, Luzzaschi, and Monteverdi all worked in Mantua or Ferrara during important periods of their lives. The brilliant musical culture there also strongly affected the compositions of the Neapolitan Gesualdo, and even touched the Roman Marenzio. The artistic ferment and high artistic standards at the two north Italian courts had a profound influence on the character of the late-sixteenth-century madrigal and hence on the disintegration of Renaissance style. Mantua and Ferrara were at least as important in determining the shape of things to come as Florence, where opera and monody were born. But if, with hindsight, we can see that those centers led the way in encouraging the exploration of new techniques and new means of expression, the contemporary observer of the Italian scene would have been aware of many other fine Italian composers whose music did not challenge older ideals quite so directly, some of whom also influenced the nature of early baroque music.

In Venice, for example, musical activities were as lively, as elegantly presented, and as influential in their own time and later as in any other Italian city. But the Venetian madrigalists after Willaert and Rore seem to have intended their works more for "entertainment and delight" (Jerome Roche's phrase) than for serious expression. Andrea Gabrieli (ca. 1533–85) wrote superb convivial, amatory, and pastoral madrigals, as well as some intended for great festival occasions; moreover, his lighter songs—such as the villanella-like *Greghesche and iustiniane* of 1571—are as light, frothy, and inconsequential as his few neoclassical choruses (such as those for the first performance of *Oedipus rex* in Vicenza) are serious in their attempt to recapture the spirit if not the techniques of the ancient world. Detailed word painting and straining after expressive effect were less important to him than choral sonority and harmonic color. His madrigals on themes of love are seldom overwrought, and his grand official manner is truly splendid. His brilliant nephew, Giovanni Gabrieli (ca. 1556–1612), the leading musician in Venice during the 1580s and 1590s, was apparently less interested in the madrigal than in the sacred music he wrote for St. Mark's, where he served as organist. Both as a composer of sumptuous polychoral motets and brilliant instrumental canzonas that were perfectly adapted to the tastes of the pleasure-loving Venetians, and as a distinguished teacher who numbered Heinrich Schütz among his students, Giovanni helped to establish the *concertato* style with its colorful mixtures of voices and instruments.

In other Italian cities as well, musical life followed its own dynamics. For example, Rome, appropriately for the capital city of Christendom, preserved its conservative image as the stronghold of the *prima prattica*. In Modena and Bologna, composers like Orazio Vecchi (1550–1605) and Adriano Banchieri (1567–1634) wrote madrigal comedies, cycles of madrigals organized loosely around a group of characters, a central narrative, and a dramatic plot. Though the preface of Vecchi's *L'Amfiparnaso* (1597) states that "this spectacle is observed with the mind, which it enters through the ears, not the eyes," suggesting perhaps that this work was not meant to be staged, some madrigal comedies were intended for the stage. Most of the plots are comic, with just enough serious moments to offer a bit of welcome contrast. Madrigal comedies are filled with characters from the commedia dell'arte, stereotyped figures like the braggart, the lecherous old doctor, the moneylender, and the clever servant, or with provincials and foreigners, like Sicilians and Germans, whose accents could be parodied. Many of them mock features of everyday life, like stuttering, or the chattering of women as they wash their clothes (as in Alessandro Striggio's *Il cicalamento delle donne al bucato*, the earliest madrigal comedy, published in 1567); and some imitate natural sounds, like the barking of dogs in Vecchi's *Le veglie di Siena* (1604) or the cuckoo, owl, cat, and dog in Banchieri's *Festino nella sera del giovedi grasso* of 1608 ("An entertainment for the eve of mardi gras"), who sing a *contrappunto bestiale* against a mock-liturgical cantus firmus.

Madrigal comedies, as delightful as they are, added few new features to the repertory of techniques available to the late-sixteenth-century composer of Italian secular music. Venetian madrigals and concertato motets include some of the greatest music of the late Renaissance; they are based on compositional procedures conservative for their times—systematic imitation and antiphonal textures, for example—although they strongly influenced the character of music in the seventeenth century. Such considerations lead us to the conclusion that descriptive terms like "Renaissance" or "baroque"—oversimple but useful and even necessary—imply ways of looking at complex situations by emphasizing elements of change while ignoring things that continue in the same tradition or change but little. Many of the innovations of the late sixteenth and early seventeenth centuries had their roots in even earlier practices. Composers at least since the late fifteenth century endeavored to write a kind of vocal music that reflected its text. The highly ornamented melodic style of the early baroque stems at least in part from composers' attempts to curb the improvisational excesses of late sixteenth-century virtuoso singers by writing out in their music precisely the notes they wished sung. Even the new basso continuo texture grew out of the habit, almost certainly a common practice even during the early years of the sixteenth century, of having a lute or a keyboard instrument double the parts in at least some vocal ensembles. There are other elements of continuity as well between the sixteenth and seventeenth centuries. Baroque culture did not come into being overnight, nor did it wipe away in an instant every trace of the lingering Renaissance.

BIBLIOGRAPHICAL NOTES

Music of the late Renaissance in Italy is given a concise and insightful treatment in Tim Carter, *Music in Late Renaissance and Early Baroque Italy* (London, 1992). A radically different approach, which brings the language of postmodern criticism to bear in its exploration of Renaissance cosmology and musical composition, is taken by Gary Tomlinson in *Music in Renaissance Magic* (Chicago, 1993).

Claude Palisca's numerous essays are fundamental to understanding late Renaissance musical humanism: see especially those collected in Palisca, *Studies in the History of Italian Music and Music Theory* (Oxford, 1994), and Palisca, *Humanism in Italian Renaissance Musical Thought* (New Haven, 1985). See, as well, Palisca, ed., *Girolamo Mei, Letters on Ancient and Modern Music to Vincenzo Galilei and Giovanni Bardi* (AIM, 1960), and his *The Florentine Camerata* (New Haven, 1989). On Vicentino and neoclassical experiment in Italy, see Henry Kaufmann, *The Life and Works of Nicola Vicentino* (1511–c. 1576) (AIM, 1966), along with Kaufmann's edition of Vicentino's complete works, also published by the American Institute of Musicology (CMM 26), and Edward E. Lowinsky's facsimile edition of Vicentino's treatise *L'antica musica ridotta alla moderna prattica* (Kassel, 1959).

On neoclassical experiment and humanism in France, see Kenneth J. Levy, "Costeley's Chromatic Chanson," *AnnM* 3 (1955); D. P. Walker, "Musical Humanism in the 16th and Early 17th Centuries," *MR* 2 (1941) and 3 (1942); Walker, "The Aims of Baïf's *Académie de Poésie et de Musique*," *Journal of Renaissance and Baroque Music* 1 (1946); Walker, "The Influence of *Musique mesurée à l'antique*, Particularly on the *Airs de cour* of the Early Seventeenth Century," *MD* 2 (1948); Walker and François Lesure, "Claude Le Jeune and Musique mesurée," *MD* 3 (1949); Walker, "Some Aspects and Problems of *Musique mesurée à l'antique*," *MD* 4 (1950); Walker, ed., *Claude Le Jeune: Airs (1608)* (AIM 1951); and Francis A. Yates, *The French Academies of the Sixteenth Century* (London, 1947). The *Complete Unpublished Chansons of Le Jeune* constitutes volume 16 of the *Sixteenth-Century Chanson*, ed. Jane Bernstein (New York, 1989). For more about Le Jeune and the aims of French musical humanism, see Richard Freedman, "Claude Le Jeune, Adrian Willaert and the Art of Musical Translation," *EMH* 13 (1994): 123–48. The *Balet comique de la royne* has been published in a facsimile edition (Turin, 1962) and in an English translation by Carol Mac-Clintock (American Institute of Musicology, 1972).

On Ronsard and music, see G. Thibault and L. Perceau, *Bibliographie des poésies de P. de Ronsard mises en musique au XVIe siècle* (Paris, 1941); Julien Tiersot, "Ronsard et la musique de son temps," *Sammelbände der internationalen Musikgesellschaft* 8 (1906–7); the special issue devoted to "Les musiciens de Ronsard" in *RdM* 74 (1988); Jeanice Brooks, "Ronsard, the Lyric Sonnet and the Late Sixteenth-Century Chanson," *EMH* 13 (1994): 65–84; and John O'Brien, "Ronsard, Belleau and Renvoisy," in *EMH* 13 (1994): 199–215.

On the virtuoso madrigalists, see Anthony Newcomb, *The Madrigal at Ferrara, 1479–1597*, 2 vols. (Princeton, 1980); and the relevant sections from the early chapters of Tomlinson, *Monteverdi and the End of the Renaissance*. Both Einstein, *The Italian Madrigal*, 3 vols. (Princeton, 1971), and Roche, *The Madrigal*, contain important insights into the virtuoso madrigalists. Iain Fenlon, *Music and Patronage in Sixteenth-Century Mantua*, 2 vols. (Cambridge, 1980–82), is an archival study that, among other things, provides a context for the composition and performance of madrigals at court. See also, on the *concerto di donne*, the excellent article by Anthony Newcomb, "Courtesans, Muses, or Musicians? Professional Women Musicians in Sixteenth-Century Italy," in *Women Making Music: The Western Art Tradition, 1150–1950,* ed. Jane Bowers and Judith Tick (Urbana and Chicago, 1986), 90–115; and on the rise of women composers, Jane Bowers, "The Emergence of Women Composers in Italy, 1566–1700," 116–67, in the same volume.

Giaches de Wert's complete works, ed. Carol MacClintock, have been published in 17 volumes (1961–77) by the American Institute of Musicology (CMM 24). On the composer's life and works, see MacClintock, *Giaches de Wert, Life and Works* (AIM, 1966); and see also Fenlon, *Music and Patronage in Sixteenth-Century Mantua,* and Newcomb, *The Madrigal at Ferrara, 1479–1597.* On aspects of Wert's music not treated elsewhere, especially his use of melodic formulae in his settings of Petrarch, see Howard Mayer Brown, "Petrarch in Naples: Notes on the Formation of Giaches de Wert's Style," in *Altro Polo: Essays on Italian Music in the Cinquecento,* ed. Richard Charteris (Sydney, 1990), 16–50. The same collection of essays also contains Kathryn Bosi, "The Ferrara Connection: Diminution in the Early Madrigals of Benedetto Pallavicino," 131–58.

Six volumes of the complete edition of the works of Luca Marenzio, *Opera Omnia,* ed. Bernhard Meier and Roland Jackson (1976–83), have appeared as CMM 72; five volumes of another edition of Marenzio's *Secular Works,* ed. Steven Ledbetter and Patricia Meyers, have been issued as well (New York, 1977–91); these supplement Marenzio, *Sämtliche Werke,* ed. Alfred Einstein (Leipzig, 1929–31); see also Marenzio, *Ten Madrigals for Mixed Voices,* ed. Denis Arnold (London, 1966). Two books on Marenzio in English are Arnold's brief but useful *Marenzio* (London, 1965) and James Chater's more extensive *Luca Marenzio and the Italian Madrigal 1577–1593,* 2 vols. (Ann Arbor, 1981). Richard Freedman, "Marenzio's *Madrigali a quattro, cinque et sei voci* of 1588: A Newly-Revealed Madrigal Cycle and Its Intellectual Context," *JM* 13 (1995): 318–54, is an insightful contribution to understanding Marenzio's late style in its social and literary context.

On Gesualdo, see Glenn Watkins, *Gesualdo: The Man and His Music,* 2d ed. (Oxford, 1991). His complete works have been edited by Glenn Watkins and Wilhelm Weismann in 10 volumes (Hamburg, 1957–66).

Claudio Monteverdi: A Guide to Research, by K. G. Adams and D. Kiel (New York, 1989), is useful but by now outdated. Gary Tomlinson, *Monteverdi and the End of the Renaissance* (Berkeley and Los Angeles, 1987), contributes in important ways to our understanding of the early madrigals of Monteverdi; in addition to the bibliography there included, see Tim Carter, "Artusi, Monteverdi, and the Poetics of Modern Music," in *Musical Humanism and Its Legacy. Essays in Honor of Claude V. Palisca,* ed. Nancy Kovaleff Baker and Barbara Russano Hanning (New York, 1992), 171–94; Suzanne Cusick, "Gendering Modern Music: Thoughts on the Monteverdi-Artusi Controversy," *JAMS* 46 (1993): 1–25; and the relevant portions of Eric Chafe, *Monteverdi's Tonal Language* (New York, 1992), and Silke Leopold, *Monteverdi: Music in Transition,* trans. Anne Smith (Oxford, 1991). An insightful consideration of Monteverdi's innovative stance is provided in Massimo Ossi, "Claudio Monteverdi's ordine novo, bello et gustevole: The Canzonetta as Dramatic Module and Formal Archetype," *JAMS* 45 (1992): 261–304. The most informative and up-to-date biographical study of Monteverdi in English is Paolo Fabbri, *Monteverdi,* trans. Tim Carter (Cambridge, 1994). Claudio Monteverdi's works have been published by G. F. Malipiero in 17 volumes (Vienna, 1926–66; 2d ed. 1954–68). A new edition of Monteverdi, *Opera Omnia,* projected to fill 20 volumes and issued by the Fondazione Claudio Monteverdi in Cremona (1970–   ), is in progress.

On Giovanni Gabrieli, see Egon Kenton, *Life and Works of Giovanni Gabrieli* (AIM, 1967). Gabrieli's complete works are published, ed. Denis Arnold and Richard Charteris, in CMM 12.

Concerning the madrigal comedies, see Martha Farahat, "On the Staging of Madrigal Comedies," *EMH* 10 (1991): 123–43; and James Haar, "On Musical Games in the 16th Century," *JAMS* 15 (1962): 22–34. Vecchi's *L'Amfiparnaso* is available, ed. Cecil Adkins, *Early Musical Masterworks* 1 (Chapel Hill, 1977).

On Caccini and the derivation of the new monody, see Palisca, "Vincenzo Galilei and Some Links between Pseudo-Monody and Monody," *MQ* 46 (1960): 344–60; Howard Mayer Brown, "The Geography of Florentine Monody: Caccini at Home and Abroad," *EM* 9 (1981): 147–68; and Giulio Caccini, *Le nuove musiche*, ed. with notes and introduction by H. Wiley Hitchcock, vol. 11 of Recent Researches in the Music of the Baroque Period (Madison, Wis., 1970).

MUSICAL EXAMPLES
AND THEIR SOURCES

Examples covered by copyright are printed with the generous permission of the publishers cited below.

1–1.   Leonel Power, *Beata progenies*. Hamm, Charles, ed., *Complete Works of Lionel Power*. Vol. 1, CMM, ser. 50. AIM, 1969– , p. 1.

1–2.   Leonel Power, *Gloriose Virginis*. Hamm, Charles, ed., *Complete Works of Lionel Power*. Vol. 1, CMM, ser. 50. AIM, 1969– , pp. 19–20.

1–3.   English figures. Hamm. Charles, "A Catalogue of Anonymous English Music in Fifteenth-Century Continental Manuscripts." MD 22 (1968): 58–59.

1–4a.   Leonel Power, *Sanctus*. Hughes, Andrew, and Margaret Bent, eds., The *Old Hall Manuscript*. Vol. 1, CMM, ser. 46. AIM, 1969, p. 346.

1–4b.   The Sarum chant Power paraphrases.

1–5.   Anonymous English carol, *There is no rose*. Stevens, John, ed., *Medieval Carols*. Vol. 4, MB. London: Stainer & Bell, 1952, pp. 10–11.

2–1.   Guillaume Dufay, *Adieu ces bons vins de Lannoy*. Dufay, Guillaume, *Opera Omnia*, ed. Heinrich Besseler. Vol. 6, CMM, ser. 1. AIM, 1948–64, p. 50.

2–2.   Guillaume Dufay, *Mille bonjours je vous present*. Dufay, Guillaume, *Opera Omnia*, ed. Heinrich Besseler. Vol. 6, CMM, ser. 1. AIM, 1948–64, p. 81.

2–3.   Guillaume Dufay, *Adieu, m'amour*. Dufay, Guillaume, *Opera Omnia*, ed. Heinrich Besseler. Vol. 6, CMM, ser. 1. AIM, 1948–64, p. 91.

2–4.   Under-third cadences in each mode.

2–5.   An octave-leap V–I cadence in the Dorian mode with 4–3 suspension.

2–6.   Guillaume Dufay, *Vasilissa ergo gaude*. Dufay, Guillaume, *Opera Omnia*, ed. Heinrich Besseler. Vol. 1, CMM, ser. 1. AIM, 1965, pp. 21–23.

2–7.   Guillaume Dufay, *Supremum est mortalibus bonum*. Dufay, Guillaume, *Opera Omnia*, ed. Heinrich Besseler. Vol. 1, CMM, ser. 1. AIM, 1965, pp. 59–60.

2–8.   Guillaume Dufay, *Nuper rosarum flores*. Dufay, Guillaume, *Opera Omnia*, ed. Heinrich Besseler. Vol. 1, CMM, ser. 1. AIM, 1965, pp. 70–72.

2–9.   Tenor of Dufay's ballade *Se la face ay pale*. Dufay, Guillaume, *Opera Omnia*, ed. Heinrich Besseler. Vol. 6, CMM, ser. 1. AIM, 1965, p. 36.

2–10.   Guillaume Dufay, *Missa Se la face ay pale*, Gloria. Dufay, Guillaume, *Opera Omnia*, ed. Heinrich Besseler. Vol. 3, CMM, ser. 1. AIM, 1965, pp. 4–5.

2–11.   Gilles Binchois, *Ave Regina caelorum, mater regis angelorum*. Binchois, Gilles, *The Sacred Music of Gilles Binchois*, ed. Philip Kaye. Oxford: Oxford University Press, 1992, p. 183.

2–12.   Gilles Binchois, *Adieu m' amour et ma maistresse*, Binchois, Gilles, *Die Chansons von Gilles Binchois*, ed. Wolfgang Rehm. Mainz: B. Schott's Söhne, 1957, p. 3.

2–13.   Gilles Binchois, *De plus en plus*, superius. Binchois, Gilles, *Die Chansons von Gilles Binchois*, ed. Wolfgang Rehm. Mainz: B. Schott's Söhne, 1957, pp. 10–11.

2–14.   Gilles Binchois, *Dueil angoisseux*. Binchois, Gilles, *Die Chansons von Gilles Binchois*, ed. Wolfgang Rehm. Mainz: B. Schott's Söhne, 1957, p. 45.

3–1.   Johannes Ockeghem, *Missa l'homme armé*, Kyrie II. Ockeghem, Johannes, *Collected Works of Johannes Ockeghem*. Vol. 1. Ed. Dragan Plamenac. American Musicological Society, 1959, p. 100.

3–2.   Johannes Ockeghem, *Missa l'homme armé*, Gloria. Ockeghem, Johannes, *Collected Works of Johannes Ockeghem*. Vol. 1. Ed. Dragan Plamenac. American Musicological Society, 1959, pp. 100–101.

3–3.   Johannes Ockeghem, *Missa Mi-mi*, Gloria. Ockeghem, Johannes, *Collected Works of Johannes Ockeghem*. Vol. 2. Ed. Dragan Plamenac. American Musicological Society, 1959, pp. 5–7.

3–4.   Johannes Ockeghem, *Ma bouche rit*. Petrucci, Ottaviano dei, *Harmonice Musices Odhecaton A*, ed. Helen Hewitt. Cambridge, Mass., 1942; reprint, New York: Da Capo Press, 1978, p. 335.

3–5.   Antoine Busnois, *Je ne fay plus*. Brown, Howard Mayer, ed., *A Florentine Chansonnier from the time of Lorenzo the Magnificent*. Vol. 7, MRM. Chicago: The University of Chicago Press, 1983, p. 109.

4–1.   Japart, *Nenciozza mia*. Petrucci, Ottaviano dei, *Harmonice Musices Odhecaton A*, ed. Helen Hewitt. Cambridge, Mass., 1942; reprint, New York: Da Capo Press, 1978, p. 233.

4–2.   Romanesca for the lira da braccio (Pesaro, Biblioteca Oliveriana MS 1144, p. 174).

4–3.   Michele Pesenti, *Modus dicendi Capitula*.

4–4.   Marco Cara, *Udite voi finestre*.

4–5.   Bartolomeo Tromboncino, *Si è debile il filo*. Disertori, Benvenuto, ed., *Le Frottole per canto e liuto intabulate da Franciscus Bossinensis*. Milan: G. Ricordi, 1964, p. 271.

4–6.   Bartolomeo Tromboncino, *Chi se fida de fortuna*. Disertori, Benvenuto, ed., *Le Frottole per canto e liuto intabulate da Franciscus Bossinensis*. Milan: G. Ricordi, 1964.

4–7.   Alessandro Coppini, *Canzona degli ucellatori alle starne*. D'Accone, Frank A., ed., *Music of the Florentine Renaissance*. Vol. 2, CMM, ser. 32. AIM, 1966– , pp. 1–2.

4–8.   Bartolomeo degli Organi, *Un dì lieto già mai*. D'Accone, Frank A., ed., *Music of the Florentine Renaissance*. Vol. 2, CMM, ser. 32. AIM, 1966– , p. 37.

4–9.   Giacomo Fogliano (or Don Nicolo?), *Vengo a te, madre Maria*. Jeppeson, Knud, ed., *Die mehrstimmige italienische Lauda um 1500*. Leipzig, 1935, p. 6.

5–1.   Josquin, *Ave Maria*. Glarean, Heinrich, *Dodecachordon*. Vol. 2. Translated and transcribed by Clement A. Miller. Vol. 6, *Musicological Studies and Documents*. AIM, 1965, pp. 436–38.

5–2.   Josquin, *Tu solus qui facis mirabilia*.

5–3.   Josquin, *Inviolata integra et casta es, Maria*. Lowinsky, Edward, ed., *The Medici Codex of 1518*. Vol. 3, MRM. Chicago: The University of Chicago Press, 1963, pp. 180–82.

5–4.   Josquin, *Missa L'homme armé sexti toni*, Gloria. Bortone, Amerigo, ed., *Messo, magnificat, motetto e inno*. Vol. 15, *Archivum musices metopolitanum mediolanense*. Milano, 1969, pp. 35–37.

5–5.   Josquin, *Plusieurs regretz*.

6–1.   Alexander Agricola, *J'ay beau huer*. Agricola, Alexander, *Opera Omnia*, ed. Edward R. Lerner. Vol. 5, CMM, ser. 22. AIM, 1961–70, pp. 28–29.

6–2.   Alexander Agricola, *De tous biens plaine*. Agricola, Alexander, *Opera Omnia*, ed. Edward R. Lerner. Vol. 5, CMM, ser. 22. AIM, 1961–70, p. 82.

6–3.   Jacob Obrecht, *Missa Fortuna desperata*, Kyrie. Obrecht, Jacob, *New Obrecht Edition*, ed. Barton Hudson. Utrecht: Vereniging voor Nederlandse Muziekgeschiedenis, 1983– , p. 49.

6–4.   Loyset Compère, *Disant adieu*. Compère, Loyset, *Opera Omnia*, ed. Ludwig Finscher. Vol. 5, CMM, ser. 15. AIM, 1958–72, pp. 18–19.

6–5.   Loyset Compère, *Mon père m'a donné mari*. Compère, Loyset, *Opera Omnia*, ed. Ludwig Finscher. Vol. 5. CMM, ser. 15. AIM, 1958–72, pp. 38–39.

6–6.   Heinrich Isaac, *Choralis Constantinus II*, Mass for Christmas Day. Isaac, Heinrich, *Choralis Constantinus. Zweite Buch & Weltliche Werke*, ed. Anton von Webern. Vol. 3, DTÖ. Graz: Akademische Druck- Verlagsanstalt, 1959, pp. 5–10. Note values halved.

6–7.   Heinrich Isaac, *Quis dabit capiti meo aquam?* Isaac, Heinrich, *Quis dabit capiti meo aquam?* ed. Harvey G. Lord. Sharon, Conn.: The Muses Gardin Music Publishers, 1976, pp. 1–3.

6–8.   Pierre de la Rue, *Lauda anima mea Dominum*. La Rue, Pierre de, *Pierre de la Rue: Vier Motetten*, ed. Nigel Davison. *Das Chorwerk*, no. 91. Wolfenbüttel, 1964, p. 16.

7–1.   Nicolas Gombert, *Expurgate vetus fermentum*. Gombert, Nicolas, *Opera Omnia*, ed. Joseph Schmidt-Görg. Vol. 8, CMM, ser. 6. AIM, 1957– , p. 67.

7–2.   Nicolas Gombert, *Beati omnes*. Gombert, Nicolas, *Opera Omnia*, ed. Joseph Schmidt-Görg. Vol. 7, CMM, ser. 6. AIM, 1957– , pp. 176–78.

7–3.   Nicolas Gombert, *Missa Beati omnes*, Kyrie I. Gombert, Nicolas, *Opera Omnia*, ed. Joseph Schmidt-Görg. Vol. 1, CMM, ser. 6. AIM, 1957– , p. 56.

7–4.   Adrian Willaert, *I piansi, hor canto*. Willaert, Adrian, *Opera Omnia*, ed. Hermann Zenck and Walter Gerstenberg. Vol. 15, CMM, ser. 3. AIM, 1950– , p. 67.

7–5.   Adrian Willaert, *Beati pauperes*. Willaert, Adrian, *Opera Omnia*, ed. Hermann Zenck and Walter Gerstenberg. Vol. 5, CMM, ser. 3. AIM, 1950– , p. 67.

7–6.   Jacob Clemens, *Fremuit spiritu Jesu*. Lowinsky, Edward, *Secret Chromatic Art in the Netherlands Motet*, trans. Carl Buchman. New York: Columbia University Press, 1946; reprint, New York: Columbia University Press, 1967, Example 22.

7–7.   Jacob Clemens, *Sancta Maria succurre miseris*. Clemens non Papa, Jacobus, *Opera Omnia*, ed. K. Ph. Bernet Kempers. Vol. 15, CMM, ser. 4. AIM, 1966, p. 18.

8–1.   Claudin de Sermisy, *Tant que vivray*. Sermisy, Claudin de, *Opera Omnia*, ed. Gaston Allaire and Isabelle Cazeaux. Vol. 4, CMM, ser. 52. AIM, 1970– , pp. 99–100.

8–2.   Jacob Clemens, *Las ie languis et si ne scay pourquoy*. Clemens, Jacob, *Opera Omnia*, ed. K. Ph. Bernet Kempers. Vol. 10, CMM, ser. 4. AIM, 1951– , pp. 104–5.

8–3.   Ninot le petit, *Et la la la*. Parvi, Johanni, *Opera Omnia*, ed. Barton Hudson. CMM, ser. 87. AIM, 1979, p. 11.

8–4.   Bernardo Pisano, *Sì è debile il filo*. D'Accone, Frank A., ed., *Music of the Florentine Renaissance*. Vol. 1, CMM, ser. 32. AIM, 1966– , p. 29.

8–5.   Costanzo Festa, *Cosi suav' è' l fuoco*. Festa, Costanzo, *Opera Omnia*, ed. Albert Seay. Vol. 8, CMM, ser. 25. AIM, 1978, pp. 14–15.

8–6.   Cipriano de Rore, *O sonno*. Rore, Cipriano de, *Opera Omnia*, ed. Bernhard Meier. Vol. 4, CMM, ser. 14. AIM, 1969, p. 66.

8–7.   Cipriano de Rore, *Da le belle contrade*. Rore, Cipriano de, *Opera Omnia*, ed. Bernhard Meier. Vol. 5, CMM, ser. 14. AIM, 1969, pp. 97–98.

8–8.   Anonymous, *In feuers hitz*. Ringmann, Herbert, ed., *Das Glogauer Liederbuch, Erster Teil: Deutscher Lieder und Spielstücke*, rev. J. Klapper. Vol. 4, *Das Erbe deutscher Musik*. Basel, 1936, p. 21.

8–9.   Ludwig Senfl, *Ich stuend an einem Morgen*. Senfl, *Deutscher Lieder zu vier bis sieben Stimmen*, ed. Arnold Geering and Wilhelm Altwegg. Vol. 4, *Sämtliche Werke*. Wolfenbüttel, 1949–74, p. 7.

8–10.   Juan de Anchieta, *Domine Jesu Christe qui hora diei ultima*. Segovia MS, fols. 94v–95.

8–11.   Pedro de Escobar, *Coraçón triste, sofrid*. Anglès, Higini, ed., *La música en la corte de los Reyes Católicos*. Vol. 10, MME. Barcelona, 1951, pp. 134–35.

8–12.   Robert Fayrfax, *Magnificat "Regale."* Lyon, Margaret, ed., *Sacred Music from the Lambeth Choirbook*. Vol. 69, RRMR. Madison, Wis.: A-R Editions, 1983, p. 54.

8–13.　John Taverner, *Magnificat in the Sixth Tone*. Taverner, John, *John Taverner: III. Ritual Music and Secular Songs*, ed. Hugh Benham. Vol. 30, *Early English Church Music*. London: Stainer & Bell, 1984, p. 43. Note values doubled.

8–14.　Thomas Tallis, *Salvator mundi*. Stevens, Denis, and Peter Le Huray, eds., *Treasury of English Church Music*. Vol. 2. London: Blanford Press, 1965, p. 14. Transposed back to original pitch level.

8–15.　Thomas Morley, *You that wont to my pipe's sound*. Morley, Thomas, *First Book of Balletts* (1595), ed. E. Fellowes, rev. T. Dart. Vol. 4, *The English Madrigalists*. London: Stainer & Bell, 1965.

8–16.　Giovanni Giacomo Gastoldi, *Vaghe Ninfe e voi pastor*. Gastoldi, Giovanni Giacomo, *Balletti a cinque voci*, ed. Michel Sanvoisin. Paris, 1968.

8–17.　Thomas Weelkes, *O care, thou wilt despatch me*. Weelkes, Thomas, *Madrigals of 5 Parts* (1600), ed. E. Fellowes, rev. T. Dart. Vol. 11, *The English Madrigals*. London: Stainer & Bell, 1968, pp. 19–24.

9–1.　Claudin de Sermisy, *Tant que vivray* (keyboard arr. by Attaingnant). Attaingnant, Pierre, *Transcriptions of Chansons for Keyboard*, ed. Albert Seay. CMM, ser. 20. AIM, 1961, pp. 99–100.

9–2.　Melchior Neusidler, *Pass' e mezo antico*. Neusidler, Melchior, *Intabolatura di Liuto*, ed. Charles Jacobs. Ottawa: The Institute of Mediaeval Music, 1994, pp. 1–3.

9–3.　Alonso Mudarra, *Fantasía que contrahaze la harpa en la manera de Luduvico*, from *Tres libros de música en cifra pare vihuela* (Seville, 1546). Transcription by John Griffiths as published in *Revista de Musicología* 9 (1986): 39–40.

10–1.　Johann Walter, *Christ lag in Todesbanden*. Walter, Johann, *Geistliches Gesangbüchlein Wittenberg 1551. Erster Teil: Deutsche Gesänge*, ed. Otto Schröder. Vol. 1, *Sämtliche Werke*. Kassel, 1953, p. 11.

11–1a.　The chant on which Palestrina's *Missa Aeterna Christi munera* is based.

11–1b.　Giovanni Pierluigi da Palestrina, *Missa Aeterna Christi munera*, Agnus Dei. Palestrina, Giovanni Pierluigi da, *Le Opere Complete di Giovanni da Palestrina*. Vol. 15. Ed. Raffaele Casimiri. Rome: Edizione Fratelli Scalera, 1941– , p. 16.

11–2.　Giovanni Pierluigi da Palestrina, *Missa Assumpta est Maria*, Sanctus. Palestrina, Giovanni Pierluigi da, *Le Opere Complete di Giovanni da Palestrina*. Vol. 25. Ed. Lino Bianchi. Rome: Edizione Fratelli Scalera, 1958, pp. 234–35.

11–3.　Giovanni Pierluigi da Palestrina, *Surgam et circuibo civitatem*. Palestrina, Giovanni Pierluigi da, *Canticum Canticorum*, ed. Antal Jancsovics. Budapest: Editio Musica, 1976, pp. 71–72.

11–4.　Orlando di Lasso, *Gustate et videte*. Lassus, *Sämtliche Werke*. Vol. 5. Ed. F. X. Haberl and A Sandberger. Leipzig: Breitkopf & Haertel, 1894, pp. 73–74.

11–5.　Orlando di Lasso, *Prophetiae Sibyllarum*, "Carmina Chromatico." Lassus, *Sämtliche Werke: neue reihe*. Vol. 21. Ed. Reinhold Schloetterer. New York: Baerenreiter, 1990, p. 3.

11–6.　Orlando di Lasso, *De profundis*. Lasso, Orlando di, *The Seven Penitential Psalms and Laudate Dominum de Caelis*, ed. Peter Bergquist. Vols. 86–87, RRMR. Madison, Wis.: A-R Editions, 1990, pp. 146–47.

11–7.　Orlando di Lasso, *La nuict froide et sombre*. Bernstein, Jane A., *The Sixteenth-Century Chanson*. Vol. 12. New York: Garland Publishing, 1987, p. 119.

11–8.   Orlando di Lasso, *Nessun visse giamai*. Lasso, Orlando di, *Sämtliche Werke*. Vol. 8. Ed. A. Sandberger. Leipzig, 1894, p. 137.

11–9.   Tomás Luis de Victoria, *O magnum mysterium*. Victoria, Tomás Luis de, *Motetes*. Vol. 1. Ed. P. Samuel Rubio. Madrid: Unión musical española, 1964, p. 7.

11–10. Tomás Luis de Victoria, *O vos omnes*. Victoria, Tomás Luis de, *Motetes*. Vol. 1. Ed. P. Samuel Rubio. Madrid: Unión musical española, 1964, pp 74–78.

11–11. William Byrd, *Domine secundum actum meum*. Byrd, William, *Cantiones Sacrae (1575)*, ed. Craig Monson. Vol. 1, *The Byrd Edition*. London: Stainer & Bell, 1991, p. 113. Transposed to pitch level of original.

11–12. William Byrd, *Susanna fair*. Byrd, William, *Madrigals, Songs, and Canons*, ed. Philip Brett. Vol. 16, *The Byrd Edition*. London: Stainer & Bell, 1976, p. 127.

11–13. William Byrd, *The Woods so Wild*. Byrd, William, *William Byrd: Keyboard Music*. 2d ed. Ed. Alan Brown. Vol. 28, MB. London: Stainer & Bell, pp. 141–43.

12–1.   Claude Le Jeune, *Revecy venir le printemps*. Rechant and beginning of Chant.

12–2.   Giaches de Wert, *Giunto alla tomba*. Wert, Giaches de, *Opera Omnia*. Ed. Carol MacClintock. Vol. 7, CMM, ser. 24. AIM, 1967, pp. 38–39.

12–3.   Giaches de Wert, *Solo e pensoso*, bass. Wert, Giaches de, *Opera Omnia*, ed. Carol MacClintock. Vol. 7, CMM, ser. 24. AIM, 1967, p. 32.

12–4.   Giaches de Wert, *Ah, dolente partita*. Wert, Giaches de, *Opera Omnia*, ed. Carol MacClintock. Vol. 12, CMM, ser. 24. AIM, 1967, pp. 1–2.

12–5.   Luca Marenzio, *Zefiro torno*. Marenzio, Luca, *Madrigali a 4 e 5 voci*, ed. Lavinio Virgili. Rome: Edizioni de Santis, 1952, pp. 3–4, 6–7.

12–6.   Luca Marenzio, *Dolorosi martir*. Marenzio, Luca, *Sämtliche Werke: Erster band*, ed. Alfred Einstein. Vol. 4, *Publikationen Älterer Musik*. Leipzig: Breitkopf & Härtel, 1929, p. 16. Note values halved.

12–7.   Carlo Gesualdo, *Ecco morirò dunque*. Gesualdo, Carlo, *Sämtliche Werke*, ed. Wilhelm Weismann and Glenn Watkins. Vol. 4. Hamburg: Ugrino Verlag, 1958, p. 59.

12–8.   Carlo Gesualdo, *Moro lasso*. Gesualdo, Carlo, *Sämtliche Werke*, ed. Wilhelm Weismann and Glenn Watkins. Vol. 6. Hamburg: Ugrino Verlag, 1957, p. 74.

12–9.   Claudio Monteverdi, *Ah, dolente partita*. Monteverdi, Claudio, *Madrigali a 5 voci. Libro Quarto*, ed. Maria Teresa Rosa Barezzani. Vol. 5, *Opera Omnia*. Cremona: The Fondazione Claudio Monteverdi, 1988, p. 93.

12–10. Claudio Monteverdi, *Cruda Amarilli*. Monteverdi, Claudio, *Madrigali a cinque. Libro V*, ed. Maria Caraci. Vol. 6, *Opera Omnia*. Cremona: Fondazione Claudio Monteverdi, 1984, p. 107.

ABBREVIATIONS

AcM	*Acta Musicologica*, 1929–.
AIM	American Institute of Musicology; publications include CMM, MD. For lists see MD 39 (1985): 169–220.
AnnM	*Annales musicologiques*, 1953–.
CMM	Corpus mensurabilis musicae, AIM, 1948–.
DTÖ	Denkmäler der Tonkunst in Oesterreich (Vienna, Artaria, 1894–1904; Leipzig: Breitkopf & Härtel, 1905–13; Vienna: Universal, 1919–38; Graz: Akademische Druck- und Verlagsanstalt, 1966–).
EM	*Early Music*, 1973–.
EMH	*Early Music History*, 1981–.
JAMS	*Journal of the American Musicological Society*, 1948–.
JLSM	*Journal of the Lute Society of America*, 1968–.
JM	*Journal of Musicology*, 1982–.
MB	Musica Britannica (London: Stainer and Bell, 1951–).
MD	*Musica Disciplina*, 1946–.
ML	*Music and Letters*, 1920–.
MME	Monumentos de la música española (Barcelona: Consejo Superior de Investigaciones Científicas, 1941–).
MQ	*The Musical Quarterly*, 1915–.
MR	*Music Review*, 1940–.

MRM	Monuments of Renaissance Music (Chicago: University of Chicago Press, 1964–).
PRMA	*Proceedings of the Royal Musical Association*, 1874–.
RBM	*Revue belge de Musicologie*, 1946–.
RdM	*Revue de Musicologie*, 1917–.
RIM	*Rivista italiana di musicologia*, 1966–.
RMF	Renaissance Music in Facsimile (New York: Garland Publishing, 1986).
RRMR	Recent Researches in the Music of the Renaissance (Madison, Wis.: A-R Editions, 1964–).
RQ	*Renaissance Quarterly*, 1948–.
RS	*Renaissance Studies*, 1987–.
SM	*Studi Musicali*, 1972–.
TNG	*The New Grove Dictionary of Music and Musicians*, ed. Stanley Sadie (London: Macmillan, 1980).
TVNM	*Tijdschrift van de Vereniging voor Nederlandse Muziekgeschiedenis*, 1882–.

INDEX